Tony Zhang

SAMS
Teach Yourself

C

in 24 Hours

SAMS

A Division of Macmillan USA
201 West 103rd Street., Indianapolis, Indiana, 46290

Sams Teach Yourself C in 24 Hours, Second Edition

Copyright ©2000 by Sams Publishing

International Standard Book Number: 0-672-31861-x

Library of Congress Catalog Card Number: 99-067311

Printed in the United States of America

First Printing: February, 2000

01 00   4   3   2

Trademarks

Warning and Disclaimer

ASSOCIATE PUBLISHER
Michael Stephens

ACQUISITIONS EDITOR
Carol Ackerman

DEVELOPMENT EDITOR
Gus A. Miklos

MANAGING EDITOR
Charlotte Clapp

PROJECT EDITOR
Andy Beaster

COPY EDITOR
Kate Givens

INDEXERS
Christine Nelsen
Deborah Hittel

PROOFREADER
Candice Hightower

TECHNICAL EDITOR
Bill Mitchell

TEAM COORDINATOR
Pamalee Nelson

INTERIOR DESIGNER
Gary Adair

COVER DESIGNER
Aren Howell

COPYWRITER
Eric Borgert

EDITORIAL ASSISTANT
Angela Boley

PRODUCTION
Stacey DeRome
Mark Walchle

Contents at a Glance

Table of Contents

About the Author

TONY ZHANG has more than 15 years experience in computer programming and enterprise-wide information system design. He is currently working for one of the "big 5" consulting firms focusing on e-business related infrastructure design, development, and implementation.

With a Masters degree in Physics, he has published dozens of research papers on lasers and computer programming. Among his broad interests are oil painting and photography, the two things that Tony enjoys most.

You can reach Tony through Sams Publishing, or by emailing him at `tyc24h@hotmail.com`.

About the Contributing Author

JOHN SOUTHMAYD is a Software Design Engineer with experience in areas ranging from systems-level programming and device drivers to Windows development and Internet technologies. He currently works as a consultant with Excell Data Corporation and lives with his wife in Kirkland, Washington.

Dedication

To my wife, Ellen, and my parents, Zhi-ying and Bing-rong, for their love and inspirations.

—*Tony Zhang*

Acknowledgments

First, I'd like to thank the readers of the first edition of the book for their encouragement, patience, comments, and especially, criticisms, which made the second edition more suitable for people who want to start a journey in the C programming world.

It's my great pleasure to work with editor Sharon Cox for the second time. I'd like to thank editors Carol Ackerman and Gus Miklos, and contributing author John Southmayd for their excellent work that made the second edition of the book more accessible, and largely, if not completely, error-free. Also, I'd like to express my appreciation to the great work of the other editing team members. Together, they made the second edition possible.

I greatly appreciate the love and support of my wife, Ellen, who inspires me to look at the technology world from different perspectives. It's always a great joy to discuss issues on philosophy and literature with her. My parents, whom I can *never* thank enough, gave me not only love and affection, but also the opportunity of receiving the best education I could ever have when I was in China.

Tell Us What You Think!

As the reader of this book, *you* are our most important critic and commentator. We value your opinion and want to know what we're doing right, what we could do better, what areas you'd like to see us publish in, and any other words of wisdom you're willing to pass our way.

As an Associate Publisher for Sams, I welcome your comments. You can fax, email, or write me directly to let me know what you did or didn't like about this book—as well as what we can do to make our books stronger.

Please note that I cannot help you with technical problems related to the topic of this book, and that due to the high volume of mail I receive, I might not be able to reply to every message.

When you write, please be sure to include this book's title and author as well as your name and phone or fax number. I will carefully review your comments and share them with the author and editors who worked on the book.

Fax: 317-581-4770
Email: michael.stephens@macmillanusa.com
Mail: Michael Stephens
         Associate Publisher
         Sams Publishing
         201 West 103rd Street
         Indianapolis, IN 46290 USA

Introduction

If one learns from others but does not think, one will be bewildered;
If one thinks but does not learn from others, one will be in peril.

—Confucius

Welcome to the second edition of *Teach Yourself C in 24 Hours*!

Based on the success of the first edition of the book and the feedback from the readers, we have re-written or modified every single chapter of the book to make the second edition more suitable for beginners like you who want to get started with the C programming language as quickly as possible.

Of course, it's very normal to spend more than 24 hours to really understand the concepts and programming skills introduced in the book. However, the good news is that this book offers many sample programs and exercises with clear explanations and answers, which makes the concepts of the C language easier to understand.

In fact, *Teach Yourself C in 24 Hours* provides a good starting point for you in C programming. It covers important topics in C programming, and lays a solid foundation for a serious beginner like you. After reading this book, you'll be able to write basic C programs on your own.

You will profit from reading the book when you start to apply C programs to real problems or move on to learn other programming languages, such as Perl, C++, and Java.

Who Should Read This Book?

If this is your first time learning C, this book is written for you. In fact, in writing this book I assume that the readers have no previous programming experience. Of course, it's always a big plus if you have some knowledge of computers.

Special Features of This Book

This book contains the following special elements that make it simpler and clearer for you to digest the rudimentary features and concepts of C as they are introduced:

- Syntax boxes
- Notes
- Cautions
- Tips

Syntax boxes explain some of the more complicated features of C, such as control structures. Each syntax box consists of a formal definition of the feature followed by an explanation. Here is an example of a syntax box:

The syntax for the `malloc()` function is

```
#include <stdlib.h>
void *malloc(size_t size);
```

Here, `size` specifies the number of bytes of storage to allocate. The header file, `stdlib.h`, has to be included before the `malloc()` function can be called. Because the `malloc()` function returns a `void` pointer, its type is automatically converted to the type of pointer on the left side of an assignment operator.

▲

(You'll learn more about the `malloc()` function later in the book.)

Notes are explanations of interesting properties of a particular C program feature. Let's have a look at the following example of a note:

> In left-justified output, the value being displayed appears at the left end of the value field. In right-justified output, the value being displayed appears at the right end of the value field.

Warnings warn you of programming pitfalls you should avoid. Here is a typical warning:

> Never use the reserved keywords in C, nor names of the C library functions as variable names in your program.

Tips are hints on how to write your C programs better. The following is an example of a tip:

> If you have a complex programming project, break it into smaller pieces. And try to make one function do one thing and do it very well.

Programming Examples

As mentioned earlier, this book contains many useful programming examples with explanations. These examples are meant to show you how to use different data types and functions provided in C.

Each example has a listing of the C program; the output generated from that listing will follow. The example also offers an analysis of how the program works. Special icons are used to point out each part of the example: Type, Input/Output, and Analysis.

In the example shown in Listing IN.1, there are some special typographic conventions. The input you enter is shown in bold monospace type, and the output generated by the executable program of Listing IN.1 is shown in plain monospace type.

TYPE   **LISTING IN.1**   Read in a Character Entered by the User

```
1:   /* INL01.c: Read input by calling getc() */
2:   #include <stdio.h>
3:
4:   main()
5:   {
6:       int ch;
7:
8:       printf("Please type in one character:\n");
9:       ch = getc(stdin);
10:      printf("The character you just entered is: %c\n", ch);
11:      return 0;
12:  }
```

The following output is displayed after the executable file, INL01.exe, is created and executed. The user enters the H character, and the program displays what the user entered.

```
Please type in one character:
H
The character you just entered is: H
```

ANALYSIS   In line 2 of Listing IN.1, the header file stdio.h is included for both the getc() and printf() functions used in the program. Lines 4–12 give the name and body of the main() function.

In line 6, an integer variable ch is declared, which is assigned to the return value from the getc() function later in line 9. Line 8 prints out a piece of message that asks the user to enter one character from the keyboard. The printf() function in line 8 uses the default standard output stdout to display messages on the screen.

In line 9, the standard input stdin is passed to the getc() function, which indicates that the file stream is from the keyboard. After the user types in a character, the getc() function returns the numeric value (that is, an integer) of the character. Note that in line 9 the numeric value is assigned to the integer variable ch.

In line 10, the character entered is displayed on the screen with the help of `printf()`. Note that the character format specifier `%c` is used within the `printf()` function in line 10.

Q&A and Workshop

Each hour (that is, each chapter) ends with a Q&A section that contains answers to common questions relating to the lesson of the chapter. Following the Q&A section there is a Workshop that consists of quiz questions and programming exercises. The answers to these quiz questions and sample solutions for the exercises are presented in Appendix D, "Answers to Quiz and Exercises."

To help you solidify your understanding of each lesson, you are encouraged to try to answer the quiz questions and finish the exercises provided in the workshop.

Conventions Used in This Book

This book uses special typefaces to help you differentiate between C code and regular English, and to identify important concepts.

- Actual C code is typeset in a special `monospace` font. You'll see this font used in listings, Input/Ouput examples, and code snippets. In the explanation of C features, commands, filenames, statements, variables, and any text you see on the screen are also typeset in this font.

- Command input and anything that you are supposed to enter appears in a **`bold monospace`** font. You'll see this mainly in the Input/Output sections of examples.

- Placeholders in syntax descriptions appear in an *`italic monospace`* font. Replace the placeholder with the actual filename, parameter, or whatever element it represents.

- *Italics* highlight technical terms when they appear for the first time in the text and are sometimes used to emphasize important points.

What You'll Learn in 24 Hours

Teach Yourself C in 24 Hours consists of five parts. In Part I, "The Basics of C," you'll learn the basics of the C language. Here is a summary of what you're going to learn:

Hour 1, "Taking the First Step," introduces you to the C language, the ANSI standard, and the basic software and hardware requirements for C programming.

Hour 2, "Your First C Program," demonstrates the entire procedure of writing, compiling, linking, and running a C program.

Hour 3, "Learning the Structure of a C Program," teaches you several important concepts, such as constants, variables, expressions, and statements. The anatomy of a function is introduced in this hour as well.

Hour 4, "Understanding Data Types and Keywords," lists all reserved C keywords. Four data types, `char`, `int`, `float`, and `double`, are introduced in detail. Also, the rules for naming a variable are explained.

Hour 5, "Handling Standard Input and Output," teaches you to receive input from the keyboard, and print output on the screen with the help of a set of C functions, such as `getc()`, `getchar()`, `putc()`, `putchar()`, and `printf()`.

Part II, "Operators and Control-flow Statements," emphasizes operators and control-flow statements in C. The following is a summary of what you'll learn:

Hour 6, "Manipulating Data," teaches you how to use arithmetic assignment operators, the unary minus operator, increment/decrement operators, relational operators, and the cast operator.

Hour 7, "Working with Loops," introduces looping (that is, iteration) with the `for`, `while`, or `do-while` statements.

Hour 8, "Using Conditional Operators," tells you about more operators, such as logical operators, bitwise operators, the `sizeof` operator, and `?:` operator, which are frequently used in C.

Hour 9, "Working with Data Modifiers and Math Functions," describes how to use data modifiers to enable or disable the sign bit, or change the size of a data type. Also, several mathematical functions provided by C are introduced.

Hour 10, "Controlling Program Flow," introduces all the control-flow statements used in C. They are the `if`, `if-else`, `switch`, `break`, `continue`, and `goto` statements.

Pointers and arrays are discussed in Part III, "Pointers and Arrays." The following is a summary of what you'll learn:

Hour 11, "Understanding Pointers," teaches you how to reference variables with pointers. Concepts such as left value and right value are also introduced.

Hour 12, "Understanding Arrays," explains how to declare and initialize arrays. The relationship between the array and the pointer in C is discussed too.

Hour 13, "Manipulating Strings" focuses on reading and writing strings. Several C library functions, such as `strlen()`, `strcpy()`, `gets()`, `puts()`, and `scanf()`, are introduced to manipulate strings.

Hour 14, "Understanding Scope and Storage Classes," introduces block scope, function scope, program scope, and file scope. In addition, storage class specifiers or modifiers, such as `auto`, `static`, `register`, `extern`, `const`, and `volatile` are explained.

Part IV, "Functions and Dynamic Memory Allocation," focuses on functions and dynamic memory allocations in C. The following is a summary of what you'll learn:

Hour 15, "Working with Functions," describes the function declaration and definition in C. The function prototyping is explained, along with the function return type specification.

Hour 16, "Applying Pointers" teaches you how to perform pointer arithmetic operations, access elements in arrays with pointers, and how to pass pointers to functions.

Hour 17, "Allocating Memory" explains the concept of allocating memory dynamically. C functions, such as `malloc()`, `calloc()`, `realloc()`, and `free()`, are introduced with regard to the dynamic memory allocation.

Hour 18, "Using Special Data Types and Functions," introduces the `enum` data type and the use of `typedef`. Function recursion and command-line arguments to the `main()` function are also taught in Hour 18.

Part V, "Structure, Union, File I/O, and More," discusses structures, unions, and disk file I/O in C. The following is a summary of what you'll learn:

Hour 19, "Understanding Structures," introduces the `structure` data type. You learn to access structure members, and pass structures to functions with the help of pointers. Nested and forward-referencing structures are also discussed in this hour.

Hour 20, "Understanding Unions," describes the `union` data type, and the difference between `union` and `structure`. The applications of unions are demonstrated in several examples.

Hour 21, "Reading and Writing with Files," explains the concepts of the file and the stream in C. The basics of disk file input and output are introduced in this first part. The following C functions, along with several examples are, introduced in this hour: `fopen()`, `fclose()`, `fgetc()`, `fputc()`, `fgets()`, `fputs()`, `fread()`, `fwrite()`, and `feof()`.

Hour 22, "Using Special File Functions," is the second part of disk file I/O, in which `fseek()`, `ftell()`, and `rewind()` are introduced to show how they can help you to get random access to disk files. In addition, the `fscanf()`, `fprintf()`, and `freopen()` functions are taught and invoked in sample programs.

Hour 23, "Compiling Programs: The C Preprocessor," describes the role played by the C preprocessor. You can learn the preprocessor directives, such as `#define`, `#undef`, `#ifdef`, `#endif`, `#ifndef`, `#if`, `#elis`, and `#else` through the examples given in this hour.

Hour 24, "Where Do You Go from Here?," summarizes the important concepts and features introduced in this book. In addition, programming style, modular programming, and debugging are explained briefly. A list of recommended C books is provided for your further reading.

Now, you're ready to start the journey of learning the C language, as the world has moved into a new millennium. Have a fun in reading this book, and enjoy programming in C!

Tony Zhang

Downingtown, Pennsylvania

January, 2000

PART I
The Basics of C

Hour

HOUR 1

Taking the First Step

A journey of a thousand miles is started by taking the first step.

—Chinese Proverb

High thoughts must have high language.

—Aristophanes

Welcome to *Teach Yourself C in 24 Hours*. In this first lesson you'll learn the following:

- What C is
- Why you need to learn C
- The ANSI standard
- Hardware and software required to write and run C programs

What Is C?

C is a programming language. The C language was first developed in 1972 by Dennis Ritchie at AT&T Bell Labs. Ritchie called his newly developed language *C* simply because there was a *B* programming language already. (As a matter of fact, the B language led to the development of C.)

C is a high-level programming language. In fact, C is one of the most popular general-purpose programming languages.

In the computer world, the further a programming language is from the computer architecture, the higher the language's level. You can imagine that the lowest-level languages are machine languages that computers understand and execute directly. The high-level programming languages, on the other hand, are closer to our human languages (see Figure 1.1).

FIGURE 1.1
The language spectrum.

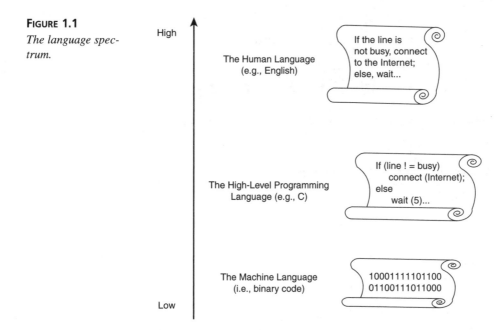

High-level programming languages, including C, have the following advantages:

- *Readability*: Programs are easy to read.
- *Maintainability*: Programs are easy to maintain.
- *Portability*: Programs are easy to port across different computer platforms.

The C language's readability and maintainability benefit directly from its relative closeness to human languages, especially English.

Each high-level language needs a *compiler* or an *interpreter* to translate instructions written in the high-level programming language into a machine language that a computer can understand and execute. Different machines may need different compilers or interpreters for the same programming language. For instance, I use Microsoft's C compiler to compile the C programs in this book for my personal computer (PC). If I need to run the C programs on a UNIX-based workstation, I have to use another type of C compiler to compile these programs. Therefore, the portability of programs written in C is realized by re-compiling the programs with different compilers for different machines (see Figure 1.2).

FIGURE 1.2

Porting programs written in C into different types of computers.

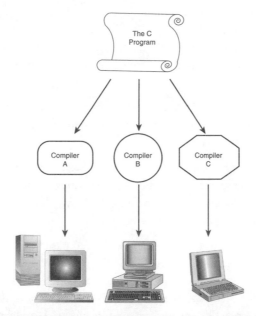

The Computer's Brain

You may know that the brain of a computer is the central processing unit (CPU). Some computers may have more than one CPU inside. A CPU has millions of transistors that make use of electronic switches. The electronic switches have only two states: off and on. (Symbolically, 0 and 1 are used to represent the two states.) Therefore, a computer can only understand instructions consisting of series of 0s and 1s. In other words, machine-readable instructions have to be in binary format.

However, a computer program written in a high-level language, such as C, Java, or Perl, is just a text file, consisting of English-like characters and words. You have to use special programs, called compilers or interpreters, to translate such a program into a machine-readable code. That is, the text format of all instructions written in a high-level language has to be converted into binary format. The code obtained after the translation is called *binary code*. Prior to the translation, a program in text format is called *source code*.

The smallest unit of binary code is called a *bit* (from binary digit), which can have a value of 0 or 1. Generally, eight bits make up one *byte*, and half a byte (four bits) is one *nibble*.

In addition, the C language has other advantages. Programs written in C can be reused. You can save parts of your C programs into a library file and invoke them in your next programming project simply by including the library file. Many common and useful programming tasks are already implemented in libraries that come included with compilers. In addition, libraries allow you to easily unleash the power and functionality of the operating system you are using. More details on using C library functions are covered in the rest of this book.

C is a relatively small programming language, which makes life easier for you. You don't have to remember many C keywords or commands before you start to write programs in C to solve problems in the real world.

For those who seek speed while still keeping the convenience and elegance of a high-level language, the C language is probably the best choice. In fact, C allows you to get control of computer hardware and peripherals. That's why the C language is sometimes called the lowest high-level programming language.

Many other high-level languages have been developed based on C. For instance, Perl is a popular programming language in World Wide Web (WWW) design across the Internet. Perl actually borrows a lot of features from C. If you understand C, learning Perl is a snap. Another example is the C++ language, which is simply an expanded version of C, although C++ makes object-oriented programming easier. Also, learning Java becomes much easier if you already know C.

There are generally two types of programming languages: *compiled* languages and *interpreted* languages.

A compiler is needed to translate a program written in a compiled language into machine-understandable code (that is, binary code) before you can run the program on your machine. When the translation is done, the binary

1

code can be saved into an application file. You can keep running the application file without the compiler unless the program (source code) is updated and you have to recompile it. The binary code or application file is also called executable code (or an executable file).

On the other hand, a program written in an interpreted language can be run immediately after you finish writing it — or for that matter, while you are writing it! But such a program always needs an interpreter to translate the high-level instructions into machine-understandable instructions (binary code) at runtime. You cannot run the program on a machine unless the right interpreter is available.

You can think of the C language as a compiled language because most C language vendors make only C compilers, as opposed to interpreters, to support programs written in C.

However, there is nothing inherent to a compiled language to prevent someone from providing an interpreter for the language; likewise, people can and often do write compilers for interpreted languages. In fact, it is not uncommon to mix the two flavors of languages, where a programmer compiles source code into a small binary file which is then executed by a runtime interpreter.

The ANSI C Standard

For many years, the de facto standard for the C programming language was the book *The C Programming Language*, written by Brian Kernighan and Dennis Ritchie in 1978. This book is commonly known in the programming community as simply K&R (referring to the initials of the authors) and finds a place on many programmers' bookshelves to this day. However, the book was written as a tutorial introduction to C, not as a comprehensive or official standard for the language. As different vendors offered varying implementations of the C language, differences between those implementations began to appear.

Fearing that C might lose its portability, a group of compiler vendors and software developers petitioned the American National Standards Institute (ANSI) to build a standard for the C language in 1983. ANSI approved the application and formed the X3J11 Technical Committee to work on the C standard. By the end of 1989, the committee approved the ANSI standard for the C programming language.

The ANSI standard for C enhances the original K&R standard and defines a group of commonly used C functions that known as the ANSI C standard library. In most cases, C compilers include the standard library, along with other libraries to provide some other compiler-specific functions.

This book focuses on the C functions defined in the ANSI standard, which is supported by all compiler vendors. All programs in this book can be compiled by any compilers that comply with the ANSI standard. If you're interested in a specific compiler, you can learn the compiler-specific functions from the compiler's reference manual.

Assumptions About You

No previous programming experience is required for you to learn the C language from this book, although some knowledge of computers helps. Also, it's up to you to determine how quickly to go through the 24 hours of this book: You could sit up with a big pot of coffee and power through the book in a sitting or you could take an hour a day for 24 days.

After you complete this book, having done all of the exercises along the way, you should be proficient and comfortable with the syntax and features of the C language. In addition, you'll already have some experience with many of the tasks that are encountered in C programming. When you're ready to undertake your own programming projects, you'll be able to use C as a tool in writing the powerful and useful programs you want to create. As you progress, you'll find that there is always more to learn—not only about C and how to leverage its power, but also about new technologies and programming ideas in general. With hard work and lots of practice, you can quickly build on the skills and technologies that you learn.

Setting Up Your System

Basically, all you need is a computer and a C compiler in order to compile and run your own C programs or the C programs from this book. The recommended hardware and software are listed in the following sections.

Hardware

Any type of computer that has or can access a C compiler is fine. The C compiler should be ANSI C compliant. Most likely, you have a PC on your desktop. A 286 PC with a 50MB hard drive and 1MB memory (RAM) is probably the minimum requirement to run a DOS-based C compiler. For a Windows-based C compiler, your computer must have a bigger hard drive and more memory. Check your compiler vendor for more details on hardware requirements.

Software

If you're using a UNIX-based workstation, you might already have a C compiler loaded on your machine, or at least you might be able to access a C compiler on a server machine. Check with your system administrator to find out how to access an ANSI C compliant compiler. On a UNIX-based machine, you should know how to use a text editor such as `vi` or `emacs` to write C programs.

If you have a PC running a Microsoft Windows operating system (such as Windows 95), you need to install a C compiler and a text editor on your PC. However, most C compilers come with a built-in editor. You can also use any text editor that may already be installed on your machine.

Borland International's Turbo C and Microsoft's Quick C used to be very popular in the C compiler market. These days, an ANSI-compliant C compiler is usually part of any commercially available C++ development package, such as Microsoft Visual C++. In addition, development packages come with an integrated development environment (IDE), which you can use to edit, compile, run, and debug your C programs all from the same window.

You can pick up any C compiler you like to compile the sample code given in the book, as long as the compiler is ANSI C compliant. You shouldn't have problems installing a C compiler on your computer if you read the manuals that come with the compiler and follow the installation instructions correctly. Most C and/or C++ compilers provide a quick tutorial that shows you how to install the compiler and set up a working development environment on your computer.

These days, the Linux operating system is becoming more and more popular among PC users. In most cases, the Linux package you get contains a C compiler. The C compiler can be installed on your PC when you're installing the Linux operating system, or can be added later after you finish the installation of Linux.

A Sample C Programming Setup

I have a Pentium 100MHz PC with 32MB memory and with a 2.5GB hard drive. (The hard drive had about 1.5GB free space before I installed a copy of Microsoft Visual C++ 5.0.) Also, I have Windows 95 as the operating system on the machine.

In this book, all C programs are developed with Microsoft Visual C++ version 5.0. The reasons I chose Visual C++ are simple: All C programs in this book are written in ANSI C and can be compiled into console-mode applications (that is, text-based programs running in a DOS window); the Visual C++ 5.0 package includes a good C compiler that is ANSI C compliant.

I set up my development environment in such a way that all C programs in this book can be compiled and made into console applications. Also, I test and run the applications made from the C programs at a DOS prompt provided by Windows 95.

In the following two sections, I'll briefly show you how to use Microsoft's and Boralnd's C compilers.

Using Microsoft's Compiler

I'm going to show you how to use the C compiler that is bundled with the Microsoft's Visual C++ package in this section. If you need to learn more details on how to install Visual C++, please follow the instructions that come with the compiler.

Now I assume you've installed a copy of Visual C++ 5.0 on your computer. To start the compiler, you can click the Start button from your Windows 95 (or 98 or NT), and choose: Programs, Microsoft Visual C++ 5.0, Microsoft Visual C++ 5.0. Or, you can simply run the application file MSDEV.EXE directly from the directory (folder) where you installed the Visual C++ package. Figure 1.3 shows an example of the integrated development environment (IDE) from Visual C++ 5.0.

FIGURE 1.3

An example of the IDE from Visual C++ version 5.0.

Then, you can open a new file within the IDE by clicking the New File button on the far left side of the toolbar, and type the following text in the space of the new file:

```c
#include <stdio.h>

main()
{
    printf ("Howdy, neighbor! This is my first C program.\n");
    return 0;
}
```

Figure 1.4 shows the IDE with the text you just typed in. Don't worry about the meaning of the text. In the next chapter, "Your First C Program," will explain it to you.

FIGURE **1.4**

*Writing code in the
Visual C++ 5.0 IDE.*

Then, you need to save the text as a file. Let's call the file MyFirstProgram.c. It is also a good idea to create a new directory on your hard drive to store your programming projects, and save the new file there. First, click the Save button on the toolbar. In the Save As dialog box, click the New Folder button and type in a name for your programming folder. Then double-click that folder to open it, type MyFirstProgram.c in the File Name box, and click Save. Note that the extension .c is used to indicate that the file you just saved is a C program file.

Now, you need to click the Build menu and choose the Compile MyFirstProgram.c option. By doing so, you ask the compiler to compile the text you just typed in and saved (see Figure 1.5). At this point, Visual C++ may prompt you to create a new workspace; just click Yes and this will be done automatically. There should be no errors or warnings in the output window after the compiler is run.

Then, click the Build menu again, and this time, choose the Build MyFirstProgram.exe option which will eventually produce an executable file called MyFirstProgram.exe. Figure 1.6 shows that there are no errors or warnings after MyFirstProgram.exe is built.

FIGURE 1.5

Compiling a C program using the IDE.

FIGURE 1.6

Creating a program executable file.

You are now ready to run the executable file, MyFirstProgram.exe, that you just compiled. You can run it from the menu path: Build, Execute MyFirstProgram.exe. Because the executable file is a console mode application, a DOS prompt window will show up when the executable file is running (see Figure 1.7).

FIGURE **1.7**

Running a C program.

You can tell that the first line in the DOS prompt window shown in Figure 1.7 is the exact line you just typed: "Howdy neighbor! This is my first C program." This is indeed your first C program output! (Note that the second line shown in the DOS prompt is just a built-in reminder from the DOS prompt window.)

Okay. I just demonstrated how to use Visual C++ compiler to write and compile a C program, and how to make the program executable. For more details, you need to read books such as *Teach Yourself Visual C++ 5 in 21 Days* that focus on teaching you how to use Visual C++ compiler.

Using Borland's Compiler

In this section, I'm going to show you how to use the C compiler that is bundled with Borland's C++ package. The procedure of the section is quite similar as the one of the previous section. If you need to learn more details on how to install Borland C++, please follow the instructions that come with the compiler.

I assume that you've installed a copy of Borland C++ 5.02 on your computer. To start the compiler, you can click the Start button from your Windows 95 (or Windows 98 or NT) task bar, and choose Programs, Borland C++ 5.02, Borland C++. Or, you can simply run the application file bcw.exe directly from the directory (folder) where you installed the Borland C++ package. Figure 1.8 shows an example of the integrated development environment (IDE) from Borland C++ 5.02.

Then, you can open a new file within the IDE, and type the following text in the space of the newly opened file:

```
#include <stdio.h>

main()
{
    printf ("Howdy, neighbor! This is my first C program.\n");
    return 0;
}
```

FIGURE **1.8**

*Creating a program
with the Borland C++
IDE.*

Figure 1.9 shows the IDE with the text you just typed. Don't worry about the meaning of
the text. The next hour will explain it to you.

FIGURE **1.9**

*Saving C program text
with Borland's IDE.*

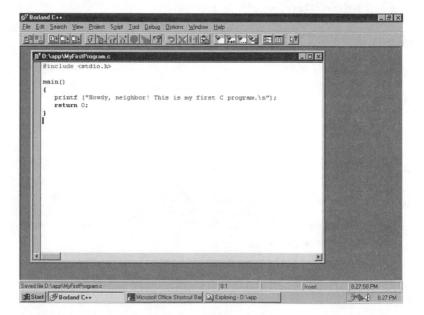

Now you need to save the text as a file. Let's call the file `MyFirstProgram.c`. Note that the extension `.c` is used to indicate that the file you just saved is a C program file.

Now, you need to click the Project menu and choose the Compile option. By doing so, you ask the compiler to start compiling the text you just typed and saved. Figure 1.10 shows that there are no errors or warnings after `MyFirstProgram.c` is compiled and `MyFirstProgram.exe` is created.

FIGURE 1.10

Compiling a C program using Borland's IDE.

You are now ready to run the executable file, `MyFirstProgram.exe`, that you just compiled. You can run it by clicking the Run button on the toolbar. Or, you can run `MyFirstProgram.exe` directly from the directory where you created it. Because the executable file is in fact a DOS application, a DOS prompt window will show up when the executable file is running (see Figure 1.11).

FIGURE 1.11

Running a C program using Borland's IDE.

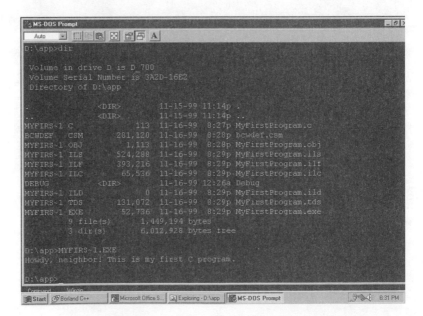

Figure 1.11 displays the output exactly as you just typed it: "Howdy neighbor! This is my first C program." This is indeed your first C program output!

If you want to learn more details on how to use Borland C++, read a book such as *Teach Yourself Borland C++ 5 in 21 Days*.

 Here is a brief note on binary code and executable files. You'll learn more details later in this book. Basically, before you can run a C program on your computer you need to use a C compiler to translate the C program into machine-understandable code (that is, binary code). When the translation is done, the binary code can be saved into an application file. The binary code or application file is called executable code, or an executable file, because it can be executed directly on your computer.

Summary

In this first lesson you learned the following basic things about the C language:

- C is a general-purpose programming language.
- C is a high-level language that has the advantages of readability, maintainability, and portability.
- C is a very efficient language that allows you to control computer hardware and peripherals.
- C is a small language that you can easily learn in a relatively short time.
- Programs written in C can be reused.
- Programs written in C must be compiled and translated into machine-readable code before the computer can execute them.
- Many other programming languages, such as Perl, C++, and Java, have adopted basic concepts and useful features from the C language. Once you learn C, learning these other languages is much easier.
- The ANSI standard for C is the standard supported by C compiler vendors to maintain the portability of C programs.
- You can use any ANSI C compliant compiler to compile all of the C programs in this book.

In the next lesson you'll learn to write your first C program.

Q&A

Q What is the lowest-level language in the computer world?

A The computer's machine language is the lowest because the machine language, made up of 0s and 1s, is the only language that the computer can understand directly.

Q What are the advantages of high-level programming languages?

A Readability, maintainability, and portability are the main advantages of high-level programming languages.

Q What is C, anyway?

A C is a general-purpose programming language. It's a high-level language that has advantages such as readability, maintainability, and portability. Also, C allows you to get down to the hardware level to increase the performance speed if needed. A C compiler is needed to translate programs written in C into machine-understandable code. The portability of C is realized by recompiling the C programs with different C compilers intended for different types of computers.

Q Can I learn C in a short time?

A Yes. C is a small programming language. There are not many C keywords or commands to remember. Also, it's very easy to read and write C programs because C is a high-level programming language that is close to human languages, especially English. You can learn C in a relatively short time.

Workshop

To help solidify your understanding of this hour's lesson, you are encouraged to answer the quiz questions provided in the workshop before you move to next lesson. The answers and hints to the questions are given in Appendix D, "Answers to Quiz Questions and Exercises."

Quiz

1. What are the lowest-level and highest-level languages mentioned in this book?

2. Can a computer directly understand a program written in C? What do you need to translate a program written in C into the machine-understandable code (that is, binary code)?

3. If needed, can a C program be reused in another C program?

4. Why do we need the ANSI standard for the C language?

Hour **2**

Writing Your First C Program

Cut your own wood and it will warm you twice.

—Chinese proverb

In Hour 1, "Taking the First Step," you learned that C is a high-level programming language and that you need a C compiler to translate your C programs into binary code that your computer can understand and execute. In this lesson you'll write your first C program and learn the basics of a C program, such as

- The #include directive
- Header files
- Comments
- The main() function
- The return statement
- The exit() function

- The newline character (\n)
- Translating a C program into an executable file
- Debugging

A Simple C Program

Let's have a look at your first C program, demonstrated in Listing 2.1. Later in this lesson you're going to write your own C program for the first time.

LISTING 2.1   A Simple C Program

```
1:  /* 02L01.c: This is my first C program */
2:  #include <stdio.h>
3:
4:  main()
5:  {
6:      printf ("Howdy, neighbor! This is my first C program.\n");
7:      return 0;
8:  }
```

This is a very simple C program, which is saved in a file called 02L01.c. Note that the name of a C program file must have an extension of .c. If you've installed a C compiler and set up the proper development environment, you should be able to compile this C program, and make it into an executable file. I'll discuss how to make an executable file later in this chapter.

In the previous hour, you learned how to enter a program into your text editor and save it as a C program file. Here, you may notice that unlike the sample in the last chapter, each line is numbered. This is only done here as a reference for when I discuss what each line of a program does. Unlike other languages such as BASIC, the C language does not have line numbers at all. In fact, if you do enter the line numbers in the listing, your program will not work! So when you enter these programs, remember not to enter the line numbers that are shown in the book.

Two things you might notice by glancing at Listing 2.1 are the semicolons and indenting on lines 6 and 7. Unlike other languages, such as BASIC, the end of a line has no special significance in C. It is perfectly legal (and in many cases, advisable) to break a statement into several lines for clarity. Generally, an individual C statement ends in a semicolon, but there is more about this later in the book. The indenting serves to identify the various levels of a program in a kind of outline format. The function main() is, well, the main level of the program, so it goes on the far left. Lines 6 and 7 are part of main() so they are indented one level to the right. Usually, you use your Tab key to indent a level before you start typing. It should be noted that indenting, like line numbers, is not enforced — or even noticed! — by the compiler. The programmer is free to use line breaks and indenting, commonly referred to as *whitespace*, to make the program look readable. It is generally a matter of style, but it's a good idea to follow generally accepted conventions so that other programmers can understand your programs and vice-versa. Take a look at the use of whitespace in the programs in this book, and feel free to develop your own style as you go.

2

I set up my development environment in such a way that all C programs in this book can be compiled and made into console applications. For instance, 02L01.exe is the name of the console application made from 02L01.c. Note that .exe is included as the extension to the name of a DOS or Windows application program (that is, an executable file).

Also, on my machine, I save all the executable files made from the C programs in this book into a dedicated directory called C:\app. Therefore, if I type in 02L01 from a DOS prompt and press the Enter key, I can run the 02L01.exe executable file and display the message Howdy, neighbor! This is my first C program. on the screen. The following output is a copy from the screen:

```
Howdy, neighbor! This is my first C program.
```

Comments

Now let's take a close look at the C program in Listing 2.1.

The first line contains a comment:

```
/* 02L01.C: This is my first C program */
```

You notice that this line starts with a combination of slash and asterisk, /*, and ends with */. In C, /* is called the *opening comment mark*, and */ is the *closing comment mark*. The C compiler ignores everything between the opening comment mark and closing comment mark. That means the comment in the first line of Listing 2.1, 02L01.C: This is my first C program, is completely ignored by the compiler.

The only purpose of including comments in your C program is to help you document what the program or some specific sections in the programs do. Remember, comments are written for yourself and other programmers. For example, when you read someone else's code, the comments in the code help you to understand what the code does, or at least what the code intends to do. As your programs get larger and more complicated, you can use comments to write notes to yourself about what you are trying to do and why.

You don't need to worry about the size or performance speed of your C program if you add many comments into it. Adding comments into a C program does not increase the size of the binary code of the program (that is, the executable file), although the size of the program itself (that is, the source code) may become larger. The performance speed of the executable file made from your C program is not affected in any way by the comments inside your C program.

The C language allows you to write a comment that crosses more than one line. For instance, you can write a comment in C like this:

```
/*
   This comment does not increase the size of
   the executable file (binary code), nor does
   it affect the performance speed.
*/
```

which is equivalent to this:

```
/* This comment does not increase the size of */
/* the executable file (binary code), nor does */
/* it affect the performance speed. */
```

These days, there is another way to put comments into a C program. C++ started using two slashes (//) to mark the beginning of a comment line; many C compilers now use this convention as well. The comment ends at the end of the line. For instance, if I write a C program in Borland C++ or Visual C++, the following two comments are identical:

```
/*
   This comment does not increase the size of
   the executable file (binary code), nor does
   it affect the performance speed.
*/
// This comment does not increase the size of
// the executable file (binary code), nor does
// it affect the performance speed.
```

Note that this new style of using // as the beginning mark of a comment has not been approved by ANSI. Make sure your C compiler supports // before you use it.

One thing that needs to be pointed out is that the ANSI standard does not support *nested comments*, that is, comments within comments. For instance, the following is not allowed by the ANSI standard:

```
/* This is the first part of the first comment
   /* This is the second comment */
   This is the second part of the first comment */
```

> You can use the opening comment mark, /*, and closing comment mark, */, to help you test and fix any errors found in your C program. This is commonly referred to as *commenting out* a block of code. You can comment out one or more C statements in your C program with /* and */ when you need to focus on other statements and watch their behaviors closely. The C compiler will ignore the statements you comment out.
>
> Later, you can always restore the previously commented-out statements simply by removing the opening comment and closing comment marks. In this way, you don't need to erase or rewrite any statements during testing and debugging.
>
> However, since you can't nest comments made with /* and */, if you attempt to comment out code that already contains these comments, your program will not compile. One reason why the //-type comments are so useful is because you can nest them, and therefore legally comment them out with /* and */.
>
> If your text editor supports color syntax highlighting, you can use this to tell at a glance if sections of code are actually commented out as you intended.

The #include Directive

Let's now move to line 2 in the C program of Listing 2.1:

```
#include <stdio.h>
```

You see that this line starts with a pound sign, #, which is followed by include. In C, #include forms a *preprocessor directive* that tells the C preprocessor to look for a file and place the contents of that file in the location where the #include directive indicates.

The preprocessor is a program that does some preparations for the C compiler before your code is compiled. More details about the C preprocessor are discussed in Hour 23, "Compiling Programs: The C Preprocessor."

Also in this line, you see that <stdio.h> follows #include. You may guess that the file the #include directive asks for is something called stdio.h. You are exactly right! Here, the #include directive does ask the C preprocessor to look for and place stdio.h at the location of the directive in the C program.

The name of the stdio.h file stands for *standard input-output header* file. The stdio.h file contains numerous prototypes and macros to perform input or output (I/O) for C programs. You'll see more program I/O in Hour 5, "Handling Standard Input and Output."

 Some operating systems distinguish between upper- and lowercase letters, while others do not. For instance, stdio.h and STDIO.H are identical file-names on a PC, while they are different in UNIX.

Header Files

The files that are included by the #include directive, like stdio.h, are called *header files* because the #include directives are almost always placed at the start, or head of C programs. Actually, the extension name of .h does mean "header" and these are sometimes referred to in conversation as dot-h files.

Besides stdio.h, there are more header files, such as stdlib.h, string.h, math.h, and so on. Appendix A, "ANSI Standard Header Files," gives a list of all the ANSI standard header files. The specific header files you need to include depend on the specific library functions you intend to call. The documentation for library functions will tell you which header file is required.

Angle Brackets (< >) and Double Quotes (" ")

In the second line of Listing 2.1, there are two angle brackets, < and >, that are used to surround stdio.h. You may be wondering what the angle brackets do. In C, the angle brackets ask the C preprocessor to look for a header file in a directory other than the current one.

For instance, the current directory containing the 02L01.C file is called C:\code on my computer. Therefore, the angle brackets around <stdio.h> tell the C preprocessor to look for stdio.h in a directory other than C:\code.

If you want to let the C preprocessor look into the current directory first for a header file before it starts to look elsewhere, you can use double quotes to surround the name of the header file. For instance, when the C preprocessor sees "stdio.h", it looks in the current directory, which is C:\code on my machine, first before it looks elsewhere for the stdio.h header file.

Normally, the header files are saved in a subdirectory called include. For instance, I install a Microsoft C compiler in the directory MSVC on my hard drive, which is labeled as the C drive. Then the path to access the header files becomes C:\MSVC\include.

The path where header files are kept is usually determined by your compiler when you install it. This is commonly referred to as the include directory or include path of your environment. Normally, you never need to worry about the include directory until you create your own header files. For now, you just need to specify the name of the header file you wish to include.

The `main()` Function

In line 4 of Listing 2.1, you see this function:

```
main ()
```

This is a very special function in C. Every C program must have a `main()` function, and every C program can only have one `main()` function. More generic discussions about functions are given in Hour 3, "Learning the Structure of a C Program."

You can put the `main()` function wherever you want in your C program. However, the execution of your program always starts with the `main()` function. If you create other functions in your program, `main()` will always execute first, even if it is at the bottom of your program file.

In Listing 2.1, the `main()` function body starts in line 4 and ends in line 8. Because this is a very simple program, the `main()` function is the only function defined in the program. Within the `main()` function body, a C library function, `printf()`, is called in order to print out a greeting message (see line 6). More details about `printf()` are covered in Hour 5.

One more important thing about `main()` is that the execution of every C program ends with `main()`. A program ends when all the statements within the `main()` function have been executed.

The Newline Character (\n)

In the `printf()` function, one thing worth mentioning at this point is the *newline* character, \n. Usually suffixed at the end of a message, the newline character tells the computer to move the cursor to the beginning of the next line so that anything printed out after the message will start on the next line on the screen.

In a UNIX environment, \n by itself goes to a new line but leaves the cursor at the position it was on the previous line. In this case, it is necessary to print \r\n rather than just \n. The \r character is the *carriage return* character. When you run the sample programs in this book, you will be able to tell right away whether the cursor is returning to the beginning of the new line; if it is not, simply use \r\n wherever you see \n in the program listings.

Exercise 3 in this lesson gives you a chance to use the newline character to break a one-line message into two lines.

The `return` Statement

All functions in C can return values. For instance, when you create a function to add two numbers, you can make such a function that returns to you the value of the addition.

The `main()` function itself returns an integer value. In C, integers are decimal numbers without fraction portions.

Therefore, in line 7 of Listing 2.1, there is a statement, `return 0;`, that indicates that `0` is returned from the `main()` function and the program is terminated normally. There are cases when you must end your program due to an error condition. When that happens, you can return values other than `0` to tell the operating system (or the program that ran your program) that there was an error.

The `exit()` Function

There is also a C library function, `exit()`, that can be used to end a program. Because the `exit()` function is defined in a header file, `stdlib.h`, you have to include the header file at the beginning of your program in order to use the function. The `exit()` function itself does not return a value to your program.

Note that `return` and `exit()` can also be used in other functions. You'll see more examples of the return keyword in the rest of the book.

Compiling and Linking

You may already be anxious to know how an executable file is made. Let's have a look how a C program is compiled and translated into an executable file. As shown in Figure 2.1, there are at least three steps needed to create an executable file.

First, a program file written in C, called *source code*, is made. The name of the source code file ends with the extension `.c`.

Then the source code file is compiled by a C *compiler*, which creates a new file. The new file is an *object file*. In UNIX operating system, the name of an object file ends with the extension `.o`; In the DOS and Windows operating systems, the extension is `.obj`.

You cannot execute the object file because there is some function code missing. You have to finish the next step: linking. Linking is done by invoking a special program called a *linker*, which normally comes with the compiler package.

A linker is used to link together the object file, the ANSI standard C library, and other user-generated libraries to produce an executable file—the binary code. In this stage, the binary code of the library functions that are called in the source code is combined with the object file; the result is saved into a new file—an executable file. As you learned in the first chapter of the book, the name of an executable file usually ends with the extension .exe in DOS and Windows. (.com is another extension used for an DOS executable filename.) In UNIX, it's not necessary to include such an extension to an executable filename.

FIGURE 2.1

Make an executable file by the compiler and linker.

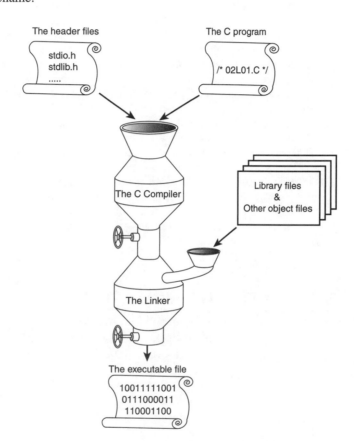

Later, you'll learn that in many cases, there may be several object files that have to be linked together in order to make an executable program.

Note that the object file and executable file are both machine-dependent. You cannot simply move an executable file from the current computer platform to another one that is operated by a different operating system, although the source code of the executable file, presumably written in ANSI C, might be machine independent (that is, portable).

Portability is an important concept in C, as it was one of the original design goals of the language. The portability of C code is what fueled its widespread use and popularity. Back in the days when applications and operating systems were hand-tailored to a specific computer system, software had to be written from scratch every time a new computer came along. The advent of the C language abstracted software away from hardware, and in a very real sense, helped give rise to the software industry as we know it today. Portability, in essence, refers to the process of porting a program to a different computer and/or operating system. Software development is an expensive and time-consuming process, and rewriting an existing program to work on a new computer is often a daunting task that is best avoided. Assuming that each operating system and compiler combination is tailored to the specific computer where it was intended to run, a C program should be easily portable with only minimal changes to the code. Portability is mentioned throughout this book, as it is important that C programs not make assumptions about the specific computer system where they are running. Fortunately, the ANSI C standard provides many features and functions that allow your program to essentially adapt to its environment, as opposed to acting on assumptions made by you, the programmer. If you get into the habit of maintaining portability early on, then as you progress with C, the idea will become second nature.

What's Wrong with My Program?

When you finish writing a C program and start to compile it, you might get some error or warning messages. Don't panic when you see error messages. We're human beings. Everybody makes mistakes. Actually, you should appreciate that your compiler catches some errors for you before you go any further.

Usually, your compiler can help you check the grammar — that is, *syntax* — of your C program and make sure you've followed the C programming rules properly. For instance, if you forget to put the ending brace on the main() function in line 8 of Listing 2.1, you'll get an error message something like this: syntax error : end of file found.

Also, the linker will issue an error message if it cannot find the missing code for a needed function in the libraries. For instance, if you misspell printf() as pprintf() in the program of Listing 2.1, you'll see an error message: '_pprintf': unresolved external (or something similar).

All errors found by the compiler and linker must be fixed before an executable file (binary code) can be made.

Debugging Your Program

In the computer world, program errors are also called *bugs*. In many cases, your C compiler and linker do not find any errors in your program, but the result made by running the executable file of the program is not what you expect. In order to find those "hidden" errors in your program, you may need to use a debugger.

Normally, your C compiler already includes a debugger software program. The debugger can execute your program one line at a time so that you can watch closely what's going on with the code in each line, or so that you can ask the debugger to stop running your program on any line. For more details about your debugger, refer to the instructions that come with your C compiler.

Later in this book, you'll learn that debugging is a very necessary and important step in writing software programs. (This topic is covered in Hour 24, "Where Do You Go From Here.")

Summary

In this lesson you learned the following concepts and statements about the C language:

- Some header files should be included at the beginning of your C program.

- Header files, such as `stdio.h` and `stdlib.h`, contain the declarations for functions used in your C program; for example, the `printf()` and `exit()` functions.

- Comments in your C programs are needed to help you in documenting your programs. You can put comments anywhere you like in your programs.

- In ANSI C, a comment starts with the opening comment mark, `/*`, and ends with the closing comment mark, `*/`.

- Every C program must have one but only one `main()` function. The program execution starts and ends with the `main()` function.

- The `return` statement can be used to return a value to indicate to the operating system whether an error has occurred. The `exit()` function terminates a program; the argument to the function indicates the error status, too.

- Compiling and linking are consecutive steps that have to be finished before an executable file is produced.

- Everybody, including you and me, makes mistakes in programming. Debugging is a very important step in your program design and coding.

In the next lesson you'll learn more about the essentials of C programs.

Q&A

Q Why do you need to put comments into your programs?

A Comments help you document what a program does. Especially when a program becomes very complex, you need to write comments to explain different parts in the program.

Q Why is the `main()` function needed in a program?

A The execution of a C program starts and ends with the `main()` function. Without the `main()` function, the computer does not know where to start to run a program.

Q What does the `#include` directive do?

A The `#include` directive is used to include header files that contain the declarations to the functions used in your C program. In other words, the `#include` directive tells the C preprocessor to look into the include path to find the specified header file.

Q Why do you need a linker?

A After compiling, some function code may still be missing in the object file of a program. A linker must then be used to link the object file to the C standard library or other user-generated libraries and include the missing function code so that an executable file can be created.

Workshop

To help solidify your understanding of this hour's lesson, you are encouraged to answer the quiz questions and finish the exercises provided in the workshop before you move to the next lesson. The answers and hints to the questions and exercises are given in Appendix D, "Answers to Quiz Questions and Exercises."

Quiz

1. Can a C compiler see the comments within your C program?
2. What kind of files does a C compiler actually produce?
3. Does the `exit()` function return a value? What about the `return` statement?
4. What is a header file?

Exercises

1. Is #include <stdio.h> the same as #include "stdio.h"?

2. It's time for you to write a program on your own. Referring to the program in Listing 2.1, write a C program that can print out a message: It's fun to write my own program in C.

3. Update the program in Listing 2.1 by adding one more newline character into the message printed out by the printf() function. You should see two lines of the message on the screen after running the updated executable file:

   ```
   Howdy, neighbor!
   This is my first C program.
   ```

4. What warning or error messages, if any, will you get when you're compiling the following program?

   ```
   #include <stdlib.h>
   #include <stdio.h>
   main()
   {
      printf ("Howdy, neighbor! This is my first C program.\n");
      exit(0);
   }
   ```

5. What error messages will you get for the following program when you're trying to compile it?

   ```
   void main()
   {
      printf ("Howdy, neighbor! This is my first C program.\n");
      return 0;
   }
   ```

2

Hour 3

Learning the Structure of a C Program

The whole is equal to the sum of its parts.

—Euclid

In Hour 2, "Writing Your First C Program," you saw and wrote some simple C programs. You also learned about the basic structure of a C program. You know that a program written in C has to be compiled before it can be executed. In this lesson you'll learn more essentials within a C program, such as

- Constants and variables
- Expressions
- Statements
- Statement blocks
- C function types and names
- Arguments to functions
- The body of a function
- Function calls

The Basics of a C Program

As a building is made of bricks, a C program is made of basic elements, such as expressions, statements, statement blocks, and function blocks. These elements are discussed in the following sections. But first, you need to learn two smaller but important elements, constant and variable, which make up expressions.

Constants and Variables

As its name implies, a *constant* is a value that never changes. A *variable*, on the other hand, can be used to present different values.

You can think of a constant as a music CD-ROM; the music saved in the CD-ROM is never changed. A variable is more like an audio cassette: You can always update the contents of the cassette by simply overwriting the old songs with new ones.

You can see many examples in which constants and variables are in the same statement. For instance, consider the following:

```
i = 1;
```

where the symbol 1 is a constant because it always has the same value (1), and the symbol i is assigned the constant 1. In other words, i contains the value of 1 after the statement is executed. Later, if there is another statement,

```
i = 10;
```

after it is executed, i is assigned the value of 10. Because i can contain different values, it's called a variable in the C language.

Expressions

An *expression* is a combination of constants, variables, and operators that are used to denote computations.

For instance, the following:

```
(2 + 3) * 10
```

is an expression that adds 2 and 3 first, and then multiplies the result of the addition by 10. (The final result of the expression is 50.)

Similarly, the expression 10 * (4 + 5) yields 90. The 80/4 expression results in 20.

Here are some other examples of expressions:

Expression	Description
6	An expression of a constant.
i	An expression of a variable.
6 + i	An expression of a constant plus a variable.
exit(0)	An expression of a function call.

Operators

As you've seen, an expression can contain symbols such as +, *, and /. In the C language, these symbols are called *arithmetic operators*. Table 3.1 lists all the arithmetic operators and their meanings.

TABLE 3.1   C Arithmetic Operators

Symbol	Meaning
+	Addition
-	Subtraction
*	Multiplication
/	Division
%	Remainder (or modulus)

You might already be familiar with all the arithmetic operators, except the remainder (%) operator. % is used to obtain the remainder of the first operand divided by the second operand. For instance, the expression

```
6 % 4
```

yields a value of 2 because 4 goes into 6 once with a remainder of 2.

The remainder operator, %, is also called the *modulus operator*.

Among the arithmetic operators, the multiplication, division, and remainder operators have a higher precedence than the addition and subtraction operators. For example, the expression

```
2 + 3 * 10
```

yields 32, not 50, because of the higher precedence of the multiplication operator.
3 * 10 is calculated first, and then 2 is added into the result of the multiplication.

As you might know, you can put parentheses around an addition (or subtraction) to force the addition (or subtraction) to be performed before a multiplication, division, or modulus computation. For instance, the expression

```
(2 + 3) * 10
```

performs the addition of 2 and 3 first before it multiplies the result by 10.

Other operators, which are used for syntax, include the comma and semicolon. The semicolon is generally used to indicate the end of a statement, as you will see later. The comma is used in certain instances where a statement is comprised of a list of expressions or declarations.

You'll learn more C language operators in Hours 6, "Manipulating Data," and 8, "Using Conditional Operators."

Identifiers

Along with numbers (such as the constant 7) and operators (such as the symbol +), expressions can also contain words that are called *identifiers*. Function names (such as exit) and variable names (such as i), as well as reserved keywords, are all *identifiers* in C.

The following is the set of characters you can use to make a valid identifier. Any characters or symbols that do not follow these rules are illegal to use in an identifier.

- Characters A through Z and a through z.
- Digit characters 0 through 9 (but these can not be used as the first character of an identifier).
- The underscore character (_).

For instance, stop_sign, Loop3, and _pause are all valid identifiers.

The following are illegal characters; that is, they do not meet the above set of rules for identifiers:

- C arithmetic signs (+, -, *, /).
- Period, or dot character (.).
- Apostrophes (') or quotes (").
- Any other special symbols such as *, @, #, ?, and so on.

Some invalid identifiers, for example, are 4flags, sum-result, method*4, and what_size?.

> Never use the reserved keywords, or the names of the standard C library functions, for variable names or function names that you create in your own C programs.

You've already seen the `return` keyword in the previous hour. Hour 4, "Understanding Data Types and Keywords," lists all of the reserved keywords.

Statements

In the C language, a *statement* is a complete instruction, ending with a semicolon. In many cases, you can turn an expression into a statement by simply adding a semicolon at the end of the expression.

For instance, the following:

```
i = 1;
```

is a statement. You might have already figured out that the statement consists of an expression of `i = 1` and a semicolon (`;`).

Here are some other examples of statements:

```
i = (2 + 3) * 10;
i = 2 + 3 * 10;
j = 6 % 4;
k = i + j;
```

Also, in the first lesson of this book you learned statements such as

```
return 0;
exit(0);
printf ("Howdy, neighbor! This is my first C program.\n");
```

Statement Blocks

A group of statements can form a *statement block* that starts with an opening brace (`{`) and ends with a closing brace (`}`). A statement block is treated as a single statement by the C compiler.

For instance, the following:

```
for(. . .) {
   s3 = s1 + s2;
   mul = s3 * c;
   remainder = sum % c;
}
```

is a statement block that starts with { and ends with }. Here for is a keyword in C that determines the statement block. The for keyword is discussed in Hour 7, "Working with Loops."

A statement block provides a way to group one or more statements together as a single statement. Many C keywords can only control one statement. If you want to put more than one statement under the control of a C keyword, you can add those statements into a statement block so that the block is considered as one statement by the C keyword.

Anatomy of a C Function

Functions are the building blocks of C programs. Besides the standard C library functions, you can also use some other functions made by you or another programmer in your C program. In Hour 2 you saw the main() function, as well as two C library functions, printf() and exit(). Now, let's have a closer look at functions.

As shown in Figure 3.1, a function consists of six parts: the function type, the function name, arguments to the function, the opening brace, the function body, and the closing brace.

FIGURE 3.1

The anatomy of a function in the C language.

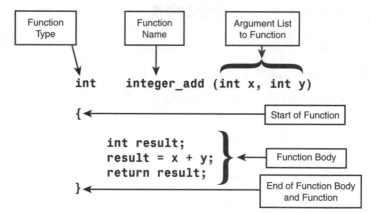

The six parts of a function are explained in the following sections.

Determining a Function's Type

The *function type* is used to signify what type of value a function is going to return after its execution. In Hour 2 for instance, you learned that the default function type of main() is int.

In C, int is used as the keyword for the integer data type. In the next hour, you'll learn more about data types.

Besides the `int` type, a function type can be one of the other types, such as the character type (keyword: `char`), the floating type (`float`), and so on. You will learn more about those types later in this book.

When you call a C function which returns a data type, the value it returns (*return value*) can then be used in an expression. You can assign it to a variable, such as

```
int a = func();
```

or use it in an expression, like this

```
a = func() + 7;
```

Giving a Function a Valid Name

A *function name* is normally given in such a way that it reflects what the function can do. For instance, the name of the `printf()` function means "print formatted data."

Since a function name is an identifier, when creating your own functions you must follow the rules for creating valid identifiers when naming your function.

In addition, you cannot use the names of standard C functions such as `printf()` or `exit()` to name your own functions. They are already defined, and it is illegal to use the same function name in defining more than one function.

Passing Arguments to C Functions

Functions are useful because you can call them over and over from different points in your program. However it's likely that you call a certain function for a slightly different reason each time.

For example, in Listing 2.1 in Hour 2, a character string, `"Howdy, neighbor! This is my first C program.\n"`, is passed to the `printf()` function, and then `printf()` prints the string on the screen. The entire purpose of `printf()` is to print a string on the screen, but each time you call it, you pass the specific string that you want it to print this time around.

Pieces of information passed to functions are known as *arguments*. As you've seen, the argument of a function is placed between the parentheses that immediately follow the function name.

The number of arguments to a function is determined by the declaration of the function, which in turn is determined by the task the function is going to perform. If a function needs more than one argument, arguments passed to the function must be separated by commas; these arguments are considered an *argument list*.

3

If no information needs to be passed to a function, you just leave the argument field between the parentheses blank. For instance, the main() function in Listing 2.1 of Hour 2 has no argument, so the field between the parentheses following the function name is empty. See the copy of Listing 3.1 below:

LISTING 3.1. A Simple C Program.

```
1:  /* 02L01.c: This is my first C program */
2:  #include <stdio.h>
3:
4:  main()
5:  {
6:      printf ("Howdy, neighbor! This is my first C program.\n");
7:      return 0;
8:  }
```

The Beginning and End of a Function

As you might have already figured out, braces are used to mark the beginning and end of a function. The *opening brace* ({) signifies the start of a function body, whereas the *closing brace* (}) marks the end of the function body.

As mentioned earlier, the braces are also used to mark the beginning and end of a statement block. You can think of it as a natural extension to use braces with functions because a function consists of one or several statements.

The Function Body

The *function body* in a function is the place that contains variable declarations and other C statements. The task of a function is accomplished by executing the statements inside the function body one at a time.

It is important to remember that any variable declarations must be placed at the beginning of the function body. It is illegal to put variable declarations anywhere other than the very beginning of a statement block.

> If your function body contains variable declarations, they must all be placed first, before any other statements.

Listing 3.2 demonstrates a function that adds two integers specified by its arguments and returns the result of the addition.

LISTING 3.2 A Function that Adds Two Integers

```
1:  /* 03L01.c: This function adds two integers and returns the result */
2:  int integer_add( int x, int y )
3:  {
4:     int result;
5:     result = x + y;
6:     return result;
7:  }
```

ANALYSIS As you learned in Hour 2, line 1 of Listing 3.1 is a comment that describes what the function can do.

In line 2, you see that the int data type is prefixed prior to the function name. Here int is used as the function type, which signifies that an integer is returned by the function. The function name shown in line 2 is integer_add. The argument list contains two arguments, int x and int y, in line 2, where the int data type specifies that the two arguments are both integers.

Line 3 contains the opening brace ({) that marks the start of the function.

The function body is in lines 4–6 in Listing 3.1. Line 4 gives the variable declaration of result, and is specified by the int data type as an integer. The statement in line 5 adds the two integers represented by x and y and assigns the computation result to the result variable. The return statement in line 6 then returns the computation result represented by result.

Last, but not least, the closing brace (}) in line 7 is used to close the function.

> When you create a function in your C program, don't assign the function too much work. If a function has too much to do, it will be very difficult to write and debug. If you have a complex programming project, break it into smaller pieces. Try your best to make sure that each function has just one task to do.

Making Function Calls

Based on what you've learned so far, you can write a C program that calls the integer_add() function to calculate an addition and then print out the result on the screen. An example of such a program is demonstrated in Listing 3.3.

LISTING 3.3   A C Program that Calculates an Addition and Prints the Result to the Screen

```
 1:  /* 03L02.c: Calculate an addition and print out the result */
 2:  #include <stdio.h>
 3:  /* This function adds two integers and returns the result */
 4:  int integer_add( int x, int y )
 5:  {
 6:     int result;
 7:     result = x + y;
 8:     return result;
 9:  }
10:
11: int main()
12: {
13:    int sum;
14:
15:    sum = integer_add(5, 12);
16:    printf("The addition of 5 and 12 is %d.\n", sum);
17:    return 0;
18: }
```

The program in Listing 3.2 is saved as a source file called `03L02.c`. After this program is compiled and linked, an executable file for `03L02.c` is created. On my machine, the executable file is named `03L02.exe`. The following is the output printed on the screen after I run the executable on my machine:

OUTPUT   The addition of 5 and 12 is 17.

ANALYSIS   Line 1 in Listing 3.2 is a comment about the program. As you learned in Hour 2, the include directive in line 2 includes the `stdio.h` header file because of the `printf()` function in the program.

Lines 3–9 represent the `integer_add()` function that adds two integers, as discussed in the previous section.

The `main()` function, prefixed with the `int` data type, starts in line 11. Lines 12 and 18 contain the opening brace and closing brace for the `main()` function, respectively. An integer variable, `sum`, is declared in line 13.

The statement in line 15 calls the `integer_add()` function that you examined in the previous section. Note that two integer constants, 5 and 12, are passed to the `integer_add()` function, and that the `sum` variable is assigned the return result from the `integer_add()` function.

You first saw the C standard library function `printf()` in Hour 2. If you thought you found something new added to the function in line 16, you're correct. This time, there are two arguments that are passed to the `printf()` function. They are the string `"The addition of 5 and 12 is %d.\n"` and the variable `sum`.

Note that a new symbol, `%d`, is added into the first argument. The second argument is the integer variable `sum`. Because the value of `sum` is going to be printed out on the screen, you might think that the `%d` has something to do with the integer variable `sum`. You're right again. `%d` tells the computer the format in which `sum` should be printed on the screen.

More details on `%d` are covered in Hour 4. The relationship between `%d` and `sum` is discussed in Hour 5, "Handling Standard Input and Output."

More importantly, you should focus on the program in Listing 3.2 and pay attention to how to call either a user-generated function or a standard C library function from the `main()` function.

Summary

In this lesson you learned the following important concepts and operators:

- A constant in C is a value that never changes. A variable, on the other hand, can present different values.
- A combination of constants, variables, and operators is called an expression in the C language. An expression is used to denote different computations.
- The arithmetic operators include +, -, *, /, and %.
- A statement consists of a complete expression suffixed with a semicolon.
- The C compiler treats a statement block as a single statement, although the statement block might contain more than one statement.
- The function type specified in the declaration of a function determines the type of the value returned by the function.
- You have to follow certain rules to make a valid function name.
- An argument contains information that you want to pass to a function. An argument list contains two or more arguments that are separated by commas.
- The opening brace ({) and closing brace (}) are used to mark the start and end of a C function.
- A function body contains variable declarations and statements.
- Usually, a function should accomplish just one task.

In the next lesson you'll learn more about data types in the C language.

Q&A

Q What is the difference between a constant and a variable?

A The major difference is that the value of a constant cannot be changed, whereas the value of a variable can. You can assign different values to a variable whenever it's necessary in your C program.

Q Why do you need a statement block?

A Many C keywords can only control one statement. A statement block provides a way to put more than one statement together, and put the statement block under the control of a C keyword. Then, the statement block is treated as a single statement.

Q Which arithmetic operators have a higher precedence?

A Among the five arithmetic operators, the multiplication, division, and remainder operators have a higher precedence than the addition and subtraction operators.

Q How many parts does a function normally have?

A A function normally has six parts: the function type, the function name, the arguments, the opening brace, the function body, and the closing brace.

Workshop

To help solidify your understanding of this hour's lesson, you are encouraged to answer the quiz questions and finish the exercises provided in the workshop before you move to the next lesson. The answers and hints to the questions and exercises are given in Appendix D, "Answers to Quiz Questions and Exercises."

Quiz

1. In the C language, is 74 a constant? How about 571?

2. Is x = 570 + 1 an expression? How about x = 12 + y?

3. Are the following function names valid?

   ```
   2methods

   m2_algorithm

   *start_function

   Room_Size

   .End_Exe

   _turbo_add
   ```

4. Is 2 + 5 * 2 equal to (2 + 5) * 2?

5. Does 7 % 2 produce the same result as 4 % 3?

Exercises

1. Given two statements, x = 3; and y = 5 + x;, how can you build a statement block with the two statements?

2. What is wrong with the following function?

```c
int 3integer_add( int x, int y, int z)
{
    int sum;
    sum = x + y + z;
    return sum;
}
```

3. What is wrong with the following function?

```c
int integer_add( int x, int y, int z)
{
    int sum;
    sum = x + y + z
    return sum;
}
```

3

4. Write a C function that can perform a multiplication of two integers and return the calculated result.

5. Write a C program that calls the C function you just wrote in Exercise 4 to calculate the multiplication of 3 times 5 and then print out the return value from the function on the screen.

Hour 4

Understanding Data Types and Keywords

What's in a name? That which we call a rose
By any other name would smell sweet.

—W. Shakespeare

You learned how to make a valid name for a C function in Hour 3, "Learning the Structure of a C Program." Now, you're going to learn more about naming a variable and the C keywords reserved by the C compiler in this hour.

Also in this hour you're going to learn about the four data types of the C language in detail:

- char data type
- int data type
- float data type
- double data type

C Keywords

The C language reserves certain words that have special meanings to the language. Those reserved words are sometimes called *C keywords*. You should not use the C keywords for your own variable, constant, or function names in your programs. Table 4.1 lists the 32 reserved C keywords.

TABLE 4.1   Reserved Keywords in C

Keyword	Description
auto	Storage class specifier
break	Statement
case	Statement
char	Type specifier
const	Storage class modifier
continue	Statement
default	Label
do	Statement
double	Type specifier
else	Statement
enum	Type specifier
extern	Storage class specifier
float	Type specifier
for	Statement
goto	Statement
if	Statement
int	Type specifier
long	Type specifier
register	Storage class specifier
return	Statement
short	Type specifier
signed	Type specifier
sizeof	Operator
static	Storage class specifier
struct	Type specifier
switch	Statement

Keyword	Description
typedef	Statement
union	Type specifier
unsigned	Type specifier
void	Type specifier
volatile	Storage class modifier
while	Statement

Don't worry if you can't remember all the C keywords the first time through. In the rest of the book, you'll become more familiar with them and start to use many of the keywords through examples and exercises.

Note that all C keywords are written in lowercase letters. As I've mentioned, C is a case-sensitive language. Therefore, int, as shown in the list here, is considered as a C keyword, but INT is not.

The char Data Type

An object of the char data type represents a single character of the character set used by your computer. For example, A is a character, and so is a. But 7 is a number.

However, a computer can only store numeric code. Therefore, characters such as A, a, B, b, and so on all have a unique numeric code that is used by computers to represent the characters. Usually, a character takes 8 bits (that is, 1 byte) to store its numeric code.

For many computers, the ASCII codes are the *de facto* standard codes to represent a character set. (ASCII, just for your information, stands for American Standard Code for Information Interchange.) The original ASCII character set has only 128 characters because it uses the lower 7 bits that can represent 2^7 (that is, 128) characters.

On IBM-compatible PCs, however, the character set is extended to contain a total of 256 (that is, 2^8) characters.

One thing I'd like to mention here is that the ANSI C standard specifies only the value of the null character, which is always zero (i.e., a byte with all bits set to 0.) The other characters' numeric values are determined by the types of computers, operating systems, and C compilers. You are encouraged to explore the character set of the computer you are using. This can be done with the program in Listing 4.1.

In the computer world, a bit is the smallest unit of data storage, and it can only have one of two values: 0 or 1. These values represent two states of electronic switches used in the computer's memory and CPU. A byte is a larger unit than a bit. In fact, eight bits are equal to one byte.

Character Variables

A variable that can represent different characters is called a *character variable*.

You can set the data type of a variable to char by using the following declaration format:

```
char   variablename;
```

where *variablename* is the name you provide in which to store values of this type.

If you have more than one variable to declare, you can either use the following format:

```
char   variablename1;
char   variablename2;
char   variablename3;
```

or this one:

```
char   variablename1, variablename2, variablename3;
```

For example, the following statement declares MyCharacter and sets it to 'A':

```
char MyCharacter = 'A';
```

Similarly, the following statements declare x, y, and z as character variables and then assign values to them:

```
char x, y, z;
x = 'A';
y = 'f';
z = '7';
```

Note the last assignment, z = '7', sets z to equal the numeric value representing the character '7' in the character set — not the actual number 7.

You'll learn more about the character variable and how to use it in your C programs later in this book.

Character Constants

A character enclosed in single quotes (') is called a *character constant*. For instance, 'A', 'a', 'B', and 'b', are all character constants that have their unique numeric values in a given character set. For instance, you may see the unique numeric values from the ASCII character set.

It is important to remember that character constants are always surrounded by single quote characters (') while a string of more than one character uses the double quote ("). If this sounds confusing, just remember that single quotes go with single characters. You saw an example of double quotes and character strings with the printf() function calls in the previous hour.

From the ASCII character set, you will find that the unique numeric (decimal) values of 'A', 'a', 'B', and 'b' are 65, 97, 66, and 98, respectively. Therefore, given x as a character variable, and given the ASCII character set, for instance, the following two assignment statements are equivalent:

```
x = 'A';
x = 65;
```

So are the following two statements:

```
x = 'a';
x = 97;
```

Later in this hour you'll see a program, shown in Listing 4.2, that converts the numeric values back to the corresponding characters.

Don't confuse x = 'a'; with x = a;. The first statement assigns the numeric value of character a to variable x, that is, x will contain the value of 97 (the ASCII value of the letter 'a') after the assignment. Statement x = a; however assigns whatever value is contained in variable a into variable x. You'll learn more about the difference later in this book.

The Escape Character (\)

Actually, you first saw the escape character (\) in Hour 2, "Your First C Program," when you learned to use the newline character (\n) to break a message into two pieces. Therefore, the backslash (\) is called the *escape character* in the ASCII character set. The escape character is used in the C language to tell the computer that a special character follows.

For instance, when the computer sees \ in the newline character \n, it knows that the next character, n, causes a sequence of a carriage return and a line feed.

Besides the newline character, some of the other special characters in the C language are as follows:

Character	Description
\b	The backspace character; moves the cursor to the left one character.
\f	The form-feed character; goes to the top of a new page.
\r	The return character; returns to the beginning of the current line.
\t	The tab character; advances to the next tab stop.

Printing Characters

You already know that the printf() function, defined in the C header file stdio.h, can be used to print out messages on the screen. (Ref. Listing 2.1 in Hour 2.) In this section, you're going to learn to use the character format specifier, %c, which indicates to the printf() function that the argument to be printed is a character. (You'll learn more about the format specifier in Hour 5, "Handling Standard Input and Output." Here, you just get your feet wet.) The important thing to know for now is that each format specifier in the string you pass to printf() will correspond to one of the variables you pass in to the function. Let's first have a look at the program in Listing 4.1, which prints out characters on the screen.

TYPE   **LISTING 4.1**   Printing Characters on the Screen

```
1:  /* 04L01.c: Printing out characters */
2:  #include <stdio.h>
3:
4:  main()
5:  {
6:     char c1;
7:     char c2;
8:
9:     c1 = 'A';
10:    c2 = 'a';
11:    printf("Convert the value of c1 to character: %c.\n", c1);
12:    printf("Convert the value of c2 to character: %c.\n", c2);
13:    return 0;
14: }
```

After the executable file of 04L01.c in Listing 4.1 is created, you can run it to see what will be printed out on the screen. On my machine, the executable file is named as 04L01.exe. The following is the output printed on the screen of my computer after I run the executable:

OUTPUT
```
Convert the value of c1 to character: A.
Convert the value of c2 to character: a.
```

ANALYSIS As you know, line 2 includes the header file, stdio.h, for the printf() function. Lines 5–15 make up the main() function body.

Lines 6 and 7 declare two character variables, c1 and c2, while lines 9 and 10 assign c1 and c2 with the character constants 'A' and 'a', respectively.

Note that the %c format specifier is used in the printf() function in lines 11 and 12, which tells the computer that the contents contained by c1 and c2 should be printed as characters. When the two statements in lines 11 and 12 are executed, two characters are formatted and output to the screen, based on the numeric values contained by c1 and c2, respectively.

Now look at the program shown in Listing 4.2. This time, %c is used to convert the numeric values back to the corresponding characters.

TYPE **LISTING 4.2** Converting Numeric Values Back to Characters

```
1:  /* 04L02.c: Converting numeric values back to characters */
2:  #include <stdio.h>
3:
4:  main()
5:  {
6:     char c1;
7:     char c2;
8:
9:     c1 =65;
10:    c2 =97;
11:    printf("The character that has the numeric value of 65 is: %c.\n", c1);
12:    printf("The character that has the numeric value of 97 is: %c.\n", c2);
13:    return 0;
14: }
```

4

The following is the output printed on the screen of my computer after I run the executable file, 04L02.exe. (You might receive different output from your computer; it is implementation-dependent. That is, it's up to the type of your computer, the operating system, and the C computer you're using):

OUTPUT
```
The character that has the numeric value of 65 is: A.
The character that has the numeric value of 97 is: a
```

ANALYSIS The program in Listing 4.2 is similar to the one in Listing 4.1 except for the two statements in lines 9 and 10. Note that in lines 9 and 10 of Listing 4.2, the character variables c1 and c2 are assigned 65 and 97, respectively.

As you know, 65 is the numeric value (decimal) of the A character in the ASCII character set; 97 is the numeric value of a. In lines 11 and 12, the %c format specifier converts the numeric values, 65 and 97, into the A and a, respectively. The A and a characters are then printed out on the screen.

The int Data Type

You saw the integer data type in Hour 3. The int keyword is used to specify the type of a variable as an integer. Integer numbers are also called *whole numbers*, which have no fractional part or decimal point. Therefore, the result of an integer division is truncated, simply because any fraction part is ignored.

Depending on the operating system and the C compiler you're using, the length of an integer varies. On most UNIX workstations, for example, an integer is 32 bits long, which means that the range of an integer is from 2147483647 (that is, $2^{31}-1$) to -2147483648. The range of a 16-bit integer is from 32767 (that is, $2^{15}-1$) to -32768. Again, this can vary among different systems, so you can check the reference materials for your compiler to be sure.

Some C compilers, such as Visual C++ 1.5, provide only the 16-bit integer, whereas other 32-bit C compilers, such as Visual C++ 5.0, support the 32-bit integer.

Declaring Integer Variables

You also saw the declaration of an integer in Hour 3. The following shows the basic declaration format:

```
int   variablename;
```

Similar to the character declaration, if you have more than one variable to declare, you can either use the format like this:

```
int   variablename1;
int   variablename2;
int   variablename3;
```

or like this:

```
int   variablename1, variablename2, variablename3;
```

Here *variablename1, variablename2,* and *variablename3* indicate the places where you put the names of int variables.

For example, the following statement declares MyInteger as an integer variable and assigns it a value:

```
int MyInteger = 2314;
```

Similarly, the following statement declares A, a, B, and b as integer variables:

```
int A, a, B, b;
A = 37;
a = -37;
B = -2418;
b = 12 ;
```

You'll learn more about the integer data type later in the book.

Showing the Numeric Values of Characters

Like the character format specifier (%c) that is used to format a single character, %d, called the *integer format specifier*, is used to format an integer. You might recall that in line 16 of Listing 3.2, %d is used in the printf() function to format the second argument to the function to an integer.

In this section you're going to study a program, shown in Listing 4.3, that can print out the numeric values of characters by using the integer format specifier %d with printf().

TYPE   **LISTING 4.3**   Showing the Numeric Values of Characters

```
1:  /* 04L03.c: Showing the numeric values of characters */
2:  #include <stdio.h>
3:
4:  main()
5:  {
6:     char c1;
7:     char c2;
8:
9:     c1 = 'A';
10:    c2 = 'a';
11:    printf("The numeric value of A is: %d.\n", c1);
12:    printf("The numeric value of a is: %d.\n", c2);
13:    return 0;
14: }
```

4

I get the following output on the screen of my computer after running the executable file, 04L03.exe. (You may get a different output if your machine is not using the ASCII character set.)

OUTPUT
```
The numeric value of A is: 65.
The numeric value of a is: 97.
```

ANALYSIS   You may find that the program in Listing 4.3 is quite similar to the one in Listing 4.1. As a matter of fact, I simply copied the source code from Listing 4.1 to Listing 4.3 and made changes in lines 11 and 12. The major change I made was to replace the character format specifier (%c) with the integer format specifier (%d).

Both format specifiers do basically the same thing — insert some data into the string you pass to printf() — but the difference is in the way printf() displays that data. The %c specifier always prints a character; the %d specifier always prints a number. Even when they refer to the exact same data, it will be printed the way you indicate in the format specifier regardless of the actual data type.

The two statements in lines 11 and 12 format the two character variables (c1 and c2) by using the integer format specifier %d, and then print out two messages showing the numeric values 65 and 97 that represent, respectively, the characters A and a in the ASCII character set.

The float Data Type

The *floating-point number* is another data type in the C language. Unlike an integer number, a floating-point number contains a decimal point. For instance, 7.01 is a floating-point number; so are 5.71 and –3.14. A floating-point number is also called a *real number*.

A floating-point number is specified by the float keyword in the C language. Floating-pointer constants can be suffixed with f or F to specify float. A floating-pointer number without a suffix is double by default. The double data type is introduced later in this lesson.

Like an integer number, a floating-point number has a limited range. The ANSI standard requires that the range be at least plus or minus 1.0×10^{37}. In most cases, a floating-point number is represented by taking 32 bits. Therefore, a floating-point number in C is of at least six digits of precision. That is, for a floating-point number, there are at least six digits (or decimal places) on the right side of the decimal point.

Unlike an integer division from which the result is truncated and the fraction is discarded, a floating-point division produces another floating-point number. A floating-point division is carried out if both the divisor and the dividend, or one of them, are floating-point numbers.

For instance, 571.2 / 10.0 produces another floating-point number, 57.12. So do 571.2 / 10 and 5712 / 10.0.

Declaring Floating-Point Variables

The following shows the declaration format for a floating-point variable:

```
float   variablename;
```

Similar to the character or integer declaration, if you have more than one variable to declare, you can either use the format like this:

```
float   variablename1;
float   variablename2;
float   variablename3;
```

or like the following one:

```
float   variablename1, variablename2, variablename3;
```

For example, the following statement declares myFloat as a float variable and assigns it a value:

```
float myFloat = 3.14;
```

Similarly, the following statement declares a, b, and c as float variables:

```
float a, b, c;
a = 10.38;
b = -32.7;
c = 12.0f;
```

The Floating-Point Format Specifier (%f)

You can also use the *floating-point format specifier* (%f) to format your output. Listing 4.4 shows an example of how to use the format specifier %f with the printf() function.

TYPE   **LISTING 4.4** Printing the Results of Integer and Floating-Point Division

```
1:  /* 04L04.c: Integer vs. floating-point divisions */
2:  #include <stdio.h>
3:
4:  main()
5:  {
6:      int int_num1, int_num2, int_num3;   /* Declare integer
            variables */
7:      float flt_num1, flt_num2, flt_num3; /* Declare floating
            -point variables */
8:
9:      int_num1 = 32 / 10;     /* Both divisor and dividend are
            integers */
10:     flt_num1 = 32 / 10;
11:     int_num2 = 32.0 / 10;  /* The divisor is an integer */
12:     flt_num2 = 32.0 / 10;
13:     int_num3 = 32 / 10.0;  /* The dividend is an integer */
14:     flt_num3 = 32 / 10.0;
15:
16:     printf("The integer divis. of 32/10 is: %d\n", int_num1);
```

continues

LISTING 4.4   continued

```
17:    printf("The floating-point divis. of 32/10 is: %f\n", flt_num1);
18:    printf("The integer divis. of 32.0/10 is: %d\n", int_num2);
19:    printf("The floating-point divis. of 32.0/10 is: %f\n", flt_num2);
20:    printf("The integer divis. of 32/10.0 is: %d\n", int_num3);
21:    printf("The floating-point divis. of 32/10.0 is: %f\n", flt_num3);
22:    return 0;
23: }
```

The following output is from the screen of my computer after the executable file, `04L04.exe`, is run on my machine:

> I did get several warning messages about type conversions while I was compiling the program in Listing 4.4, but I ignored them all because I wanted to create an executable file in order to show you the differences between the int data type and the float data type.

OUTPUT

```
The integer divis. of 32/10 is: 3
The floating-point divis. of 32/10 is: 3.000000
The integer divis. of 32.0/10 is: 3
The floating-point divis. of 32.0/10 is: 3.200000
The integer divis. of 32/10.0 is: 3
The floating-point divis. of 32/10.0 is: 3.200000
```

ANALYSIS   Inside the `main()` function, the two statements in lines 6 and 7 declare three integer variables, `int_num1`, `int_num2`, and `int_num3`, and three floating-point variables, `flt_num1`, `flt_num2`, and `flt_num3`.

Lines 9 and 10 assign the result of `32/10` to `int_num1` and `flt_num1`, respectively; `32.0/10` to `int_num2` and `flt_num2` in lines 11 and 12, and `32/10.0` to `int_num3` and `flt_num3` in lines 13 and 14.

Then, lines 16–21 print out the values contained by the three int variables and the three floating-point variables. Note that `%d` is used for the integer variables, and the floating-point specifier (`%f`) is used for formatting the floating-point variables in the `printf()` function.

Because the truncation occurs in the integer division of `32/10`, `flt_num1` contains `3.000000`, not `3.200000`, which you can see from the second line of the output. However, `flt_num2` and `flt_num3` are assigned `3.200000` because both `32.0/10` and `32/10.0` are considered as the floating-point division.

But `int_num2` and `int_num3`, as integer variables, discard respectively the fraction parts of the floating-point divisions of `32.0/10` and `32/10.0`. Therefore, you just see the integer `3` in both the third and fifth lines of the output.

The `double` Data Type

In the C language, a floating-point number can also be represented by another data type, called the *double data type*. In other words, you can specify a variable by the `double` keyword, and assign the variable a floating-point number.

The difference between a `double` data type and a `float` data type is that the former uses twice as many bits as the latter. Therefore, a `double` floating-point number is of at least 10 digits of precision, although the ANSI standard does not specify it for the `double` data type.

In Hour 8, "Using Conditional Operators," you'll learn to use the `sizeof` operator to obtain the length in bytes of a data type, such as `char`, `int`, `float`, or `double`, specified on your computer system.

Using Scientific Notation

The C language uses *scientific notation* to help you write lengthy floating-point numbers.

In scientific notation, a number can be represented by the combination of the *mantissa* and the *exponent*. The format of the notation is that the mantissa is followed by the exponent, which is prefixed by e or E. Here are two examples:

mantissaeexponent

and

mantissaEexponent

Please note that `mantissa` and `exponent` above are both placeholders and you need to replace them with numerical values.

For instance, `5000` can be represented by `5e3` in scientific notation. Likewise, `-300` can be represented by `-3e2`, and `0.0025` by `2.5e-3`.

Correspondingly, the format specifier, `%e` or `%E`, is used to format a floating-point number in scientific notation. The usage of `%e` or `%E` in the `printf()` function is the same as `%f`.

4

Naming a Variable

There are a few things to keep in mind when creating your own variable names. Remember that since variable names are identifiers, you must follow the rules for identifiers that were outlined in the previous hour.

Just as function names should ideally reflect the task that the function performs, variable names should describe the value stored in the variable and what purpose it serves in your program or function. Most of the code samples so far have used single-letter variable names such as i, but as you write larger programs and more complicated functions it becomes increasingly more important to give your variables meaningful names.

Never use the C keywords reserved in the C language, or the names of the standard C library functions, as variable names in your C program.

Summary

In this lesson you learned about the following important C keywords and data types:

- The C keywords reserved in the C language
- The char data type and the %c format specifier
- The int data type and the %d format specifier
- The float data type and the %f format specifier
- Floating-point numbers can be suffixed with f or F to specify float. A floating-point number without a suffix is double by default.
- The possible ranges of the char, int, and float data types
- The double data type
- Scientific notation and the %e and %E format specifiers
- The rules you have to follow to make a valid variable name

In the next lesson you'll learn more about the printf() function and other functions to deal with input and output.

Q&A

Q Why do characters have their unique numeric values?

A Characters are stored in computers in the form of bits. The combinations of bits can be used to represent different numeric values. A character has to have a unique

numeric value in order to distinguish itself. Many computer systems support the ASCII character set, which contains a set of unique numeric values for up to 256 characters.

Please note that your computer may use a different character set than the ASCII character set. Then, all characters used by the C language except the null character may have different numeric values from the values represented by the ASCII character set.

Q How can you declare two character variables?

A There are two ways to do the declaration. The first one is

```
...char variable-name1, variable-name2;
```

The second one is

```
char   variable-name1;
char   variable-name2;
```

Q What are %c, %d, and %f?

A These are format specifiers. %c is used to obtain the character format; %d is for the integer format; %f is for the floating-point format. %c, %d, and %f are often used with C functions such as printf().

Q What are the main differences between the int data type (integer) and the float data type (floating-point)?

A First, an integer does not contain any fraction parts, but a floating-point number does. A floating-point number must have a decimal point. In C, the float data type takes more bits than the int data type. In other words, the float data type has a larger range of numeric values than the int data type.

Also, the integer division truncates the fraction part. For instance, the integer division of 16/10 produces a result of 1, not 1.6.

Workshop

To help solidify your understanding of this hour's lesson, you are encouraged to answer the quiz questions and finish the exercises provided in the workshop before you move to the next lesson. The answers and hints to the questions and exercises are given in Appendix C, "Answers to Quiz Questions and Exercises."

Quiz

1. Are the integer divisions of 134/100 and 17/10 equal?
2. Is the result of 3000 + 1.0 a floating-point number? How about 3000/1.0?

3. How can you represent the following numbers in scientific notation?

   - 3500

   - 0.0035

   - −0.0035

4. Are the following variable names valid?

   - 7th_calculation

   - Tom's_method

   - _index

   - Label_1

Exercises

1. Write a program that prints out the numeric values of characters Z and z.

2. Given two numeric values, 72 and 104, write a program to print out the corresponding two characters.

3. For a 16-bit integer variable, can you assign the variable with an integer value of 72368?

4. Given the declaration double dbl_num = 123.456;, write a program that prints out the value of dbl_num in both floating-point and scientific notation formats.

5. Write a program that can print out the numeric value of the newline character (\n). (Hint: assign '\n' to a character variable.)

HOUR 5

Handling Standard Input and Output

I/O, I/O, it's off to work we go...

—The Seven Dwarfs (sort of)

In the last lesson you learned how to print out characters, integers, and float-ing-point numbers to the screen by calling the printf() function. In this lesson you're going to learn more about printf(), as well as about the fol-lowing functions, which are necessary to receive the input from the user or to print the output to the screen:

- The getc() function
- The putc() function
- The getchar() function
- The putchar() function

Before we jump into these new functions, let's first get an idea about stan-dard input and output (I/O) in C.

Understanding Standard I/O

A file contains related characters and numbers. Because all characters and numbers are represented in bits on computers, and a byte is a series of bits, the C language treats a file as a series of bytes. A series of bytes is also called a *stream*. In fact, the C language treats all file streams equally, although some of the file streams may come from a disk or tape drive, from a terminal, or even from a printer.

Additionally, in C, there are three file streams that are pre-opened for you — that is to say, they are always available for use in your programs:

- stdin—The standard input for reading.
- stdout—The standard output for writing.
- stderr—The standard error for writing error messages.

Usually, the standard input (stdin) file stream links to your keyboard, while the standard output (stdout) and the standard error (stderr) file streams point to your terminal screen. Also, many operating systems allow the user to redirect these file streams.

In fact, you've already used stdout. When you called the printf() function in the last lesson, you were actually sending the output to the default file stream, stdout, which points to your screen.

You'll learn more on stdin and stdout in the following sections.

> The C language provides many functions to manipulate file reading and writing (I/O). The header file stdio.h contains the declarations for those functions. Therefore, always include the header file stdio.h in your C program before doing anything with file I/O.

Getting Input from the User

These days, typing on the keyboard is still the de facto standard way to input information into computers. The C language has several functions to tell the computer to read input from the user (typically through the keyboard.) In this lesson the getc() and getchar() functions are introduced.

Using the getc() Function

The getc() function reads the next character from a file stream, and returns the character as an integer.

SYNTAX

Syntax Entry

The syntax for the `getc()` function is
```
#include <stdio.h>
int getc(FILE *stream);
```

Here *FILE *stream* declares a file stream (that is, a variable). The function returns the numeric value of the character read. If an end-of-file or error occurs, the function returns EOF.

For now, don't worry about the FILE structure. More details about it are introduced in Hours 21, "Reading and Writing with Files," and 22, "Using Special File Functions." In this section, the standard input stream stdin is used as the file stream specified by *FILE *stream*.

> Defined in the header file stdio.h, EOF is a constant. EOF stands for *end-of-file*. Usually, the value of EOF is -1. But keep using EOF, instead of -1, to indicate the end-of-file in your programs. That way, if you later use a compile or operating system that uses a different value, your program will still work.

Listing 5.1 shows an example that reads a character typed in by the user from the keyboard and then displays the character on the screen.

TYPE   **LISTING 5.1**   Reading in a Character Entered by the User

```
 1:  /* 05L01.c: Reading input by calling getc() */
 2:  #include <stdio.h>
 3:
 4:  main()
 5:  {
 6:      int ch;
 7:
 8:      printf("Please type in one character:\n");
 9:      ch = getc( stdin );
10:      printf("The character you just entered is: %c\n", ch);
11:      return 0;
12: }
```

The following is the output displayed on the screen of my computer after I run the executable file, 05L01.exe, enter the character H, and press the Enter key:

OUTPUT
```
Please type in one character:
H
The character you just entered is: H
```

5

ANALYSIS You see in line 2 of Listing 5.1 that the header file `stdio.h` is included for both the `getc()` and `printf()` functions used in the program. Lines 4–12 give the name and body of the `main()` function.

In line 6, an integer variable, `ch`, is declared; it is assigned the return value from the `getc()` function later in line 9. Line 8 prints out a message that asks the user to enter one character from the keyboard. As I mentioned earlier in this lesson, the `printf()` function call in line 8 uses the default standard output `stdout` to display messages on the screen.

In line 9, the standard input stream `stdin` is passed to the `getc()` function, which indicates that the file stream is from the keyboard. After the user types in a character, the `getc()` function returns the numeric value (that is, an integer) of the character. You see that, in line 9, the numeric value is assigned to the integer variable `ch`.

Then, in line 10, the character entered by the user is displayed on the screen via the help of `printf()`. Note that the character format specifier (`%c`) is used within the `printf()` function call in line 10. (Exercise 1 in this lesson asks you to use `%d` in a program to print out the numeric value of a character entered by the user.)

Using the `getchar()` Function

The C language provides another function, `getchar()`, that performs a similar function to `getc()`. More precisely, the `getchar()` function is equivalent to `getc(stdin)`.

SYNTAX

Syntax Entry

The syntax for the `getchar()` function is
```
#include <stdio.h>
int getchar(void);
```

Here *void* indicates that no argument is needed for calling the function. The function returns the numeric value of the character read. If an end-of-file or error occurs, the function returns `EOF`.

The program in Listing 5.2 demonstrates how to use the `getchar()` function to read the input from the user.

TYPE   **LISTING 5.2**   Reading in a Character by Calling `getchar()`

```
1:  /* 05L02.c: Reading input by calling getchar() */
2:  #include <stdio.h>
3:
4:  main()
5:  {
6:     int ch1, ch2;
7:
```

```
8:      printf("Please type in two characters together:\n");
9:      ch1 = getc( stdin );
10:     ch2 = getchar( );
11:     printf("The first character you just entered is: %c\n", ch1);
12:     printf("The second character you just entered is: %c\n", ch2);
13:     return 0;
14: }
```

After running the executable file, 05L02.exe, and entering two characters (H and i) together without spaces, I press the Enter key and have the following output displayed on the screen of my computer:

OUTPUT
```
Please type in two character together:
Hi
The first character you just entered is: H
The second character you just entered is: i
```

ANALYSIS The program in Listing 5.2 is quite similar to the one in Listing 5.1, except that this one reads in two characters.

The statement in line 6 declares two integers, ch1 and ch2. Line 8 displays a message asking the user to enter two characters together.

Then, the getc() and getchar() functions are called in lines 9 and 10, respectively, to read in two characters entered by the user. Note that in line 10, nothing is passed to the getchar() function. This is because, as mentioned earlier, getchar() uses the default input file stream—stdin. You can replace the getchar() function in line 10 with getc(stdin) because getc(stdin) is equivalent to getchar().

Lines 11 and 12 send two characters (kept by ch1 and ch2, respectively) to the screen.

Printing Output on the Screen

Besides getc() and getchar() for reading, the C language also provides two functions, putc() and putchar(), for writing. The following two sections introduce these functions.

Using the putc() Function

The putc() function writes a character to the specified file stream, which, in your case, is the standard output pointing to your screen.

5

SYNTAX

Syntax Entry

The syntax for the putc() function is
#include <stdio.h>
int putc(*int c, FILE *stream*);

Here the first argument, *int c*, indicates that the output is a character saved in an integer variable *c*; the second argument, *FILE *stream*, specifies a file stream. If successful, putc() returns the character written; otherwise, it returns EOF.

In this lesson the standard output stdout is specified as the output file stream in putc().

The putc() function is used in Listing 5.3 to put the character A on the screen.

TYPE **LISTING 5.3** Putting a Character on the Screen

```
1:  /* 05L03.c: Outputting a character with putc() */
2:  #include <stdio.h>
3:
4:  main()
5:  {
6:     int ch;
7:
8:     ch = 65;   /* the numeric value of A */
9:     printf("The character that has numeric value of 65 is:\n");
10:    putc(ch, stdout);
11:    return 0;
12: }
```

The following output is what I get from my machine:

OUTPUT
The character that has numeric value of 65 is:
A

ANALYSIS As mentioned, the header file stdio.h, containing the declaration of putc(), is included in line 2.

The integer variable, ch, declared in line 6, is assigned the numeric value of 65 in line 8. The numeric value of character A is 65 in the ASCII character set.

Line 9 displays a message to remind the user of the numeric value of the character that is going to be put on the screen. Then, the putc() function in line 10 puts character A on the screen. Note that the first argument to the putc() function is the integer variable (ch) that contains 65, and the second argument is the standard output file stream, stdout.

Another Function for Writing: `putchar()`

Like `putc()`, `putchar()` can also be used to put a character on the screen. The only difference between the two functions is that `putchar()` needs only one argument to contain the character. You don't need to specify the file stream because the standard output (`stdout`) is set as the file stream to `putchar()`.

SYNTAX

Syntax Entry

The syntax for the `putchar()` function is
```
#include <stdio.h>
int putchar(int c);
```

Here `int c` is the argument that contains the numeric value of a character. The function returns `EOF` if an error occurs; otherwise, it returns the character that has been written.

An example of using `putchar()` is demonstrated in Listing 5.4.

TYPE **LISTING 5.4** Outputting Characters with `putchar()`.

```
1:  /* 05L04.c: Outputting characters with putchar() */
2:  #include <stdio.h>
3:
4:  main()
5:  {
6:     putchar(65);
7:        putchar(10);
8:           putchar(66);
9:              putchar(10);
10:          putchar(67);
11:       putchar(10);
12:    return 0;
13: }
```

After running the executable file, `05L04.exe`, I get the following output:

OUTPUT
```
A
B
```

ANALYSIS The way to write the program in Listing 5.4 is a little bit different. There is no variable declared in the program. Rather, integers are passed to `putchar()` directly, as shown in lines 6–11.

As you might have figured out, 65, 66, and 67 are, respectively, the numeric values of characters A, B, and C in the ASCII character set. From exercise 5 of Hour 4, "Understanding Data Types and Keywords," you can find out that 10 is the numeric value of the newline character (\n).

5

Therefore, respectively, lines 6 and 7 put character A on the screen and cause the computer to start at the beginning of the next line. Likewise, line 8 puts B on the screen, and line 9 starts a new line. Then, line 10 puts C on the screen, and line 11 starts another new line. Accordingly, A, B, and C, are put at the beginning of three consecutive lines, as shown in the output section.

Revisiting the `printf()` Function

The `printf()` function is the first C library function you used in this book to print out messages on the screen. `printf()` is a very important function in C, so it's worth it to spend more time on it.

SYNTAX

Syntax Entry

The syntax for the `printf()` function is
```
#include <stdio.h>
int printf(const char *format-string, . . .);
```

Here *const char *format-string* is the first argument that contains the format specifier(s); . . . indicates the expression section that contains the expression(s) to be formatted according to the format specifiers. The number of expressions is determined by the number of the format specifiers inside the first argument. The function returns the number of expressions formatted if it succeeds. It returns a negative value if an error occurs.

const char * is explained later in this book. For the time being, consider the first argument to the `printf()` function as a string (a series of characters surrounded with double quotes) with some format specifiers inside. For instance, you can pass "The sum of two integers %d + %d is: %d.\n" to the function as the first argument.

Figure 5.1 shows the relationship between the format string and expressions. Note that the format specifiers and the expressions are matched in order from left to right.

FIGURE 5.1

The relation between the format string and the expressions in `printf()`.

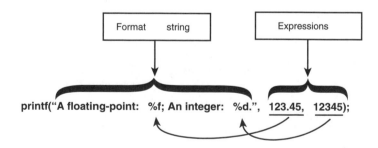

Please remember that you should use exactly the same number of expressions as the number of format specifiers within the format string.

The following are all the format specifiers that can be used in printf():

%c	The character format specifier.
%d	The integer format specifier.
%i	The integer format specifier (same as %d).
%f	The floating-point format specifier.
%e	The scientific notation format specifier (note the lowercase e).
%E	The scientific notation format specifier (note the uppercase E).
%g	Uses %f or %e, whichever result is shorter.
%G	Uses %f or %E, whichever result is shorter.
%o	The unsigned octal format specifier.
%s	The string format specifier.
%u	The unsigned integer format specifier.
%x	The unsigned hexadecimal format specifier (note the lowercase x).
%X	The unsigned hexadecimal format specifier (note the uppercase X).
%p	Displays the corresponding argument that is a pointer.
%n	Records the number of characters written so far.
%%	Outputs a percent sign (%).

Among the format specifiers in this list, %c, %d, %f, %e, and %E have been introduced so far. Several others are explained later in this book. The next section shows you how to convert decimal numbers to hexadecimal numbers by using %x or %X.

Converting to Hex Numbers

Since all data in a computer consists of binary data (a series of zeroes and ones), any data we work with or print out is really just some kind of human-readable representation of the binary data. As a programmer, it is often necessary to deal with binary data directly, but it is extremely time consuming to decipher a string of zeroes and ones and try to convert them to meaningful numeric or character data.

The solution to this problem is *hexadecimal notation* (or hex), which is a kind of short-hand to represent binary numbers. Hex is a compromise between the computer-readable base-2 (or binary) number system, and our more familiar base-10 (or decimal) system. Converting numbers from hex to decimal (or from binary to hex) and back is far easier (not to mention quicker) than converting directly from binary to decimal or vice-versa.

The difference between a decimal number and a hexadecimal number is that the hexadecimal is a base-16 numbering system. A hexadecimal number can be represented by four bits. (2^4] is equal to 16, which means four bits can produce 16 unique numbers.)

The hexadecimal numbers 0 through 9 use the same numeric symbols found in the decimal numbers 0 through 9. A, B, C, D, E, and F are used to represent, respectively, the numbers 10 through 15 in uppercase. (Similarly, in lowercase, a, b, c, d, e, and f are used to represent these hex numbers. Uppercase and lowercase hex are interchangeable and really just a matter of style.)

Listing 5.5 provides an example of converting decimal numbers to hex numbers by using %x or %X in the printf() function.

TYPE   **LISTING 5.5**   Converting to Hex Numbers

```
1:  /* 05L05.c: Converting to hex numbers */
2:  #include <stdio.h>
3:
4:  main()
5:  {
6:      printf("Hex(uppercase)    Hex(lowercase)    Decimal\n");
7:      printf("%X                %x                %d\n", 0, 0, 0);
8:      printf("%X                %x                %d\n", 1, 1, 1);
9:      printf("%X                %x                %d\n", 2, 2, 2);
10:     printf("%X                %x                %d\n", 3, 3, 3);
11:     printf("%X                %x                %d\n", 4, 4, 4);
12:     printf("%X                %x                %d\n", 5, 5, 5);
13:     printf("%X                %x                %d\n", 6, 6, 6);
14:     printf("%X                %x                %d\n", 7, 7, 7);
15:     printf("%X                %x                %d\n", 8, 8, 8);
16:     printf("%X                %x                %d\n", 9, 9, 9);
17:     printf("%X                %x                %d\n", 10, 10, 10);
18:     printf("%X                %x                %d\n", 11, 11, 11);
19:     printf("%X                %x                %d\n", 12, 12, 12);
20:     printf("%X                %x                %d\n", 13, 13, 13);
21:     printf("%X                %x                %d\n", 14, 14, 14);
22:     printf("%X                %x                %d\n", 15, 15, 15);
23:     return 0;
24: }
```

The following output is obtained by running the executable file, 05L05.exe, on my computer:

OUTPUT

Hex(uppercase)	Hex(lowercase)	Decimal
0	0	0
1	1	1
2	2	2
3	3	3
4	4	4
5	5	5
6	6	6
7	7	7
8	8	8
9	9	9
A	a	10
B	b	11
C	c	12
D	d	13
E	e	14
F	f	15

ANALYSIS Don't panic when you see so many printf() function calls being used in Listing 5.5. In fact, the program in Listing 5.5 is very simple. The program has just one function body from lines 5–23.

The printf() function in line 6 prints out a headline that contains three fields: Hex(uppercase), Hex(lowercase), and Decimal.

Then, lines 7–22 print out the hex and decimal numbers 0 through 15. Sixteen printf()calls are made to accomplish the job. Each of the printf() calls has a format string as the first argument followed by three integers as three expressions. Note that the hex format specifiers %X and %x are used within the format string in each of the printf() calls to convert the corresponding expressions to the hex format (both uppercase and lowercase).

In reality, nobody would write a program like the one in Listing 5.5. Instead, a loop can be used to call the printf() function repeatedly. Looping (or iteration) is introduced in Hour 7, "Working with Loops."

Specifying the Minimum Field Width

The C language allows you to add an integer between the percent sign (%) and the letter in a format specifier. The integer is called the *minimum field width specifier* because it specifies the minimum field width and ensures that the output reaches the minimum width. For example, in %10f, 10 is a minimum field width specifier that ensures that the output is at least 10 character spaces wide. This is especially useful when printing out a column of numbers.

5

The example in Listing 5.6 shows how to use the minimum field width specifier.

TYPE   **LISTING 5.6**   Specifying the Minimum Field Width

```
1:  /* 05L06.c: Specifying minimum field width */
2:  #include <stdio.h>
3:
4:  main()
5:  {
6:     int num1, num2;
7:
8:     num1 = 12;
9:     num2 = 12345;
10:    printf("%d\n", num1);
11:    printf("%d\n", num2);
12:    printf("%5d\n", num1);
13:    printf("%05d\n", num1);
14:    printf("%2d\n", num2);
15:    return 0;
16: }
```

The following is the output I obtain by running the executable file 05L06.exe:

OUTPUT
```
12
12345
   12
00012
12345
```

ANALYSIS   In Listing 5.6, two integer variables, num1 and num2, are declared in line 6, and assigned 12 and 12345, respectively, in lines 8 and 9.

Without using any minimum field width specifiers, lines 10 and 11 print out the two integers by calling the printf() function. You can see in the output section that the output from the statement in line 10 is 12, which takes two character spaces, while the output 12345 from line 11 takes five character spaces.

In line 12, a minimum field width, 5, is specified by %5d. The output from line 12 therefore takes five character spaces, with three blank spaces plus two character spaces of 12. (See the third output line in the output section.)

The %05d in printf(), shown in line 13, indicates that the minimum field width is 5, and the 0 indicates that zeros are used to fill, or "pad," the spaces. Therefore, you see the output made by the execution of the statement in line 13 is 00012.

The %2d in line 14 sets the minimum field width to 2, but you still see the full-size output of 12345 from line 14. This means that when the minimum field width is shorter than the width of the output, the latter is taken, and the output is still printed in full.

Aligning Output

As you might have noticed in the previous section, all output is right-justified. In other words, by default, all output is placed on the right edge of the field, as long as the field width is longer than the width of the output.

You can change this and force output to be left-justified. To do so, you need to prefix the minimum field specifier with the minus sign (-). For example, %-12d specifies the minimum field width as 12, and justifies the output from the left edge of the field.

Listing 5.7 gives an example aligning output by left- or right-justification.

TYPE   **LISTING 5.7**   Left- or Right-Justified Output

```
1:  /* 05L07.c: Aligning output */
2:  #include <stdio.h>
3:
4:  main()
5:  {
6:      int num1, num2, num3, num4, num5;
7:
8:      num1 = 1;
9:      num2 = 12;
10:     num3 = 123;
11:     num4 = 1234;
12:     num5 = 12345;
13:     printf("%8d  %-8d\n", num1, num1);
14:     printf("%8d  %-8d\n", num2, num2);
15:     printf("%8d  %-8d\n", num3, num3);
16:     printf("%8d  %-8d\n", num4, num4);
17:     printf("%8d  %-8d\n", num5, num5);
18:     return 0;
19: }
```

I get the following output displayed on the screen of my computer after I run the executable 05L07.exe:

OUTPUT
```
       1  1
      12  12
     123  123
    1234  1234
   12345  12345
```

In Listing 5.7, there are five integer variables, num1, num2, num3, num4, and num5, that are declared in line 6 and are assigned values in lines 8–12.

These values represented by the five integer variables are then printed out by the printf() functions in lines 13–17. Note that all the printf() calls have the same first argument: "%8d %-8d\n". Here the first format specifier, %8d, aligns the output at the right edge of the field, and the second specifier, %-8d, aligns the output to the left edge of the field.

After the execution of the statements in lines 13–17, the alignment is accomplished and the output is put on the screen like this:

```
    1  1
   12  12
  123  123
 1234  1234
12345  12345
```

Using the Precision Specifier

You can put a period . and an integer right after the minimum field width specifier. The combination of the period (.) and the integer makes up a *precision specifier*. You can use the precision specifier to determine the number of decimal places for floating-point numbers, or to specify the maximum field width (or length) for integers or strings. (Strings in C are introduced in Hour 13, "Manipulating Strings.")

For instance, with %10.3f, the minimum field width length is specified as 10 characters long, and the number of decimal places is set to 3. (Remember, the default number of decimal places is 6.) For integers, %3.8d indicates that the minimum field width is 3, and the maximum field width is 8.

Listing 5.8 gives an example of using precision specifiers.

TYPE **LISTING 5.8** Using Precision Specifiers

```
1:  /* 05L08.c: Using precision specifiers */
2:  #include <stdio.h>
3:
4:  main()
5:  {
6:      int int_num;
7:      double flt_num;
8:
9:      int_num = 123;
10:     flt_num = 123.456789;
11:     printf("Default integer format:   %d\n", int_num);
```

```
12:     printf("With precision specifier:  %2.8d\n", int_num);
13:     printf("Default float format:      %f\n", flt_num);
14:     printf("With precision specifier:  %-10.2f\n", flt_num);
15:     return 0;
16: }
```

After running the executable file 05L08.exe on my computer, I get the following output on the screen:

OUTPUT

```
Default integer format:    123
With precision specifier:  00000123
Default float format:      123.456789
With precision specifier:  123.46
```

ANALYSIS The program in Listing 5.8 declares one integer variable, int_num, in line 6, and one floating-point number, flt_num, in line 7. Lines 9 and 10 assign 123 and 123.456789 to int_num and flt_num, respectively.

In line 11, the default integer format is specified for the integer variable, int_num, while the statement in line 12 specifies the integer format with a precision specifier that indicates that the maximum field width is eight characters long. Therefore, you see that five zeros are padded prior to the integer 123 in the second line of the output.

For the floating-point variable, flt_num, line 13 prints out the floating-point value in the default format, and line 14 reduces the decimal places to two by putting the precision specifier .2 within the format specifier %-10.2f. Note here that left-justification is also specified by the minus sign (-) in the floating-point format specifier.

The floating-point number 123.46 in the fourth line of the output is produced by the statement in line 14 with the precision specifier for two decimal places. Therefore, 123.456789 rounded to two decimal places becomes 123.46.

Summary

In this lesson you've learned the following important concepts, specifiers, and functions:

- The C language treats a file as a series of bytes.
- stdin, stdout, and stderr are three file streams that are pre-opened and always available for you to use.
- The C library functions getc() and getchar() can be used to read in one character from the standard input.
- The C library functions putc() and putchar() can be used to write one character to the standard output.

5

- %x or %X can be used to convert decimal numbers to hex numbers.
- A minimum field width can be specified and ensured by adding an integer into a format specifier.
- An output can be aligned at either the left or right edge of the output field.
- A precision specifier can be used to specify the decimal place number for floating-point numbers, or the maximum field width for integers or strings.

In next lesson you'll learn about some important operators in C.

Q&A

Q What are `stdin`, `stdout`, and `stderr`?

A In C, a file is treated as a series of bytes that is called file stream. `stdin`, `stdout`, and `stderr` are all pre-opened file streams. `stdin` is the standard input for reading; `stdout` is the standard output for writing; `stderr` is the standard error for outputting error messages.

Q How much is the hex number 32?

A Hexadecimal, or hex for short, is a base-16 numerical system. Therefore, 32 (hex) is equal to $3*16^1+2*16^0$, or 50 in decimal.

Q Are `getc(stdin)` and `getchar()` equivalent?

A Because the `getchar()` function reads from the file stream `stdin` by default, `getc(stdin)` and `getchar()` are equivalent in this case.

Q In the function `printf("The integer %d is the same as the hex %x", 12, 12)`, what is the relation between the format specifiers and the expressions?

A The two format specifiers, `%d` and `%x`, specify the formats of numeric values contained in the expression section. Here the first numeric value of 12 is going to be printed out in integer format, while the second 12 (in the expression section) will be displayed in the hex format. Generally speaking, the number of format specifiers in the format section should match the number of expressions in the expression section.

Workshop

To help solidify your understanding of this hour's lesson, you are encouraged to answer the quiz questions and finish the exercises provided in the workshop before you move to the next lesson. The answers and hints to the questions and exercises are given in Appendix D, "Answers to Quiz Questions and Exercises."

Quiz

1. Can you align your output at the left edge, rather than the right edge, of the output field?

2. What is the difference between putc() and putchar()?

3. What does getchar() return?

4. Within %10.3f, which part is the minimum field width specifier, and which one is the precision specifier?

Exercises

1. Write a program to put the characters B, y, and e together on the screen.

2. Display the two numbers 123 and 123.456 and align them at the left edge of the field.

3. Given three integers, 15, 150, and 1500, write a program that prints the integers on the screen in the hex format.

4. Write a program that uses getchar() and putchar() to read in a character entered by the user and write the character to the screen.

5. If you compile the following C program, what warning or error messages will you get?

```
main()
{
    int ch;
    ch = getchar();
    putchar(ch);
    return 0;
}
```

5

PART II

Operators and Control-flow Statements

Hour

HOUR 6

Manipulating Data

"The question is," said Humpty Dumpty,
"which is to be master—that's all."

—L. Carroll

You can think of operators as verbs in C that let you manipulate data (which are like nouns). In fact, you've learned some operators, such as + (addition), - (subtraction), * (multiplication), / (division), and % (remainder), in Hour 3, "Learning the Structure of a C Program." The C language has a rich set of operators. In this hour, you'll learn about more operators, such as

- Arithmetic assignment operators
- Unary minus operator
- Increment and decrement operators
- Relational operators
- Cast operator

Arithmetic Assignment Operators

Before jumping into the arithmetic assignment operators, let's first take a closer look at the assignment operator itself.

The Assignment Operator (=)

In the C language, the = operator is called an *assignment operator*, which you've seen and used for several hours.

The general statement form to use an assignment operator is

```
left-hand-operand = right-hand-operand;
```

Here the statement causes the value of the `right-hand-operand` to be assigned (or written) to the memory location of the `left-hand-operand`. Thus, after the assignment, `left-hand-operand` will be equal to the value of `right-hand-operand`. Additionally, the entire assignment expression evaluates to the same value that is assigned to the `left-hand-operand`.

For example, the statement a = 5; writes the value of the right-hand operand (5) into the memory location of the integer variable a (which is the left-hand operand in this case).

Similarly, the statement b = a = 5; assigns 5 to the integer variable a first, and then to the integer variable b. After the execution of the statement, both a and b contain the value of 5.

It is important to remember that the left-hand operand of the assignment operator must be an expression to which you can legally write data. An expression such as 6 = a, although it may look correct at a glance, is actually backwards and will not work. The = operator always works from right to left; therefore the value on the left must be some form of a variable that can receive the data from the expression on the right.

Don't confuse the assignment operator (=) with the relational operator, == (called the *equal-to operator*). The == operator is introduced later in this hour.

Combining Arithmetic Operators with =

Consider this example: Given two integer variables, x and y, how do you assign the addition of x and y to another integer variable, z?

By using the assignment operator (=) and the addition operator (+), you get the following statement:

```
z = x + y;
```

As you can see, it's pretty simple. Now, consider the same example again. This time, instead of assigning the result to the third variable, z, let's write the result of the addition back to the integer variable, x:

```
x = x + y;
```

Remember, the = operator always works from right to left, so the right side will be evaluated first. Here, on the right side of the assignment operator (=), the addition of x and y is executed; on the left side of =, the previous value of x is replaced with the result of the addition from the right side.

The C language gives you a new operator, +=, to do the addition and the assignment together. Therefore, you can rewrite the statement x = x + y; as

```
x += y;
```

The combinations of the assignment operator (=) with the arithmetic operators, +, -, *, /, and %, give you another type of operators—*arithmetic assignment operators*:

Operator	Description
+=	Addition assignment operator
-=	Subtraction assignment operator
*=	Multiplication assignment operator
/=	Division assignment operator
%=	Remainder assignment operator

The following shows the equivalence of statements:

```
x += y; is equivalent to x = x + y;
x -= y; is equivalent to x = x - y;
x *= y; is equivalent to x = x * y;
x /= y; is equivalent to x = x / y;
x %= y; is equivalent to x = x % y;
```

Note that the statement

6

z = z * x + y;

is not equivalent to the statement

z *= x + y;

because

z *= x + y

multiplies z by the entire right-hand side of the statement, so the result would be the same as

z = z * (x + y);

Listing 6.1 gives an example of using some of the arithmetic assignment operators.

TYPE   **LISTING 6.1**   Using Arithmetic Assignment Operators

```
 1:  /* 06L01.c: Using arithemtic assignment operators */
 2:  #include <stdio.h>
 3:
 4:  main()
 5:  {
 6:     int x, y, z;
 7:
 8:     x = 1;   /* initialize x */
 9:     y = 3;   /* initialize y */
10:     z = 10;  /* initialize z */
11:     printf("Given x = %d, y = %d, and z = %d,\n", x, y, z);
12:
13:     x = x + y;
14:     printf("x = x + y  assigns %d to x;\n", x);
15:
16:     x = 1;  /* reset x */
17:     x += y;
18:     printf("x += y  assigns %d to x;\n", x);
19:
20:     x = 1;  /* reset x */
21:     z = z * x + y;
22:     printf("z = z * x + y  assigns %d to z;\n", z);
23:
24:     z = 10;  /* reset z */
25:     z = z * (x + y);
26:     printf("z = z * (x + y) assigns %d to z;\n", z);
27:
28:     z = 10;  /* reset z */
29:     z *= x + y;
30:     printf("z *= x + y assigns %d to z.\n", z);
31:
32:     return 0;
33: }
```

After this program is compiled and linked, an executable file is created. On my machine, this executable file is named as 06L01.exe. The following is the output displayed after I run the executable:

OUTPUT

```
Given x = 1, y = 3, and z = 10,
x = x + y   assigns 4 to x;
x += y   assigns 4 to x;
z = z * x + y   assigns 13 to z;
z = z * (x + y) assigns 40 to z;
z *= x + y assigns 40 to z.
```

ANALYSIS Line 2 in Listing 6.1 includes the header file stdio.h by using the include directive. The stdio.h header file is needed for the printf() function used in lines 4–33.

Lines 8–10 initialize three integer variables, x, y, and z, which are declared in line 6. Line 11 then prints out the initial values assigned to x, y, and z.

The statement in line 13 uses one addition operator and one assignment operator to add the values contained by x and y, and then assigns the result to x. Line 14 displays the result on the screen.

Similarly, lines 17 and 18 do the same addition and display the result again, after the variable x is reset to the value 1 in line 16. This time, the arithmetic assignment operator, +=, is used.

The value of x is reset again in line 20. Line 21 performs a multiplication and an addition and saves the result to the integer variable z; that is, z = z * x + y;. The printf() call in line 22 displays the result, 13, on the screen. Again, the x = 1; statement in line 20 resets the integer variable, x.

Lines 24–30 display two results from two computations. The two results are actually the same (that is, 40) because the two computations in lines 25 and 29 are equivalent. The only difference between the two statements in lines 25 and 29 is that the arithmetic assignment operator, *=, is used in line 29.

6

Getting Negations of Numeric Values

If you want to change the sign of a number, you can put the minus operator (-) right before the number. For instance, given an integer of 7, you can get its negative value by changing the sign of the integer like this: -7. Here, - is the minus operator.

The - symbol used in this way is called the *unary minus operator*. This is because the operator takes only one operand: the expression to its immediate right. The data type of the operand can be any integer or floating-point number.

You can apply the unary minus operator to an integer or a floating-point variable as well. For example, given x = 1.234, -x equals -1.234. Or, given x = -1.234, -x equals 1.234 since negating a negative value results in a positive number.

Don't confuse the unary minus operator with the subtraction operator, although both operators use the same symbol. For instance, the following statement:

z = x - -y;

is actually the same as this statement:

z = x - (-y);

or this one:

z = x + y;

Here, in both statements, the first - symbol is used as the subtraction operator, while the second - symbol is the unary minus operator.

Incrementing or Decrementing by One

The increment and decrement operators are very handy to use when you want to add or subtract 1 from a variable. The symbol for the increment operator is ++. The decrement operator is --.

For instance, you can rewrite the statement x = x + 1; as ++x;, or you can replace x = x - 1; with --x;.

Actually, there are two versions of the increment and decrement operators. In the ++x; statement, where ++ appears before its operand, the increment operator is called the *pre-increment operator*. This refers to the order in which things happen: the operator first adds 1 to x, and then yields the new value of x. Likewise, in the statement --x;, the *pre-decrement operator* first subtracts 1 from x and then yields the new value of x.

If you have an expression like x++, where ++ appears after its operand, you're using the *post-increment operator*. Similarly, in x--, the decrement operator is called the *post-decrement operator*.

For example, in the statement y = x++;, y is assigned the original value of x first, then x is increased by 1.

The post-decrement operator has a similar story. In the statement y = x--; the assignment of y to the value of x takes place first, then x is decremented. The program in Listing 6.2 shows the differences between the two versions of increment operators and decrement operators.

| TYPE | LISTING 6.2   Using Pre- or Post-Increment and Decrement Operators |

```
1:  /* 06L02.c: pre- or post-increment(decrement) operators */
2:  #include <stdio.h>
3:
4:  main()
5:  {
6:      int w, x, y, z, result;
7:
8:      w = x = y = z = 1;   /* initialize x and y */
9:      printf("Given w = %d, x = %d, y = %d, and z = %d,\n", w, x, y, z);
10:
11:     result = ++w;
12:     printf("++w evaluates to %d and w is now %d\n", result, w);
13:     result = x++;
14:     printf("x++ evaluates to %d and x is now %d\n", result, x);
15:     result = --y;
16:     printf("--y evaluates to %d and y is now %d\n", result, y);
17:     result = z--;
18:     printf("z-- evaluates to %d and z is now %d\n", result, z);
19:     return 0;
20: }
```

The following result is obtained by running the executable file 06L02.exe:

| OUTPUT |
```
Given w = 1, x = 1, y = 1, and z = 1,
++w evaluates to 2 and w is now 2
x++ evaluates to 1 and x is now 2
--y evaluates to 0 and y is now 0
z-- evaluates to 1 and z is now 0
```

| ANALYSIS | Inside the main() function, line 8 in Listing 6.2 assigns 1 to each of the integer variables, w, x, y, and z. The printf() call in line 9 displays the values contained by the four integer variables.

Then, the statement in line 11 is executed and the result of the pre-increment of w is assigned to the integer variable result. In line 12, the value of result, which is 2, is printed out to the screen, along with the value of w after the pre-increment statement. Note that w is still 2 since the increment took place before the new value of w was assigned to result.

Lines 13 and 14 get the post-increment of x and print out the result. As you know, the result is obtained before the value of x is increased. Therefore, you see the value 1 (the old value of x) from the result of x++, while the new value of x is 2 since it was incremented after the assignment to result in line 13 The pre-decrement operator in line 15 causes the value of y to be reduced by 1 before the new value is assigned to the integer variable result. Therefore, you see 0 as the result of --y shown on the screen, which reflects the new value of y, which is also 0.

6

In line 17, however, the post-decrement operator has no effect on the assignment because
the original value of z is given to the integer variable result before z is decreased by 1.
The post-decrement acts as if line 17 was simply result = z, with z then being decremented by 1 after the statement was executed. Line 18 thus prints out the result 1, which
is of course the original value of z, along with 0, the value of z after the post-decrement.

Greater Than or Less Than?

There are six types of relations between two expressions: equal to, not equal to, greater
than, less than, greater than or equal to, and less than or equal to. Accordingly, the C language provides these six *relational operators*:

Operator	Description
==	Equal to
!=	Not equal to
>	Greater than
<	Less than
>=	Greater than or equal to
<=	Less than or equal to

All the relational operators have lower precedence than the arithmetic operators.
Therefore, all arithmetic operations on either side of a relational operator are carried out
before any comparison is made. You should use parentheses to enclose operations of
operators that have to be performed first.

Among the six relational operators, the >, <, >=, and <= operators have higher precedence
than the == and != operators.

For example, the expression

x * y < z + 3

is interpreted as

(x * y) < (z + 3)

Another important point is that all relational expressions produce a result of either 0 or 1.
In other words, a relational expression evaluates to 1 if the specified relationship holds.
Otherwise, 0 is yielded.

Given x = 3 and y = 5, for instance, the relational expression x < y gives a result of 1.

Listing 6.3 shows more examples of using relational operators.

When several different operators appear together in an expression, the operands in between are associated with operators in a given order. *Operator precedence* refers to the order in which operators and operands are grouped together. Operators that have the highest precedence within an expression are grouped with their operands first,

For example, in the expression

```
z + x * y - 3
```

The * operator has higher precedence than the + and - operators. Therefore, x * y will be evaluated first, and its result becomes the right-hand operand of the + operator. The result of that is then given to the - operator as its left-hand operand.

If you want to override the default operator precedence, you can use parentheses to group operands within an expression. If, for example, you actually wanted to multiply z + x by y - 3, you could rewrite the above expression as

```
(z + x) * (y - 3)
```

In addition, you can always use the parentheses when you aren't quite sure about the effects of operator precedence, or you just want to make your code easier to read.

TYPE **LISTING 6.3** Results Produced by Relational Expressions

```
1:  /* 06L03.c: Using relational operators */
2:  #include <stdio.h>
3:
4:  main()
5:  {
6:     int x, y;
7:     double z;
8:
9:     x = 7;
10:    y = 25;
11:    z = 24.46;
12:    printf("Given x = %d, y = %d, and z = %.2f,\n", x, y, z);
13:    printf("x >= y  produces: %d\n", x >= y);
14:    printf("x == y  produces: %d\n", x == y);
15:    printf("x < z   produces: %d\n", x < z);
16:    printf("y > z   produces: %d\n", y > z);
17:    printf("x != y - 18  produces: %d\n", x != y - 18);
18:    printf("x + y != z   produces: %d\n", x + y != z);
19:    return 0;
20: }
```

6

After the executable 06L03.exe is executed, the following output is displayed on the screen of my computer:

OUTPUT

```
Given x = 7, y = 25, and z = 24.46,
x >= y   produces: 0
x == y   produces: 0
x < z    produces: 1
y > z    produces: 1
x != y - 18  produces: 0
x + y != z   produces: 1
```

ANALYSIS There are two integer variables, x and y, and one floating-point variable z, declared in lines 6 and 7, respectively.

Lines 9–11 initialize the three variables. Line 12 prints out the values assigned to the variables.

Because the value of x is 7 and the value of y is 25, y is greater than x. Therefore, line 13 prints out 0, which is the result yielded by the relational expression x >= y.

Likewise, in line 14, the relational expression x == y yields 0.

Lines 15 and 16 print out the result of 1, which is yielded by the evaluations of both x < z and y > z.

The statement in line 17 displays 0, which is the result of the relational expression x != y - 18. Since y - 18 yields 7, and the value of x is 7, the != relationship does not hold. In line 18, the expression x + y != z produces 1, which is displayed on the screen.

Be careful when you compare two values for equality. Because of truncation or rounding, some relational expressions, which are algebraically true, might yield 0 stead of 1. For example, look at the following relational expression:

1 / 2 + 1 / 2 == 1

This is algebraically true and one would expect it to evaluate to 1.

The expression, however, yields 0, which means that the equal-to relationship does not hold. This is because the truncation of the integer division—that is, 1 / 2—produces an integer: 0, not 0.5.

Another example is 1.0 / 3.0, which produces 0.33333.... This is a number with infinite number of decimal places. But the computer can only hold a limited number of decimal places. Therefore, the expression

1.0 / 3.0 + 1.0 / 3.0 + 1.0 / 3.0 == 1.0

might not yield 1 on some computers, although the expression is algebraically true.

Using the Cast Operator

In C, you can convert the data type of a variable, expression, or constant to a different one by prefixing the cast operator. This conversion does not change the operand itself; when the cast operator is evaluated, it yields the same value (but represented as a different type), which you can then use in the rest of an expression.

The general form of the cast operator is

```
(data-type) x
```

Here data-type specifies the new data type you want. x is a variable (or constant or expression) of a different data type. You have to include the parentheses (and) around the new data type to make a cast operator.

For example, the expression (float)5 converts the integer 5 to a floating-point number, 5.0.

The program in Listing 6.4 shows another example of using the cast operator.

TYPE   **LISTING 6.4** Playing with the Cast Operator

```
1:  /* 06L04.c: Using the cast operator */
2:  #include <stdio.h>
3:
4:  main()
5:  {
6:     int x, y;
7:
8:     x = 7;
9:     y = 5;
10:    printf("Given x = %d, y = %d\n", x, y);
11:    printf("x / y produces: %d\n",  x / y);
12:    printf("(float)x / y produces: %f\n",  (float)x / y);
13:    return 0;
14: }
```

The following output is obtained by running the executable 06L04.exe on my computer:

OUTPUT
```
Given x = 7, y = 5
x / y produces: 1
(float)x / y produces: 1.400000
```

ANALYSIS   In Listing 6.4, there are two integer variables, x and y, declared in line 6, and initialized in lines 8 and 9, respectively. Line 10 then displays the values contained by the integer variables x and y.

6

The statement in line 11 prints out the integer division of x/y. Because the fractional part is truncated, the result of the integer division is 1.

However, in line 12, the cast operator (float) converts the value of x to a floating-point value. Therefore, the (float)x/y expression becomes a floating-point division that returns a floating-point number. That's why you see the floating-point number 1.400000 shown on the screen after the statement in line 12 is executed.

Summary

In this lesson you learned about the following important operators:

- The assignment operator =, which has two operands (one on each side). The value of the right-side operand is assigned to the operand on the left side. The operand on the left side must be some form of a variable which can accept the new value.
- The arithmetic assignment operators +=, -=, *=, /=, and %=, which are combinations of the arithmetic operators with the assignment operator.
- The unary minus operator (-), which evaluates to the negation of a numeric value.
- The two versions of the increment operator, ++. You know that in ++x, the ++ operator is called the pre-increment operator; and in x++, ++ is the post-increment operator.
- The two versions of decrement operator, --. You have learned that, for example, in --x, the -- operator is the pre-decrement operator, and in x--, -- is called the post-decrement operator.
- The six relational operators in C: == (equal to), != (not equal to), > (greater than), < (less than), >= (greater than or equal to), and <= (less than or equal to).
- How to change the data type of an expression by prefixing a cast operator to the data.

In the next lesson, you'll learn about loops in the C language.

Q&A

Q What is the difference between the pre-increment operator and the post-increment operator?

A The pre-increment operator increases the operand's value by 1 first, and then yields the modified value. On the other hand, the post-increment operator yields the original value of its operand first, then increments the operand. For instance, given x = 1, the ++x expression yields 2, whereas the expression x++ evaluates to 1 before actually modifying x.

Q Is the unary minus operator (-) the same as the subtraction operator (-)?

A No, they are not the same, although the two operators share the same symbol. The meaning of the symbol is determined by the context in which it appears. The unary minus operator is used to change the sign of a numeric value. In other words, the unary minus operator yields the negation of the value. The subtraction operator is an arithmetic operator that performs a subtraction between its two operands.

Q Which one has a higher precedence, a relational operator or an arithmetic operator?

A An arithmetic operator has a higher precedence than a relational operator. For instance, in the expression x * y + z > x + y, the operator precedence from highest to lowest goes from * to + and finally >. The entire expression is therefore interpreted as ((x * y) + z) > (x + y).

Q What value is yielded by a relational expression?

A A relational expression evaluates to either 0 or 1. If the relation indicated by a relational operator in an expression is true, the expression evaluates to 1; otherwise, the expression evaluates to 0.

Workshop

To help solidify your understanding of this hour's lesson, you are encouraged to answer the quiz questions and finish the exercises provided in the workshop before you move to the next lesson. The answers and hints to the questions and exercises are given in Appendix C, "Answers to Quiz Questions and Exercises."

Quiz

1. What is the difference between the = operator and the == operator?
2. In the expression x + - y - - z, which operator(s) are subtraction operators, and which one(s) are unary minus operator(s)?
3. Given x = 15 and y = 4, what values do the expressions x / y and (float)x / y yield, respectively?
4. Is the expression y *= x + 5 equivalent to the expression y = y * x + 5?

Exercises

1. Given x = 1 and y = 3, write a program to print out the results of these expressions: x += y, x += -y, x -= y, x -= -y, x *= y, and x *= -y.

6

2. Given x = 3 and y = 6, what is the value of z after the statement

   ```
   z = x * y == 18;
   ```

   is executed?

3. Write a program that initializes the integer variable x with 1 and outputs results with the following two statements:

   ```
   printf("x++ produces:    %d\n", x++);
   printf("Now x contains: %d\n", x);
   ```

4. Rewrite the program you wrote in exercise 3. This time, include the following two statements:

   ```
   printf("x = x++ produces: %d\n", x = x++);
   printf("Now x contains:    %d\n", x);
   ```

   What do you get after running the executable of the program? Can you explain why you get such a result?

5. The following program is supposed to compare the two variables, x and y, for equality. What's wrong with the program? (Hint: Run the program to see what it prints out.)

   ```
   #include <stdio.h>

   main()
   {
      int x, y;

      x = y = 0;
      printf("The comparison result is: %d\n",  x = y);
      return 0;
   }
   ```

HOUR 7

Working with Loops

Heaven and earth:
Unheard sutra chanting
Repeated...
—Zen saying

In the previous lessons, you learned the basics of the C program, several important C functions, standard I/O, and some useful operators. In this lesson you'll learn a very important feature of the C language—looping. Looping, also called *iteration*, is used in programming to perform the same set of statements over and over until certain specified conditions are met.

Three statements in C are designed for looping:

- The `while` statement
- The `do-while` statement
- The `for` statement

The following sections explore these statements.

The while Loop

The purpose of the while keyword is to repeatedly execute a statement over and over while a given condition is true. When the condition of the while loop is no longer logically true, the loop terminates and program execution resumes at the next statement following the loop.

The general form of the while statement is

```
while (expression)
   statement;
```

Here *expression* is the condition of the while statement. This expression is evaluated first. If the expression evaluates to a *nonzero* value, then *statement* is executed. After that, *expression* is evaluated once again. The statement is then executed one more time if the expression still evaluates to a nonzero value. This process is repeated over and over until *expression* evaluates to zero, or logical false.

The idea is that the code inside the loop, (*statement;* above) will eventually cause *expression* to be logically false the next time it is evaluated, thus terminating the loop.

Of course, you often want to use a while keyword to control looping over several statements. When this is the case, use a statement block surrounded by braces { and }. Each time the while expression is evaluated, the entire statement block will be executed if the expression evaluates as true.

Now, let's look at an example of using the while statement. The program in listing 7.1 uses a while loop to continually read, and then display, character input *while* the character input does not equal 'x'.

TYPE   **LISTING 7.1**   Using a while Loop

```
1:  /* 07L01.c: Using a while loop */
2:  #include <stdio.h>
3:
4:  main()
5:  {
6:     int c;
7:
8:     c = ' ';
9:     printf("Enter a character:\n(enter x to exit)\n");
10:    while (c != 'x') {
11:       c = getc(stdin);
12:       putchar(c);
13:    }
14:    printf("\nOut of the while loop. Bye!\n");
15:    return 0;
16: }
```

The following is a copy of the output from my computer's screen. (Note that the characters I entered are in bold.)

OUTPUT

```
Enter a character:
(enter x to exit)
H
H
i
i
x
x
Out of the while loop. Bye!
```

ANALYSIS   As you can see in the output, the program prints back every character that is typed in, and then stops after x.

Line 8 sets the variable c to the value ' ' (a space character). This is known as *initializing* the variable, and we just need to initialize it to something other than 'x'.

Line 10 is the while statement. The condition inside the parentheses, c != 'x', means the loop will continue executing over and over until c is actually equal to 'x'. Since we had just initialized c to equal the ' ' character, the relation c != x is of course true. Following the closing parenthesis is an opening brace, so the loop will execute until a closing brace is encountered.

Line 11 and line 12 read a character and print it back out, and in doing so assign the character's value to the variable c. Line 13 is the closing brace, so the loop is done and execution goes back to line 10, the while statement. If the character that was typed is anything other than "x" the loop will continue; otherwise, c != x will be logically false, and execution goes to the next statement after the closing brace at line 13. In this case it moves on to the printf() call at line 14.

The do-while Loop

In the while statement that we've seen, the conditional expression is set at the very top of the loop. However, in this section, you're going to see another statement used for looping, do-while, which puts the expression at the bottom of the loop. In this way, the statements in the loop are guaranteed to be executed at least once before the expression is tested. Note that statements in a while loop are not executed at all if the conditional expression evaluates to zero the first time through.

The general form for the do-while statement is

```
do {
    statement1;
    statement2;
        .
        .
        .
} while (expression);
```

Here, the statements inside the statement block are executed once, and then *expression* is evaluated in order to determine whether the looping is to continue. If the expression evaluates to a nonzero value, the do-while loop continues; otherwise, the looping stops and execution proceeds to the next statement following the loop.

Note that the do-while statement ends with a semicolon, which is an important distinction from the if and while statements.

The program in Listing 7.2 displays the characters A through G by using a do-while loop to repeat the printing and adding.

TYPE   **LISTING 7.2**   Using a do-while Loop

```
 1:  /* 07L02.c: Using a do-while loop */
 2:  #include <stdio.h>
 3:
 4:  main()
 5:  {
 6:      int i;
 7:
 8:      i = 65;
 9:      do {
10:          printf("The numeric value of %c is %d.\n", i, i);
11:          i++;
12:      } while (i<72);
13:      return 0;
14:  }
```

After running the executable 07L02.exe of Listing 7.6, I have the characters A through G, along with their numeric values, shown on the screen as follows:

OUTPUT
```
The numeric value of A is 65.
The numeric value of B is 66.
The numeric value of C is 67.
The numeric value of D is 68.
The numeric value of E is 69.
The numeric value of F is 70.
The numeric value of G is 71.
```

ANALYSIS The statement in line 8 of Listing 7.6 initializes the integer variable i with 65. The integer variable was declared in line 6.

Lines 9–12 contain the do-while loop. The expression i<72 is at the bottom of the loop in line 12. When the loop first starts, the two statements in lines 10 and 11 are executed before the expression is evaluated. Because the integer variable i contains the initial value of 65, the printf() function in line 10 displays the numeric value as well as the corresponding character A on the screen.

After the integer variable i is increased by 1 in line 11, the program control reaches the bottom of the do-while loop. Then the expression i<72 is evaluated. If the relationship in the expression still holds, the program control jumps up to the top of the do-while loop, and then the process is repeated. When the expression evaluates to 0 after i is increased to 72 (i then equals 72 and is therefore not less than 72), the do-while loop is terminated immediately.

Looping Under the for Statement

The general form of the for statement is

```
for (expression1; expression2; expression3) {
   statement;
}
```

or

```
for (expression1; expression2; expression3) {
   statement1;
   statement2;
   .
   .
   .
}
```

You see from this example that the for statement uses three expressions (*expression1*, *expression2*, and *expression3*) that are separated by semicolons.

A for loop can control just one statement as in the first example, or several statements, such as *statement1* and *statement2*, placed within the braces ({ and }).

The first time the for statement is executed, it first evaluates *expression1*, which is typically used to initialize one or more variables.

The second expression, *expression2*, acts in the same way as the conditional expression of a do or do-while loop. This second expression is evaluated immediately after *expression1*, and then later is evaluated again after each successful looping by the for statement. If *expression2* evaluates to a nonzero (logical true) value, the statements within the braces are executed. Otherwise the looping is stopped and the execution resumes at the next statement after the loop.

The third expression in the for statement, *expression3*, is not evaluated when the for statement is first encountered. However, *expression3* is evaluated after each looping and before the statement goes back to test *expression2* again.

In Hour 5, "Handling Standard Input and Output," you saw an example (Listing 5.5) that converts the decimal numbers 0 through 15 into hex numbers. Back then, the conversions had to be written in separate statements. Now, with the for statement, you can rewrite the program in Listing 5.5 in a very efficient way. Listing 7.3 shows the rewritten version of the program.

TYPE   **LISTING 7.3**   Converting 0 through 15 to Hex Numbers

```
1:  /* 07L03.c: Converting 0 through 15 to hex numbers */
2:  #include <stdio.h>
3:
4:  main()
5:  {
6:      int i;
7:
8:      printf("Hex(uppercase)    Hex(lowercase)    Decimal\n");
9:      for (i=0; i<16; i++){
10:         printf("%X                %x                %d\n", i, i, i);
11:     }
12:     return 0;
13: }
```

After creating the executable file 07L03.exe, I obtain the following output by running 07L03.exe. (The output is in fact the same as the one from 05L05.exe in Hour 5.)

OUTPUT

Hex(uppercase)	Hex(lowercase)	Decimal
0	0	0
1	1	1
2	2	2
3	3	3
4	4	4
5	5	5
6	6	6
7	7	7
8	8	8
9	9	9
A	a	10
B	b	11

C	c	12
D	d	13
E	e	14
F	f	15

ANALYSIS Now, let's have a look at the code in Listing 7.3. As you know, line 2 includes the header file stdio.h for the printf() function used later in the program.

Inside the body of the main() function, the statement in line 6 declares an integer variable, i. Line 8 displays the headline of the output on the screen.

Lines 9–11 contain the for statement. Note that the first expression in the for statement is i = 0, which is an assignment expression that initializes the integer variable i to 0.

The second expression in the for statement is i < 16, which is a relational expression. This expression evaluates to nonzero (true) as long as the relation indicated by the less-than operator (<) holds. As mentioned earlier, the second expression is evaluated by the for statement each time after a successful looping. If the value of i is less than 16, which means the relational expression remains true, the for statement will start another loop. Otherwise, it will stop looping and exit.

The third expression in the for statement is i++. When this expression is evaluated, the integer variable i is increased by 1. This is done after each statement inside the body of the for statement is executed. Here it doesn't make a big difference whether the post-increment operator (i++) or the pre-increment operator (++i) is used in the third expression.

In other words, when the for loop is first encountered, i is set to 0, the expression i<16 is evaluated and found to be true, and therefore the statements within the body of the for loop are executed. Following execution of the for loop, the third expression i++ is executed incrementing i to 1, and i<16 is again evaluated and found to be true, thus the body of the loop is executed again. The looping lasts until the conditional expression i<16 is no longer true.

There is only one statement inside the for statement body, as you can see in line 10. The statement contains the printf() function, which is used to display the hex numbers (both uppercase and lowercase) converted from the decimal values by using the format specifiers, %X and %x.

The decimal value is provided by the integer variable i. As explained earlier, i contains the initial value of 0 right before and during the first looping. After each looping, i is increased by 1 because of the third expression, i++, in the for statement. The last value provided by i is 15. When i reaches 16, the relation indicated by the second expression, `i<16`, is no longer true. Therefore, the looping is stopped and the execution of the `for` statement is completed.

Then, the statement in line 12 returns `0` to indicate a normal termination of the program, and finally, the `main()` function ends and returns the control back to the operating system.

As you see, with the `for` statement you can write a very concise program. In fact, the program in Listing 7.3 is more than 10 lines shorter than the one in Listing 5.5, although the two programs end up doing exactly the same thing.

Actually, you can make the program in Listing 7.3 even shorter by discarding the braces ({ and }) since there is only one statement inside the statement block.

The Null Statement

As you may notice, the `for` statement does not end with a semicolon. The `for` statement has within it either a statement block that ends with the closing brace (}), or a single statement that ends with a semicolon. The following `for` statement contains a single statement:

```
for (i=0; i<8; i++)
      sum += i;
```

Note that the braces ({ and }) are discarded because the `for` statement only contains one statement.

Now let us consider a statement like this:

```
for (i=0; i<8; i++);
```

Here the `for` statement is followed by a semicolon immediately.

In the C language, there is a special statement called the *null statement*. A null statement contains nothing but a semicolon. In other words, a null statement is a statement with no expression.

Therefore, when you review the statement `for (i=0; i<8; i++);`, you can see that it is actually a `for` statement with a null statement. In other words, you can rewrite it as

```
for (i=0; i<8; i++)
   ;
```

Because the null statement has no expression, the `for` statement actually does nothing but loop. You'll see some examples using the null statement with the `for` statement later in the book.

> Because the null statement is perfectly legal in C, you should pay attention to placing semicolons in your `for` statements. For example, suppose you intended to write a `for` loop like this:
>
> ```
> for (i=0; i<8; i++)
>    sum += i;
> ```
>
> If you accidentally put a semicolon at the end of the `for` statement like this, however,
>
> ```
> for (i=0; i<8; i++);
>    sum += i;
> ```
>
> your C compiler will still accept it, but the results from the two `for` statements will be quite different. (See exercise 1 in this lesson for an example.)

7

Just remember that the `do-while` loop is the only looping statement that uses a semicolon immediately after it as part of its syntax. The `while` and `for` statements are followed immediately by a loop, which could be a single statement followed by a semicolon, a statement block which has no semicolon afterwards, or just a semicolon (null statement) by itself.

Using Complex Expressions in a `for` Statement

The C language allows you to use the comma operator to combine multiple expressions into the three parts of the `for` statement.

For instance, the following form is valid in C:

```
for (i=0, j=10; i!=j; i++, j--){
   /* statement block */
}
```

Here, in the first expression, the two integer variables i and j are initialized, respectively, with 0 and 10 when the `for` statement is first encountered. Then, in the second field, the relational expressions i!=j is evaluated and tested. If it evaluates to zero (false), the loop is terminated. After each iteration of the loop, i is increased by 1 and j is reduced by 1 in the third expression. Then the expression i!=j is evaluated to determine whether or not to execute the loop again.

Now, let's look at a real program. Listing 7.4 shows an example of using multiple expressions in the `for` statement.

TYPE **LISTING 7.4**   Adding Multiple Expressions to the for Statement

---

```
1:  /* 07L04.c: Multiple expressions */
2:  #include <stdio.h>
3:
4:  main()
5:  {
6:     int i, j;
7:
8:     for (i=0, j=8; i<8; i++, j--)
9:        printf("%d  +  %d  =  %d\n", i, j, i+j);
10:    return 0;
11: }
```

I get the following output displayed on the screen after running the executable file,
`07L04.exe`:

OUTPUT
```
0  +  8  =  8
1  +  7  =  8
2  +  6  =  8
3  +  5  =  8
4  +  4  =  8
5  +  3  =  8
6  +  2  =  8
7  +  1  =  8
```

ANALYSIS   In Listing 7.4, line 6 declares two integer variables, i and j, which are used in a
for loop.

In line 8, i is initialized with 0 and j is set to 8 in the first expression of the for statement. The second expression contains a condition, i < 8, which tells the computer to
keep looping as long as the value of i is less than 8.

Each time, after the statement controlled by for in line 9 is executed, the third expression is evaluated, causing i is increase (increment) by 1 while j is reduced
(decremented) by 1. Because there is only one statement inside the for loop, no braces
({ and }) are used to form a statement block.

The statement in line 9 displays the addition of i and j on the screen during the looping,
which outputs eight results during the looping by adding the values of the two variables,
i and j.

Adding multiple expressions into the for statement is a very convenient way to manipulate more than one variable in a loop. To learn more about using multiple expressions in
a for loop, look at the example in Listing 7.5.

TYPE **LISTING 7.5**   Another Example of Using Multiple Expressions in the for Statement

```
1:  /* 07L05.c: Another example of multiple expressions */
2:  #include <stdio.h>
3:
4:  main()
5:  {
6:     int i, j;
7:
8:     for (i=0, j=1; i<8; i++, j++)
9:        printf("%d - %d = %d\n", j, i, j - i);
10:    return 0;
11: }
```

The following output is displayed on the screen after the executable 07L05.exe is run on my machine:

OUTPUT
```
1 - 0 = 1
2 - 1 = 1
3 - 2 = 1
4 - 3 = 1
5 - 4 = 1
6 - 5 = 1
7 - 6 = 1
8 - 7 = 1
```

ANALYSIS   In the program shown in Listing 7.5, two integer variables, i and j, are declared in line 6.

Note that in line 8, there are two assignment expressions, i=0 and j=1, in the first expression of the for statement. These two assignment expressions initialize the i and j integer variables, respectively.

There is one relational expression, i<8, in the second field, which is the condition that has to be met before the looping can be carried out. Because i starts at 0 and is incremented by 1 after each loop, there are total of 8 loops that will be performed by the for statement.

The third expression contains two expressions, i++ and j++, that increase the two integer variables by 1 each time after the statement in line 9 is executed.

The printf() function in line 9 displays the subtraction of the two integer variables, j and i, within the for loop. Because there is only one statement in the statement block, the braces ({ and }) are not needed.

Using Nested Loops

It's often necessary to create a loop even when you are already in a loop. You can put a loop (an inner loop) inside another one (an outer loop) to make *nested loops*. When the program reaches an inner loop, it will run just like any other statement inside the outer loop.

Listing 7.6 is an example of how nested loops work.

TYPE   **LISTING 7.6**   Using Nested Loops

```
1:  /* 07L06.c: Demonstrating nested loops */
2:  #include <stdio.h>
3:
4:  main()
5:  {
6:     int i, j;
7:
8:     for (i=1; i<=3; i++) {   /* outer loop */
9:        printf("The start of iteration %d of the outer loop.\n", i);
10:       for (j=1; j<=4; j++)   /* inner loop */
11:          printf("   Iteration %d of the inner loop.\n", j);
12:       printf("The end of iteration %d of the outer loop.\n", i);
13:    }
14:    return 0;
15: }
```

The following result is obtained by running the executable file 07L06.exe:

OUTPUT
```
The start of iteration 1 of the outer loop.
   Iteration 1 of the inner loop.
   Iteration 2 of the inner loop.
   Iteration 3 of the inner loop.
   Iteration 4 of the inner loop.
The end of iteration 1 of the outer loop.
The start of iteration 2 of the outer loop.
   Iteration 1 of the inner loop.
   Iteration 2 of the inner loop.
   Iteration 3 of the inner loop.
   Iteration 4 of the inner loop.
The end of iteration 2 of the outer loop.
The start of iteration 3 of the outer loop.
   Iteration 1 of the inner loop.
   Iteration 2 of the inner loop.
   Iteration 3 of the inner loop.
   Iteration 4 of the inner loop.
The end of iteration 3 of the outer loop.
```

ANALYSIS In Listing 7.6, two for loops are nested together. The outer for loop starts in line 8 and ends in line 13, while the inner for loop starts in line 10 and ends in line 11.

The inner loop is only one statement that prints out the iteration number according to the numeric value of the integer variable j. As you see in line 10, j is initialized with 1, and is increased by 1 after each looping (that is, iteration). The execution of the inner loop stops when the value of j is greater than 4.

Besides the inner loop, the outer loop has two statements in lines 9 and 12, respectively. The printf() function in line 9 displays a message showing the beginning of an iteration from the outer loop. An ending message is sent out in line 12 to show the end of the iteration from the outer loop.

From the output, you can see that the inner loop is finished before the outer loop starts another iteration. When the outer loop begins another iteration, the inner loop is encountered and run again. The output from the program in Listing 7.6 clearly shows the execution orders of the inner and outer loops.

Don't confuse the two relational operators (< and <=) and misuse them in the expressions of loops.

For instance, the following

```
for (j=1; j<10; j++){
    /* statement block */
}
```

means if j is less than 10, keep looping. Thus, the total number of iterations is 9. However, in the following example,

```
for (j=1; j<=10; j++){
    /* statement block */
}
```

the total number of iterations is 10 because the relational expression j<=10 is evaluated in this case. Note that the expression evaluates to 1 (logical true) as long as j is less than or equal to 10.

Therefore, you see the difference between the operators < and <= causes the looping in the first example to be one iteration shorter than the looping in the second example.

Summary

In this lesson you learned the following important concepts and statements:

- Looping can be used to perform the same set of statements over and over until specified conditions are met.
- Looping makes your program more concise.
- There are three statements, while, and do-while, and for, that are used for looping in C.
- The while statement contains one expression, which is the conditional expression which controls the loop.
- The while statement does not end with a semicolon.
- The do-while statement places its conditional expression at the bottom of the loop.
- The do-while statement ends with a semicolon.
- There are three expressions in the for statement. The second expression is the conditional expression.
- The for statement does not end with a semicolon.
- Multiple expressions, combined via commas, can be used as one expression in the for statement.
- In a nested loop, inner loop finishes before the outer loop resumes its iteration in nested loops.

In the next lesson you'll learn about more operators used in the C language.

Q&A

Q What is the difference between the while and do-while statements?

A The main difference is that in the while statement, the conditional expression is evaluated at the top of the loop, while in the do-while statement, the conditional expression is evaluated at the bottom of the loop. Therefore, the statements controlled by the do-while statement are guaranteed to be executed at least once whereas the loop in a while statement may never be executed at all.

Q How does a for loop work?

A There are three expressions in the for statement. The first field contains an initializer that is evaluated first and only once before the iteration. The second expression the conditional expression that must evaluate to nonzero (logical true) before the statements controlled by the for statement are executed. If the conditional expression evaluates to a nonzero (true) value, which means the specified condition is met, one iteration of the for loop is carried out. After each iteration, the third expression is evaluated, and then the second field is evaluated again. This process with the second and third expressions is repeated until the conditional expression evaluates to zero (logical false).

Q Can the while statement end with a semicolon?

A By definition, the while statement does not end with a semicolon. However, it's legal in C to put a semicolon right after the while statement like this: while(*expression*);, which means there is a null statement controlled by the while statement. Remember that the result will be quite different from what you expect if you accidentally put a semicolon at the end of the while statement.

Q If two loops are nested together, which one must finish first, the inner loop or the outer loop?

A The inner must finish first. Then the outer loop will continue until the end, and then start another iteration if its specified condition is still met.

Workshop

To help you solidify your understanding of this hour's lesson, you are encouraged to try to answer the quiz questions and finish the exercises provided in the workshop before you move to next lesson. The answers and hints to the questions and exercises are given in Appendix D, "Answers to Quizzes and Exercises."

Quiz

1. Can the following while loop print out anything?

```
int k = 100;
while (k<100){
    printf("%c", k);
    k++;
}
```

2. Can the following do-while loop print out anything?

```
int k = 100;
do {
    printf("%c", k);
    k++;
} while (k<100);
```

3. Do the following two for loops have the same number of iterations?

```
for (j=0; j<8; j++);
for (k=1; k<=8; k++);
```

4. Is the following `for` loop

```
for (j=65; j<72; j++) printf("%c", j);
```

equivalent to the following `while` loop?

```
int k = 65;
while (k<72)
    printf("%c", k);
    k++;
}
```

Exercises

1. What is the difference between the following two pieces of code?

```
for (i=0, j=1; i<8; i++, j++)
    printf("%d  +  %d  =  %d\n", i, j, i+j);

for (i=0, j=1; i<8; i++, j++);
    printf("%d  +  %d  =  %d\n", i, j, i+j);
```

2. Write a program that contains the two pieces of code shown in Exercise 1, and then execute the program. What are you going to see on the screen?

3. Rewrite the program in Listing 7.1. This time, you want the `while` statement to keep looping until the user enters the character K.

4. Rewrite the program shown in Listing 7.2 by replacing the `do-while` loop with a `for` loop.

5. Rewrite the program in Listing 7.6. This time, use a `while` loop as the outer loop, and a `do-while` loop as the inner loop.

Hour **8**

Using Conditional Operators

Civilization advances by extending the number of important operations we can perform without thinking about them.

—A. N. Whitehead

In Hour 6, "Manipulating Data," you learned about some important operators in C, such as the arithmetic assignment operators, the unary minus operator, the increment and decrement operators, and the relational operators. In this lesson you'll learn more operators that are very important in C programming, including

- The `sizeof` operator
- Logical operators
- Bit-manipulation operators
- The conditional operator

Measuring Data Sizes

You may remember in Hour 4, "Understanding Data Types and Keywords," I mentioned that each data type has its own size. Depending on the operating system and the C compiler you're using, the size of a data type varies. For example, on most UNIX workstations, an integer is 32 bits long, whereas most C compilers only support 16-bit integers on a DOS-based machine.

So, how do you know the size of a data type on your machine? The answer is that you can measure the data type size by using the sizeof operator provided by C.

The general form of the sizeof operator is

sizeof (*expression*)

Here *expression* is the data type or variable whose size is measured by the sizeof operator. The sizeof operator evaluates the size, in bytes, of its operand. The operand of the sizeof operator may be a C language keyword naming a data type (such as int, char, or float), or it may be an expression which refers to a data type whose size can be determined (such as a constant or the name of a variable).

The parentheses are optional in the general form of the operator. If the expression is not a C keyword for a data type, the parentheses can be discarded. For instance, the following statement:

size = sizeof(int);

Places the size, in bytes, of the int data type into a variable named size. The program in Listing 8.1 finds the sizes of the char, int, float, and double data types on my machine.

TYPE   LISTING 8.1   Using the sizeof Operator

```
 1:   /* 08L01.c: Using the sizeof operator */
 2:   #include <stdio.h>
 3:
 4:   main()
 5:   {
 6:       char   ch = ' ';
 7:       int    int_num = 0;
 8:       float  flt_num = 0.0f;
 9:       double dbl_num = 0.0;
10:
11:       printf("The size of char is: %d-byte\n", sizeof(char));
12:       printf("The size of ch is: %d-byte\n", sizeof ch );
13:       printf("The size of int is: %d-byte\n", sizeof(int));
14:       printf("The size of int_num is: %d-byte\n", sizeof int_num);
```

```
15:    printf("The size of float is: %d-byte\n", sizeof(float));
16:    printf("The size of flt_num is: %d-byte\n", sizeof flt_num);
17:    printf("The size of double is: %d-byte\n", sizeof(double));
18:    printf("The size of dbl_num is: %d-byte\n", sizeof dbl_num);
19:    return 0;
20: }
```

After this program is compiled and linked, an executable file, 08L01.exe, is created. The following is the output printed on the screen after the executable is run on my machine:

OUTPUT

```
The size of char is: 1-byte
The size of ch is: 1-byte
The size of int is: 2-byte
The size of int_num is: 2-byte
The size of float is: 4-byte
The size of flt_num is: 4-byte
The size of double is: 8-byte
```

The size of dbl_num is: 8-byte[ic:analysis]Line 2 in Listing 8.1 includes the header file stdio.h for the printf() function used in the statements inside the main() function body. Lines 6–9 declare a char variable (ch), an int variable (int_num), a float variable (flt_num), and a double variable (dbl_num), respectively. Also, these four variables are initialized. Note that in line 8, the initial value to flt_num is suffixed with f to specify float. (As you learned in Hour 4, you can use f or F to specify the float type for a floating-point number.)

Lines 11 and 12 display the size of the char data type, as well as the char variable ch. Note that the sizeof operator is used in both line 11 and line 12 to obtain the number of bytes the char data type or the variable ch can have. Because the variable ch is not a keyword in C, the parentheses are discarded for the sizeof operator in line 12.

The first two lines in the output are printed out by the two statements in lines 11 and 12, respectively. From the output, you see that the size of the char data type is 1 byte, which is the same as the size of the variable ch. This is not surprising because the variable ch is declared as the char variable.

Likewise, lines 13 and 14 print out the sizes of the int data type and the int variable int_num by using the sizeof operator. You see that the size of each is 2 bytes.

Also, by using the sizeof operator, lines 15–18 give the sizes of the float data type, the float variable flt_num, the double data type, and the double variable dbl_num, respectively. The results in the output section show that the float data type and the variable flt_num have the same size (4 bytes). The sizes of the double data type and the variable dbl_num are both 8 bytes.

Everything Is Logical

Now, it's time to learn about a new set of operators: *logical operators.*

There are three logical operators in the C language:

&&   The logical AND operator

¦¦   The logical OR operator

!   The logical NEGATION operator

The first two, the AND and OR operators, are binary operators; that is, they both take two operands (one to the left and one to the right of the operator). The logical AND operator (&&) is used to evaluate the truth or falsity of a pair of expressions. If either expression evaluates to 0 (that is, logically false), the operator yields a value of 0. Otherwise, if — and only if — both operand expressions evaluate to nonzero values, the logical AND operator yields a value of 1 (logically true).

The logical OR operator (¦¦) yields a value of 1 whenever one or both of the operand expressions evaluates to nonzero (logically true). The ¦¦ operator yields 0 only if both operand expressions evaluate to 0 (false). The logical negation operator (!) is a unary operator; that is, it only takes one operand (the expression to its right). If the operand evaluates to any nonzero value, the ! operator yields 0 (logically false); only when the operand expression evaluates to 0, does the operator yield 1 (logically true).

The following three sections contain examples that show you how to use the three logical operators.

The Logical AND Operator (&&)

A general format of the logical AND operator is:

exp1 && *exp2*

where *exp1* and *exp2* are two operand expressions evaluated by the AND operator.

A good way to understand the AND operator is to look at a table that shows the values yielded by the AND operator depending on the possible values of *exp1* and *exp2*. See Table 8.1, which can be called the *truth table* of the AND operator.

TABLE 8.1   The Values Returned by the AND Operator

exp1	exp2	&& Yields
nonzero	nonzero	1
nonzero	0	0
	nonzero	0
0	0	0

8

Listing 8.2 is an example of using the logical AND operator (&&).

TYPE   **LISTING 8.2**   Using the Logical AND Operator (&&)

```
 1:  /* 08L02.c: Using the logical AND operator */
 2:  #include <stdio.h>
 3:
 4:  main()
 5:  {
 6:      int   num;
 7:
 8:      num = 0;
 9:      printf("The AND operator yields: %d\n",
10:              (num%2 == 0) && (num%3 == 0));
11:      num = 2;
12:      printf("The AND operator yields: %d\n",
13:              (num%2 == 0) && (num%3 == 0));
14:      num = 3;
15:      printf("The AND operator yields: %d\n",
16:              (num%2 == 0) && (num%3 == 0));
17:      num = 6;
18:      printf("The AND operator yields: %d\n",
19:              (num%2 == 0) && (num%3 == 0));
20:
21:      return 0;
22:  }
```

After this program is compiled and linked, an executable file, 08L02.exe, is created. The following output is displayed after the executable is run on my machine:

OUTPUT
```
The AND operator yields: 1
The AND operator yields: 0
The AND operator yields: 0
The AND operator yields: 1
```

ANALYSIS   In Listing 8.2, an integer variable, num, is declared in line 6 and initialized for the first time in line 8. Lines 9 and 10 print out the value yielded by the logical AND operator in the following expression:

`(num%2 == 0) && (num%3 == 0)`

Here you see two relational expressions, num%2 == 0 and num%3 == 0. In Hour 3 "Learning the Structure of a C Program," you learned that the arithmetic operator % can be used to obtain the remainder after its first operand is divided by the second operand. Therefore, num%2 yields the remainder of num divided by 2. The relational expression num%2 == 0 yields 1 if the remainder is equal to 0—that is, the value of num can be divided by 2 completely. Likewise, if the value of num can be divided by 3, the relational

expression num%3 == 0 yields 1 as well. Then, according to the truth table of the &&
operator (see Table 8.1), you know that the combination of the logical AND operator (&&)
and the two relational expressions yields 1 if the two relational expressions both evaluate
to nonzero; otherwise, it yields 0.

In our case, when num is initialized to 0 in line 8, both 0%2 and 0%3 yield remainders of
zero so that the two relational expressions evaluate to 1. Therefore, the logical AND
operator yields 1.

However, when num is assigned the value of 2 or 3 as shown in lines 11 and 14, the logical AND operator in line 13 or line 16 yields 0. The reason is that 2 or 3 can not be
divided by both 2 and 3.

Line 17 then assigns num the value of 6. Because 6 is a multiple of both 2 and 3, the logical AND operator in line 19 yields 1 which is printed out by the printf() function in
lines 18 and 19.

The Logical OR Operator (¦¦)

As mentioned earlier, the logical OR operator yields 1 (logically true) if one or both
of the expressions evaluates to a nonzero value. The ¦¦ operator yields 0 if (and only if)
both expressions yield 0.

A general format of the logical OR operator is:

exp1 ¦¦ *exp2*

where *exp1* and *exp2* are two operand expressions evaluated by the OR operator.

Table 8.2 is the truth table of the OR operator.

TABLE 8.2   The Values Returned by the OR Operator

exp1	exp2	¦¦ Yields
nonzero	nonzero	1
nonzero	0	1
0	nonzero	1
0	0	0

The program in Listing 8.3 shows how to use the logical OR operator (¦¦).

TYPE   **LISTING 8.3**   Using the Logical OR Operator ¦¦

```
1:  /* 08L03.c: Using the logical OR operator */
2:  #include <stdio.h>
```

```
3:
4:  main()
5:  {
6:      int   num;
7:
8:      printf("Enter a single digit that can be divided\nby both 2 and 3:\n");
9:      for (num = 1; (num%2 != 0) || (num%3 != 0); )
10:         num = getchar() - '0';
11:     printf("You got such a number: %d\n", num);
12:     return 0;
13: }
```

The following is the output displayed after the executable file 08L03.exe is run on my machine. The numbers in bold are what I entered. (The Enter key is pressed each time after one of the numbers is entered.) In the range of 0–9, 0 and 6 are the only two numbers that can be completely divided by both 2 and 3:

OUTPUT

```
Enter a single digit that can be divided
by both 2 and 3:
2
3
4
5
6
```

ANALYSIS You got such a number: 6 In Listing 8.3, an integer variable, num, is declared in line 6. Line 8 of Listing 8.3 prints out two headlines asking the user to enter a single digit.

In line 9, the integer variable num is initialized in the first expression of the for statement. The reason to initialize num with 1 is because 1 is such a number that is divisible by neither 2 nor 3. This way, the for loop is guaranteed to be executed at least once.

The key part of the program in Listing 8.3 is the logical expression in the for statement:

```
(num%2 != 0) || (num%3 != 0)
```

Here the two relational expressions num%2 != 0 and num%3 != 0 are evaluated. According to the truth table of the || operator (see Table 8.2), you know that if one of the relational expression evaluates to nonzero, indicating in this case that the value of num cannot be divided completely by either 2 or 3, then the logical OR expression evaluates to 1, which allows the for loop to continue.

The for loop stops only if the user enters a digit that can be divided by both 2 and 3. In other words, when both of the relational expressions evaluate to 0, the logical OR operator yields 0, which causes the termination of the for loop.

The Logical NEGATION Operator (!)

The general format of using the logical NEGATION operator is:

!expression

where expression is the operand of the NEGATION operator.

The truth table of the NEGATION operator is shown in Table 8.3.

TABLE 8.3   The Values Returned by the ! Operator

expression	Value Returned by !
nonzero	0
0	1

Now, let's take a look at the example shown in Listing 8.4, which demonstrates how to use the logical negation operator (!).

TYPE   **LISTING 8.4**   Using the Logical Negation Operator (!)

```
1:   /* 08L04.c: Using the logical negation operator */
2:   #include <stdio.h>
3:
4:   main()
5:   {
6:      int    num;
7:
8:      num = 7;
9:      printf("Given num = 7\n");
10:     printf("!(num < 7)  yields: %d\n", !(num < 7));
11:     printf("!(num > 7)  yields: %d\n", !(num > 7));
12:     printf("!(num == 7) yields: %d\n", !(num == 7));
13:     return 0;
14: }
```

The following result is displayed by running the executable file 08L04.exe:

OUTPUT
```
Given num = 7
!(num < 7)  returns: 1
!(num > 7)  returns: 1
!(num == 7) returns: 0
```

ANALYSIS   In line 8, note that an integer variable num is initialized to 7, which is then displayed by the printf() function in line 9.

8

In line 10, the relational expression num < 7 evaluates to 0 because the value of num is not less than 7. However, by using the logical negation operator, !(num < 7) yields 1. (Refer to the truth table of the ! operator shown in Table 8.3.)

Similarly, the logical expression !(num > 7) evaluates to 1 in line 11.

Because num has the value of 7, the relational expression num == 7 yields 1; however, the logical expression !(num == 7) in line 12 evaluates to 0.

Manipulating Bits

In previous hours, you learned that computer data and files are made of bits. In this section, you'll learn about a set of operators that enable you to access and manipulate specific bits. But before we go further, let us learn more about binary and hex numbers, and how to convert a decimal number to its binary or hex representation.

Converting Decimal to Hex or Binary

As I mentioned before, a bit is the smallest storage unit in the computer world. A bit can only hold the values 0 and 1 (0 and 1 are used to represent the off and on states of electronic switches that make up a computer's CPU and memory.) Each digit of a hex number consists of 4 bits. It is easy to convert a decimal number into a hex or a binary number. Table 8.4 shows the hex numbers from 0 to F and their corresponding binary and decimal representations.

TABLE 8.4 Numbers Expressed in Different Formats

Hex	Binary	Decimal
0	0000	0
1	0001	1
2	0010	2
3	0011	3
4	0100	4
5	0101	5
6	0110	6
7	0111	7
8	1000	8
9	1001	9
A	1010	10

continues

TABLE 8.4   continued

Hex	Binary	Decimal
B	1011	11
C	1100	12
D	1101	13
E	1110	14
F	1111	15

Let's see how to convert a decimal number into a binary or a hex number, or vice versa. As you know, binary is a 2-based numbering system. Each digit in a binary number is called a bit and can be 1 or 0. If the position of a bit in a binary number is n, the bit can have a value of either 0 or 2 to the power of n. The position of a bit in a binary number is counted from the right of the binary number. The rightmost bit is at the position of zero. Thus, given a binary number 1000 (its hex value is 8), we can calculate its decimal value like this:

$$1000 \rightarrow 1 * 2^3 + 0 * 2^2 + 0 * 2^1 + 0 * 2^0 \rightarrow 2^3 \rightarrow 8 \text{ (decimal)}$$

That is, the decimal value of the binary number 1000 is 8.

Similarly, given a binary number 1110, its hex value is E, you can calculate its decimal value like this:

$$1110 \rightarrow 1 * 2^3 + 1 * 2^2 + 1 * 2^1 + 0 * 2^0 \rightarrow 2^3 \rightarrow 14 \text{ (decimal)}$$

In other words, the decimal value of the binary number 1110 is 14.

If you want to convert a decimal number, for example 10, to its binary counterpart, you have the following process:

$$10 \rightarrow 2^3 + 2^1 \rightarrow 1 * 2^3 + 0 * 2^2 + 1 * 2^1 + 0 * 2^0 \rightarrow 1010 \text{ (binary) or A (hex)}$$

Likewise, you can convert the rest of decimal numbers in Table 8.4 to their binary counterparts, or vice versa.

Using Bitwise Operators

There are six bit-manipulation operators in the C language:

Operator	Description
&	The bitwise AND operator
¦	The bitwise OR operator
^	The bitwise exclusive OR (XOR) operator

Operator	Description
~	The bitwise complement operator
>>	The right-shift operator
<<	The left-shift operator

This section and the next one give explanations and examples of the bit-manipulation operators.

The general forms of the bitwise operators are as follows:

```
x & y
x ¦ y
x ^ y
~x
```

Here *x* and *y* are operands.

The & operator compares each bit of *x* to the corresponding bit in *y*. If both bits are 1, 1 is placed at the same position of the bit in the result. If one or both of the bits is 0, 0 is placed in the result.

For instance, the expression with two binary operands, 01 & 11, yields 01.

The ¦ operator places 1 in the result if either operand is 1. For example, the expression 01 ¦ 11 yields 11. The ¦ operator yields a 0 bit if — and only if — both operand bits are 0.

The ^ operator places 1 in the result if exactly one operand, but not both, is 1. Therefore, the expression 01 ^ 11 yields 10.

Finally, the ~ operator takes just one operand. This operator reverses each bit in the operand. For instance, ~01 gives 10.

Table 8.5 shows more examples of using the bitwise operators in decimal, hex, and binary formats (in the left three columns). The corresponding results, in binary, hex, and decimal formats, are listed in the right three columns. The hex numbers are prefixed with 0x.

TABLE 8.5 Examples Using Bitwise Operators

	Expressions		Results		
Decimal	Hex	Binary	Decimal	Hex	Binary
12 & 10	0x0C & 0x0A	1100 & 1010	8	0x08	1000
12 ¦ 10	0x0C ¦ 0x0A	1100 ¦ 1010	14	0x0E	1110
12 ^ 10	0x0C ^ 0x0A	1100 ^ 1010	6	0x06	0110
~12	~0x000C	~0000000000001100	65523	FFF3	1111111111110011

Note that the complementary value of 12 is 65523 because the unsigned integer data type (16-bit) has the maximum number 65535. In other words, 65,523 is the result of subtracting 12 from 65,535. (The unsigned data modifier is introduced in Hour 9, "Working with Data Modifiers and Math Functions.")

The program in Listing 8.5 demonstrates the usage of the bitwise operators.

TYPE   **LISTING 8.5**   Using Bitwise Operators

```
 1:  /* 08L05.c: Using bitwise operators */
 2:  #include <stdio.h>
 3:
 4:  main()
 5:  {
 6:     int   x, y, z;
 7:
 8:     x = 4321;
 9:     y = 5678;
10:     printf("Given x = %u, i.e., 0X%04X\n", x, x);
11:     printf("      y = %u, i.e., 0X%04X\n", y, y);
12:     z = x & y;
13:     printf("x & y  returns: %6u, i.e., 0X%04X\n", z, z);
14:     z = x ¦ y;
15:     printf("x ¦ y  returns: %6u, i.e., 0X%04X\n", z, z);
16:     z = x ^ y;
17:     printf("x ^ y  returns: %6u, i.e., 0X%04X\n", z, z);
18:     printf("  ~x   returns: %6u, i.e., 0X%04X\n", ~x, ~x);
19:     return 0;
20:  }
```

After the executable file, 08L05.exe, is created and run on my computer, the following output is shown on the screen:

OUTPUT
```
Given x = 4321, i.e., 0X10E1
      y = 5678, i.e., 0X162E
x & y  returns:  4128, i.e., 0X1020
x ¦ y  returns:  5871, i.e., 0X16EF
x ^ y  returns:  1743, i.e., 0X06CF
  ~x   returns: 61214, i.e., 0XEF1E
```

ANALYSIS   In Listing 8.5, three integer variables, x, y, and z, are declared in line 6. Lines 8 and 9 set x and y to 4321 and 5678, respectively. Lines 10 and 11 then print out the values of x and y in both decimal and hex formats. The hex numbers are prefixed with 0X.

The statement in line 12 assigns the result of the operation made by the bitwise AND operator (&) with the variables x and y. Then, line 13 displays the result in both decimal and hex formats.

Lines 14 and 15 perform the operation specified by the bitwise OR operator ($\vert$) and print out the result in both decimal and hex formats. Similarly, lines 16 and 17 give the result of the operation made by the bitwise XOR operator (^).

Last, the statement in line 18 prints out the complementary value of x by using the bitwise complement operator (~). The result is displayed on the screen in both decimal and hex formats.

Note that the unsigned integer format specifier with a minimum field width of 6, %6u, and the uppercase hex format specifier with the minimum width of 4, %04X, are used in the printf() function. The unsigned integer data type is used here so that the complementary value of an integer can be shown and understood easily. More details on the unsigned data modifier are introduced in Hour 9.

> Don't confuse the *bitwise* operators & and $\vert$ with the *logical* operators && and $\vert\vert$. For instance,
>
> (x=1) & (y=10)
>
> is a completely different expression from
>
> (x=1) && (y=10)

Using Shift Operators

There are two shift operators in C. The >> operator shifts the bits of an operand to the right; the << operator shifts the bits to the left.

The general forms of the two shift operators are

```
x >> y
x << y
```

Here *x* is an operand that is going to be shifted. *y* contains the specified number of places to shift.

For instance, the expression 8 >> 2 tells the computer to shift the operand 8 to the right 2 bits, which yields the number 2 in decimal. The following:

$\quad$ 8 >> 2 which is equivalent to $(1 * 2^3 + 0 * 2^2 + 0 * 2^1 + 0 * 2^0)$ >> 2

produces the following:

$\quad$ $(0 * 2^3 + 0 * 2^2 + 1 * 2^1 + 0 * 2^0)$ which is equivalent to 0010 (in the binary format) or 2 (in the decimal format).

Likewise, the 5 << 1 expression shifts the operand 5 to the left 1 bit, and yields 10 in decimal.

The program in Listing 8.6 prints out more results by using the shift operators.

TYPE   **LISTING 8.6**   Using the Shift Operators

```
 1:  /* 08L06.c: Using shift operators */
 2:  #include <stdio.h>
 3:
 4:  main()
 5:  {
 6:      int   x, y, z;
 7:
 8:      x = 255;
 9:      y = 5;
10:      printf("Given x = %4d, i.e., 0X%04X\n", x, x);
11:      printf("      y = %4d, i.e., 0X%04X\n", y, y);
12:      z = x >> y;
13:      printf("x >> y  yields: %6d, i.e., 0X%04X\n", z, z);
14:      z = x << y;
15:      printf("x << y  yields: %6d, i.e., 0X%04X\n", z, z);
16:      return 0;
17:  }
```

The following output is obtained by running the executable file 08L06.exe on my computer:

OUTPUT
```
Given x =  255, i.e., 0X00FF
      y =    5, i.e., 0X0005
x >> y  yields:      7, i.e., 0X0007
x << y  yields:   8160, i.e., 0X1FE0
```

ANALYSIS   Three integer variables, x, y, and z, are declared in line 6 of Listing 8.6. x is initialized to 255 in line 8; y is initialized to 5 in line 9. Then, lines 10 and 11 display the values of x and y on the screen.

The statement in line 12 shifts y bits of the operand x to the right, and then assigns the result to z. Line 13 prints out the result of the shifting made in line 12. The result is 7 in decimal, or 0X0007 in hex.

Lines 14 and 15 shift the operand x to the left by y bits, and display the result on the screen too. The result of the left-shifting is 8160 in decimal, or 0x1FE0 in hex.

> The operation of the shift-right operator (>>) is equivalent to dividing by powers of two. In other words, the following:
>
> x >> y
>
> is equivalent to the following:
>
> x / 2
>
> Here x is a non-negative integer.
>
> On the other hand, shifting to the left is equivalent to multiplying by powers of two; that is,
>
> x << y
>
> is equivalent to
>
> x * 2

8

What Does x?y:z Mean?

The operator ?: is called the *conditional operator*, which is the only operator that takes three operands. The general form of the conditional operator is

x ? y : z

Here x, y, and z are three operand expressions. Among them, x contains the test condition, and y and z represent the two possible final values of the expression. If x evaluates to nonzero (logically true), then y is chosen; otherwise, z is the result yielded by the conditional expression. The conditional operator is used as a kind of shorthand for an if statement.

For instance, the expression

x > 0 ? 'T' : 'F'

evaluates to 'T' if the value of x is greater than 0. Otherwise, the conditional expression evaluates to the value 'F'.

Listing 8.7 demonstrates the usage of the conditional operator.

TYPE **LISTING 8.7** Using the Conditional Operator

```
1:  /* 08L07.c: Using the ?: operator */
2:  #include <stdio.h>
3:
4:  main()
5:  {
```

continues

LISTING 8.7   continued

```
 6:     int    x;
 7:
 8:     x = sizeof(int);
 9:     printf("%s\n",
10:        (x == 2)
11:        ? "The int data type has 2 bytes."
12:        : "int doesn't have 2 bytes.");
13:     printf("The maximum value of int is: %d\n",
14:        (x != 2) ? ~(1 << x * 8 - 1) : ~(1 << 15) );
15:     return 0;
16: }
```

The following output is displayed on the screen when I run the executable file 08L07.exe on my machine:

OUTPUT
```
The int data type has 2 bytes
The maximum value of int is: 32767
```

ANALYSIS
In Listing 8.7, the size of the int data type is measured first in line 8 by using the sizeof operator, and the number of bytes is assigned to the integer variable x.

Lines 9–12 contain one statement, in which the conditional operator (?:) is used to test whether the number of bytes saved in x is equal to 2, and the result is printed. If the x == 2 expression evaluates to nonzero, the string The int data type has 2 bytes is printed out by the printf() function in the statement. Otherwise, the second string, int doesn't have 2 bytes, is displayed on the screen.

In addition, the statement in lines 11 and 12 tries to find out the maximum value of the int data type on the current machine. The x != 2 expression is evaluated first in the statement. If the expression returns nonzero (that is, the byte number of the int data type is not equal to 2), the ~(1 << x * 8 - 1) expression is evaluated, and the result is chosen as the return value. Here the ~(1 << x * 8 - 1) expression is a general form to calculate the maximum value of the int data type, which is equivalent to $2^{[ic:super](x * 8 - 1)} - 1$. (The complement operator, ~, and the shift operator, <<, were introduced in the previous sections of this hour.)

On the other hand, if the test condition x != 2 in line 12 returns 0, which means the value of x is indeed equal to 2, the result of the ~(1 << 15) expression is chosen. Here you may have already figured out that ~(1 << 15) is equivalent to $2^{15}-1$, which is the maximum value that the 16-bit int data type can have.

The result displayed on the screen shows that the int data type on my machine is 2 bytes (or 16 bits) long, and the maximum value of the int data type is 32767.

Summary

In this lesson you learned the following very important logical and bit-manipulation operators in C:

- The `sizeof` operator evaluates to the number of bytes that a specified data type has. You can use this operator to measure the size of a data type on your machine.

- The logical AND operator (`&&`) yields 1 (`logical true`) only if both of its two operand expressions) evaluate to nonzero values. Otherwise, the operator yields 0.

- The logical OR operator (`¦¦`) yields 0 only if both of its two operands evaluate to 0. Otherwise, the operator yields 1.

- The logical negation operator (`!`) yields 0 when its operand evaluates to nonzero, and yields 1 only if its operand evaluates to 0.

- There are six bit-manipulation operators: the bitwise AND operator (`&`), the bitwise OR operator (`¦`), the bitwise XOR operator (`^`), the bitwise complement operator `~`), the right-shift operator (`>>`), and the left-shift operator (`<<`).

- The conditional operator (`?:`) is the only operator in C that can take three operands.

In the next lesson you'll learn about the data type modifiers in the C language.

Q&A

Q Why do we need the `sizeof` operator?

A The `sizeof` operator can be used to measure the sizes of all data types defined in C. When you write a portable C program that needs to know the size of an integer variable, it's a bad idea to hard-code the size based on the machine you are currently using. The better way to tell the program the size of the variable is to use the `sizeof` operator, which yields the size of the integer variable at runtime.

Q What's the difference between `¦` and `¦¦`?

A `¦` is the bitwise OR operator that takes two operands. The `¦` operator compares each bit of one operand to the corresponding bit in another operand. If both bits are 0, 0 is placed at the same position of the bit in the result. Otherwise, 1 is placed in the result.

On the other hand, `¦¦`, as the logical OR operator, requires two operands (or expressions). The operator yields 0 only if both of its operands evaluate to 0. Otherwise, the operator yields 1.

Q Why is 1 << 3 equivalent to 1 * 2³?

A The 1 << 3 expression tells the computer to shift 3 bits of the operand 1 to the left. The binary format of the operand is 0001. (Note that only the lowest four bits are shown here.) After being shifted 3 bits to left, the binary number becomes 1000, which is equivalent to $1 * 2^3 + 0 * 2^2 + 0 * 2^1 + 0 * 2^0$; that is, $1 * 2^3$.

Q What can the conditional operator (?:) do?

A If there are two possible answers under certain conditions, you can use the ?: operator to pick up one of the two answers based on the result made by testing the conditions. For instance, the expression (age > 65) ? "Retired" : "Not retired" tells the computer that if the value of age is greater than 65, the string of Retired should be chosen; otherwise, Not retired is chosen.

Workshop

To help solidify your understanding of this hour's lesson, you are encouraged to answer the quiz questions and finish the exercises provided in the workshop before you move to the next lesson. The answers and hints to the questions and exercises are given in Appendix D, "Answers to Quiz Questions and Exercises."

Quiz

1. What do the (x=1) && (y=10) and (x=1) & (y=10) expressions yield, respectively?

2. Given x = 96, y = 1, and z = 69, to what does the expression !y ? x == z : y evaluate?

3. If you have two int variables x and y, with x set to the binary value 0011000000111001 and y set to the binary value 1100111111000110, what values are yielded by the two expressions ~x and ~y?

4. Given x=9, what does (x%2==0)||(x%3==0) yield? How about (x%2==0)&&(x%3==0)?

5. Is 8 >> 3 equivalent to $8 / 2^3$? How about 1 << 3?

Exercises

1. Given x = 0xEFFF and y = 0x1000 (that is, EFFF and 1000 as hex values), what hex values do you get by evaluating ~x and ~y?

2. Taking the values of x and y assigned in Exercise 1, write a program that prints out the values of !x and !y by using both the %d and %u formats in the printf() function.

3. Given x = 123 and y = 4, write a program that displays the results of the expressions x << y and x >> y.

4. Write a program that shows the values (in hex) of the expressions 0xFFFF^0x8888, 0xABCD & 0x4567, and 0xDCBA ¦ 0x1234.

5. Use the ?: operator and the for statement to write a program that keeps taking the characters entered by the user until the character q is accounted. (Hint: Put x!='q' ? 1 : 0 expression as the second expression in a for statement.)

8

Hour 9

Working with Data Modifiers and Math Functions

If at first you don't succeed, transform your data.

—Murphy's Laws of Computers

In Hour 4, "Understanding Data Types and Keywords," you learned about several data types, such as char, int, float, and double, in the C language. In this hour, you'll learn about four data modifiers that enable you to have greater control over the data. The C keywords for the four data modifiers are

- signed
- unsigned
- short
- long

You're also going to learn about several mathematical functions provided by the C language, such as

- The sin() function
- The cos() function
- The tan() function
- The pow() function
- The sqrt() function

Enabling or Disabling the Sign Bit

As you know, it's very easy to express a negative number in decimal. All you need to do is put a minus sign in front of the absolute value of the number. (The absolute value being the distance of the number from zero.) But how does the computer represent a negative number in the binary format?

Normally, one bit can be used to indicate whether the value of a number represented in the binary format is negative. This bit is called the *sign bit*. The following two sections introduce two data modifiers, signed and unsigned, that can be used to enable or disable the sign bit.

It should be noted that some computers may not express negative numbers in the manner described; in fact the C language standard makes no requirement that a sign bit be used, although this is a common method. The important thing to understand is the differences between signed and unsigned data types.

The signed Modifier

For integers, the leftmost bit can be used as the sign bit. For instance, if the int data type is 16 bits long and the rightmost bit is counted as bit 0, you can use bit 15 as a sign bit. When the sign bit is set to 1, the C compiler knows that the value represented by the data variable is negative.

There are several ways to represent a negative value of the float or double data types. The implementations of the float and double data types are beyond the scope of this book. You can refer to Kernighan and Ritchie's book *The C Programming Language* for more details on the implementations of negative values of the float or double type.

The C language provides a data modifier, signed, that can be used to indicate to the compiler that the integer data types (char, int, short int, and long int) use the sign bit. (The short and long modifiers are introduced later in this chapter). By default, all the integer data types except the `char` data type are signed quantities. But the ANSI standard does not require the `char` data type be signed; it's up to the compiler vendors. Therefore, if you want to use a signed character variable, and make sure the compiler knows it, you can declare the character variable like this:

```
signed char ch;
```

so that the compiler knows that the character variable `ch` is signed, which means the variable can hold both negative and positive values. If the `char` type is 8 bits in length, then a `signed char` would hold values from -128 (that is, 2^7) to 127 (2^7-1). By contrast, an unsigned character in this case would range from 0 to 255 (2^8-1).

The `unsigned` Modifier

The C language also gives you the `unsigned` modifier, which can be used to tell the C compiler that the specified data type is only capable of holding non-negative values.

Like the `signed` modifier, the `unsigned` modifier is meaningful only to the `integer` data types (`char`, `int`, `short int`, and `long int`).

For instance, the declaration

```
unsigned int x;
```

tells the C compiler that the integer variable x can only assume positive values from 0 to 65535 (that is, 2^{16}-1), if the `int` data type is 16 bits long; a (signed) `int` would hold values from -32768 (-2^{15}-1) to 32767 (2^{15}).

In fact, `unsigned int` is equivalent to `unsigned` (by itself) according to the ANSI standard. In other words, `unsigned int x;` is the same as `unsigned x;`.

Also, the ANSI standard allows you to indicate that a constant is of type `unsigned` by suffixing u or U to the constant. For instance,

```
unsigned int x, y;
x = 12345U;
y = 0xABCDu;
```

Here, the unsigned integer constants `12345U` and `0xABCDu` are assigned to variables x and y, respectively.

The program in Listing 9.1 is an example of using the `signed` and `unsigned` modifiers.

LISTING 9.1   Modifying Data with signed and unsigned

```
1:  /* 09L01.c: Using signed and unsigned modifiers */
2:  #include <stdio.h>
3:
4:  main()
5:  {
6:     signed char  ch;
7:     int          x;
8:     unsigned int y;
9:
10:    ch = 0xFF;
11:    x = 0xFFFF;
12:    y = 0xFFFFu;
13:    printf("The decimal of signed 0xFF is %d.\n", ch);
14:    printf("The decimal of signed 0xFFFF is %d.\n", x);
15:    printf("The decimal of unsigned 0xFFFFu is %u.\n", y);
16:    printf("The hex of decimal 12345 is 0x%X.\n", 12345);
17:    printf("The hex of decimal -12345 is 0x%X.\n", -12345);
18:    return 0;
19: }
```

On my machine, the executable file of the program in Listing 9.1 is named 09L01.exe. (Note that when you compile the program in Listing 9.1, you may see a warning message regarding the assignment statement ch = 0xFF; in line 10 due to the fact that ch is declared as a signed char variable. You can ignore the warning message.)

The following is the output displayed on the screen after I run the executable on my computer:

OUTPUT
```
The decimal of signed 0xFF is -1
The decimal of signed 0xFFFF is -1.
The decimal of unsigned 0xFFFFu is 65535.
The hex of decimal 12345 is 0x3039.
The hex of decimal -12345 is 0xCFC7.
```

ANALYSIS   As you see in Listing 9.1, line 6 declares a signed char variable, ch. The int variable x and the unsigned int variable y are declared in lines 7 and 8, respectively. The three variables, ch, x, and y, are initialized in lines 10–12. Note that in line 12, u is suffixed to 0xFFFF to indicate that the constant is an unsigned integer.

The statement in line 13 displays the decimal value of the signed char variable ch. The output on the screen shows that the corresponding decimal value of 0xFF is -1 for the signed char variable ch.

Lines 14 and 15 print out the decimal values of the int variable x (which is signed by default) and the unsigned int variable y, respectively. Note that for the variable y, the unsigned integer format specifier %u is used in the printf() function in line 15.

(Actually, you might recall that %u was used to specify the unsigned int data type as the display format in the previous hour.)

Based on the output, you see that 0xFFFF is equal to -1 for the signed int data type, and 65535 for the unsigned int data type. Here, the integer data type is 16 bits long.

Lines 16 and 17 print out 0x3039 and 0xCFC7, which are the hex formats of the decimal values of 12345 and -12345, respectively. According to the method mentioned in the last section, 0xCFC7 is obtained by adding 1 to the complemented value of 0x3039.

You may receive different results from this example, depending on the width of the various data types on your system. The important thing to understand is the difference between signed and unsigned data types.

Changing Data Sizes

Sometimes, you want to reduce the memory taken by variables, or you need to increase the storage space of certain data types. Fortunately, the C language gives you the flexibility to modify sizes of data types. The two data modifiers, short and long, are introduced in the following two sections.

The short Modifier

A data type can be modified to take less memory by using the short modifier. For instance, you can apply the short modifier to an integer variable that is 32 bits long, which might reduce the memory taken by the variable to as little as 16 bits.

You can use the short modifier like this:

```
short x;
```

or

```
unsigned short y;
```

By default, a short int data type is a signed number. Therefore, in the short x; statement, x is a signed variable of short integer.

The long Modifier

If you need more memory to keep values from a wider range, you can use the long modifier to define a data type with increased storage space.

For instance, given an integer variable x that is 16 bits long, the declaration

```
long int x;
```

increases the size of x to at least 32 bits.

The ANSI standard allows you to indicate that a constant has type long by suffixing 1 or L to the constant:

```
long int x, y;
x = 1234567891;
y = 0xABCD1234L;
```

Here, the constants of the long int data type, 1234567891 and 0xABCD1234L, are assigned to variables x and y, respectively.

Also, you can declare a long integer variable simply like this:

```
long x;
```

which is equivalent to

```
long int x;
```

Listing 9.2 contains a program that can print out the numbers of bytes provided by the C compiler used to compile the program for different modified data types.

LISTING 9.2　Modifying Data with short and long

```
 1:  /* 09L02.c: Using short and long modifiers */
 2:  #include <stdio.h>
 3:
 4:  main()
 5:  {
 6:     printf("The size of short int is: %d.\n",
 7:         sizeof(short int));
 8:     printf("The size of long int is: %d.\n",
 9:         sizeof(long int));
10:     printf("The size of float is: %d.\n",
11:         sizeof(float));
12:     printf("The size of double is: %d.\n",
13:         sizeof(double));
14:     printf("The size of long double is: %d.\n",
15:         sizeof(long double));
16:     return 0;
17:  }
```

I obtain the following output after I run the executable 09L02.exe on my computer:

```
The size of short int is: 2.
The size of long int is: 4.
The size of float is: 4.
The size of double is: 8.
The size of long double is: 10.
```

ANALYSIS In Listing 9.2, the `sizeof` operator and `printf()` function are used to measure the sizes of the modified data types and display the results on the screen.

For instance, lines 6 and 7 obtain the size of the `short int` data type and print out the number of bytes, 2, on the screen. From the output, you know that the `short int` data type is 2 bytes long on my machine.

Likewise, lines 8 and 9 find the size of the `long int` data type is 4 bytes long, which is the same length as the `float` data type obtained in lines 10 and 11.

Lines 12 and 13 obtain the size of the `double` data type, which is 8 bytes on my machine. Then, after being modified by the `long` modifier, the size of the `double` data type is increased to 10 bytes (that is, 80 bits), which is printed out by the `printf()` call in lines 14 and 15.

As with the previous example, your results will likely be different if your system supports data widths that are different from the ones on my machine. By running this program on your own machine, you can determine the widths of these data types for your system.

Adding `h`, `l`, or `L` to `printf` and `fprintf` Format Specifiers

The `printf` and `fprintf` functions need to know the exact data type of the arguments passed to them in order to properly evaluate those arguments and print their values in a meaningful way. The format string for the `printf` and `fprintf` functions uses the conversion specifiers `d`, `i`, `o`, `u`, `x`, or `X` to indicate that the corresponding argument is an integer, and is of type `int` or unsigned `int`.

You can add `h` into the integer format specifier (like this: `%hd`, `%hi`, or `%hu`) to specify that the corresponding argument is a `short int` or unsigned `short int`.

On the other hand, using `%ld` or `%Ld` specifies that the corresponding argument is `long int`. `%lu` or `%Lu` is then used for the `long unsigned int` data.

The program in Listing 9.3 shows the usage of `%hd`, `%lu`, and `%ld`.

LISTING 9.3   Using `%hd`, `%ld`, and `%lu`

```
1:   /* 09L03.c: Using %hd, %ld, and %lu specifiers */
2:   #include <stdio.h>
3:
4:   main()
5:   {
6:      short int        x;
```

continues

LISTING 9.3   continued

```
7:      unsigned int      y;
8:      long int          s;
9:      unsigned long int t;
10:
11:     x = 0xFFFF;
12:     y = 0xFFFFU;
13:     s = 0xFFFFFFFFl;
14:     t = 0xFFFFFFFFL;
15:     printf("The short int of 0xFFFF is %hd.\n", x);
16:     printf("The unsigned int of 0xFFFF is %u.\n", y);
17:     printf("The long int of 0xFFFFFFFF is %ld.\n", s);
18:     printf("The unsigned long int of 0xFFFFFFFF is %lu.\n", t);
19:     return 0;
20: }
```

After the executable file 09L03.exe is created and run on my machine, the following output is displayed on the screen:

OUTPUT

```
The short int of 0xFFFF is -1.
The unsigned int of 0xFFFF is 65535.
The long int of 0xFFFFFFFF is -1.
The unsigned long int of 0xFFFFFFFF is 4294967295
```

ANALYSIS   There are four data types declared in Listing 9.3: the short int variable x, the unsigned int variable y, the long int variable s, and the unsigned long int variable t. The four variables are initialized in lines 6–9.

To display the decimal values of x, y, s, and t, the format specifiers %hd, %u, %ld, and %lu are used, respectively, in lines 15–18 to convert the corresponding hex numbers to decimal numbers. The output from the program in Listing 9.3 shows that values contained by x, y, s, and t have been correctly displayed on the screen.

Mathematical Functions in C

Basically, the math functions provided by the C language can be classified into three groups:

- Trigonometric and hyperbolic functions, such as acos(), cos(), and cosh().
- Exponential and logarithmic functions, such as exp(), pow(), and log10().
- Miscellaneous math functions, such as ceil(), fabs(), and floor().

You have to include the header file math.h in your C program before you can use any math functions defined in the header file.

The following two sections introduce several math functions and describe how to use them in your programs.

Calling `sin()`, `cos()`, and `tan()`

You may skip the following two sections if you are not a math fan, as they are not vital to understanding the C language itself. However, if you do need to make mathematical calculations, you may appreciate that C gives you this set of math functions.

For instance, given an angle x in radians, the `sin` expression returns the sine of the angle.

The following formula can be used to convert the value of an angle in degrees into the value in radians:

```
radians = degree * (3.141593 / 180.0).
```

Here, `3.141593` is the approximate value of pi. If needed, you can use more decimal digits from pi.

Now, let's look at the syntax of the `sin()`, `cos()`, and `tan()` functions.

SYNTAX

The syntax for the `sin()` function is

```
#include <math.h>
double sin(double x);
```

Here, the `double` variable x contains the value of an angle in radians. The `sin()` function returns the sine of x in the `double` data type.

SYNTAX

The syntax for the `cos()` function is

```
#include <math.h>
double cos(double x);
```

Here, the `double` variable x contains the value of an angle in radians. The `cos()` function returns the cosine of x in the `double` data type.

SYNTAX

The syntax for the `tan()` function is

```
#include <math.h>
double tan(double x);
```

Here, the `double` variable x contains the value of an angle in radians. The `tan()` function returns the tangent of x in the `double` data type.

Listing 9.4 demonstrates how to use the `sin()`, `cos()`, and `tan()` functions.

LISTING 9.4 Calculating Trigonometric Values with `sin()`, `cos()`, and `tan()`

```
1:  /* 09L04.c: Using sin(), cos(), and tan() functions */
2:  #include <stdio.h>
3:  #include <math.h>
4:
```

continues

LISTING 9.4   continued

```
 5:  main()
 6:  {
 7:     double x;
 8:
 9:     x = 45.0;                     /* 45 degree */
10:     x *= 3.141593 / 180.0;    /* convert to radians */
11:     printf("The sine of 45 is:    %f.\n", sin);
12:     printf("The cosine of 45 is:  %f.\n", cos);
13:     printf("The tangent of 45 is: %f.\n", tan);
14:     return 0;
15:  }
```

The following output is displayed on the screen when the executable file 09L04.exe is executed:

```
The sine of 45 is:    0.707107.
The cosine of 45 is:  0.707107.
The tangent of 45 is: 1.000000.
```

ANALYSIS   Note that the header file math.h is included in line 3, which is required by the C math functions.

The double variable x in Listing 9.4 is initialized with 45.0 in line 9. Here, 45.0 is the value of the angle in degrees, which is converted into the corresponding value in radians in line 10.

Then, the statement in line 11 calculates the sine of x by calling the sin() function and prints out the result on the screen. Similarly, line 12 obtains the cosine of x and shows it on the screen as well. Because x contains the value of a 45-degree angle, it's not surprising to see that both the sine and cosine values are the same, about 0.707107.

Line 13 gives the tangent value of x by using the tan() function. As you might know, the tangent of x is equal to the sine of x divided by the cosine of x. Because the sine of a 45-degree angle is the same as the cosine of a 45-degree angle, the tangent of a 45-degree angle is equal to 1. The result (in the floating-point format) of 1.000000, in the third line of the listing's output, proves it.

To make things simpler, you could declare a variable PI initialized to 3.141593, and another variable initialized to 180.0, and use those in your calculations. Or, simply declare a single constant initialized to the result of 3.141593/180.0.

Calling pow() and sqrt()

The pow() and sqrt() functions are two other useful math functions in C. Unlike some other languages, C has no intrinsic operator for raising a number to a power.

SYNTAX

The syntax for the pow() function is

```
#include <math.h>
double pow(double x, double y);
```

Here, the value of the double variable x is raised to the power of y. The pow() function returns the result in the double data type.

SYNTAX

The syntax for the sqrt() function is

```
#include <math.h>
double sqrt(double x);
```

Here, the sqrt() function returns the non-negative square root of x in the double data type. An error occurs if x is negative.

If you pass 0.5 to the pow() function as its second argument, and x contains a non-negative value, the two expressions, pow(x, 0.5) and sqrt, are equivalent.

Now, take a look at how to call the pow() and sqrt() functions in the program shown in Listing 9.5.

LISTING 9.5   Applying the pow() and sqrt() Functions

```
 1:   /* 09L05.c: Using pow() and sqrt() functions */
 2:   #include <stdio.h>
 3:   #include <math.h>
 4:
 5:   main()
 6:   {
 7:       double x, y, z;
 8:
 9:       x = 64.0;
10:       y = 3.0;
11:       z = 0.5;
12:       printf("pow(64.0, 3.0) returns: %7.0f\n", pow(x, y));
13:       printf("sqrt(64.0) returns:    %2.0f\n", sqrt);
14:       printf("pow(64.0, 0.5) returns: %2.0f\n", pow(x, z));
15:       return 0;
16:   }
```

Then, the following output is displayed on the screen after the executable file 09L05.exe is executed:

OUTPUT
```
pow(64.0, 3.0) returns: 262144
sqrt(64.0) returns:    8
pow(64.0, 0.5) returns: 8
```

ANALYSIS   The three double variables in Listing 9.5, x, y, and z, are initialized with 64.0, 3.0, and 0.5, respectively, in lines 9–11.

The pow() function in line 12 takes x and y and then calculates the value of x raised to the power of y. Because the result is a double, yet I know the fractional part will be all decimal digits of 0s, the format specifier %7.0f is used in the printf() function to convert only the non-fractional part of the value. The result is shown on the screen as 262144.

In line 13, the non-negative square root of x is calculated by calling the sqrt() function. As in line 12, the format specifier %2.0f is used in line 13 to convert the non-fractional part of the value returned from the sqrt() function because the fractional part consists of all 0s. As you see in the output, the non-negative square root of x is 8.

As I mentioned earlier, the expression pow(x, 0.5) is equivalent to the expression sqrt. Thus, it's no surprise to see that pow(x, z) in the statement of line 14 produces the same result as sqrt does in line 13.

All floating-point calculations, including both the float and double data types, are done in double-precision arithmetic. That is, a float data variable must be converted to a double in order to carry on the calculation. After the calculation, the double has to be converted back to a float before the result can be assigned to the float variable. Therefore, a float calculation may take more time.

The main reason that C supports the float data type at all is to save memory space because the double data type takes twice as much memory space for storage as the float data type does. In many cases, precision beyond what is provided by float is simply unnecessary.

Summary

In this lesson you learned the following important modifiers and math functions:

- The signed modifier can be used to declare char and int data types that are able to hold negative as well as non-negative values.

- All int variables in C are signed by default.

- The unsigned modifier can be used to declare char and int data types that are not able to hold negative values. Doing this effectively doubles the range of positive values that the variable can hold.

- The memory space taken by a data variable may be reduced or increased by using the short or long data modifier, respectively.

- There is a set of C library functions, such as sin(), cos(), and tan(), that can be used to perform trigonometric or hyperbolic computations.

- There is another group of math functions in C—for example, pow()—that can perform exponential and logarithmic calculation.

- The sqrt() function returns a non-negative square root. The expression sqrt is equivalent to the pow(x, 0.5) expression, if x has a non-negative value. You cannot pass a negative value to the sqrt() function, as this will cause an error.

- The header file math.h must be included in your C program if you call any math functions declared in that header file.

In the next lesson you'll learn several very important control flow statements in C.

Q&A

Q Which bit can be used as the sign bit in an integer?

A The leftmost bit can be used as the sign bit for an integer. For instance, assume the int data type is 16 bits long. If you count the bit position from right to left, and the first bit counted is bit 0, then bit 15 is the leftmost bit that can be used as the sign bit.

Q What can the %lu format specifier do?

A The %lu format specifier can be used in a printf() string to convert the corresponding argument to the unsigned long int data type. In addition, the %lu format specifier is equivalent to %Lu.

Q When do I use short and long?

A If you need to save memory space, and you know the value of an integer data variable stays within a smaller range, you can try to use the short modifier to tell the C compiler to reduce the default memory space assigned to the variable, for instance, from 32 bits to 16 bits.

On the other hand, if a variable has to hold a number that is beyond the current range of a data type, you can use the long modifier to increase the storage space of the variable in order to hold the number.

Q Does the sin() function take a value in degrees or in radians?

A Like other trigonometric math functions in C, the sin() function takes a value in radians. If you have an angle in degrees, you have to convert it into the form of radians. The formula is:

```
radians = degree * (3.141593 / 180.0).
```

Workshop

To help solidify your understanding of this hour's lesson, you are encouraged to answer the quiz questions and finish the exercises provided in the workshop before you move to the next lesson. The answers and hints to the questions and exercises are given in Appendix D, "Answers to Quiz Questions and Exercises."

Quiz

1. Given an int variable x and an unsigned int variable y, as well as x = 0x8765 and y = 0x8765, and if the leftmost bit is used as a sign bit, is x equal to y?

2. What should you do if you try to assign a large value to an int variable, but the value you assign is too large and you end up with a negative number that you didn't expect?

3. Which format specifier, %ld or %lu, should be used to specify an unsigned long int variable?

4. What is the name of the header file you have to include if you're calling some C math functions from your C program?

Exercises

1. Given the following statements,
   ```
   int x;
   unsigned int y;
   x = 0xAB78;
   y = 0xAB78;
   ```
   write a program to display the decimal values of x and y on the screen.

2. Write a program to measure the sizes of short int, long int, and long double on your machine.

3. Write a program to multiply two signed int variables with positive values, and display the result as a long int.

4. Write a program to display negative integers in hex format along with their signed int equivalents.

5. Given an angle of 30 degrees, write a program to calculate its sine and tangent values.

6. Write a program to calculate the non-negative square root of 0x19A1.

HOUR 10

Controlling Program Flow

It is harder to command than to obey.

—F. Nietzsche

In Hour 7, "Working with Loops," you learned to use the `while`, `do-while`, and `for` statements to do the same things over and over. These three statements can be grouped into the category of *looping* statements that are used for *control flow* in C.

In this lesson you'll learn about the statements that belong to another group of the control flow statements—*conditional branching* (or *jumping*), such as

- The `if` statement
- The `if-else` statement
- The `switch` statement
- The `break` statement
- The `continue` statement
- The `goto` statement

Always Saying "if..."

If life were a straight line, it would be very boring. The same thing is true for programming. It would be too dull if the statements in your program could only be executed in the order in which they appear.

In fact, an important task of a program is to instruct the computer to *branch* (that is, jump) to different portions of the code and work on different jobs whenever the specified conditions are met.

However, in most cases, you don't know in advance what will come next. What you do know is that something is bound to happen if certain conditions are met. Therefore, you can just write down tasks and conditions in the program. The decisions of when to perform the tasks are made by the conditional branching statements.

In C, the if statement is the most popular conditional branching statement; it can be used to evaluate the conditions as well as to make the decision whether the block of code controlled by the statement is going to be executed.

The general form of the if statement is

```
if (expression) {
   statement1;
   statement2;
      .
      .
      .
}
```

Here *expression* is the conditional criterion. If *expression* evaluates to a nonzero value, the statements inside the braces ({ and }), such as *statement1* and *statement2*, are executed. If *expression* evaluates to a value of zero, the statements are skipped.

Note that the braces ({ and }) form a block of statements that is under the control of the if statement. If there is only one statement inside the block, the braces can be omitted. The parentheses ((and)), however, must be always used to enclose the conditional expression.

For instance, the following expression:

```
if (x > 0.0)
  printf("The square root of x is: %f\n", sqrt);
```

tells the computer that if the value of the floating point variable x is greater than 0.0 (that is, positive), it should calculate the square root of x by calling the sqrt() function, and then print out the result. Here the conditional criterion is the relational expression x > 0.0, which evaluates to a value of 1 (logically true) if x is greater than zero, and evaluates to a value of 0 (logically false) if x is less than or equal to zero.

Listing 10.1 gives you another example of using the if statement.

LISTING 10.1   Using the if Statement in Decision Making

```
1:  /* 10L01.c  Using the if statement */
2:  #include <stdio.h>
3:
4:  main()
5:  {
6:     int i;
7:
8:     printf("Integers that can be divided by both 2 and 3\n");
9:     printf("(within the range of 0 to 100):\n");
10:    for (i=0; i<=100; i++){
11:       if ((i%2 == 0) && (i%3 == 0))
12:          printf("   %d\n", i);
13:    }
14:    return 0;
15: }
```

10

After 10L01.exe, the executable of the program in Listing 10.1, is created and run, the following output is displayed on the screen:

OUTPUT

```
Integers that can be divided by both 2 and 3
(within the range of 0 to 100):
   0
   6
   12
   18
   24
   30
   36
   42
   48
   54
   60
   66
   72
   78
   84
   90
   96
```

ANALYSIS   As you see in Listing 10.1, line 6 declares an integer variable, i. Lines 8 and 9 print out two headlines. Starting in line 10, the for statement keeps looping 101 times.

Within the for loop, the if statement in lines 11 and 12 evaluates the logical expression (i%2 == 0) && (i%3 == 0). If the expression evaluates to 1 (that is, the value of i can be divided by both 2 and 3 completely), the value of i is displayed on the screen by calling the printf() function in line 12. Otherwise, the statement in line 12 is skipped.

Note that the braces ({ and }) are not used because there is only one statement under the control of the if statement.

The result shown on the screen gives all integers within the range of 0 to 100 that can be evenly divided by both 2 and 3.

The if-else Statement

In the if statement, when the conditional expression evaluates to a nonzero value, the computer will jump to the statements controlled by the if statement and execute them right away. If the expression evaluates to a value of zero, the computer will ignore those statements controlled by the if statement.

You will often want the computer to execute an alternate set of statements when the conditional expression of the if statement evaluates to logically false. To do so, you can use another conditional branching statement in C—the if-else statement.

As an expansion of the if statement, the if-else statement has the following form:

```
if (expression) {
   statement1;
   statement2;
   .
   .
   .
}
else {
   statement_A;
   statement_B;
   .
   .
   .
}
```

If expression evaluates to a nonzero value, the statements controlled by if, including statement1 and statement2, are executed. However, if expression evaluates to a value of zero, statement_A and statement_B following the else keyword are executed instead.

The program in Listing 10.2 shows how to use the if-else statement.

LISTING 10.2   Using the if-else Statement

```
1:  /* 10L02.c  Using the if-else statement */
2:  #include <stdio.h>
3:
4:  main()
5:  {
6:     int i;
7:
8:     printf("Even Number    Odd Number\n");
9:     for (i=0; i<10; i++)
10:       if (i%2 == 0)
11:          printf("%d", i);
12:       else
13:          printf("%14d\n", i);
14:
15:     return 0;
16: }
```

The following result is obtained by running the executable file 10L02.exe:

OUTPUT

```
Even Number   Odd Number
0             1
2             3
4             5
6             7
8             9
```

ANALYSIS Line 6 of Listing 10.2 declares an integer variable, i. The printf() function in line 8 displays a headline on the screen.

The integer variable i is initialized in the first expression of the for statement in line 9. Controlled by the for statement, the if-else statement in lines 10–13 is executed 10 times. According to the if-else statement, the printf() call in line 11 prints out even numbers if the relational expression i%2 == 0 in line 10 evaluates to 1 (logically true). If the relational expression evaluates to 0 (logically false), the printf() call controlled by the else keyword in line 13 outputs odd numbers to the standard output.

Because the if-else statement is treated as a single statement, the braces { and } are not needed to form a block of statements under the for statement. Likewise, there are no braces used in the if-else statement because the if and else keywords each control a single statement in lines 11 and 13 respectively.

Note that the minimum width of 14 is specified in the printf() function in line 13, so the output of the odd numbers is listed to the right side of the even numbers, as you can see in the output section. The program in Listing 10.2 checks numbers in a range of 0 to 9, and shows that 0, 2, 4, 6, and 8 are even numbers, and 1, 3, 5, 7, and 9 are odd ones.

10

Nested `if` Statements

As you saw in the previous sections, one `if` statement enables a program to make one decision. In many cases, a program has to make a series of related decisions. For this purpose, you can use nested `if` statements.

Listing 10.3 demonstrates the usage of nested `if` statements.

LISTING 10.3   Using Nested `if` Statements

```
1:  /* 10L03.c  Using nested if statements */
2:  #include <stdio.h>
3:
4:  main()
5:  {
6:     int i;
7:
8:     for (i=-5; i<=5; i++){
9:        if (i > 0)
10:           if (i%2 == 0)
11:              printf("%d is an even number.\n", i);
12:           else
13:              printf("%d is an odd number.\n", i);
14:        else if (i == 0)
15:           printf("The number is zero.\n");
16:        else
17:           printf("Negative number: %d\n", i);
18:     }19:    return 0;
20: }
```

After running the executable file `10L03.exe`, I obtain the following output:

OUTPUT
```
Negative number: -5
Negative number: -4
Negative number: -3
Negative number: -2
Negative number: -1
The number is zero.
1 is an odd number.
2 is an even number.
3 is an odd number.
4 is an even number.
5 is an odd number.
```

ANALYSIS   Listing 10.3 contains a `for` loop, starting in line 8 and ending in line 18. According to the expressions of the `for` statement in line 8, any tasks controlled by the `for` statement are executed up to 11 times.

First, a decision has to be made based on the evaluation of the relational expression i > 0 in the if statement of line 9. The i > 0 expression is used to test whether the value of i is positive or anything else (negative numbers including zero.) If the expression evaluates to 1, the computer jumps to the second (that is, nested) if statement in line 11.

Note that line 11 contains another relational expression, i%2 == 0, which tests whether the integer variable i is even or odd. Therefore, the second decision of displaying even numbers or odd numbers has to be made according to the evaluation of the second relational expression, i%2 == 0. If this evaluation yields 1, the printf() call in line 11 prints out an even number. Otherwise, the statement in line 13 is executed, and an odd number is shown on the screen.

The computer branches to line 14 if the i > 0 expression from line 9 evaluates to 0; that is, if the value of i is not greater than 0. In line 14, another if statement is nested within an else phrase, and the relational expression i == 0 is evaluated. If i == 0 evaluates to logically true, which means i does contain the value of zero, the string The number is zero is displayed on the screen. Otherwise, the value of i must be negative, according to the previous evaluation of the i > 0 expression in line 9. The statement in line 17 then outputs the negative number to the standard output.

As you can see in the example, the value of i is within the range of 5 to -5. Thus, -5, -4, -3, -2, and -1 are printed out as negative numbers. Then a message is printed when i is zero, and then the odd numbers 1, 3, and 5, as well as the even numbers 2 and 4 are printed out.

The switch Statement

In the last section, you saw that nested if statements are used when there are successive, related decisions to be made. However, the nested if statements can become very complex if there are many decisions that need to be made. Sometimes, a programmer will have problems just keeping track of a series of complex nested if statements.

Fortunately there is another statement in C, the switch statement, which you can use to make unlimited decisions or choices based on the value of a conditional expression and specified cases.

The general form of the switch statement is

```
switch (expression) {
   case constant-expression1:
       statement1;

   case constant-expression2:
```

```
        statement2;

    .
    .
    .
  default:
      statement-default;
}
```

Here the conditional expression, *expression*, is evaluated first. The switch statement will then jump to the proper case label and execute, in order, whatever statements follow. If *expression* yields a value equal to the constant expression constant-expression1, the statement *statement1* is executed, followed by *statement2* and everything on down to *statement-default*. If the value yielded by *expression* is the same as the value of constant-expression2, *statement2* is executed first. If, however, the value of *expression* is not equal to any values of the constant expressions labeled by the case keyword, the statement (*statement-default*) following the default keyword is executed.

You have to use the case keyword to label each case. Note that each case label ends with a *colon*, not a semicolon. This is the syntax for labels in C. The default keyword should be used for the "default" case — that is, when no case label matches with the conditional expression. Note that none of the constant expressions associated with case labels may be identical within the switch statement.

In C, a *label* is used as a kind of bookmark in your code for use by the conditional branching statement. A label is not, itself, a statement; rather, it points to a place to jump when you want to depart from the normal top-down flow of execution.

The proper syntax for a label is a unique identifier followed by a colon — not a semicolon . In this chapter you will see several ways to use labels, as well as the reserved label names case *expression*: and default:.

The program in Listing 10.4 gives you an example of using the switch statement. The program also demonstrates an important feature of the switch statement.

LISTING 10.4   Using the switch Statement

```
1:  /* 10L04.c  Using the switch statement */
2:  #include <stdio.h>
3:
4:  main()
5:  {
6:      int day;
```

```
7:
8:     printf("Please enter a single digit for a day\n");
9:     printf("(within the range of 1 to 3):\n");
10:    day = getchar();
11:    switch (day){
12:       case '1':
13:          printf("Day 1\n");
14:       case '2':
15:          printf("Day 2\n");
16:       case '3':
17:          printf("Day 3\n");
18:       default:
19:          ;
20:    }
21:    return 0;
22: }
```

10

If I run the executable file 10L04.exe and enter 3, I obtain the following output:

OUTPUT
```
Please enter a single digit for a day
(within the range of 1 to 3):
3
Day 3
```

ANALYSIS As you can see in line 6, an int variable, day, is declared; it is assigned the input entered by the user in line 10.

In line 11, the value of the integer variable day is evaluated in the switch statement. If the value is equal to one of the values of the constant expressions, the computer starts to execute statements from there. The constant expressions are labeled by prefixing case in front of them.

For instance, I entered 3 and then pressed the Enter key. The numeric value of 3 is assigned to day in line 10. Then, after finding a case in which the value of the constant expression matches the value contained by day, the computer jumps to line 17 to execute the printf() function and display Day 3 on the screen.

Note that under the default label in Listing 10.4, there is an empty (that is, null) statement ending with semicolon in line 19. The computer does nothing with the empty statement. This means that if none of the constant expressions apply, then the switch statement ends up doing nothing at all.

However, if I enter 1 from my keyboard and then press the Enter key when running executable file 10L04.exe, I get the following output:

```
Please enter a single digit for a day
```

(within the range of 1 to 3):
1
Day 1
Day 2
Day 3

From the output, you can see that the statement controlled by the selected case, case 1, and the statements controlled by the rest of the cases, are executed, because Day 1, Day 2, and Day 3 are displayed on the screen. Likewise, if I enter 2 from my keyboard, I have Day 2 and Day 3 shown on the screen.

This is an important feature of the switch statement: The computer continues to execute the statements following the selected case until the end of the switch statement.

You're going to learn how to exit early from the execution of the switch statement in the next section.

The break Statement

If you want to exit the switch entirely after each case label, you can add a break statement at the end of the statement list that follows every case label. The break statement simply exits the switch and resumes execution after the end of the switch statement block.

The program in Listing 10.5 looks similar to the one in Listing 10.4, but this time, the break statement is used and there are different results.

LISTING 10.5   Adding the break Statement

```
1:  /* 10L05.c  Adding the break statement */
2:  #include <stdio.h>
3:
4:  main()
5:  {
6:     int day;
7:
8:     printf("Please enter a single digit for a day\n");
9:     printf("(within the range of 1 to 7):\n");
10:    day = getchar();
11:    switch (day){
12:       case '1':
13:          printf("Day 1 is Sunday.\n");
14:          break;
15:       case '2':
16:          printf("Day 2 is Monday.\n");
17:          break;
18:       case '3':
19:          printf("Day 3 is Tuesday.\n");
```

```
20:            break;
21:         case '4':
22:            printf("Day 4 is Wednesday.\n");
23:            break;
24:         case '5':
25:            printf("Day 5 is Thursday.\n");
26:            break;
27:         case '6':
28:            printf("Day 6 is Friday.\n");
29:            break;
30:         case '7':
31:            printf("Day 7 is Saturday.\n");
32:            break;
33:         default:
34:            printf("The digit is not within the range of 1 to 7.\n");
35:            break;
36:      }
37:      return 0;
38: }
```

10

With help from the break statement, I can run the executable file 10L05.exe and obtain only the output of the selected case:

OUTPUT

```
Please enter a single digit for a day
(within the range of 1 to 7):
1
Day 1 is Sunday.
```

ANALYSIS This program has seven case labels followed by the constant expressions of '1', '2', '3', '4', '5', '6', and '7', respectively. (See lines 12, 15, 18, 21, 24, 27, and 30.)

In each case, there is one statement followed by a break statement. As mentioned, the break statements will exit the switch construct before the computer ever gets to the next case label and the statements that follow it.

For example, after the int variable day is assigned the value of 1 and evaluated in the switch statement, the case with '1' is selected, and the statement in line 13 is executed. Then, the break statement in line 14 is executed, which breaks the control of the switch statement and returns the control to the next statement outside the switch construct. In Listing 10.5, the next statement is the return statement in line 37, which ends the main function.

The printf() call in line 13 outputs a string of Day 1 is Sunday. on the screen.

Note that in a switch statement, braces are not needed to group the statements within an individual case, since case is just a label and does not control the statements that follow it. They are simply executed in order, starting with the label.

Breaking an Infinite Loop

You can also use the break statement to break an infinite loop. An infinite loop is one in which the conditional expression is left out entirely; thus, it is up to the code inside the loop to determine the conditions for ending the loop. The following are examples of infinite for and while loops:

```
for (;;){
   statement1;
   statement2;
      .
      .
      .
}

while {
   statement1;
   statement2;
      .
      .
      .
}
```

The for loop above leaves out all three expressions. This causes the for statement to always execute the loop. The while statement uses 1 as its conditional expression, and since this of course never evaluates to 0, the while statement always continues the loop.

The program in Listing 10.6 shows an example of using the break statement in an infinite while loop.

LISTING **10.6**   Breaking an Infinite Loop

```
1:   /* 10L06.c: Breaking an infinite loop */
2:   #include <stdio.h>
3:
4:   main()
5:   {
6:      int c;
7:
8:      printf("Enter a character:\n(enter x to exit)\n");
9:      while  {
10:        c = getc(stdin);
11:        if (c == 'x')
12:           break;
13:     }
14:     printf("Break the infinite while loop. Bye!\n");
15:     return 0;
16: }
```

The following is the result I got after running the executable file (10L06.exe) on my machine:

OUTPUT
```
Enter a character:
(enter x to exit)
H
I
x
Break the infinite while loop. Bye!
```

ANALYSIS There is an infinite while loop in Listing 10.6, which starts in line 9 and ends in line 13. Within the infinite loop, the characters entered by the user are assigned, one at a time, to the integer variable c (see line 10.)

The relational expression c == 'x' in the if statement (see line 11) is evaluated each time during the looping. If the expression evaluates to a value of 0 (that is, the user has not entered the letter x), the looping continues. Otherwise, the break statement in line 12 is executed, which causes the computer to jump out of the infinite loop and start executing the next statement, which is shown in line 14.

You can see in the sample output, the while loop continues until I have entered the letter x, which causes the infinite loop to be broken and a message, Break the infinite while loop. Bye!, to be displayed on the screen.

The continue Statement

Instead of breaking a loop, there are times when you want to stay in a loop but skip over some statements within the loop. To do this, you can use the continue statement. The continue statement causes execution to jump to the bottom of the loop immediately.

For example, Listing 10.7 demonstrates how to use the continue statement in a loop doing sums.

LISTING 10.7   Using the continue Statement

```
1:  /* 10L07.c: Using the continue statement */
2:  #include <stdio.h>
3:
4:  main()
5:  {
6:      int i, sum;
7:
8:      sum = 0;
9:      for (i=1; i<8; i++){
10:         if ((i==3) || (i==5))
11:             continue;
```

continues

Listing 10.7   continued

```
12:        sum += i;
13:    }
14:    printf("The sum of 1, 2, 4, 6, and 7 is: %d\n", sum);
15:    return 0;
16: }
```

After the executable file `10L07.exe` is run on my computer, the following output is
shown on the screen:

OUTPUT   The sum of 1, 2, 4, 6, and 7 is: 20

ANALYSIS   In Listing 10.7, we want to calculate the sum of the integer values of 1, 2, 4, 6,
and 7. Because the integers are almost consecutive, a `for` loop is built in lines
9–13. The statement in line 12 sums all consecutive integers from 1 to 7 (except for 3
and 5, which aren't in the listing and are skipped in the `for` loop).

To skip these two numbers, the expression `(i==3) || (i==5)` is evaluated in the `if`
statement of line 10. If the expression evaluates to 1 (that is, the value of `i` is equal to
either 3 or 5), the `continue` statement in line 11 is executed, which causes the sum operation in line 12 to be skipped, and another iteration to be started at the `for` statement. In
this way, you obtain the sum of the integer values of 1, 2, 4, 6, and 7, but skip 3 and 5,
automatically by using one `for` loop.

After the `for` loop, the value of `sum`, 20, is displayed on the screen by the `printf()` call
in the statement of line 14.

The goto Statement

This book would not be complete without mentioning the `goto` statement, although I do
not recommend that you use the `goto` statement. The main reason that the `goto` statement
is discouraged is because its usage is likely to make the C program unreliable and hard to
debug.

Programmers are often tempted to use the `goto` statement, especially if they have used
other languages without the rich set of structured conditional branching statements that
C provides. The fact is, any use of `goto` can be avoided entirely by using the other
branching statements.

If nothing else, you should know what a `goto` statement is so that you can properly
cringe when you see one in somebody else's code.

The following is the general form of the goto statement:

```
labelname:
    statement1;
    statement2;
    .
    .
    .
    goto    labelname;
```

Here *labelname* is a label name that tells the goto statement where to jump. You have to place *labelname* in two places: One is at the place where the goto statement is going to jump (note that a colon must follow the label name), and the other is the place following the goto keyword.

The label for the goto statement to jump to can appear either before or after the statement.

10

One of the best things about C is that it encourages *structured programming*. Programs should act predictably and their behavior should be reasonably evident from merely reading over the source code.

Of course, one of the other best things about C is that the language itself does not enforce this ideal. It is left up to you, the programmer, to use the tools you are given to write clean, elegant, readable, structured code.

In this chapter we have seen the break, continue, and goto statements. The improper use of these branching statements can lead to what is known as "spaghetti code." (If you printed out the source code and drew arrows on the page to indicate the flow of execution, you would end up with a drawing of spaghetti.) When a program's execution jumps around in unpredictable ways, it makes it very difficult (or for a large, complex project, often nearly impossible) to determine the intended or actual behavior of a program.

The use of the goto statement can easily lead to spaghetti code, especially if it is used to jump backwards, or jump out of flow-control statements. When you see a random label just sitting there in the code, you know only that some other code is going to jump there using goto — you just don't know when, or why, without stopping to search the rest of the function.

The effects of the continue statement, at least, are limited to the looping statement where it is used. However, complex loops can be hard to decipher unless you know exactly when and why the loop will terminate.

The same goes for break. Aside from switch statements, it can be used to jump out of for, while, or do-while loops. Generally, this should only be used to break out of an infinite loop. Otherwise, use your conditional expression to terminate the loop.

Summary

In this lesson you learned the following important statements and keywords for conditional branching and looping in C:

- An important task of a program is to instruct the computer to jump to different portions of the code according to the specified branch conditions.
- The if statement is a very important statement for conditional branching in C.
- The if statement can be nested for making a series of related decisions in your program.
- The if-else statement is an expansion of the if statement.
- The switch statement helps you to keep your program more readable when there are more than just a couple of related decisions to be made in your code.
- The case keyword, followed by a colon and an integral constant value, is used as a label in the switch statement. The default: label is used at the end of a switch statement when no case applies to the condition.
- The break statement can be used to exit the switch construct or a loop (usually, an infinite loop).
- The continue statement is used to let you stay within a loop while skipping over some statements.
- The goto statement is to enable the computer to jump to some other spot in your code. Using this statement is not recommended because it may make your program unreliable and hard to debug.

In the next lesson you'll learn about a very important concept—pointers.

Q&A

Q How many expressions are there in the if statement?

A The if statement takes only one expression to hold the conditional criteria. When the expression evaluates to a nonzero value (that is, the conditions are met), the statements controlled by the if statement are executed. Otherwise, these statements are skipped and the next statement following the if statement block is executed.

Q Why is the if-else statement an expansion of the if statement?

A When the conditional expression in the if statement evaluates to a value of zero, the program control flow is returned back to the original track. However, when the conditional expression in the if-else statement evaluates to zero, the program control flow branches to the statement block under the else keyword and returns to its original track after the statements controlled by `else` are executed. In other words, the `if` statement allows a single statement block to be executed or skipped entirely, whereas the `if-else` statement executes one of the two statement blocks under the control of the `if-else` statement.

Q Why do you normally need to add the `break` statement into the `switch` statement?

A When one of the `cases` within the `switch` statement is selected, the program control will branch to the `case` and execute all statements within the selected `case` and the rest of the `cases` that follow it. Therefore, you might get more results than you expected. To tell the computer to execute only the statements inside a selected `case`, you can put a `break` statement at the end of the `case` so that the program control flow will exit the `switch` construct after the statements within the `case` are executed.

Q What can the `continue` statement do inside a loop?

A When the `continue` statement inside a loop is executed, the program control is branched to the end of the loop so that the controlling `while` or `for` statement can be executed and another iteration can be started if the conditional expression still holds. Inside the loop, any statements following the `continue` statement will be skipped over each time the `continue` statement is executed.

Workshop

To help solidify your understanding of this hour's lesson, you are encouraged to answer the quiz questions and finish the exercises provided in the workshop before you move to the next lesson. The answers and hints to the questions and exercises are given in Appendix B, "Answers to Quiz Questions and Exercises."

Quiz

1. Given x = 0, will the arithmetic operations inside the following `if` statement be performed?
```
if (x != 0)
   y = 123 / x + 456;
```

2. Given x = 4, y = 2, and operator = '-', what is the final value of x after the following `switch` statement is executed?
```
switch (operator){
   case '+':  x += y;
   case '-':  x -= y;
   case '*':  x *= y;
```

```
    case '/':   x /= y;
    default:    break;
}
```

3. Similar to question 2, using x = 4, y = 2, and operator = '-', what is the final value of x after the following switch statement is executed?

```
switch (operator){
    case '+':   x += y; break;
    case '-':   x -= y; break;
    case '*':   x *= y; break;
    case '/':   x /= y; break;
    default:    break;
}
```

4. What is the value of the integer variable x after the following code is executed?

```
x = 1;
for (i=2; i<10; i++){
    if (i%3 == 0)
        continue;
    x += i;
}
```

Exercises

1. Rewrite the program in Listing 10.1. This time, use the logical expression i%6 == 0 in the if statement.

2. Rewrite the program in Listing 10.1 by using nested if statements.

3. Write a program to read characters from the standard I/O. If the characters are A, B, and C, display their numeric values on the screen. (The switch statement is required.)

4. Write a program that keeps reading characters from the standard input until the character q is entered.

5. Rewrite the program in Listing 10.7. This time, instead of skipping 3 and 5, skip the integer that can be evenly divided by both 2 and 3.

PART III

Pointers and Arrays

Hour

HOUR **11**

Understanding Pointers

The duties of the Pointer were to point out, by calling their names, those in the congregation who should take note of some point made in the sermon.

—H. B. Otis, Simple Truth

You've learned about many important C data types, operators, functions, and loops in the past 10 hours. In this lesson you'll learn about one of the most important and powerful features in C: pointers. The topics covered in this hour are

- Pointer variables
- Memory addresses
- The concept of indirection
- Declaring a pointer
- The address-of operator
- The dereference operator

More examples of applying pointers will be demonstrated in the next several hours of the book, especially in Hour 16, "Applying Pointers."

What Is a Pointer?

Understanding pointers is vital to being an effective C programmer. Until now, you have only dealt with variables directly, by assigning values to them. This hour introduces a new concept, known as *indirection*.

Instead of assigning values directly to variables, you can indirectly manipulate a variable by creating a variable called a *pointer*, which contains the memory address of another variable.

So, why is this so important? For starters, using the memory address of your data is often the quickest and simplest way to access it. There are many things that are difficult, if not outright impossible, to do without pointers, such as dynamically allocating memory, passing large data structures between functions, even talking to your computer's hardware.

In fact, you have already used a pointer — in Hour 1, of this book "Taking the First Step"! Do you remember the string `"Howdy, neighbor! This is my first C program.\n"`? A string is actually an array, which is itself a kind of pointer.

There is a lot more discussion later on in this book about arrays, memory allocation, and the wonderful things you can do with pointers. For now, the first step is to understand what a pointer is, and how to work with one in your programs.

From the definition of a pointer, you know two things: first, that a pointer is a variable, so you can assign different values to a pointer variable, and second, that the value contained by a pointer must be an address that indicates the location of another variable in the memory. That's why a pointer is also called an *address variable*.

Address (Left Value) Versus Content (Right Value)

As you might know, the memory inside your computer is used to hold the binary code of your program, which consists of statements and data, as well as the binary code of the operating system on your machine.

Each memory location must have a unique address so that the computer can read from or write to the memory location without any confusion. This is similar to the concept that each house in a city must have a unique address.

When a variable is declared, a piece of unused memory will be reserved for the variable, and the unique address to the memory will be associated with the name of the variable. The address associated with the variable name is usually called the *left value* of the variable.

Then, when the variable is assigned a value, the value is stored into the reserved memory location as the content. The content is also called the *right value* of the variable.

For instance, after the integer variable x is declared and assigned to a value like this:

```
int x;
x = 7;
```

the variable x now has two values:

Left value: 1000

Right value: 7

Here the left value, 1000, is the address of the memory location reserved for x. The right value, 7, is the content stored in the memory location. Note that depending on computers and operating systems, the left value of x can be different from one machine to another.

You can imagine that the variable x is the mailbox in front of your house, which has the address (normally the street number) 1000. The right value, 7, can be thought of as a letter delivered to the mailbox.

Note that when your C program is being compiled and a value is being assigned to a variable, the C compiler has to check the left value of the variable. If the compiler cannot find the left value, it will issue an error message saying that the variable is undefined in your program. That's why, in C, you have to declare a variable before you can use it. (Imagine a letter carrier complaining that he or she cannot drop the letters addressed to you because you haven't built a mailbox yet.)

By using a variable's left value, the C compiler can easily locate the appropriate memory storage reserved for a variable, and then read or write the right value of the variable.

The Address-of Operator (&)

The C language even provides you with an operator, &, in case you want to know the left value of a variable. This operator is called the *address-of operator* because it evaluates to the address (that is, the left value) of a variable.

The following code, for example,

```
long int x;
long int *y;
y = &x;
```

assigns the address of the long integer variable x to a pointer variable, y. (More on this and the significance of *y will be discussed later in this chapter.)

Listing 11.1 shows another example of obtaining addresses (that is, left values) of variables.

TYPE   **LISTING 11.1**   Obtaining the Left Values of Variables

```
1:   /* 11L01.c: Obtaining addresses */
2:   #include <stdio.h>
3:
4:   main()
5:   {
6:      char  c;
7:      int   x;
8:      float y;
9:
10:     printf("c: address=%p, content=%c\n", &c, c);
11:     printf("x: address=%p, content=%d\n", &x, x);
12:     printf("y: address=%p, content=%5.2f\n", &y, y);
13:     c = 'A';
14:     x = 7;
15:     y = 123.45;
16:     printf("c: address=%p, content=%c\n", &c, c);
17:     printf("x: address=%p, content=%d\n", &x, x);
18:     printf("y: address=%p, content=%5.2f\n", &y, y);
19:     return 0;
20:  }
```

After the executable file (11L01.exe) of this program is created and run on my computer, the following output is displayed on the screen:

> You might get different result, depending on your computer and operating system, and especially depending on the memory situation in your computer when you're running the program.

OUTPUT
```
c: address=0x1AF4, content=@
x: address=0x1AF2, content=-32557
y: address=0x1AF6, content=0.00
c: address=0x1AF4, content=A
x: address=0x1AF2, content=7
y: address=0x1AF6, content=123.45
```

ANALYSIS   As you can see in Listing 11.1, there are three variables, c, x, and y, declared in lines 6–8, respectively.

The statement in line 10 displays the address (that is, the left value) and the content (that is, the right value) of the character variable c on the screen. Here the &c expression produces the address of c.

Note that the format specifier %p is used in the printf() function of line 10 for displaying the address produced by &c.

Likewise, lines 11 and 12 print out the addresses of x and y, as well as the contents of x and y. From the first part of the output, you see that the addresses of c, x, and y are 0x1AF4, 0x1AF2, and 0x1AF6. My computer printed these addresses in hex format. However, the %p format specifier does not guarantee to print the addresses in hex format, just to convert the addresses to a sequence of printable characters. You should consult the manual for your C compiler to see what format to expect. Because these three variables have not been initialized yet, the contents contained in their memory locations are left there from the last memory writing.

However, after the initializations that are carried out in lines 13–15, the memory slots reserved for the three variables have the contents of the initial values. Lines 16–18 display the addresses and contents of c, x, and y after the initialization.

You can see in the second part of the output, the contents of c, x, and y are now 'A', 7, and 123.45, respectively, with the same memory addresses.

The format specifier %p used in the printf() function is supported by the ANSI standard. If, somehow, your compiler does not support %p, you can try to use %u or %lu in the printf() function to convert and print out a left value (that is, an address).

Also, the addresses printed out by the examples in this lesson are obtained by running the examples on my machine. The values may be different from what you can get by running the examples on your machine. This is because the address of a variable may vary from one type of computer to another.

Declaring Pointers

As mentioned at the beginning of this lesson, a pointer is a variable, which means that a pointer has a left value and a right value as well. However, both the left and right values are addresses. The left value of a pointer is used to refer to the pointer itself, whereas the right value of a pointer, which is the content of the pointer, is the address of another variable.

The general form of a pointer declaration is

```
data-type  *pointer-name;
```

Here *data-type* specifies the type of data to which the pointer points. *pointer-name* is the name of the pointer variable, which can be any valid variable name in C.

Note that right before the pointer name is an asterisk *, which indicates that the variable is a pointer. When the compiler sees the asterisk in the declaration, it makes a note that the variable can be used as a pointer.

The following shows different types of pointers:

```
char *ptr_c;    /* declare a pointer to a character */

int  *ptr_int; /* declare a pointer to an integer */

float *ptr_flt; /* declare a pointer to a floating-point */
```

The program in Listing 11.2 demonstrates how to declare pointers and assign values to them.

TYPE   **LISTING 11.2**   Declaring and Assigning Values to Pointers

```
 1:  /* 11L02.c: Declaring and assign values to pointers */
 2:  #include <stdio.h>
 3:
 4:  main()
 5:  {
 6:     char  c, *ptr_c;
 7:     int   x, *ptr_x;
 8:     float y, *ptr_y;
 9:
10:     c = 'A';
11:     x = 7;
12:     y = 123.45;
13:     printf("c: address=%p, content=%c\n", &c, c);
14:     printf("x: address=%p, content=%d\n", &x, x);
15:     printf("y: address=%p, content=%5.2f\n", &y, y);
16:     ptr_c = &c;
17:        printf("ptr_c: address=%p, content=%p\n", &ptr_c, ptr_c);
18:        printf("*ptr_c => %c\n", *ptr_c);
19:     ptr_x = &x;
20:        printf("ptr_x: address=%p, content=%p\n", &ptr_x, ptr_x);
21:        printf("*ptr_x => %d\n", *ptr_x);
22:     ptr_y = &y;
23:        printf("ptr_y: address=%p, content=%p\n", &ptr_y, ptr_y);
24:        printf("*ptr_y => %5.2f\n", *ptr_y);
25:     return 0;
26:  }
```

I get the following output displayed on the screen after running the executable file
11L02.exe from on my machine:

OUTPUT

```
c: address=0x1B38, content=A
x: address=0x1B36, content=7
y: address=0x1B32, content=123.45
ptr_c: address=0x1B30, content=0x1B38
*ptr_c => A
ptr_x: address=0x1B2E, content=0x1B36
*ptr_x => 7
ptr_y: address=0x1B2C, content=0x1B32
*ptr_y => 123.45
```

ANALYSIS In Listing 11.2, there are three variables, c, x, and y, and three pointer variables,
ptr_c, ptr_x, and ptr_y, declared in lines 6–8, respectively.

The statements in lines 10–12 initialize the three variables c, x, and y. Then, lines 13–15
print out the addresses as well as the contents of the three variables.

In line 16, the left value of the character variable c is assigned to the pointer variable
ptr_c. The output made by the statement in line 17 shows that the pointer variable ptr_c
contains the address of c. In other words, the content (that is, the right value) of ptr_c is
the address (that is, the left value) of c.

Then in line 18, the value referred to by the pointer *ptr_c is printed out. The output
proves that the pointer *ptr_c does point to the memory location of c.

Line 19 assigns the left value of the integer x to the integer pointer variable ptr_x. The
statements in lines 20 and 21 print out the left value and right value of the pointer variable ptr_x, as well as the value referred to by the pointer *ptr_x.

Similarly, the left value of the float variable y is assigned to the float pointer variable
ptr_y in line 22. To prove that ptr_y contains the address of y, and *ptr_y gives the content held by y, lines 23 and 24 print out the right values of ptr_y and *ptr_y, respectively.

The statements in lines 16, 19, and 22 show you how to assign the value of one variable
to another—in an indirect way. In other words, the left value of a variable can be
assigned to another variable so that the latter can be used as a pointer variable to obtain
the right value of the former. In this case, the variable name and the pointer refer to the
same memory location. Accordingly, if either the variable name or the pointer is used in
an expression to change the contents of the memory location, the contents of the memory
location have also changed for the other.

To help you understand the indirection of assigning values, Figure 11.1 demonstrates the
memory image of the relationships between c and ptr_c, x and ptr_x, and y and ptr_y,
based on the output obtained on my machine.

11

FIGURE 11.1
The memory image of variables and their pointers.

The Dereference Operator (*)

You've seen the asterisk (*) in the declaration of a pointer. In C, the asterisk is called the *dereference operator* when it is used as a unary operator. (Sometimes, it's also called the *indirection operator*.) The value of a variable can be referenced by the combination of the * operator and its operand, which contains the address of the variable.

For instance, in the program shown in Listing 11.2, after the address of the character variable c is assigned to the pointer variable ptr_c, the expression *ptr_c refers to the value contained by c. Therefore, you can use the *ptr_c expression, instead of using the variable c directly, to obtain the value of c.

Likewise, given an integer variable x and x = 1234, you can declare an integer pointer variable, ptr_x, for instance, and assign the left value (address) of x to ptr_x—that is, ptr_x = &x. Then, the expression *ptr_x produces 1234, which is the right value (content) of x.

Don't confuse the dereference operator with the multiplication operator, although they share the same symbol, *.

The *dereference operator* is a unary operator, which takes only one operand. The operand contains the address (that is, left value) of a variable.

On the other hand, the *multiplication operator* is a binary operator that requires two operands to perform the operation of multiplication.

The meaning of the * symbol is determined by the context in which you use it.

Null Pointers

A pointer is said to be a *null pointer* when its right value is 0. Remember, a null pointer can never point to valid data. For this reason, you can test a pointer to see if it's assigned to 0; if it is, you know that it is a null pointer and isn't valid.

To set a null pointer, simply assign 0 to the pointer variable. For example:

```
char *ptr_c;
int  *ptr_int;

ptr_c = ptr_int = 0;
```

Here ptr_c and ptr_int become null pointers after the integer value of 0 is assigned to them.

You'll see applications of null pointers used in control-flow statements and arrays later in this book.

Updating Variables via Pointers

As you learned in the previous section, as long as you link up a variable to a pointer variable, you can obtain the value of the variable by using the pointer variable. In other words, you can read the value by pointing to the memory location of the variable and using the dereferencing operator.

This section shows you that you can write a new value to the memory location of a variable using a pointer that contains the left value of the variable. Listing 11.3 shows an example.

TYPE   **LISTING 11.3**   Changing Variable Values Via Pointers

```
1:  /* 11L03.c: Changing values via pointers */
2:  #include <stdio.h>
3:
4:  main()
5:  {
6:     char  c,  *ptr_c;
7:
8:     c = 'A';
9:     printf("c: address=%p, content=%c\n", &c, c);
10:    ptr_c = &c;
11:       printf("ptr_c: address=%p, content=%p\n", &ptr_c, ptr_c);
12:       printf("*ptr_c => %c\n", *ptr_c);
13:    *ptr_c = 'B';
14:       printf("ptr_c: address=%p, content=%p\n", &ptr_c, ptr_c);
```

continues

LISTING 11.3   continued

```
15:        printf("*ptr_c => %c\n", *ptr_c);
16:     printf("c: address=%p, content=%c\n", &c, c);
17:     return 0;
18: }
```

After running the executable file 11L03.exe on my machine, I get the following output displayed on the screen:

OUTPUT
```
c: address=0x1828, content=A
ptr_c: address=0x1826, content=0x1828
*ptr_c => A
ptr_c: address=0x1826, content=0x1828
*ptr_c => B
c: address=0x1828, content=B
```

ANALYSIS A char variable, c, and a char pointer variable, ptr_c, are declared in line 6 of Listing 11.3.

The variable c is initialized with 'A' in line 8, which is printed out, along with the address of the variable, by the printf() function in line 9.

In line 10, the pointer variable ptr_c is assigned the left value (address) of c. It's not surprising to see the output printed out by the statements in lines 11 and 12, where the right value of ptr_c is the left value of c, and the pointer *ptr_c points to the right value of c.

In line 13 the expression *ptr_c = 'B' asks the computer to write 'B' to the location pointed to by the pointer ptr_c. The output printed by the statement in line 15 proves that the content of the memory location pointed to by ptr_c is updated. The statement in line 14 prints out the left and right values of the pointer variable ptr_c and shows that these values remain the same. As you know, the location pointed to by ptr_c is where the character variable c resides. Therefore, the expression *ptr_c = 'B' actually updates the content (that is, the right value) of the variable c to 'B'. To prove this, the statement in line 16 displays the left and right values of c on the screen. Sure enough, the output shows that the right value of c has been changed.

Pointing to the Same Memory Location

A memory location can be pointed to by more than one pointer. For example, given that c = 'A' and that ptr_c1 and ptr_c2 are two character pointer variables, ptr_c1 = &c and ptr_c2 = &c set the two pointer variables to point to the same location in the memory.

The program in Listing 11.4 shows another example of pointing to the same thing with several pointers.

TYPE

LISTING 11.4   Pointing to the Same Memory Location with More Than One Pointer

```
1:  /* 11L04.c: Pointing to the same thing */
2:  #include <stdio.h>
3:
4:  main()
5:  {
6:     int x;
7:     int *ptr_1, *ptr_2, *ptr_3;
8:
9:     x = 1234;
10:    printf("x: address=%p, content=%d\n", &x, x);
11:    ptr_1 = &x;
12:    printf("ptr_1: address=%p, content=%p\n", &ptr_1, ptr_1);
13:       printf("*ptr_1 => %d\n", *ptr_1);
14:    ptr_2 = &x;
15:    printf("ptr_2: address=%p, content=%p\n", &ptr_2, ptr_2);
16:       printf("*ptr_2 => %d\n", *ptr_2);
17:    ptr_3 = ptr_1;
18:    printf("ptr_3: address=%p, content=%p\n", &ptr_3, ptr_3);
19:       printf("*ptr_3 => %d\n", *ptr_3);
20:    return 0;
21: }
```

11

The following output is displayed on the screen by running the executable file `11L04.exe` on my machine (note that you might get different address values depending on the your system):

OUTPUT

```
x: address=0x1838, content=1234
ptr_1: address=0x1834, content=0x1838
*ptr_1 => 1234
ptr_2: address=0x1836, content=0x1838
*ptr_2 => 1234
ptr_3: address=0x1832, content=0x1838
*ptr_3 => 1234
```

ANALYSIS   As shown in Listing 11.4, line 6 declares an integer variable, x, and line 7 declares three integer pointer variables, ptr_1, ptr_2, and ptr_3.

The statement in line 10 prints out the left and right values of x. On my machine, the left value (address) of x is 0x1838. The right value (content) of x is 1234, which is the initial value assigned to x in line 9

Line 11 assigns the left value of x to the pointer variable ptr_1 so that ptr_1 can be used to refer to the right value of x. To make sure that the pointer variable ptr_1 now contains the address of x, line 12 prints out the right value of ptr_1, along with its left value. The output shows that ptr_1 does hold the address of x, 0x1838. Then, line 13 prints out the value 1234, which is referred to by the *ptr_1 expression. Note that the asterisk * in the expression is the dereference operator

In line 14, the *ptr_2 = &x expression assigns the left value of x to another pointer variable, ptr_2; that is, the pointer variable ptr_2 is now linked with the address of x. The statement in line 16 displays the integer 1234 on the screen by using the dereference operator * and its operand, ptr_2. In other words, the memory location of x is referred to by the second pointer *ptr_2.

In line 17, the pointer variable ptr_3 is assigned the right value of ptr_1. Because ptr_1 now holds the address of x, the expression ptr_3 = ptr_1 is equivalent to ptr_3 = &x. Then, from the output made by the statements in lines 18 and 19, you see the integer 1234 again on the screen. This time the integer is referred to by the third pointer, ptr_3.

Summary

In this lesson you learned the following very important concepts about pointers in C:

- A pointer is a variable whose value points to another variable.
- A variable declared in C has two values: the left value and the right value.
- The left value of a variable is the address; the right value is the content of the variable.
- The address-of operator (&) can be used to obtain the left value (address) of a variable.
- The asterisk (*) in a pointer declaration tells the compiler that the variable is a pointer variable.
- The dereference operator (*) is a unary operator; as such, it requires only one operand.
- The *ptr_name expression evaluates to the value pointed to by the pointer variable ptr_name, where ptr_name can be any valid variable name in C.
- If the pointer variable's right value has been assigned the value 0, the pointer is a null pointer. A null pointer cannot point to valid data.
- You can update the value of a variable referred by a pointer variable.
- Several pointers can point to the same location of a variable in the memory.

You will see more examples of using pointers in the rest of the book.

In the next lesson you'll learn about an aggregate type—an array, which is closely related to pointers in C.

Q&A

Q What are the left and right values?

A The left value is the address of a variable, and the right value is the content stored in the memory location of a variable. There are two ways to get the right value of a variable: use the variable name directly, or use the left value of the variable and the dereference operator to refer to where the right value resides. The second way is also called the indirect way.

Q How can you obtain the address of a variable?

A By using the address-of operator, &. For instance, given an integer variable x, the &x expression evaluates to the address of x. To print out the address of x, you can use the %p format specifier in the printf() function.

Q What is the concept of indirection in terms of using pointers?

A Before this hour, the only way you knew for reading from or writing to a variable was to invoke the variable directly. For instance, if you wanted to write a decimal, 16, to an integer variable x, you could use the statement x = 16;.

As you learned in this hour, C allows you to access a variable in another way—using pointers. Therefore, to write 16 to x, you can first declare an integer pointer (ptr) and assign the left value (address) of x to ptr—that is, ptr = &x;. Then, instead of executing the statement x = 16;, you can use another statement:

```
*ptr = 16;
```

Here the pointer *ptr refers to the memory location reserved by x, and the content stored in the memory location is updated to 16 after the statement is executed. So, you see, making use of pointers to access the memory locations of variables is a way of indirection.

Q Can a null pointer point to valid data?

A No. A null pointer cannot point to valid data. This is because the value contained by a null pointer has been set to 0. You'll see examples of using null pointers in arrays, strings, and memory allocation later in the book.

Workshop

To help solidify your understanding of this hour's lesson, you are encouraged to answer the quiz questions and finish the exercises provided in the workshop before you move to the next lesson. The answers and hints to the questions and exercises are given in Appendix B, "Answers to Quiz Questions and Exercises."

Quiz

1. How can you obtain the left value of a character variable ch?

2. In the following expressions, which asterisk (*) is a dereference operator, and which one is a multiplication operator?

    - *ptr
    - x * y
    - y *= x + 5
    - *y *= *x + 5

3. Given that x = 10, the address of x is 0x1A38, and ptr_int = &x, what will ptr_int and *ptr_int produce, respectively?

4. Given that x = 123, and ptr_int = &x after the execution of *ptr_int = 456, what does x contain?

Exercises

1. Given three integer variables, x = 512, y = 1024, and z = 2048, write a program to print out their left values as well as their right values.

2. Write a program to update the value of the double variable flt_num from 123.45 to 543.21 by using a double pointer.

3. Given a character variable ch and ch = 'A', write a program to update the value of ch to decimal 66 by using a pointer.

4. Given that x=5 and y=6, write a program to calculate the multiplication of the two integers and print out the result, which is saved in x, all in the way of indirection (that is, using pointers).

Hour **12**

Understanding Arrays

Gather up the fragments that remain, that nothing be lost.

—John 6:12

In last hour's lesson you learned about pointers and the concept of indirection. In this lesson you'll learn about arrays, which are collections of similar data items and are closely related to pointers. The main topics covered in this lesson are

- Single-dimension arrays
- Indexing arrays
- Pointers and arrays
- Character arrays
- Multidimensional arrays
- Unsized arrays

What Is an Array?

You now know how to declare a variable with a specified data type, such as char, int, float, or double. In many cases, you have to declare a set of variables that have the same data type. Instead of declaring them individually, C allows you to declare a set of variables of the same data type collectively as an array.

An *array* is a collection of variables that are of the same data type. Each item in an array is called an *element*. All elements in an array are referenced by the name of the array and are stored in a set of consecutive, adjacent memory slots.

Declaring Arrays

The following is the general form to declare an array:

```
data-type  Array-Name[Array-Size];
```

Here data-type is the type specifier that indicates what data type the declared array will be. Array-Name is the name of the declared array. Array-Size defines how many elements the array can contain. Note that the brackets ([and]) are required in declaring an array. The bracket pair ([and]) is also called the *array subscript operator*.

For example, an array of integers is declared in the following statement,

```
int array_int[8];
```

where int specifies the data type of the array whose name is array_int. The size of the array is 8, which means that the array can store eight elements (that is, integers in this case).

In C, you have to declare an array explicitly, as you do for other variables, before you can use it.

Indexing Arrays

After you declare an array, you can access each of the elements in the array separately.

For instance, the following declaration declares an array of characters:

```
char day[7];
```

You can access the elements in the array of day one after another. To do this, you use the array name in an expression followed by a number, called an *index*, enclosed in brackets.

The important thing to remember is that all arrays in C are indexed starting at 0. In other words, the index to the first element in an array is 0, not 1. Therefore, the first element in the array of day is day[0]. Because there are 7 elements in the day array, the last element is day[6], not day[7].

The seven elements of the array have the following expressions: day[0], day[1], day[2], day[3], day[4], day[5], and day[6].

Because these expressions reference the elements in the array, they are sometimes called *array element references*.

Initializing Arrays

With the help of the array element references, you can initialize each element in an array.

For instance, you can initialize the first element in the array of day, which was declared in the last section, like this:

```
day[0] = 'S';
```

Here the numeric value of S is assigned to the first element of day, day[0].

Likewise, the statement day[1] = 'M'; assigns 'M' to the second element, day[1], in the array.

The second way to initialize an array is to initialize all elements in the array together. For instance, the following statement initializes an integer array, arInteger:

```
int arInteger[5] = {100, 8, 3, 365, 16};
```

Here the integers inside the braces ({ and }) are correspondingly assigned to the elements of the array arInteger. That is, 100 is given to the first element (arInteger[0]), 8 to the second element (arInteger[1]), 3 to the third (arInteger[2]), and so on.

Listing 12.1 gives another example of initializing arrays.

12

TYPE   **LISTING 12.1**   Initializing an Array

```
 1:  /* 12L01.c: Initializing an array */
 2:  #include <stdio.h>
 3:
 4:  main()
 5:  {
 6:     int i;
 7:     int list_int[10];
 8:
 9:     for (i=0; i<10; i++){
10:        list_int[i] = i + 1;
11:        printf( "list_int[%d] is initialized with %d.\n", i, list_int[i]);
12:     }
13:     return 0;
14: }
```

The following output is displayed on the screen after the executable (`12L01.exe`) of the program in Listing 12.1 is created and run on my computer:

```
list_int[0] is initialized with 1.
list_int[1] is initialized with 2.
list_int[2] is initialized with 3.
list_int[3] is initialized with 4.
list_int[4] is initialized with 5.
list_int[5] is initialized with 6.
list_int[6] is initialized with 7.
list_int[7] is initialized with 8.
list_int[8] is initialized with 9.
list_int[9] is initialized with 10.
```

ANALYSIS As you can see in Listing 12.1, there is an integer array, called `list_int`, which is declared in line 7. The array `list_int` contains `10` elements.

Lines 9–12 make up a `for` loop that iterates `10` times. The statement in line 10 initializes `list_int[i]`, the ith element of the array `list_int`, with the result of the expression `i + 1`.

Line 11 then prints out the name of the element, `list_int[i]`, and the value assigned to the element.

The Size of an Array

As mentioned earlier in this lesson, an array consists of consecutive memory locations. Given an array, like this:

```
data-type  Array-Name[Array-Size];
```

you can then calculate the total bytes of the array by the following expression:

```
sizeof(data-type) * Array-Size
```

Here `data-type` is the data type of the array; `Array-Size` specifies the total number of elements the array can take. This expression evaluates to the total number of bytes the array takes.

Another way to calculate the total bytes of an array is simpler; it uses the following expression:

```
sizeof(Array-Name)
```

Here `Array-Name` is the name of the array.

The program in Listing 12.2 shows how to calculate the memory space taken by an array.

TYPE   **LISTING 12.2**   Calculating the Size of an Array

```
1:   /* 12L02.c: Total bytes of an array */
2:   #include <stdio.h>
3:
4:   main()
5:   {
6:      int total_byte;
7:      int list_int[10];
8:
9:      total_byte = sizeof (int) * 10;
10:     printf( "The size of int is %d-byte long.\n", sizeof (int));
11:     printf( "The array of 10 ints has total %d bytes.\n", total_byte);
12:     printf( "The address of the first element: %p\n", &list_int[0]);
13:     printf( "The address of the last element:  %p\n", &list_int[9]);
14:     return 0;
15: }
```

After running the executable 12L02.exe, I have the following output displayed on the screen of my computer:

OUTPUT
```
The size of int is 2-byte long.
The array of 10 ints has total 20 bytes
The address of the first element: 0x1806
The address of the last element:  0x1818
```

ANALYSIS   Note that you might get different address values when you run the program in Listing 12.2 on your machine. However, the difference between the address of the first element and the address of the last element should equal the total number of bytes in the array.

In Listing 12.2, there is an integer array, list_int, which is declared in line 7. The total memory space taken by the array is the result of multiplying the size of int and the total number of elements in the array. As declared in this example, there are a total of 10 elements in the array list_int.

The statement in line 10 prints out the size of int on my machine. You can see from the output that each integer element in the array takes 2 bytes. Therefore, the total memory space (in bytes) taken by the array is 10 * 2. In other words, the statement in line 9 assigns the value of 20, produced by the expression sizeof (int) * 10, to the integer variable total_byte. Line 11 then displays the value contained by the total_byte variable on the screen.

To prove that the array does take the consecutive memory space of 20 bytes, the address of the first element in the array is printed out by the statement in line 12. Note that the ampersand (&), which was introduced as the address-of operator in Hour 11, "Understanding Pointers," is used in line 12 to obtain the address of the first element,

12

list_int[0], in the array. Here the address of the first element is the starting address of the array. From the output, you can see that the address of the list_int[0] element is 0x1806 on my machine.

Then, the &list_int[9] expression in line 13 evaluates to the address of the final element in the array, which is 0x1818 on my machine. Thus, the distance between the last element and the first element is 0x1818–0x1806, or 18 bytes.

As mentioned earlier in the book, hexadecimal is a 16-based numbering system. We know that 0x1818 minus 0x1806 produces 0x0012 (that is, 0x12). Then 0x12 in hexadecimal is equal to 1*16 + 2 that yields 18 in decimal.

Because each element takes 2 bytes, and the address of the final element is the beginning of that 2-byte element, the total number of bytes taken by the array list_int is indeed 20 bytes. You can calculate it another way: The distance between the last element and the first element is 18 bytes. The total number of bytes taken by the array should be counted from the very first byte in the first element to the last byte in the last element. Therefore, the total number bytes taken by the array is equal to 18 plus 2, that is 20 bytes.

Figure 12.1 shows you the memory space taken by the array list_int

FIGURE 12.1

The memory space taken by the array list_int.

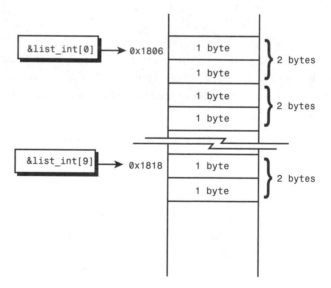

Arrays and Pointers

As I mentioned earlier in this hour, pointers and arrays have a close relationship in C. In fact, you can make a pointer that refers to the first element of an array by simply assigning the array name to the pointer variable. If an array is referenced by a pointer, the elements in the array can be accessed with the help of the pointer.

For instance, the following statements declare a pointer and an array, and assign the address of the first element to the pointer variable:

```
char  *ptr_c;
char  list_c[10];
ptr_c = list_c;
```

Because the address of the first element in the array list_c is the beginning address of the array, the pointer variable ptr_c is actually now referencing the array via the beginning address.

Listing 12.3 demonstrates how to reference an array with a pointer.

TYPE   LISTING 12.3   Referencing an Array with a Pointer

```
1:   /* 12L03.c: Referencing an array with a pointer */
2:   #include <stdio.h>
3:
4:   main()
5:   {
6:       int *ptr_int;
7:       int list_int[10];
8:       int i;
9:
10:      for (i=0; i<10; i++)
11:         list_int[i] = i + 1;
12:      ptr_int = list_int;
13:      printf( "The start address of the array: %p\n", ptr_int);
14:      printf( "The value of the first element: %d\n", *ptr_int);
15:      ptr_int = &list_int[0];
16:      printf( "The address of the first element: %p\n", ptr_int);
17:      printf( "The value of the first element: %d\n", *ptr_int);
18:      return 0;
19:  }
```

After the executable 12L03.exe is run on my computer, the following output is displayed on the screen:

OUTPUT
```
The start address of the array: 0x1802
The value of the first element: 1
The address of the first element: 0x1802
The value of the first element: 1
```

ANALYSIS   In Listing 12.3, an integer pointer variable, ptr_int, is declared in line 6. Then, an integer array, list_int, which is declared in line 7, is initialized by the list_int[i] = i + 1 expression in a for loop. (See lines 10 and 11.)

The statement in line 12 assigns the address of the first element in the array to the pointer variable ptr_int. To do so, the name of the array list_int is simply placed on the right side of the assignment operator (=) in line 12.

Line 13 displays the address assigned to the pointer variable ptr_int. The output shows that 0x1802 is the start address of the array. (You might get a different address on your machine.) The *ptr_int expression in line 14 evaluates to the value referenced by the pointer. This value is the same value contained by the first element of the array, which is the initial value, 1, assigned in the for loop. You can see that the output from the statement in line 14 shows the value correctly.

The statement in line 15 is equivalent to the one in line 12, which assigns the address of the first element to the pointer variable. Lines 16 and 17 then print out the address and the value kept by the first element, 0x1802 and 1, respectively.

In Hour 16, "Applying Pointers," you'll learn to access an element of an array by incrementing or decrementing a pointer.

Displaying Arrays of Characters

This subsection focuses on arrays of characters. The char data type takes one byte. Therefore, each element in a character array is one byte long. The total number of elements in a character array is the total number of bytes the array takes in the memory.

More importantly in C, a *character string* is defined as a contiguous sequence of characters terminated by, and including, the first null character ('\0'). Hour 13, "Manipulating Strings," introduces more details about strings.

In Listing 12.4, you see various ways to display an array of characters on the screen.

TYPE   **LISTING 12.4**   Printing an Array of Characters

```
1:  /* 12L04.c: Printing out an array of characters */
2:  #include <stdio.h>
3:
4:  main()
5:  {
6:     char array_ch[7] = {'H', 'e', 'l', 'l', 'o', '!', '\0'};
7:     int i;
8:
9:     for (i=0; i<7; i++)
10:       printf("array_ch[%d] contains: %c\n", i, array_ch[i]);
11:    /*--- method I ---*/
12:    printf( "Put all elements together(Method I):\n");
13:    for (i=0; array_ch[i] != '\0' && i<7; i++)
14:       printf("%c", array_ch[i]);
```

```
15:    /*---  method II ---*/
16:    printf( "\nPut all elements together(Method II):\n");
17:    printf( "%s\n", array_ch);
18:
19:    return 0;
20: }
```

When I run executable 12L04.exe, the following output is displayed:

OUTPUT

```
array_ch[0] contains: H
array_ch[1] contains: e
array_ch[2] contains: l
array_ch[3] contains: l
array_ch[4] contains: o
array_ch[5] contains: !
array_ch[6] contains:
Put all elements together(Method I):
Hello!
Put all elements together(Method II):
Hello!
```

ANALYSIS As you can see from Listing 12.4, a character array, array_ch, is declared and initialized in line 6. Each element in the character array is printed out by the printf() call in a for loop shown in lines 9 and 10. There is a total of seven elements in the array; they contain the following character constants: 'H', 'e', 'l', 'l', 'o', '!', and '\0'.

There are two ways to display this array: display all the characters individually, or treat them as a character string.

Lines 12–14 show the first way, which fetches each individual element, array_ch[i], consecutively in a loop, and prints out one character next to another by using the character format specifier %c in the printf() call in line 14.

Whenever you are dealing with a character array, as was mentioned earlier, the null character '\0' signals the end of the string (even though it may not yet be the end of the array). It is a good idea to watch for the null character so you know when to stop printing, so the conditional expression in line 13 will terminate the for loop if the current element is a null character.

The second way is simpler. You simply tell the printf() function where to find the first element the array (the address of its first element). Also, you need to use the string format specifier %s in the printf() call as shown in line 17. Note that the array_ch expression in line 17 contains the address of the first element in the array—that is, the starting address of the array. The name of the array, by itself, is a shorthand way of saying array_ch[0]; they mean the same thing.

12

You may be wondering how the printf() function knows where the end of the character array is. Do you remember that the last element in the character array array_ch is a '\0' character? It's this null character that marks the end of the string. As I mentioned earlier, a contiguous sequence of characters ending with a null character is called a character string in C. We don't tell printf() how many elements are in the array, so the %s format specifier tells printf() to keep printing characters until it finds a null character—just as we did, ourselves, in the first method.

The Null Character ('\0')

The null character ('\0') is treated as one character in C; it is a special character that marks the end of a string. Therefore, when functions like printf() act on a character string, they process one character after another until they encounter the null character. (You'll learn more about strings in Hour 13.)

The null character ('\0'), which is always evaluated as a value of zero, can also be used for a logical test in a control-flow statement. Listing 12.5 shows an example of using the null character in a for loop.

TYPE   **LISTING 12.5**   Ending Output at the Null Character

```
1:  /* 12L05.c: Stopping at the null character */
2:  #include <stdio.h>
3:
4:  main()
5:  {
6:     char array_ch[15] = {'C', ' ',
7:                          'i', 's', ' ',
8:                          'p', 'o', 'w', 'e', 'r',
9:                          'f', 'u', 'l', '!', '\0'};
10:    int i;
11:    /*  array_ch[i] in logical test */
12:    for (i=0; array_ch[i]; i++)
13:       printf("%c", array_ch[i]);
14:
15:    printf("\n");
16:    return 0;
17: }
```

By running the executable 12L05.exe, I obtain the following output:

OUTPUT   C is powerful!

ANALYSIS In Listing 12.5, a character array, `array_ch`, is declared and initialized, with the characters (including the space characters) from the string `C is powerful!`, in lines 6–9.

Note that the last element in the array contains the null character (`'\0'`), which is needed to terminate the string.

The `for` loop in lines 12 and 13 prints out each element in the array `array_ch` to show the string `C is powerful!` on the screen. So in the first expression of the `for` statement, the integer variable `i`, which is used as the index to the array, is initialized to `0`.

Then, the conditional expression, `array_ch[i]`, is evaluated. If the expression evaluates to a nonzero value, the `for` loop iterates; otherwise, the loop stops. Starting at the first element in the array, the `array_ch[i]` expression keeps producing a nonzero value until the null character is encountered. Therefore, the `for` loop can put all characters of the array on the screen, and stop printing right after the `array_ch[i]` expression produces a value of zero, when it finds the null character

Multidimensional Arrays

So far, all the arrays you've seen have been one-dimensional arrays, in which the dimension sizes are placed within a pair of brackets (`[` and `]`).

In addition to one-dimensional arrays, the C language also supports multidimensional arrays. You can declare arrays with as many dimensions as your compiler allows.

The general form of declaring a *N*-dimensional array is

```
data-type  Array-Name[Array-Size1][Array-Size2]. . . [Array-SizeN];
```

where *N* can be any positive integer.

Because the two-dimensional array, which is widely used, is the simplest form of the multidimensional array, let's focus on two-dimensional arrays in this section. Anything you learn from this section can be applied to arrays of more than two dimensions, however.

For example, the following statement declares a two-dimensional integer array:

```
int  array_int[2][3];
```

Here there are two pairs of brackets that represent two dimensions with a size of 2 and 3 integer elements, respectively.

You can initialize the two-dimensional array `array_int` in the following way:

```
array_int[0][0] = 1;
array_int[0][1] = 2;
```

12

```
array_int[0][2] = 3;
array_int[1][0] = 4;
array_int[1][1] = 5;
array_int[1][2] = 6;
```

which is equivalent to the statement

```
int array_int[2][3] = {1, 2, 3, 4, 5, 6};
```

Also, you can initialize the `array_int` array in the following way:

```
int array_int[2][3] = {{1, 2, 3}, {4, 5, 6}};
```

Note that `array_int[0][0]` is the first element in the two-dimensional array `array_int`; `array_int[0][1]` is the second element in the array; `array_int[0][2]` is the third element; `array_int[1][0]` is the fourth element; `array_int[1][1]` is the fifth element; and `array_int[1][2]` is the sixth element in the array.

The program in Listing 12.6 shows a two-dimensional integer array that is initialized and displayed on the screen.

TYPE   **LISTING 12.6**   Printing a Two-Dimensional Array

```
 1:   /* 12L06.c: Printing out a 2-D array */
 2:   #include <stdio.h>
 3:
 4:   main()
 5:   {
 6:      int two_dim[3][5] = {1, 2, 3, 4, 5,
 7:                           10, 20, 30, 40, 50,
 8:                           100, 200, 300, 400, 500};
 9:      int i, j;
10:
11:      for (i=0; i<3; i++){
12:         printf("\n");
13:         for (j=0; j<5; j++)
14:            printf("%6d", two_dim[i][j]);
15:      }
16:      printf("\n");
17:      return 0;
18:   }
```

The following output is obtained by running the executable `12L06.exe`:

OUTPUT

```
      1     2     3     4     5
     10    20    30    40    50
    100   200   300   400   500
```

ANALYSIS As you can see in Listing 12.6, there is a two-dimensional integer array, `two_dim`, declared and initialized in lines 6–8.

In lines 11–15, two `for` loops are nested together. The outer `for` loop increments the integer variable `i` and prints out the newline character '\n' in each iteration. Here the integer variable `i` is used as the index to the first dimension of the array, `two_dim`.

The inner `for` loop in lines 13 and 14 prints out each element, represented by the expression `two_dim[i][j]`, by incrementing the index to the second dimension of the array. Therefore, I obtain the following output:

```
  1    2    3    4    5
 10   20   30   40   50
100  200  300  400  500
```

after the two nested `for` loops are run successfully.

Unsized Arrays

As you've seen, the size of a dimension is normally given during the declaration of an array. It means that you have to count each element in an array to determine the size. It could be tedious to do so, though, especially if there are many elements in an array.

The good news is that the C compiler can actually calculate a dimension size of an array automatically if an array is declared as an *unsized array*. For example, when the compiler sees the following unsized array:

```
int  list_int[] = { 10, 20, 30, 40, 50, 60, 70, 80, 90};
```

it will create an array big enough to store all the elements.

Likewise, you can declare a multidimensional unsized array. However, you have to specify all but the leftmost (that is, the first) dimension size. For instance, the compiler can reserve enough memory space to hold all elements in the following two-dimensional unsized array:

```
char list_ch[][2] = {
        'a', 'A',
        'b', 'B',
        'c', 'C',
        'd', 'D',
        'e', 'E',
        'f', 'F',
        'g', 'G'};
```

The program in Listing 12.7 initializes a one-dimensional character unsized array and a two-dimensional unsized integer array, and then measures the memory spaces taken for storing the two arrays.

12

TYPE **LISTING 12.7** Initializing Unsized Arrays

```
1:  /* 12L07.c: Initializing unsized arrays */
2:  #include <stdio.h>
3:
4:  main()
5:  {
6:      char array_ch[] = {'C', ' ',
7:                         'i', 's', ' ',
8:                         'p', 'o', 'w', 'e', 'r',
9:                         'f', 'u', 'l', '!', '\0'};
10:     int list_int[][3] = {
11:              1, 1, 1,
12:              2, 2, 8,
13:              3, 9, 27,
14:              4, 16, 64,
15:              5, 25, 125,
16:              6, 36, 216,
17:              7, 49, 343};
18:
19:     printf("The size of array_ch[] is %d bytes.\n", sizeof (array_ch));
20:     printf("The size of list_int[][3] is %d bytes.\n", sizeof (list_int));
21:     return 0;
22: }
```

The following output is obtained when the executable 12L07.exe is run on my computer:

OUTPUT
```
The size of array_ch[] is 15 bytes.
The size of list_int[][3] is 42 bytes.
```

ANALYSIS A character unsized array, array_ch, is declared and initialized in lines 6–9. In lines 10–17, a two-dimensional unsized integer array, list_int, is declared and initialized too.

The statement in line 19 measures and prints out the total memory space (in bytes) taken by the array array_ch. The result shows that the unsized character array is assigned 15 bytes in memory to hold all its elements after compiling. When you calculate the total number of the elements in the character array manually, you find that there are indeed 15 elements. Because each character takes one byte in the memory, the character array array_ch takes total of 15 bytes accordingly.

Likewise, the statement in line 20 gives the total number of bytes reserved in the memory for the unsized two-dimensional integer array list_int. Because there are a total of 21 integer elements in the array, and an integer takes 2 bytes on my machine, the compiler should allocate 42 bytes for the integer array list_int. The result printed out by the printf() function in line 20 proves that there are 42 bytes reserved in the memory for the two-dimensional integer array. (If the size of int is different on your machine, you may get different values for the size of the list_int array in program Listing 12.7.)

Summary

In this lesson you learned the following very important concepts about arrays in C:

- An array is a collection of variables that are of the same data type.
- In C, the index to an array starts at 0.
- You can initialize each individual element of an array after the declaration of the array, or you can place all initial values into a data block surrounded by { and } during the declaration of an array.
- The memory storage taken by an array is determined by multiplying the size of the data type and the dimensions of the array.
- A pointer is said to *refer to* an array when the address of the first element in the array is assigned to the pointer. The address of the first element in an array is also called the start address of the array.
- To assign the start address of an array to a pointer, you can put either the combination of the address-of operator (&) and the first element name of the array, or simply use the array name on the right side of an assignment operator (=).
- The null character ('\0') marks the end of a string. C functions, such as printf(), will stop processing the string when the null character is encountered.
- C supports multidimensional arrays, too. An empty pair of brackets (the array subscript operator—[and]) indicates a dimension.
- The compiler can automatically calculate the memory space needed by an unsized array.

In the next lesson you'll learn more about strings in C.

12

Q&A

Q Why do you need to use arrays?

A In many cases, you need to declare a set of variables that are of the same data type. Instead of declaring each variable separately, you can declare all variables collectively in the format of an array. Each variable, as an element of the array, can be accessed either through the array element reference or through a pointer that references the array.

Q What is the minimum index in an array?

A In C, the minimum index of a one-dimensional array is 0, which marks the first element of the array. For instance, given an integer array,

```
int array_int[8];
```

the first element of the array is `array_int[0]`.

Likewise, for a multidimensional array, the minimum index of each dimension starts at 0.

Q How do you reference an array by using a pointer?

A You can use a pointer to reference an array by assigning the start address of an array to the pointer. For example, given a pointer variable `ptr_ch` and a character array `array_ch`, you can use one of the following statements to reference the array by the pointer:

```
ptr_ch = array_ch;
```

or

```
ptr_ch = &array_ch[0];
```

Q What can the null character do?

A The null character (`'\0'`) in C can be used to mark the end of a string. For instance, the `printf()` function keeps putting the next character on the screen until the null character is encountered. Also, the null character always evaluates to a value of zero.

Workshop

To help solidify your understanding of this hour's lesson, you are encouraged to answer the quiz questions and finish the exercises provided in the workshop before you move to the next lesson. The answers and hints to the questions and exercises are given in Appendix B, "Answers to Quiz Questions and Exercises."

Quiz

1. What does the following statement do?

   ```
   int array_int[4] = {12, 23, 9, 56};
   ```

2. Given an array, `int data[3]`, what's wrong with the following initialization?

   ```
   data[1] = 1;
   data[2] = 2;
   data[3] = 3;
   ```

3. How many dimensions do the following arrays have?

   • `char array1[3][19];`

   • `int array2[];`

   • `float array3[][8][16];`

   • `char array4[][80];`

4. What's wrong with the following declaration?

```
char list_ch[][] = {
        'A', 'a',
        'B', 'b',
        'C', 'c',
        'D', 'd',
```

Exercises

1. Given this character array:

   ```
   char array_ch[5] = {'A', 'B', 'C', 'D', 'E'};
   ```

   write a program to display each element of the array on the screen.

2. Rewrite the program in Exercise 1, but this time use a `for` loop to initialize the character array with `'a'`, `'b'`, `'c'`, `'d'`, and `'e'`, and then print out the value of each element in the array.

3. Given this two-dimensional unsized array:

   ```
   char list_ch[][2] = {
           '1', 'a',
           '2', 'b',
           '3', 'c',
           '4', 'd',
           '5', 'e',
           '6', 'f'};
   ```

   write a program to measure the total bytes taken by the array, and then print out all elements of the array.

4. Rewrite the program in Listing 12.5. This time put a string of characters, `I like C!`, on the screen.

5. Given the following array:

   ```
   double list_data[6] = {
           1.12345,
           2.12345,
           3.12345,
           4.12345,
           5.12345};
   ```

   use the two equivalent ways taught in this lesson to measure the total memory space taken by the array, and then display the results on the screen.

12

HOUR 13

Manipulating Strings

I have made this letter longer than usual, because I lack the time to make it short.

—B. Pascal

In the last hour's lesson you learned how to use arrays to collect variables of the same type. You also learned that a character string is actually a character array, with a null character \0 marking the end of the string. In this lesson you'll learn more about strings, and C functions that can be used to manipulate strings. The following topics are covered:

- Declaring a string
- The length of a string
- Copying strings
- Reading strings with scanf()
- The gets() and puts() functions

Declaring Strings

This section teaches you how to declare and initialize strings, as well as the difference between string constants and character constants. First, let's review the definition of a string.

What Is a String?

As introduced in Hour 12, "Understanding Arrays," a *string* is a character array, with a null character (\0) used to mark the end of the string. (The length of a string can be shorter than its character array.)

For instance, a character array, array_ch, declared in the following statement, is considered as a character string:

```
char array_ch[7] = {'H', 'e', 'l', 'l', 'o', '!', '\0'};
```

In C, the null character is used to mark the end of a string, and it always evaluates to 0. C treats \0 as one character. Each character in a string takes only 1 byte.

A series of characters enclosed in double quotes ("") is called a *string constant*. The C compiler will automatically add a null character (\0) at the end of a string constant to indicate the end of the string.

For example, the character string "A character string." is considered a string constant; so is "Hello!".

Initializing Strings

As taught in the last lesson, a character array can be declared and initialized like this:

```
char arr_str[6] = {'H', 'e', 'l', 'l', 'o', '!'};
```

Here the array arr_str is treated as a character array. However, if you add a null character (\0) into the array, you can have the following statement:

```
char arr_str[7] = {'H', 'e', 'l', 'l', 'o', '!', '\0'};
```

Here the array arr_str is expanded to hold seven elements; the last element contains a null character. Now, the character array arr_str is considered a character string because of the null character that is appended (added to the end) of the character data.

You can also initialize a character array with a string constant, instead of a list of character constants. For example, the following statement initializes a character array, str, with a string constant, "Hello!":

```
char str[7] = "Hello!";
```

The compiler will automatically append a null character (\0) to the end of "Hello!", and treat the character array as a character string. Note that the size of the array is specified to hold up to seven elements, although the string constant has only six characters enclosed in double quotes. The extra space is reserved for the null character that will be added later by the compiler.

You can declare an unsized character array if you want the compiler to calculate the total number of elements in the array. For instance, the following statement:

```
char str[] = "I like C.";
```

initializes an unsized character array:, str, with a string constant. Later, when the compiler sees the statement, it will figure out the total memory space needed to hold the string constant plus an extra null character added by the compiler itself.

If you like, you can also declare a char pointer and then initialize the pointer with a string constant. The following statement is an example:

```
char *ptr_str = "I teach myself C.";
```

> Don't specify the size of a character array as too small. Otherwise, it cannot hold a string constant plus an extra null character. For instance, the following declaration is considered illegal:
>
> ```
> char str[4] = "text";
> ```
>
> Note that many C compilers will not issue a warning or an error message on this incorrect declaration. The runtime errors that could eventually arise as a result could be very difficult to debug. Therefore, it's your responsibility to make sure to specify enough space for a string.
>
> The following statement is a correct one, because it specifies the size of the character array str that is big enough to hold the string constant plus an extra null character:
>
> ```
> char str[5] = "text";
> ```

13

String Constants versus Character Constants

As you already know, a string constant is a series of characters enclosed in double quotes (" "). On the other hand, a character constant is a character enclosed in single quotes (' ').

When a character variable ch and a character array str are initialized with the same character, x, such as the following:

```
char ch = 'x';
char str[] = "x";
```

1 byte is reserved for the character variable ch, and two bytes are allocated for the character array str. The reason that an extra byte is needed for str is that the compiler has to append a null character to the array.

Another important thing is that a string, since it is an array, is really a char pointer. Therefore, you can assign a character string to a pointer variable directly, like this:

```
char *ptr_str;
ptr_str = "A character string.";
```

However, you cannot assign a character constant to the pointer variable, as shown in the following :

```
ptr_str = 'x';   /* It's wrong. */
```

In other words, the character constant 'x' contains a right value, and the pointer variable ptr_str expects a left value. But C requires the same kinds of values on both sides of an assignment operator =.

It's legal to assign a character constant to a dereferenced char pointer like this:

```
char *ptr_str;
*ptr_str = 'x';
```

Now the values on both sides of the = operator are of the same type.

The program in Listing 13.1 demonstrates how to initialize, or assign, character arrays with string constants.

LISTING 13.1   Initializing Strings

```
1:  /* 13L01.c: Initializing strings */
2:  #include <stdio.h>
3:
4:  main()
5:  {
6:     char str1[] = {'A', ' ',
7:                    's', 't', 'r', 'i', 'n', 'g', ' ',
8:                    'c', 'o', 'n', 's', 't', 'a', 'n', 't', '\0'};
9:     char str2[] = "Another string constant";
10:    char *ptr_str;
11:    int i;
12:
13:    /* print out str1 */
14:    for (i=0; str1[i]; i++)
15:       printf("%c", str1[i]);
```

```
16:     printf("\n");
17:     /* print out str2 */
18:     for (i=0; str2[i]; i++)
19:         printf("%c", str2[i]);
20:     printf("\n");
21:     /* assign a string to a pointer */
22:     ptr_str = "Assign a string to a pointer.";
23:     for (i=0; *ptr_str; i++)
24:         printf("%c", *ptr_str++);
25:     return 0;
26: }
```

The following output is displayed after the executable 13L01.exe of the program in
Listing 13.1 is created and run.

```
A string constant
Another string constant
Assign a string to a pointer.
```

 As you can see from Listing 13.1, there are two character arrays, str1 and str2,
that are declared and initialized in lines 6–9. In the declaration of str1, a set of
character constants, including a null character, is used to initialize the array. For str2, a
string constant is assigned to the array in line 9. The compiler will append a null character to str2. Note that both str1 and str2 are declared as unsized arrays for which the
compiler will automatically figure out how much memory is needed. The statement in
line 10 declares a char pointer variable, ptr_str.

The for loop in lines 14 and 15 then prints out all the elements in str1. Because the last
element contains a null character (\0) that is evaluated as 0, str1[i] is used as the conditional expression of the for statement. The expression str1[i] evaluates to nonzero
for each element in str1 except the one holding the null character. After the execution of
the for loop, the string A string constant is shown on the screen..

Likewise, another for loop in lines 18 and 19 displays the string constant assigned to
str2 by putting every element of the array on the screen. Because the compiler appends
a null character to the array, the expression str2[i] is evaluated in the for statement.
The for loop stops iterating when str2[i] evaluates to 0. By that time, the content of
the string constant, Another string constant, has already been displayed on the
screen.

The statement in line 22 assigns a string constant, "Assign a string to a pointer.",:
to the char pointer variable ptr_str. Also, a for loop is used to print out the string constant by putting every character in the string on the screen (see lines 23 and 24). Note that
the dereferenced pointer *ptr_str is used to refer to one of the characters in the string

13

constant. When the null character appended to the string is encountered, `*ptr_str` evaluates to `0`, which causes the iteration of the `for` loop to stop. In line 24, the expression `*ptr_str++` moves the pointer to the next character of the string after the current character referred to by the pointer is fetched. In Hour 16, "Applying Pointers," you'll learn more about pointer arithmetic.

How Long Is a String?

Sometimes, you need to know how many bytes are taken by a string, since its length can be less than the length of its `char` array. In C, you can use a function called `strlen()` to measure the length of a string.

The `strlen()` Function

Let's have a look of the syntax of the `strlen()` function.

▼ SYNTAX

The syntax for the `strlen()` function is

```
#include <string.h>
size_t strlen(const char *s);
```

Here `s` is a `char` pointer variable. The return value from the function is the number of bytes in the string, not counting the null character `'\0'`. `size_t` is a data type defined in the `string.h` header file. The size of the data type depends on the particular computer system. Note that `string.h` has to be included in your program before you can call the `strlen()` function.

▲

Listing 13.2 gives an example of using the `strlen()` function to measure string lengths.

LISTING 13.2   Measuring String Lengths

```
 1:  /* 13L02.c: Measuring string length */
 2:  #include <stdio.h>
 3:  #include <string.h>
 4:
 5:  main()
 6:  {
 7:     char str1[] = {'A', ' ',
 8:                    's', 't', 'r', 'i', 'n', 'g', ' ',
 9:                    'c', 'o', 'n', 's', 't', 'a', 'n', 't', '\0'};
10:     char str2[] = "Another string constant";
11:     char *ptr_str = "Assign a string to a pointer.";
12:
13:     printf("The length of str1 is: %d bytes\n", strlen(str1));
14:     printf("The length of str2 is: %d bytes\n", strlen(str2));
15:     printf("The length of the string assigned to ptr_str is: %d bytes\n",
16:        strlen(ptr_str));
```

```
17:    return 0;
18: }
```

I get the following output by running the executable, `13L02.exe`, of the program in Listing 13.2.

```
The length of str1 is: 17 bytes
The length of str2 is: 23 bytes
The length of the string assigned to ptr_str is: 29 bytes
```

In Listing 13.2, two `char` arrays, `str1` and `str2`, and one pointer variable, `ptr_str`, are declared and initialized in lines 7–11, respectively.

Then, the statement in line 13 obtains the length of the string constant held by `str1`, and prints out the result. From the result, you can see that the null character (`\0`) at the end of `str1` is not counted by the `strlen()` function.

In lines 14–16, the lengths of the string constants referenced by `str2` and `ptr_str` are measured and shown on the screen. The results indicate that the `strlen()` function does not count the null characters appended to the two string constants by the compiler, either.

Copying Strings with `strcpy()`

If you want to copy a string from one array to another, you can copy each item of the first array to the corresponding element in the second array, or you can simply call the C function `strcpy()` to do the job for you.

▼ SYNTAX

The syntax for the `strcpy()` function is

```
#include <string.h>
char *strcpy(char *dest, const char *src);
```

Here the content of the string *src* is copied to the array referenced by *dest*. The `strcpy()` function returns the value of *src* if it is successful. The header file `string.h` must be included in your program before the `strcpy()` function is called.

▲

The program in Listing 13.3 demonstrates how to copy a string from one array to another by either calling the `strcpy()` function or doing it yourself.

LISTING 13.3 Copying Strings

```
1: /* 13L03.c: Copying strings */
2: #include <stdio.h>
3: #include <string.h>
4:
5: main()
```

continues

13

LISTING 13.3   continued

```
 6:  {
 7:      char str1[] = "Copy a string.";
 8:      char str2[15];
 9:      char str3[15];
10:      int  i;
11:
12:      /* with strcpy() */
13:      strcpy(str2, str1);
14:      /* without strcpy() */
15:      for (i=0; str1[i]; i++)
16:          str3[i] = str1[i];
17:      str3[i] = '\0';
18:      /* display str2 and str3 */
19:      printf("The content of str2 using strcpy: %s\n", str2);
20:      printf("The content of str3 without using strcpy: %s\n", str3);
21:      return 0;
22:  }
```

After the executable, 13L03.exe, is created and run, the following output is displayed:

OUTPUT
```
The content of str2 using strcpy: Copy a string.
The content of str3 without using strcpy: Copy a string.
```

ANALYSIS   Three char arrays, str1, str2, and str3, are declared in Listing 13.3. In addition, str1 is initialized with a string constant, "Copy a string.", in line 7.

The statement in line 13 calls the strcpy() function to copy the content of str1 (including the null character appended by the compiler) to the array referenced by str2.

Lines 15–17 demonstrate another way to copy the content of str1 to an array referenced by str3. To do so, the for loop in lines 15 and 16 keeps copying characters of str1 to the corresponding elements in str3 one after another, until the null character (\0) appended by the compiler is encountered. When the null character is encountered, the str1[i] expression used as the condition of the for statement in line 15 evaluates to 0, which terminates the loop.

Because the for loop does not copy the null character from str1 to str3, the statement in line 17 appends a null character to the array referenced by str3. In C, it's very important to make sure that any array that is used to store a string has a null character at the end of the string.

To prove that the string constant referenced by str1 has been copied to str2 and str3 successfully, the contents held by str2 and str3 are displayed on the screen. Note that the string format specifier %s and the start addresses of str2 and str3 are passed to the printf() call in lines 19 and 20 to print out all characters, except the null character, stored in str2 and str3. The results displayed on the screen show that str2 and str3 have the exact same content as str1.

Reading and Writing Strings

Now let's focus on how to read or write strings with the standard input and output streams—that is, stdin and stdout. In C, there are several functions you can use to deal with reading or writing strings. The following subsections introduce some of these functions.

The gets() and puts() Functions

The gets() function can be used to read characters from the standard input stream.

The syntax for the gets() function is

```
#include <stdio.h>
char *gets(char *s);
```

Here the characters read from the standard input stream are stored in the character array identified by s. The gets() function stops reading, and appends a null character \0 to the array, when a newline or end-of-file (EOF) character is encountered. The function returns s if it concludes successfully. Otherwise, a null pointer is returned.

The puts() function can be used to write characters to the standard output stream (that is, stdout).

The syntax for the puts function is

```
#include <stdio.h>
int puts(const char *s);
```

Here s refers to the character array that contains a string. The puts() function writes the string to stdout. If the function is successful, it returns 0. Otherwise, a nonzero value is returned.

The puts() function appends a newline character to replace the null character at the end of a character array.

Both the gets() and puts() functions require the header file stdio.h. In Listing 13.4, you can see the application of the two functions.

SYNTAX

SYNTAX

13

LISTING 13.4   Using the `gets()` and `puts()` Functions

```
 1:  /* 13L04.c: Using gets() and puts() */
 2:  #include <stdio.h>
 3:
 4:  main()
 5:  {
 6:      char str[80];
 7:      int i, delt = 'a' - 'A';
 8:
 9:      printf("Enter a string less than 80 characters:\n");
10:      gets( str );
11:      i = 0;
12:      while (str[i]){
13:        if ((str[i] >= 'a') && (str[i] <= 'z'))
14:            str[i] -= delt;   /* convert to upper case */
15:        ++i;
16:      }
17:      printf("The entered string is (in uppercase):\n");
18:      puts( str );
19:      return 0;
20:  }
```

While running the executable `13L04.exe`, I enter a line of characters (in bold below) from the keyboard and have the characters (all in uppercase) shown on the screen.

OUTPUT

```
Enter a string less than 80 characters:
This is a test.
The entered string is (in uppercase):
THIS IS A TEST.
```

ANALYSIS   The program in Listing 13.4 accepts a string of characters entered from the keyboard (that is, `stdin`), and then converts all lowercase characters to uppercase ones. Finally, the modified string is put back to the screen..

In line 6, a character array (`str`) is declared that can hold up to 80 characters. The `gets()` function in line 10 reads any characters entered by the user from the keyboard until the user presses the Enter key, which is interpreted as a newline character. The characters read in by the `gets()` function are stored into the character array indicated by `str`. The newline character is not saved into `str`. Instead, a null character is appended to the array as a terminator.

The `while` loop in lines 12–15 has a conditional expression, `str[i]`. The `while` loop keeps iterating as long as `str[i]` evaluates to a nonzero value. Within the loop, the value of each character represented by `str[i]` is evaluated in line 13, to find out whether the character is a lowercase character within the range of a through z. If the character is one of the lowercase characters, it is converted into uppercase by subtracting the value of an int variable, delt, from its current value in line 14. The delt variable is initialized in line 7 by the value of the expression 'a' - 'A', which is the difference between the numeric value of a lowercase character and its uppercase counterpart. In other words, by subtracting the difference of 'a' and 'A' from the lower case integer value, we obtain the uppercase integer value.

Then the puts() function in line 18 outputs the string with all uppercase characters to stdout, which goes to the screen by default. A newline character is appended by the puts() function when it encounters the null character at the end of the string..

Using %s with the printf() Function

We've used the printf() function in many program examples in this book. As you know, many format specifiers can be used with the printf() function to specify different display formats for data of various types.

For instance, you can use the string format specifier, %s, with the printf() function to display a character string saved in an array. (Refer to the example in Listing 13.3.)

In the next section, the scanf() function is introduced as a way to read values of various data types with different format specifiers, including the format specifier %s.

The scanf() Function

The scanf() function provides another way to read strings from the standard input stream. Moreover, this function can actually be used to read various types of input data. The formats of arguments to the scanf() function are quite similar to those used in the printf() function.

▼ SYNTAX

The syntax for the scanf() function is

```
#include <stdio.h>
int scanf(const char *format,...);
```

Here various format specifiers can be included inside the format string referenced by the char pointer variable *format*. If the scanf() function concludes successfully, it returns the number of data items read from stdin. If an error occurs, the scanf() function returns EOF (end-of-file).

▲

13

Using the string format specifier %s tells the scanf() function to continue reading characters until a space, a newline, a tab, a vertical tab, or a form feed is encountered. Characters read by the scanf() function are stored into an array referenced by the corresponding argument. The array should be big enough to store the input characters.

A null character is automatically appended to the array after the string is read.

Note that with scanf(), unlike printf(), you must pass pointers to your arguments so that the scanf() function can modify their values.

The program in Listing 13.5 shows how to use various format specifiers with the scanf() function.

LISTING 13.5 Using the scanf() Function with Various Format Specifiers

```
1:  /* 13L05.c: Using scanf() */
2:  #include <stdio.h>
3:
4:  main()
5:  {
6:     char str[80];
7:     int x, y;
8:     float z;
9:
10:    printf("Enter two integers separated by a space:\n");
11:    scanf("%d  %d", &x, &y);
12:    printf("Enter a floating-point number:\n");
13:    scanf("%f", &z);
14:    printf("Enter a string:\n");
15:    scanf("%s", str);
16:    printf("Here are what you've entered:\n");
17:    printf("%d  %d\n%f\n%s\n", x, y, z, str);
18:    return 0;
19: }
```

The following output is displayed on the screen after I run the executable 13L05.exe and enter data (which appears in bold) from my keyboard:

OUTPUT
```
Enter two integers separated by a space:
10  12345
Enter a floating-point number:
1.234567
Enter a string:
Test
Here are what you've entered:
10  12345
1.234567
Test
```

ANALYSIS   In Listing 13.5, there are one char array (str), two int variables (x and y), and a float variable declared in lines 6–8.

Then, the scanf() function in line 11 reads in two integers entered by the user and saves them into the memory locations reserved for the integer variables x and y. The address-of operator is used to obtain the memory addresses of the variables. The statement in line 13 reads and stores a floating-point number into z. Note that the format specifiers, %d and %f, are used to specify proper formats for entered numbers in lines 11 and 13.

Line 15 uses the scanf() function and the format specifier %s to read a series of characters entered by the user, and then saves the characters (plus a null character as the terminator) into the array pointed to by str. The address-of operator is not used here, since str itself points to the starting address of the array.

To prove that the scanf() function reads all the numbers and characters entered by the user, the printf() function in line 17 displays the contents saved in x, y, z, and str on the screen. Sure enough, the result shows that the scanf() has done its job.

One thing you need to be aware of is that the scanf() function doesn't actually start reading the input until the Enter key is pressed. Data entered from the keyboard is placed in an input buffer. When the Enter key is pressed, the scanf() function looks for its input in the buffer. You'll learn more about buffered input and output in Hour 21, "Reading and Writing with Files."

Summary

In this lesson you learned the following important functions and concepts about strings in C:

- A string is a character array with a null character marking the end of the string.
- A string constant is a series of characters enclosed by double quotes.
- The C compiler automatically appends a null character to a string constant that has been used to initialize an array.
- You cannot assign a string constant to a dereferenced char pointer.
- The strlen() function can be used to measure the length of a string. This function does not count the null character.
- You can copy a string from one array to another by calling the C function strcpy().
- The gets() function can be used to read a series of characters. This function stops reading when the newline character or end-of-file (EOF) is encountered. The function adds a null character to the end of the string.

13

- The puts() function sends all characters, except the null character, in a string to the stdout, and appends a newline character to the output.
- You can read different data items with the scanf() function by using various format specifiers.

In the next lesson you'll learn about the concepts of scope and storage in C.

Q&A

Q What is a string? How do you know its length?

A In C, a string is stored in a character array and is terminated by a null character ('\0'). The null character tells the string functions (such as puts() and strcpy) that they have reached the end of the string.

The C function strlen() can be used to measure the length of a string. If it is successful, the strlen() function returns the total number of bytes taken by the string; however, the null character in the string is not counted.

Q What are the main differences between a string constant and a character constant?

A A string constant is a series of characters enclosed by double quotes, while a character constant is a single character surrounded by single quotes. The compiler will append a null character to the string when it is used to initialize an array. Therefore, an extra byte has to be reserved for the null character. On the other hand, a character constant takes only 1 byte in memory and is not stored in an array.

Q Does the gets() function save the newline character from the standard input stream?

A No. The gets() function keeps reading characters from the standard input stream until a newline character or end-of-file is encountered. Instead of saving the newline character, the gets() function appends a null character to the string and stores it in the array that is referenced by the argument to the gets() function.

Q What types of data can the scanf() function read?

A Depending on the printf()-style format specifiers that you pass to the function, scanf() can read various types of data, such as a series of characters, integers, or floating-point numbers. Unlike gets(), scanf() stops reading the current input item (and moves to the next input item if there is any) when it encounters a space, a newline, a tab, a vertical tab, or a form feed.

Workshop

To help solidify your understanding of this hour's lesson, you are encouraged to answer the quiz questions and finish the exercises provided in the workshop before you move to the next lesson. The answers and hints to the questions and exercises are given in Appendix B, "Answers to Quiz Questions and Exercises."

Quiz

1. In the following list, which statements are legal?

   - `char str1[5] = "Texas";`
   - `char str2[] = "A character string";`
   - `char str3[2] = "A";`
   - `char str4[2] = "TX";`

2. Given a `char` pointer variable `ptr_ch`, are the following statements legal?

   - `*ptr_ch = 'a';`
   - `ptr_ch = "A character string";`
   - `ptr_ch = 'x';`
   - `*ptr_ch = "This is Quiz 2.";`

3. Can the `puts()` function print out the null character in a character array?

4. Which format specifier do you use with the `scanf()` function to read in a string, and which one do you use to read a floating-point number?

Exercises

1. Given a character array in the following statement,

   `char str1[] = "This is Exercise 1.";`

   write a program to copy the string from `str1` to another array, called `str2`.

2. Write a program to measure the length of a string by evaluating the elements in a character array one by one until you reach the null character. To prove you get the right result, you can use the `strlen()` function to measure the same string again.

3. Rewrite the program in Listing 13.4. This time, convert all uppercase characters to their lowercase counterparts.

4. Write a program that uses the `scanf()` function to read in two integers entered by the user, adds the two integers, and then prints out the sum on the screen.

13

HOUR 14

Understanding Scope and Storage Classes

Nobody owns anything and all anyone has is the use of his presumed possessions.

—P. Wylie

In the previous hours, you learned how to declare variables of different data types, as well as to initialize and use those variables. It's been assumed that you can access variables from anywhere. Now, the question is: Can you declare variables that are accessible only to certain portions of a program? In this lesson you'll learn about the scope and storage classes of data in C. The main topics covered in this lesson are

- Block scope
- Function scope
- File scope
- Program scope

- The auto specifier
- The static specifier
- The register specifier
- The extern specifier
- The const modifier
- The volatile modifier

Hiding Data

To solve a complex problem in practice, the programmer normally breaks the problem into smaller pieces and deals with each piece of the problem by writing one or two functions (or routines). Then, all the functions are put together to form a complete program that can be used to solve the complex problem.

In the complete program, there might be variables that have to be shared by all the functions. On the other hand, the use of some other variables might be limited to only certain functions. That is, the visibility of those variables is limited, and values assigned to those variables are hidden from many functions.

Limiting the scope of variables is very useful when several programmers are working on different pieces of the same program. If they limit the scope of their variables to their pieces of code, they do not have to worry about conflicting with variables of the same name used by others in other parts of the program.

In C, you can declare a variable and indicate its visibility level by designating its scope. Thus, variables with local scope can only be accessed within the block in which they are declared.

The following sections teach you how to declare variables with different scopes.

Block Scope

In this section, a *block* refers to any sets of statements enclosed in braces ({ and }). A variable declared within a block has *block scope*. Thus, the variable is active and accessible from its declaration point to the end of the block. Sometimes, block scope is also called *local scope*.

For example, the variable i declared within the block of the following main function has block scope:

```
int main()
{
   int i;   /* block scope */
```

```
         .
         .
         .
      return 0;
   }
```

Usually, a variable with block scope is called a *local variable*. Note that local variables must be declared at the beginning of the block, before other statements.

Nested Block Scope

You can also declare variables within a nested block. If a variable declared in the outer block shares the same name with one of the variables in the inner block, the variable within the outer block is hidden by the one within the inner block. This is true for the scope of the inner block.

Listing 14.1 shows an example of variable scopes in nested blocks.

TYPE   **LISTING 14.1**   Printing Variables with Different Scope Levels

```
1:  /* 14L01.c: Scopes in nested block */
2:  #include <stdio.h>
3:
4:  main()
5:  {
6:     int i = 32;    /* block scope 1*/
7:
8:     printf("Within the outer block: i=%d\n", i);
9:
10:    {    /* the beginning of the inner block */
11:      int i, j;    /* block scope 2, int i hides the outer int i*/
12:
13:      printf("Within the inner block:\n");
14:      for (i=0, j=10; i<=10; i++, j--)
15:         printf("i=%2d, j=%2d\n", i, j);
16:    }    /* the end of the inner block */
17:    printf("Within the outer block:  i=%d\n", i);
18:    return 0;
19: }
```

The following output is displayed on the screen after the executable (14L01.exe) of the program in Listing 14.1 is created and run:

OUTPUT
```
Within the outer block: i=32
Within the inner block:
i= 0, j=10
i= 1, j= 9
i= 2, j= 8
```

14

```
i= 3, j= 7
i= 4, j= 6
i= 5, j= 5
i= 6, j= 4
i= 7, j= 3
i= 8, j= 2
i= 9, j= 1
i=10, j= 0
Within the outer block: i=32
```

ANALYSIS The purpose of the program in Listing 14.1 is to show you the different scopes of variables in nested blocks. As you can see, there are two nested blocks in Listing 14.1. The integer variable i declared in line 6 is visible within the outer block enclosed by the braces ({ and }) in lines 5 and 19. Two other integer variables, i and j, are declared in line 11 and are visible only within the inner block from line 10 to line 16.

Although the integer variable i within the outer block has the same name as one of the integer variables within the inner block, the two integer variables cannot be accessed at the same time due to their different scopes.

To prove this, line 8 prints out the value, 32, contained by i within the outer block for the first time. Then, the for loop in lines 14 and 15 displays 10 pairs of values assigned to i and j within the inner block. At this point, there is no sign that the integer variable i within the outer block has any effects on the one within the inner block. When the inner block is exits, the variables within the inner block are no longer accessible. In other words, any attempt to access j from the outer block would be illegal.

Finally, the statement in line 17 prints out the value of i within the outer block again to find out whether the value has been changed due to the integer variable i within the inner block. The result shows that these two integer variables hide from each other, and no conflict occurs..

Function Scope

Function scope indicates that a variable is active and visible from the beginning to the end of a function.

In C, only a goto label has function scope. For example, the goto label, start, shown in the following code portion has function scope:

```
int main()
{
   int i;   /* block scope */
   .
   .
   .
   start:   /* A goto label has function scope */
```

```
   .
   .
   .
   goto  start;  /* the goto statement */
   .
   .
   .
   return 0;
}
```

Here the label start is visible from the beginning to the end of the main() function. Therefore, there should not be more than one label having the same name within the main() function.

Program Scope

A variable is said to have *program scope* when it is declared outside a function. For instance, look at the following code:

```
int x = 0;       /* program scope */
float y = 0.0;   /* program scope */
int main()
{
   int i;   /* block scope */
   .
   .
   .
   return 0;
}
```

Here the int variable x and the float variable y have program scope.

Variables with program scope are also called *global variables*, which are visible among all the source files that make up an executable program. Note that a global variable is declared with an initializer outside a function.

The program in Listing 14.2 demonstrates the relationship between variables with program scope and variables with block scope.

LISTING 14.2 The Relationship Between Program Scope and Block Scope

TYPE

```
1:   /* 14L02.c: Program scope vs block scope */
2:   #include <stdio.h>
3:
4:   int x = 1234;        /* program scope */
5:   double y = 1.234567; /* program scope */
```

14

continues

LISTING 14.2   continued

```
 6:
 7:  void function_1()
 8:  {
 9:     printf("From function_1:\n   x=%d, y=%f\n", x, y);
10: }
11:
12: main()
13: {
14:    int x = 4321;    /* block scope 1*/
15:
16:    function_1();
17:    printf("Within the main block:\n   x=%d, y=%f\n", x, y);
18:    /* a nested block */
19:    {
20:       double y = 7.654321;   /* block scope 2 */
21:       function_1();
22:       printf("Within the nested block:\n   x=%d, y=%f\n", x, y);
23:    }
24:    return 0;
25: }
```

I have the following output shown on the screen after the executable 14L02.exe is created and run on my machine:

OUTPUT

```
From function_1:
   x=1234, y=1.234567
Within the main block:
   x=4321, y=1.234567
From function_1:
   x=1234, y=1.234567
Within the nested block:
   x=4321, y=7.654321
```

ANALYSIS   As you can see in Listing 14.2, there are two global variables, x and y, with program scope; they are declared in lines 4 and 5.

In lines 7–10, a function, called function_1(), is declared. (More details about function declarations and prototypes are taught in the next hour.) The function_1() function contains only one statement; it prints out the values held by both x and y. Because there is no variable declaration made for x or y within the function block, the values of the global variables x and y are used for the statement inside the function. To prove this, function_1() is called twice in lines 16 and 21, respectively, from two nested blocks. The output shows that the values of the two global variables x and y are passed to printf() within the function_1() function body.

Then, line 14 declares another integer variable, x, with block scope, which can replace the global variable x within the block of the main() function. The result made by the statement in line 17 shows that the value of x is the value of the local variable x with block scope, whereas the value of y is still that of the global variable y.

There is a nested block in lines 19 and 23, within which another double variable y, with block scope, is declared and initialized. Like the variable x within the main() block, this variable, y, within the nested block replaces the global variable y. The statement in line 22 displays the values of the local variables x and y on the screen

> Because a global variable is visible among different source files of a program, using global variables increases your program's complexity, which in turn makes your program hard to maintain or debug. Generally, it's not recommended that you declare and use global variables, unless it's absolutely necessary. For instance, you can declare a global variable whose value is used (but never changed) by several subroutines in your program. (In Hour 23, "Compiling Programs: The C Preprocessor," you'll learn to use the #define directive to define constants that are used in many places in a program.)

Before I introduce file scope, let me first talk about the storage class specifiers.

The Storage Class Specifiers

In C, the *storage class* of a variable refers to the combination of its spatial and temporal regions.

You've learned about scope, which specifies the spatial region of a variable. Now, let's focus on *duration*, which indicates the temporal region of a variable.

There are four specifiers and two modifiers that can be used to indicate the duration of a variable. These specifiers and modifiers are introduced in the following sections.

The auto Specifier

The auto specifier is used to indicate that the memory location of a variable is temporary. In other words, a variable's reserved space in the memory can be erased or relocated when the variable is out of its scope.

Only variables with block scope can be declared with the auto specifier. The auto keyword is rarely used in practice, however, because the duration of a variable with block scope is temporary by default.

14

The static Specifier

The static specifier, on the other hand, can be applied to variables with either block scope or program scope. When a variable within a function is declared with the static specifier, the variable has a permanent duration. In other words, the memory storage allocated for the variable is not destroyed when the scope of the variable is exited, the value of the variable is maintained outside the scope. If execution ever returns to the scope of the variable, the last value stored in the variable is still there.

For instance, in the following code portion:

```
int main()
{
   int i;         /* block scope and temporary duration */
   static int j;  /* block scope and permanent duration */
   .
   .
   return 0;
}
```

the integer variable i has temporary (auto) duration by default. But the other integer variable, j, has permanent duration due to the storage class specifier static.

The program in Listing 14.3 shows the effect of the static specifier on variables.

TYPE   **LISTING 14.3**   Using the static Specifier

```
 1:  /* 14L03.c: Using the static specifier */
 2:  #include <stdio.h>
 3:  /* the add_two function */
 4:  int add_two(int x, int y)
 5:  {
 6:     static int counter = 1;
 7:
 8:     printf("This is the function call of %d,\n", counter++);
 9:     return (x + y);
10:  }
11:  /* the main function */
12:  main()
13:  {
14:     int i, j;
15:
16:     for (i=0, j=5; i<5; i++, j--)
17:        printf("the addition of %d and %d is %d.\n\n",
18:               i, j, add_two(i, j));
19:     return 0;
20:  }
```

The following output is displayed on the screen after the executable (14L03.exe) is run:

OUTPUT

```
This is the function call of 1,
the addition of 0 and 5 is 5.

This is the function call of 2,
the addition of 1 and 4 is 5.

This is the function call of 3,
the addition of 2 and 3 is 5.

This is the function call of 4,
the addition of 3 and 2 is 5.

This is the function call of 5,
the addition of 4 and 1 is 5.
```

ANALYSIS The purpose of the program in Listing 14.3 is to call a function to add two integers and then print out the result returned by the function on the screen. The function is called several times. A counter is set to keep track of how many times the function has been called.

This function, called add_two(), is declared in lines 4–10. There are two int arguments, x and y, that are passed to the function, and the addition of the two arguments is returned in line 9. Note that there is an integer variable, counter, which is declared with the static specifier in line 6. Values stored by counter are retained because the duration of the variable is permanent. In other words, although the scope of counter is within the block of the add_two() function, the memory location of counter and value saved in the location are not changed after the add_two() function is called and the execution control is returned back to the main() function. Note that the initialization of counter to 1 only takes place the first time add_two() is called; after that, it retains its previous value each time the function is called.

Therefore, the counter variable is used as a counter to keep track of the number of calls received by the add_two() function. In fact, the printf() function in line 8 prints out the value saved by the counter variable each time the add_two() function is called. In addition, counter is incremented by one each time after the printf() function is executed.

The for loop, declared in lines 16–18 within the main() function, calls the add_two() function five times. The values of the two integer variables, i and j, are passed to the add_two() function where they are added. Then, the return value from the add_two() function is displayed on the screen by the printf() call in lines 17 and 18.

From the output, you can see that the value saved by counter is indeed incremented by one each time the add_two() function is called, and is retained after the function exits because the integer variable counter is declared with static. You can see that counter is only initialized to 1 once, when the add_two() function is called for the first time.

14

File Scope and the Hierarchy of Scopes

In the first part of this hour, I mentioned three of the four types of scopes: block scope, function scope, and program scope. It's time now to introduce the fourth scope—*file scope.*

In C, a global variable declared with the `static` specifier is said to have file scope. A variable with file scope is visible from its declaration point to the end of the file. Here the file refers to the program file that contains the source code. Most large programs consist of several program files.

The following portion of source code shows variables with file scope:

```
int x = 0;              /* program scope */
static int y = 0;       /* file scope */
static float z = 0.0;   /* file scope */
int main()
{
   int i;   /* block scope */
   .
   .
   .
   return 0;
}
```

Here the `int` variable y and the `float` variable z both have file scope.

Figure 14.1 shows the hierarchy of the four scopes. As you can see, a variable with block scope is the most limited and is not visible outside the block within which the variable is declared. On the other hand, a variable with program scope is visible within all files, functions, and other blocks that make up the program.

FIGURE 14.1

The hierarchy of the four scopes.

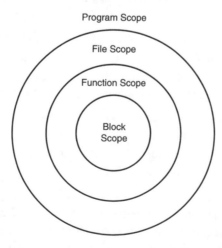

Program Scope

File Scope

Function Scope

Block Scope

The register Specifier

The word *register* is borrowed from computer hardware terminology. Each computer has a certain number of registers to hold data and perform arithmetic or logical calculations. Because registers are located within the CPU (central processing unit) chip, it's much quicker to access a register than a memory location which resides outside the chip. Therefore, storing variables in registers might help to speed up your program.

The C language provides you with the register specifier. You can apply this specifier to variables when you think it's necessary to put the variables into the computer registers.

However, the register specifier only gives the compiler a suggestion. In other words, a variable specified by the register keyword is not guaranteed to be stored in a register. The compiler can ignore the suggestion if there is no register available, or if some other restrictions apply.

It's illegal to take the address of a variable that is declared with the register specifier because the variable is intended to be stored in a register, not in memory. A CPU register does not have a memory address that you can access.

In the following portion of code, the integer variable i is declared with the register specifier:

```
int main()
{
   /* block scope with the register specifier */
   register int i;
   . . .
   for (i=0; i<MAX_NUM; i++){
      /* some statements */
   }
   . . .
   return 0;
}
```

The declaration of i suggests that the compiler stores the variable in a register. Because i is intensively used in the for loop, storing i in a register might increase the speed of the code shown here.

The extern Specifier

As introduced in the section titled "Program Scope," earlier in this hour, a variable with program scope is visible through all source files that make up an executable program. A variable with program scope is also called a *global variable*.

Here is a question: How can a global variable declared in file A be seen in file B? In other words, how does the compiler know that the variable used in file B is actually the same variable declared in file A?

14

The solution is to use the `extern` specifier provided by the C language to allude to a global variable defined elsewhere. In this case, you declare a global variable in file A, and then declare the variable again using the `extern` specifier in file B. This isn't a separate declaration, but specifies the original declaration in file A.

For instance, suppose you have two global `int` variables, y and z, that are defined in one file, and then, in another file, you might have the following declarations:

```
int x = 0;          /* a global variable */
extern int y;       /* an allusion to a global variable y */
int main()
{
   extern int z;   /* an allusion to a global variable z */
   int i;          /* a local variable */
   .
   .
   .
   return 0;
}
```

As you can see, there are two integer variables, y and z, that are declared with the `extern` specifier, both outside and inside the `main()` function, respectively. When the compiler sees the two declarations, it knows that the declarations are actually allusions to the global variables y and z that are defined elsewhere.

> To make your program portable across different computer platforms, you can apply the following rules in your program when you declare or allude to global variables:
>
> - You can ignore the `extern` specifier, but include an initializer, when you declare a global variable.
> - You should use the `extern` specifier (without an initializer) when you allude to a global variable defined elsewhere.

The Storage Class Modifiers

Besides the four storage class specifiers introduced in the previous sections, C also provides you with two storage class modifiers (or *qualifiers*, as they're sometimes called) that you can use to indicate to the C compiler how variables might be accessed.

The `const` Modifier

If you declare a variable with the `const` modifier, the content of the variable cannot be changed after it is initialized.

For instance, the following expression indicates to the compiler that `circle_ratio` is a variable whose value should not be changed:

```
const double circle_ratio = 3.141593;
```

Likewise, the value of the character array `str` declared in the following statement cannot be changed, either:

```
const char str[] = "A string constant";
```

Therefore, it's illegal to do something like this:

```
str[0] = 'a';   /* It's not allowed here. */
```

In addition, you can declare a pointer variable with the `const` modifier so that an object pointed to by the pointer cannot be changed. For example, consider the following pointer declaration with the `const` modifier:

```
char const *ptr_str = "A string constant";
```

After the initialization, you cannot change the content of the string pointed by the pointer `ptr_str`. For instance, the following statement is not allowed:

```
*ptr_str = 'a';      /* It's not allowed here. */
```

However, the `ptr_str` pointer itself can be assigned a different address of a string that is declared with `char const`.

The `volatile` Modifier

Sometimes, you want to declare a variable whose value can be changed without any explicit assignment statement in your program. This is especially true when you are dealing directly with hardware. For instance, you might declare a global variable that contains characters entered by the user. The address of the variable is passed to a device register that accepts characters from the keyboard. However, when the C compiler optimizes your program automatically, it intends to not update the value held by the variable unless the variable is on the left side of an assignment operator (=). In other words, the value of the variable is likely not changed even though the user is typing in characters from the keyboard.

To ask the compiler to turn off certain optimizations on a variable, you can declare the variable with the `volatile` specifier. For instance, in the following code portion, a variable, `keyboard_ch`, declared with the `volatile` specifier, tells the compiler not to optimize any expressions of the variable because the value saved by the variable might be changed without execution of any explicit assignment statement:

```
void read_keyboard()
{
```

14

```
    volatile char keyboard_ch;   /* a volatile variable */
    .
    .
    .
}
```

Summary

In this lesson you learned the following important concepts about scopes and storage classes in C:

- A variable declared within a block has block scope. Such a variable is also called a local variable and is only visible within the block.

- A goto label has function scope, which means that it is visible through the whole block of the function within which the label is placed. No two goto labels share the same name within a function block.

- A variable declared with the static specifier outside a function has file scope, which means that it is visible throughout the entire source file in which the variable is declared.

- A variable declared outside a function is said to have program scope. Such a variable is also called a global variable. A global variable is visible in all source files that make up an executable program.

- A variable with block scope has the most limited visibility. On the other hand, a variable with program scope is the most visible, and can be seen through all files, functions, and other blocks that make up the program.

- The storage class of a variable refers to the combination of its spatial and temporal regions (that is, its scope and duration.)

- By default, a variable with block scope has an auto duration, and its memory storage is temporary.

- A variable declared with the static specifier has permanent memory storage, even after the function in which the variable is declared has been called and the function scope has exited.

- A variable declared with the register specifier might be stored in a register to speed up the performance of a program; however, the compiler can ignore the specifier if there is no register available or if some other restrictions apply.

- You can also allude to a global variable defined elsewhere by using the extern specifier from the current source file.

- To make sure the value saved by a variable cannot be changed, you can declare the variable with the `const` modifier.
- If you want to let the compiler know that the value of a variable can be changed without an explicit assignment statement, declare the variable with the `volatile` modifier so that the compiler will turn off optimizations on expressions involving the variable.

In the next lesson you'll learn about function declarations and prototypes in C.

Q&A

Q Can a global variable be hidden by a local variable with block scope?

A Yes. If a local variable shares the same name with a global variable, the global variable can be hidden by the local variable for the scope of the block within which the local variable is defined with block scope. However, outside the block, the local variable cannot be seen, but the global variable becomes visible again.

Q Why do you need the `static` specifier?

A In many cases, the value of a variable is needed, even if the scope of the block, in which the variable is declared, has exited. By default, a variable with block scope has a temporary memory storage—that is, the lifetime of the variable starts when the block is executed and the variable is declared, and ends when the execution of that block is finished. Therefore, to declare a variable with permanent duration, you have to use the `static` specifier to indicate to the compiler that the memory location of the variable and the value stored in the memory location should be retained after the execution of the block.

Q Does using the `register` specifier guarantee to improve the performance of a program?

A Not really. Declaring a variable with the `register` specifier only suggests to the compiler that the variable should be stored in a register. But there is no guarantee that the variable *will* be stored in a register. The compiler can ignore the request based on the availability of registers or other restrictions.

Q When you declare a variable with the `extern` specifier, do you define the variable or allude to a global variable elsewhere?

A When a variable is declared with the `extern` specifier, the compiler considers the declaration of the variable as an allusion rather than a definition. The compiler will therefore look somewhere else to find a global variable to which the variable with `extern` alludes.

14

Workshop

To help solidify your understanding of this lesson, you are encouraged to answer the quiz questions and finish the exercises provided in the workshop before you move to the next lesson. The answers and hints to the questions and exercises are given in Appendix B, "Answers to Quiz Questions and Exercises."

Quiz

1. Given the following code portion, which variables are global variables, and which ones are local variables with block scope?

```
int x = 0;
float y = 0.0;
int myFunction()
{
    int i, j;
    float y;
    . . .
    {
        int x, y;
        . . .
    }
    . . .
}
```

2. When two variables with the same name are defined, how does the compiler know which one to use?

3. Identify the storage class of each declaration in the following code portion:

```
int i = 0;
static int x;
extern float y;
int myFunction()
{
    int i, j;
    extern float z;
    register long s;
    static int index;
    const char str[] = "Warning message.";
    . . .
}
```

4. Given the following declaration:

```
const char ch_str[] = "The const specifier";
```

is the ch_str[9] = '-'; statement legal?

Exercises

1. Given the following:

   - An `int` variable with block scope and temporary storage
   - A constant character variable with block scope
   - A `float` local variable with permanent storage
   - A register `int` variable
   - A `char` pointer initialized with a null character

   write declarations for all of them.

2. Rewrite the program in Listing 14.2. This time, pass the `int` variable x and the `float` variable y as arguments to the `function_1()` function. What do you get on your screen after running the program?

3. Compile and run the following program. What do you get on the screen, and why?

   ```c
   #include <stdio.h>
   int main()
   {
      int i;

      for (i=0; i<5; i++){
         int x = 0;
         static int y = 0;
         printf("x=%d, y=%d\n", x++, y++);
      }
      return 0;
   }
   ```

4. Rewrite the `add_two()` function in Listing 14.3 to print out the previous result of the addition, as well as the counter value.

14

PART IV

Functions and Dynamic Memory Allocation

Hour

HOUR 15

Working with Functions

Form follows function.

—L. H. Sullivan

In Hour 14, "Understanding Scope and Storage Classes," you might have noticed that a function definition is always given first, before the function is called from a `main()` function. In fact, you can put a function definition anywhere you want, as long as you put the function declaration before the first place where the function is called. You'll learn about many features of functions from the following topics covered in this lesson:

- Function declarations
- Prototyping
- Values returned from functions
- Arguments to functions
- Structured programming

In addition, several C library functions and macros, such as `time()`, `localtime()`, `asctime()`, `va_start()`, `va_arg()`, and `va_end()` are introduced in this hour.

Declaring Functions

As you know, you have to declare or define a variable before you can use it. This is also true for functions. In C, you have to declare or define a function before you can call it.

Declaration Versus Definition

According to the ANSI standard, the *declaration* of a variable or function specifies the interpretation and attributes of a set of identifiers. The *definition*, on the other hand, requires the C compiler to reserve storage for a variable or function named by an identifier.

A variable declaration is a definition, but a function declaration is not. A function declaration alludes to a function that is defined elsewhere and specifies what kind of value is returned by the function. A function definition defines what the function does, as well as gives the number and type of arguments passed to the function.

A function declaration is not a function definition. If a function definition is placed in your source file before the function is first called, you don't need to make the function declaration. Otherwise, the declaration of a function must be made before the function is invoked.

For example, I've used the printf() function in almost every sample program in this book. Each time, I had to include a header file, stdio.h, because the header file contains the declaration of printf(), which indicates to the compiler the return type and prototype of the function. The definition of the printf() function is placed somewhere else. In C, the definition of this function is saved in a library file that is invoked during the linking states.

Specifying Return Types

A function can be declared to return any data type, except an array or function. The return statement used in a function definition returns a single value whose type should match the one declared in the function declaration.

By default, the return type of a function is int, if no explicit data type is specified for the function. A data type specifier is placed prior to the name of a function like this:

```
data_type_specifier  function_name();
```

Here data_type_specifier specifies the data type that the function should return. function_name is the function name that should follow the rules of naming identifiers in C.

In fact, this declaration form represents the traditional function declaration form before the ANSI standard was created. After setting up the ANSI standard, the function prototype is added to the function declaration.

15

Using Prototypes

Before the ANSI standard was created, a function declaration only included the return type of the function. With the ANSI standard, the number and types of arguments passed to a function can be added into the function declaration. The number and types of an argument are called the *function prototype*.

The general form of a function declaration, including its prototype, is as follows:

```
data_type_specifier  function_name(
    data_type_specifier argument_name1,
    data_type_specifier argument_name2,
    data_type_specifier argument_name3,
    .
    .
    .
    data_type_specifier argument_nameN,
);
```

The purpose of using a function prototype is to help the compiler check whether the data types of arguments passed to a function match what the function expects. The compiler issues an error message if the data types do not match.

Although argument names, such as *argument_name1*, *argument_name2*, and so on, are optional, it is recommended that you include them so that the compiler can identify any mismatches of argument names.

Making Function Calls

As shown in Figure 15.1, when a function call is made, the program execution jumps to the function and finishes the task assigned to the function. Then the program execution resumes after the called function returns.

A *function call* is an expression that can be used as a single statement or within other statements.

Listing 15.1 gives an example of declaring and defining functions, as well as making function calls.

TYPE   **LISTING 15.1** Calling Functions After They Are Declared and Defined

```
1:  /* 15L01.c: Making function calls */
2:  #include <stdio.h>
3:
4:  int function_1(int x, int y);
5:  double function_2(double x, double y)
6:  {
7:     printf("Within function_2.\n");
```

continues

LISTING 15.1   continued

```
8:     return (x - y);
9: }
10:
11: main()
12: {
13:    int x1 = 80;
14:    int y1 = 10;
15:    double x2 = 100.123456;
16:    double y2 = 10.123456;
17:
18:    printf("Pass function_1  %d and %d.\n", x1, y1);
19:    printf("function_1 returns %d.\n", function_1(x1, y1));
20:    printf("Pass function_2  %f and %f.\n", x2, y2);
21:    printf("function_2 returns %f.\n", function_2(x2, y2));
22:    return 0;
23: }
24: /* function_1() definition */
25: int function_1(int x, int y)
26: {
27:    printf("Within function_1.\n");
28:    return (x + y);
29: }
```

FIGURE 15.1

Program execution jumps to an invoked function when a function call is made.

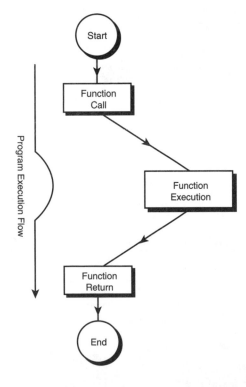

15

The following output is displayed after the executable (15L01.exe) of the program in Listing 15.1 is created and run:

OUTPUT

```
Pass function_1  80 and 10.
Within function_1.
function_1 returns 90.
Pass function_2  100.123456. and 10.123456.
Within function_2.
function_2 returns 90.000000.
```

ANALYSIS The purpose of the program in Listing 15.1 is to show you how to declare and define functions. The statement in line 4 is a function declaration with a prototype. The declaration alludes to the function_1 defined later in Listing 15.1. The return type of function_1 is int, and the function prototype includes two int variables, called x and y.

In lines 5–9, the second function, function_2, is defined before it is called. As you can see, the return type of function_2 is double, and two double variables are passed to the function. Note that the names of the two variables are also x and y. Don't worry because function_1 and function_2 share the same argument names. There is no conflict because these arguments are in different function blocks and arguments to functions have block scope.

Then, in the main() function defined in lines 11–23, two int variables, x1 and y1, and two double variables, x2 and y2, are declared and initialized in lines 13–16, respectively. The statement in line 18 shows the values of x1 and y1 that are passed to the function_1 function. Line 19 calls function_1 and displays the return value from function_1.

Likewise, lines 20 and 21 print out the values of x2 and y2 that are passed to function_2, as well as the value returned by function_2 after the function is called and executed.

Lines 25–29 contain the definition of the function_1 function, specifying that the function can perform an addition of two integer variables (see line 28) and print out the string of Within function_1. in line 27.

Prototyping Functions

In the following subsections, you're going to study three cases regarding arguments passed to functions. The first case is that functions take no argument; the second one is that functions take a fixed number of arguments; the third case is that functions take a variable number of arguments.

Functions with No Arguments

The first case is a function that takes no argument. For instance, the C library function getchar() does not need any arguments. It can be used in a program like this:

```
int c;
c = getchar();
```

As you can see, the second statement is left blank between the parentheses ((and)) when the function is called.

In C, the declaration of the getchar() function can be something like this:

```
int getchar(void);
```

Note that the keyword void is used in the declaration to indicate to the compiler that no argument is needed by this function. The compiler will issue an error message if there is any argument passed to getchar() later in a program when this function is called.

Therefore, for a function with no argument, the void data type is used as the prototype in the function declaration.

The program in Listing 5.2 shows another example of using void in function declarations.

TYPE   **LISTING 15.2**   Using void in Function Declarations

```
 1:  /* 15L02.c: Functions with no arguments */
 2:  #include <stdio.h>
 3:  #include <time.h>
 4:
 5:  void GetDateTime(void);
 6:
 7:  main()
 8:  {
 9:     printf("Before the GetDateTime() function is called.\n");
10:     GetDateTime();
11:     printf("After the GetDateTime() function is called.\n");
12:     return 0;
13:  }
14:  /* GetDateTime() definition */
15:  void GetDateTime(void)
16:  {
17:     time_t now;
18:
19:     printf("Within GetDateTime().\n");
20:     time(&now);
21:     printf("Current date and time is: %s\n",
22:        asctime(localtime(&now)));
23:  }
```

15

I obtain the following output after I run the executable file, 15L02.exe, of the program in
Listing 15.2:

OUTPUT

```
Before the GetDateTime() function is called.
Within GetDateTime().
Current date and time is: Sat Apr 05 11:50:10 1997

After the GetDateTime() function is called.
```

ANALYSIS   The purpose of the program in Listing 15.2 is to show you how .to declare and
call a function without passing arguments. The program prints out the current
date and time on your computer by calling the function GetDateTime(), declared in line
5. Because no argument needs to be passed to the function, the void data type is used as
the prototype in the declaration of GetDateTime().

Additionally, another void keyword is used in front of the name of the GetDateTime()
function to indicate that this function does return any value either (see line 5.)

The statements in lines 9 and 11 print out messages both before and after the
GetDateTime() function is called from within the main() function.

In line 10, the function is called by the statement GetDateTime();. Note that no argument should be passed to this function because the function prototype is void.

The definition of GetDateTime() is in lines 15–23; it obtains the calendar time and converts it into a character string by calling several C library functions: time(), local-
time(), and asctime(). Then, the character string containing the current date and time is
printed out on the screen by the printf() function with the format specifier %s. As you
can see, the output on my screen shows that at the moment the executable file 15L02.exe
is being executed, the date and time are

```
Sat Apr 05 11:50:10 1997
```

time(), localtime(), and asctime() are date and time functions provided by the C language. These functions are discussed in the following subsection. You might notice that
the header file time.h is included at the beginning of the program in Listing 15.2 before
these time functions can be used.

Using time(), localtime(), and asctime()

There is a group of C functions known as *date and time functions*. The declarations of all
date and time functions are included in the header file time.h. These functions can give
three types of date and time:

- Calendar time
- Local time
- Daylight savings time

Here *calendar time* gives the current date and time based on the Gregorian calendar. *Local time* represents the calendar time in a specific time zone. *Daylight savings time* is the local time under the daylight savings rule.

In this section, three date and time functions—time(), localtime(), and asctime()—are briefly introduced.

The time() function returns the calendar time.

The syntax for the time() function is

```
#include <time.h>
time_t time(time_t *timer);
```

Here *time_t* is the arithmetic type that is used to represent time. *timer* is a pointer variable pointing to a memory storage that can hold the calendar time returned by this function. The time() function returns -1 if the calendar time is not available on the computer.

The localtime() function returns the local time converted from the calendar time.

The syntax for the localtime() function is

```
#include <time.h>
struct tm *localtime(const time_t *timer);
```

Here tm is a structure that contains the components of the calendar time. struct is the keyword for structure, which is another data type in C. (The concept of structures is introduced in Hour 19, "Understanding Structures.") *timer* is a pointer variable pointing to a memory storage that holds the calendar time returned by the time() function.

To convert the date and time represented by the structure tm, you can call the asctime() function..

The syntax for the asctime() function is

```
#include <time.h>
char *asctime(const struct tm *timeptr);
```

Here *timeptr* is a pointer referencing the structure *tm* returned by date and time functions like localtime(). The asctime() function converts the date and time represented by *tm* into a character string..

As shown in Listing 15.2, the statement in line 17 declares a time_t variable called now. Line 20 stores the calendar time in the memory location referenced by the now variable. Note that the argument passed to the time() function should be the left value of a variable; therefore, the address-of operator (&) is used prior to now. Then, the expression in line 22, `asctime(localtime(&now))`, obtains the local time expression of the calendar time by calling `localtime()`, and converts the local time into a character string with help from `asctime()`. The character string representing the date and time is then printed out by the `printf()` call in lines 21 and 22, which has the following format:

```
Sat Apr 05 11:50:10 1997\n\0
```

Note that there is a newline character appended right before the null character in the character string that is converted and returned by the `asctime()` function..

Functions with a Fixed Number of Arguments

You have actually seen several examples that declare and call functions with a fixed number of arguments. For instance, in Listing 15.1, the declaration of the `function_1()` function in line 4

```
int function_1(int x, int y);
```

contains the prototype of two arguments, x and y.

To declare a function with a fixed number of arguments, you need to specify the data type of each argument. Also, it's recommended to indicate the argument names so that the compiler can check to make sure that the argument types and names declared in a function declaration match with the implementation in the function definition.

Prototyping a Variable Number of Arguments

As you may remember, the syntax of the `printf()` function is

```
int printf(const char *format[, argument, ...]);
```

Here the ellipsis token ... (that is, three dots) represents a variable number of arguments. In other words, besides the first argument that is a character string, the `printf()` function can take an unspecified number of additional arguments, as many as the compiler allows. The brackets (`[` and `]`) indicate that the unspecified arguments are optional.

The following is a general form to declare a function with a variable number of arguments:

```
data_type_specifier  function_name(
     data_type_specifier argument_name1, ...
);
```

Note that the first argument name is followed by the ellipsis (`...`) that represents the rest of unspecified arguments.

For instance, the declaration of the `printf()` function would look something like this:

```
int printf(const char *format, ...);
```

Processing Variable Arguments

There are three routines declared in the header file `stdarg.h` that enable you to write functions that take a variable number of arguments. They are `va_start()`, `va_arg()`, and `va_end()`.

Also included in `stdarg.h` is a data type, `va_list`, which defines an array type suitable for containing data items needed by `va_start()`, `va_arg()`, and `va_end()`.

To initialize a given array that is needed by `va_arg()` and `va_end()`, you have to use the `va_start()` macro routine before any arguments are processed.

The syntax for the `va_start()` macro is

```
#include <stdarg.h>
void va_start(va_list ap, lastfix);
```

Here *ap* is the name of the array that is about to be initialized by the `va_start()` macro routine. *lastfix* should be the argument before the ellipsis (...) in the function declaration.

By using the `va_arg()` macro, you're able to deal with an expression that has the type and value of the next argument. In other words, the `va_arg()` macro can be used to get the next argument passed to the function.

The syntax for the `va_arg()` macro is

```
#include <stdarg.h>
type va_arg(va_list ap, data_type);
```

Here *ap* is the name of the array that is initialized by the `va_start()` macro routine. *data_type* is the data type of the argument passed to function.

To facilitate a normal return from your function, you have to use the `va_end()` function in your program after all arguments have been processed.

The syntax for the `va_end()` function is

```
#include <stdarg.h>
void va_end(va_list ap);
```

Here *ap* is the name of the array that is initialized by the `va_start()` macro routine.

Remember to include the header file `stdarg.h` in your program before you call `va_start()`, `va_arg()`, or `va_end()`.

15

Listing 5.3 demonstrates how to use va_start(), va_arg(), and va_end() in a function that takes a variable number of arguments.

TYPE   **LISTING 15.3**   Processing Variable Arguments

```
1:  /* 15L03.c: Processing variable arguments */
2:  #include <stdio.h>
3:  #include <stdarg.h>
4:
5:  double AddDouble(int x, ...);
6:
7:  main ()
8:  {
9:     double d1 = 1.5;
10:    double d2 = 2.5;
11:    double d3 = 3.5;
12:    double d4 = 4.5;
13:
14:    printf("Given an argument: %2.1f\n", d1);
15:    printf("The result returned by AddDouble() is: %2.1f\n\n",
16:       AddDouble(1, d1));
17:    printf("Given arguments: %2.1f and %2.1f\n", d1, d2);
18:    printf("The result returned by AddDouble() is: %2.1f\n\n",
19:       AddDouble(2, d1, d2));
20:    printf("Given arguments: %2.1f, %2.1f and %2.1f\n", d1, d2, d3);
21:    printf("The result returned by AddDouble() is: %2.1f\n\n",
22:       AddDouble(3, d1, d2, d3));
23:    printf("Given arguments: %2.1f, %2.1f, %2.1f, and %2.1f\n",
24:          d1, d2, d3, d4);
25:    printf("The result returned by AddDouble() is: %2.1f\n",
26:       AddDouble(4, d1, d2, d3, d4));
27:    return 0;
28: }
29: /* definition of AddDouble() */
30: double AddDouble(int x, ...)
31: {
32:    va_list   arglist;
33:    int i;
34:    double result = 0.0;
35:
36:    printf("The number of arguments is: %d\n", x);
37:    va_start (arglist, x);
38:    for (i=0; i<x; i++)
39:       result += va_arg(arglist, double);
40:    va_end (arglist);
41:    return result;
42: }
```

The following output is displayed on the screen after the executable file, 15L03.exe, is run:

OUTPUT

```
Given an argument: 1.5
The number of arguments is: 1
The result returned by AddDouble() is: 1.5

Given arguments: 1.5 and 2.5
The number of arguments is: 2
The result returned by AddDouble() is: 4.0

Given arguments: 1.5, 2.5, and 3.5
The number of arguments is: 3
The result returned by AddDouble() is: 7.5

Given arguments: 1.5, 2.5, 3.5, and 4.5
The number of arguments is: 4
The result returned by AddDouble() is: 12.0
```

ANALYSIS
The program in Listing 15.3 contains a function that can take a variable number of double arguments, perform the operation of addition on these arguments, and then return the result to the main() function.

The declaration in line 5 indicates to the compiler that the AddDouble() function takes a variable number of arguments. The first argument to AddDouble() is an integer variable that holds the number of the rest of the arguments passed to the function each time AddDouble() is called. In other words, the first argument indicates the number of remaining arguments to be processed.

The definition of AddDouble() is given in lines 29–41, in which a va_list array, arglist, is declared in line 31. As mentioned, the va_start() macro has to be called before the arguments are processed. Thus, line 36 invokes va_start() to initialize the array arglist. The for loop in lines 37 and 38 fetches the next double argument saved in the array arglist by calling va_arg(). Then, each argument is added into a local double variable called result.

The va_end() function is called in line 39 after all arguments saved in arglist have been fetched and processed. Then, the value of result is returned back to the caller of the AddDouble() function, which is the main() function in this case.

The va_end() function must be called in a C program to end variable argument processing. Otherwise, the behavior of the program is undefined.

As you can see, within the main() function, AddDouble() is called four times, with a different number of arguments each time. These arguments passed to AddDouble() are displayed by the printf() calls in lines 14, 17, 20, and 23. Also, the four different results returned by AddDouble() are printed out on the screen.

Learning Structured Programming

Now you've learned the basics of function declaration and definition. Before we go to the next hour, let's talk a little bit about *structured programming* in program design.

Structured programming is one of the best programming methodologies. Basically, there are two types of structured programming: top-down programming and bottom-up programming.

When you start to write a program to solve a problem, one way to do it is to work on the smallest pieces of the problem. First, you define and write functions for each piece. After each function is written and tested, you begin to put them together to build a program that can solve the problem. This approach is normally called *bottom-up programming*.

On the other hand, to solve a problem, you can first work out an outline and start your programming at a higher level. For instance, you can work on the main() function at the beginning, and then move to the next lower level until the lowest-level functions are written. This type of approach is called *top-down programming*.

You'll find that it's useful to combine these two types of structured programming and use them alternately in order to solve real problems.

Summary

In this lesson you learned the following important concepts about functions in C:

- A function declaration alludes to a function that is defined elsewhere, and specifies what type of arguments and values are passed to and returned from the function as well.

- A function definition reserves the memory space and defines what the function does, as well as the number and type of arguments passed to the function.

- A function can be declared to return any data type, except an array or a function.

- The return statement used in a function definition returns a single value whose type must be matched with the one declared in the function declaration.

- A function call is an expression that can be used as a single statement or within other expressions or statements.

- The void data type is needed in the declaration of a function that takes no argument.

- To declare a function that takes a variable number of arguments, you have to specify at least the first argument, and use the ellipsis (. . .) to represent the rest of the arguments passed to the function.

15

- `va_start()`, `va_arg()`, and `va_end()`, all included in `stdarg.h`, are needed in processing a variable number of arguments passed to a function.
- `time()`, `localtime()`, and `asctime()` are three time functions provided by C. They can be used together to obtain a character string that contains information about the local date and time based on the calendar time.

In the next lesson you'll learn more about pointers and their applications in C.

Q&A

Q What is the main difference between a function declaration and a function definition?

A The main difference between a function declaration and a function definition is that the former does not reserve any memory space, nor does it specify what a function does. A function declaration only alludes to a function definition that is placed elsewhere. It also specifies what type of arguments and values are passed to and returned from the function. A function definition, on the other hand, reserves the memory space and specifies tasks the function can complete.

Q Why do we need function prototypes?

A By declaring a function with prototypes, you specify not only the data type returned by the function, but also the types and names of arguments passed to the function. With the help of a function prototype, the compiler can automatically perform type checking on the definition of the function, which saves you time in debugging the program.

Q Can a function return a pointer?

A Yes. In fact, a function can return a single value that can be any data type except an array or a function. A pointer value—that is, the address—returned by a function can refer to a character array, or a memory location that stores other types of data. For instance, the C library function `asctime()` returns a character pointer that points to a character string converted from a date-time structure.

Q Can you use top-down programming and bottom-up programming together to solve a problem?

A Yes. In practice, you can find that it's actually a good idea to combine the top-down and bottom-up programming approaches together to solve problems. Using the two types of structured programming can make your program easy to write and understand.

Workshop

To help solidify your understanding of this hour's lesson, you are encouraged to answer the quiz questions and finish the exercises provided in the workshop before you move to the next lesson. The answers and hints to the questions and exercises are given in Appendix B, "Answers to Quiz Questions and Exercises."

Quiz

1. Given the following function declarations, which ones are functions with fixed number of arguments, which ones are functions with no arguments, and which ones are functions with a variable number of arguments?

   - `int function_1(int x, float y);`

   - `void function_2(char *str);`

   - `char *asctime(const struct tm *timeptr);`

   - `int function_3(void);`

   - `char function_4(char c, ...);`

   - `void function_5(void);`

2. Which one in the following two expressions is a function definition?
   ```
   int function_1(int x, int y);
   int function_2(int x, int y){return x+y;}
   ```

3. What is the data type returned by a function when a type specifier is omitted?

4. In the following function declarations, which ones are illegal?

   - `double function_1(int x, ...);`

   - `void function_2(int x, int y, ...);`

   - `char function_3(...);`

   - `int function_4(int, int, int, int);`

Exercises

1. Rewrite the program in Listing 15.2. This time use the format specifier %c, instead of %s, to print out the character string of the local time on your computer.

2. Declare and define a function, called MultiTwo(), that can perform multiplication on two integer variables. Call the MultiTwo() function from the main() function and pass two integers to MultiTwo(). Then print out the result returned by the MultiTwo() function on the screen.

3. Rewrite the program in Listing 15.3. This time, make a function that takes a variable number of `int` arguments and performs the operation of multiplication on these arguments.

4. Rewrite the program in Listing 15.3 again. This time, print out all arguments passed to the `AddDouble()` function. Does `va_arg()` fetch each argument in the same order (that is, from left to right) of the argument list passed to `AddDouble()`?

Hour **16**

Applying Pointers

Think twice and do once.

—Chinese proverb

In Hour 11, "Understanding Pointers," you learned the basics of using pointers in C. Because pointers are very useful in programming, it's worth spending another hour to learn more about them. In this lesson, the following topics are discussed:

- Pointer arithmetic
- Passing arrays to functions
- Passing pointers to functions
- Pointing to functions

Pointer Arithmetic

In C, you can move the position of a pointer by adding or subtracting integers to or from the pointer. For example, given a character pointer variable `ptr_str`, the following expression:

```
ptr_str + 1
```

moves the pointer to the memory location that is one byte away from the current position of `ptr_str`.

Note that for pointers of different data types, the integers added to or subtracted from the pointers have different sizes. In other words, adding (or, subtracting) 1 to a pointer is not necessarily instructing the compiler to add (or subtract) one byte to the address, but rather to adjust the address so that it skips over one element of the type of the pointer. You'll see more details in the following sections.

The Scalar Size of Pointers

The general format to change the position of a pointer is

pointer_name + n

Here *n* is an integer whose value can be either positive or negative. *pointer_name* is the name of a pointer variable that has the following declaration:

*data_type_specifier *pointer_name*;

When the C compiler reads the expression *pointer_name + n*, it interprets it as

*pointer_name + n * sizeof(data_type_specifier)*

Note that the `sizeof` operator is used to obtain the number of bytes of the specified data type. Therefore, for the `char` pointer variable `ptr_str`, the expression `ptr_str + 1` actually means

`ptr_str + 1 * sizeof(char)`.

Because the size of a character is one byte long, `ptr_str + 1` tells the compiler to move to the memory location that is 1 byte after the current location referenced by the pointer.

The program in Listing 16.1 shows how the scalar sizes of different data types affect the offsets added to or subtracted from pointers.

TYPE   **LISTING 16.1**   Moving Pointers of Different Data Types

```
1:  /* 16L01.c: Pointer arithmetic */
2:  #include <stdio.h>
3:
4:  main()
5:  {
6:     char *ptr_ch;
7:     int *ptr_int;
8:     double *ptr_db;
9:     /* char pointer ptr_ch */
10:    printf("Current position of ptr_ch: %p\n", ptr_ch);
```

```
11:     printf("The position after ptr_ch + 1: %p\n", ptr_ch + 1);
12:     printf("The position after ptr_ch + 2: %p\n", ptr_ch + 2);
13:     printf("The position after ptr_ch - 1: %p\n", ptr_ch - 1);
14:     printf("The position after ptr_ch - 2: %p\n", ptr_ch - 2);
15:     /* int pointer ptr_int */
16:     printf("Current position of ptr_int: %p\n", ptr_int);
17:     printf("The position after ptr_int + 1: %p\n", ptr_int + 1);
18:     printf("The position after ptr_int + 2: %p\n", ptr_int + 2);
19:     printf("The position after ptr_int - 1: %p\n", ptr_int - 1);
20:     printf("The position after ptr_int - 2: %p\n", ptr_int - 2);
21:     /* double pointer ptr_ch */
22:     printf("Current position of ptr_db: %p\n", ptr_db);
23:     printf("The position after ptr_db + 1: %p\n", ptr_db + 1);
24:     printf("The position after ptr_db + 2: %p\n", ptr_db + 2);
25:     printf("The position after ptr_db - 1: %p\n", ptr_db - 1);
26:     printf("The position after ptr_db - 2: %p\n", ptr_db - 2);
27:
28:     return 0;
29: }
```

The following output is obtained by running the executable file 16L01.exe of the program in Listing 16.1 on my machine. You might get different addresses on your computer, as well as different offsets depending on the sizes of the data types on your system:

OUTPUT

```
Current position of ptr_ch: 0x000B
The position after ptr_ch + 1: 0x000C
The position after ptr_ch + 2: 0x000D
The position after ptr_ch - 1: 0x000A
The position after ptr_ch - 2: 0x0009
Current position of ptr_int: 0x028B
The position after ptr_int + 1: 0x028D
The position after ptr_int + 2: 0x028F
The position after ptr_int - 1: 0x0289
The position after ptr_int - 2: 0x0287
Current position of ptr_db: 0x0128
The position after ptr_db + 1: 0x0130
The position after ptr_db + 2: 0x0138
The position after ptr_db - 1: 0x0120
The position after ptr_db - 2: 0x0118
```

ANALYSIS

As you can see in Listing 16.1, there are three pointers of different types—ptr_ch, ptr_int, and ptr_db—declared in lines 6–8. Among them, ptr_ch is a pointer to a character, ptr_int is a pointer to an integer, and ptr_db is a pointer to a double.

Then the statement in line 10 shows the memory address, 0x000B, contained by the char pointer variable ptr_ch. Lines 11 and 12 display the two addresses, 0x000C and 0x000D, when ptr_ch is added with 1 and 2, respectively. Similarly, lines 13 and 14 give 0x000A and `0x0009` when `ptr_ch` is moved down to lower memory addresses. Because the size of `char` is 1 byte, `ptr_ch+1` means to move to the memory location that is 1 byte higher than the current memory location, `0x000B`, referenced by the pointer `ptr_ch`.

Line 16 shows the memory location referenced by the `int` pointer variable `ptr_int` at `0x028B`. Because the size of `int` is 2 bytes long on my system, the expression `ptr_int+1` moves `ptr_int` to the memory location that is 2 bytes higher than the current one pointed to by `ptr_int`. That's exactly the result you see in line 17. Likewise, line 18 shows that `ptr_int+2` moves the reference to `0x028F`, which is 4 bytes higher (`2*sizeof(int)`) than `0x028B`. The memory location `0x0289` is referenced by the expression `ptr_int-1` in line 19; `0x0287` is referenced by `ptr_int-2` in line 20.

The size of the `double` data type is 8 bytes long on my system. Therefore, the expression `ptr_db+1` is interpreted as the memory address referenced by `ptr_db` plus 8 bytes—that is, `0x0128+8`, which gives `0x0130` in hex format ,as you can see in line 23.

Lines 24–26 print out the memory addresses referenced by `ptr_db+2`, `ptr_db-1`, and `ptr_db-2`, respectively, which prove that the compiler has used the same scalar size of `double` in the pointer arithmetic.

Pointers are very useful when used properly. However, a pointer can get you into trouble quickly if it contains the wrong value. A common error, for instance, is to assign a right value to a pointer that actually expects a left one. Fortunately, many C compilers will find such errors and issue a warning message.

There is another common error that the compiler does not always pick up for you: using uninitialized pointers. For example, the following code has a potential problem:

```
int x, *ptr_int;
x = 8;
*ptr_int = x;
```

The problem is that the `ptr_int` pointer is not initialized; it points to some unknown memory location. Therefore, assigning a value, like 8 in this case, to an unknown memory location is dangerous. It may overwrite some important data that are already saved at the memory location, thus causing a serious problem. The solution is to make sure that a pointer is pointing at a legal and valid memory location before it is used.

You can rewrite the above code to avoid the potential problem like this:

```
int x, *ptr_int;
x = 8;
ptr_int = &x;    /* initialize the pointer */
```

Pointer Subtraction

You can subtract one pointer value from the other to obtain the distance between the two memory locations. For instance, given two char pointer variables, ptr_str1 and ptr_str2, you can calculate the offset between the two memory locations pointed to by the two pointers like this:

ptr_str2 - ptr_str1

To get meaningful results, it is best to only subtract pointers of the same data type.

Listing 16.2 shows an example of performing subtraction on an int pointer variable.

TYPE   **LISTING 16.2**   Performing Subtraction on Pointers

```
1:  /* 16L02.c: Pointer subtraction */
2:  #include <stdio.h>
3:
4:  main()
5:  {
6:     int *ptr_int1, *ptr_int2;
7:
8:     printf("The position of ptr_int1: %p\n", ptr_int1);
9:     ptr_int2 = ptr_int1 + 5;
10:    printf("The position of ptr_int2 = ptr_int1 + 5: %p\n", ptr_int2);
11:    printf("The subtraction of ptr_int2 - ptr_int1: %d\n", ptr_int2 -
ptr_int1);
12:    ptr_int2 = ptr_int1 - 5;
13:    printf("The position of ptr_int2 = ptr_int1 - 5: %p\n", ptr_int2);
14:    printf("The subtraction of ptr_int2 - ptr_int1: %d\n", ptr_int2 -
ptr_int1);
15:
16:    return 0;
17: }
```

After running the executable (16L02.exe) of the program in Listing 16.2 on my machine, I have the following output shown on the screen:

OUTPUT
```
The position of ptr_int1: 0x0128
The position of ptr_int2 = ptr_int1 + 5: 0x0132
The subtraction of ptr_int2 - ptr_int1: 5
The position of ptr_int2 = ptr_int1 - 5: 0x011E
The subtraction of ptr_int2 - ptr_int1: -5
```

ANALYSIS   The program in Listing 16.2 declares two int pointer variables, ptr_int1 and ptr_int2, in line 6. The statement in line 8 prints out the memory position held by ptr_int1. Line 9 assigns the memory address referenced by ptr_int1+5 to ptr_int2. Then, the content of ptr_int2 is printed out in line 10.

The statement in line 11 shows the difference between the two int pointers—that is, the subtraction of ptr_int2 and ptr_int1. The result is 5.

Line 12 then assigns another memory address, referenced by the expression ptr_int1-5, to the ptr_int2 pointer. Now, ptr_int2 points to a memory location that is 10 bytes lower than the memory location pointed by ptr_int1 (see the output made by line 13.) The difference between ptr_int2 and ptr_int1 is obtained by the subtraction of the two pointers, which is -5 (since an int on my machine is two bytes) as printed out by the statement in line 14.

Pointers and Arrays

As indicated in previous lessons, pointers and arrays have a close relationship. You can access an array through a pointer that contains the start address of the array. The following subsection introduces how to access array elements through pointers.

Accessing Arrays via Pointers

Because an array name that is not followed by a subscript is interpreted as a pointer to the first element of the array, you can assign the start address of the array to a pointer of the same data type; then you can access any element in the array by adding a proper integer to the pointer. The value of the integer you use is the same as the subscript value of the element that you want to access.

In other words, given an array, array, and a pointer, ptr_array, if array and ptr_array are of the same data type, and ptr_array contains the start address of the array, that is

```
ptr_array = array;
```

then the expression array[n] is equivalent to the expression

```
*(ptr_array + n)
```

Here n is a subscript number in the array.

Listing 16.3 demonstrates how to access arrays and change values of array elements by using pointers.

TYPE   **LISTING 16.3**   Accessing Arrays by Using Pointers

```
1:  /* 16L03.c: Accessing arrays via pointers */
2:  #include <stdio.h>
3:
4:  main()
5:  {
```

```
 6:      char str[] = "It's a string!";
 7:      char *ptr_str;
 8:      int list[] = {1, 2, 3, 4, 5};
 9:      int *ptr_int;
10:
11:      /* access char array */
12:      ptr_str = str;
13:      printf("Before the change, str contains: %s\n", str);
14:      printf("Before the change, str[5] contains: %c\n", str[5]);
15:      *(ptr_str + 5) = 'A';
16:      printf("After the change, str[5] contains: %c\n", str[5]);
17:      printf("After the change, str contains: %s\n", str);
18:      /* access int array */
19:      ptr_int = list;
20:      printf("Before the change, list[2] contains: %d\n", list[2]);
21:      *(ptr_int + 2) = -3;
22:      printf("After the change, list[2] contains: %d\n", list[2]);
23:
24:      return 0;
25: }
```

The following output is displayed after the executable file 16L03.exe is created and run on my computer:

OUTPUT

```
Before the change, str contains: It's a string!
Before the change, str[5] contains: a
After the change, str[5] contains: A
After the change, str contains: It's A string!
Before the change, list[2] contains: 3
After the change, list[2] contains: -3
```

ANALYSIS The purpose of the program in Listing 16.3 is to show you how to access a char array, str, and an int array, list. In lines 6 and 8, str and list are declared and initialized with a string and a set of integers, respectively. A char pointer, ptr_str, and an int pointer, ptr_int, are declared in lines 7 and 9.

Line 12 assigns the start address of the str array to the ptr_str pointer. The statements in lines 13 and 14 demonstrate the content of the string saved in the str array, as well as the character contained by the str[5] element in the array before any changes are made to str.

The statement in line 15 shows that the character constant, 'A', is assigned to the element of the str array pointed by the expression

```
*(ptr_str + 5)
```

To verify that the content of the element in str has been updated, lines 16 and 17 print out the element and the whole string, respectively. The output indicates that 'A' has replaced the original character constant, 'a'.

The start address of the int array list is assigned to the ptr_int pointer in line 19. Before I do anything with the list[2] element of the list array, I print out its value, which is 3 at this moment (see the output made by line 20). In line 21, the list[2] element is given another value, -3, through the dereferenced pointer *(ptr_int + 2). The printf() call in line 22 prints the updated value of list[2] .

Pointers and Functions

Before I start to talk about passing pointers to functions, let's first have a look how to pass arrays to functions.

Passing Arrays to Functions

In practice, it's usually awkward if you pass more than five or six arguments to a function. One way to save the number of arguments passed to a function is to use arrays. You can put all variables of the same type into an array, and then pass the array as a single argument.

The program in Listing 16.4 shows how to pass an array of integers to a function.

TYPE   **LISTING 16.4**   Passing Arrays to Functions

```
 1:  /* 16L04.c: Passing arrays to functions */
 2:  #include <stdio.h>
 3:
 4:  int AddThree(int list[]);
 5:
 6:  main()
 7:  {
 8:     int sum, list[3];
 9:
10:     printf("Enter three integers separated by spaces:\n");
11:     scanf("%d%d%d", &list[0], &list[1], &list[2]);
12:     sum = AddThree(list);
13:     printf("The sum of the three integers is: %d\n", sum);
14:
15:     return 0;
16:  }
17:
18:  int AddThree(int list[])
19:  {
20:     int i;
21:     int result = 0;
22:
23:     for (i=0; i<3; i++)
24:        result += list[i];
25:     return result;
26:  }
```

The following output is obtained after I run the executable, 16L04.exe, and enter three integers, 10, 20, and 30, on my machine:

OUTPUT
```
Enter three integers separated by spaces:
10  20  30
The sum of the three integers is: 60
```

ANALYSIS The purpose of the program in Listing 16.4 is to obtain three integers entered by the user, and then pass the three integers as an array to a function called AddThree() to perform the operation of addition.

Line 4 gives the declaration of the AddThree() function. Note that the unsized array, list[], is used in the argument expression, which indicates that the argument contains the start address of the list array.

The list array and an integer variable, sum, are declared in line 8. The printf() call in line 10 displays a message asking the user to enter three integers. Then, line 11 uses scanf() to retrieve the integers entered by the user and stores them into the three memory locations of the elements in the integer array referenced by &list[0], &list[1], and &list[2], respectively.

The statement in line 12 calls the AddThree() function with the name of the array as the argument. The AddThree(list) expression is actually passing the start address of the list array (&list[0]) to the AddThree() function.

The definition of the AddThree() function is in lines 18–26; it adds the values of all three elements in the list array and returns the result of the addition. The result returned from the AddThree() function is assigned to the integer variable sum in line 12 and is printed out in line 13.

You can also specify the size of an array that is passed to a function. For instance, the following:

```
function(char str[16]);
```

is equivalent to the following statement:

```
function(char str[]);
```

Remember that the compiler can figure out the size for the unsized array str[].

For multidimensional arrays, the format of an unsized array should be always used in the declaration. (See the section titled "Passing Multidimensional Arrays as Arguments," later in this hour.)

Passing Pointers to Functions

As you know, an array name that is not followed by a subscript is interpreted as a pointer to the first element of the array. In fact, the address of the first element in an array is the start address of the array. Therefore, you can assign the start address of an array to a pointer, and then pass the pointer name, instead of the unsized array, to a function.

Listing 16.5 shows an example of passing pointers to functions, which is similar to passing arrays that are passed to functions.

TYPE   **LISTING 16.5**   Passing Pointers to Functions

```
1:  /* 16L05.c: Passing pointers to functions */
2:  #include <stdio.h>
3:
4:  void ChPrint(char *ch);
5:  int DataAdd(int *list, int max);
6:  main()
7:  {
8:     char str[] = "It's a string!";
9:     char *ptr_str;
10:    int list[5] = {1, 2, 3, 4, 5};
11:    int *ptr_int;
12:
13:    /* assign address to pointer */
14:    ptr_str = str;
15:    ChPrint(ptr_str);
16:    ChPrint(str);
17:
18:    /* assign address to pointer */
19:    ptr_int = list;
20:    printf("The sum returned by DataAdd(): %d\n",
21:            DataAdd(ptr_int, 5));
22:    printf("The sum returned by DataAdd(): %d\n",
23:            DataAdd(list, 5));
24:    return 0;
25: }
26: /* function definition */
27: void ChPrint(char *ch)
28: {
29:    printf("%s\n", ch);
30: }
31: /* function definition */
32: int DataAdd(int *list, int max)
33: {
34:    int i;
35:    int sum = 0;
36:
```

```
37:    for (i=0; i<max; i++)
38:        sum += list[i];
39:    return sum;
40: }
```

After executing the 16L05.exe program, I obtain the following output displayed on the screen of my computer:

OUTPUT

```
It's a string!
It's a string!
The sum returned by DataAdd(): 15
The sum returned by DataAdd(): 15
```

16

ANALYSIS The purpose of the program in Listing 16.5 is to demonstrate how to pass two pointers—an integer pointer that points to an integer array and a character pointer that references a character string—to two functions that are declared in lines 4 and 5.

Note that expressions such as char *ch and int *list are used as arguments in the function declarations, which indicates to the compiler that a char pointer and an int pointer are respectively passed to the functions ChPrint() and DataAdd().

Inside the main() function body, lines 8 and 9 declare a char array (str) that is initialized with a character string, and a char pointer variable (ptr_str). Line 10 declares and initializes an int array (list) with a set of integers. An int pointer variable, ptr_int, is declared in line 11.

The start address of the str array is assigned to the ptr_str pointer by the assignment statement in line 14. Then, the ptr_str pointer is passed to the ChPrint() function as the argument in line 15. According to the definition of ChPrint() in lines 27–30, the content of the str array whose start address is passed to the function as the argument is printed out by the printf() call inside the ChPrint() function in line 29.

In fact, you can still use the name of the str array as the argument and pass it to the ChPrint() function. Line 16 shows that the start address of the character array is passed to ChPrint() via the name of the array.

The statement in line 19 assigns the start address of the integer array list to the integer pointer ptr_int. Then, the ptr_int pointer is passed to the DataAdd() function in line 21, along with 5, which is the maximum number of elements contained by the list array. The max argument is used because the function can't determine the size of the array given only the start address. From the definition of the DataAdd() function in lines 32–40, you can see that DataAdd() adds all the integer elements in list and returns the sum to the caller. Thereafter, the statement in lines 20 and 21 prints out the result returned from DataAdd().

The expression in line 23 also invokes the DataAdd() function, but this time, the name of the list array is used as the argument to the function. Not surprisingly, the start address of the list array is passed to the DataAdd() function successfully, and the printf() statement in lines 22 and 23 displays the correct result on the screen.

Passing Multidimensional Arrays as Arguments

In Hour 12, "Understanding Arrays," you learned about multidimensional arrays. In this section, you're going to see how to pass multidimensional arrays to functions.

As you might have guessed, passing a multidimensional array to a function is similar to passing a one-dimensional array to a function. You can either pass the unsized format of a multidimensional array or a pointer that contains the start address of the multidimensional array to a function. Listing 16.6 is an example of these two methods.

TYPE   **LISTING 16.6**   Passing Multidimensional Arrays to Functions

```
1:  /* 16L06.c: Passing multidimensional arrays to functions */
2:  #include <stdio.h>
3:  /* function declarations */
4:  int DataAdd1(int list[][5], int max1, int max2);
5:  int DataAdd2(int *list, int max1, int max2);
6:  /* main() function */
7:  main()
8:  {
9:     int list[2][5] = {1, 2, 3, 4, 5,
10:                        5, 4, 3, 2, 1};
11:    int *ptr_int;
12:
13:    printf("The sum returned by DataAdd1(): %d\n",
14:           DataAdd1(list, 2, 5));
15:    ptr_int = &list[0][0];
16:    printf("The sum returned by DataAdd2(): %d\n",
17:           DataAdd2(ptr_int, 2, 5));
18:
19:    return 0;
20: }
21: /* function definition */
22: int DataAdd1(int list[][5], int max1, int max2)
23: {
24:    int i, j;
25:    int sum = 0;
26:
27:    for (i=0; i<max1; i++)
28:      for (j=0; j<max2; j++)
29:        sum += list[i][j];
30:    return sum;
31: }
```

```
32: /* function definition */
33: int DataAdd2(int *list, int max1, int max2)
34: {
35:     int i, j;
36:     int sum = 0;
37:
38:     for (i=0; i<max1; i++)
39:         for (j=0; j<max2; j++)
40:             sum += *(list + i*max2 + j);
41:     return sum;
42: }
```

16

The following output is displayed on the screen of my computer after the executable (16L06.exe) is executed:

OUTPUT
```
The sum returned by DataAdd1(): 30
The sum returned by DataAdd2(): 30
```

ANALYSIS   At the beginning of the program in Listing 16.6, I declare two functions, DataAdd1() and DataAdd2(), in lines 4 and 5. Note that the first argument to DataAdd1() in line 4 is the unsized array of list. In fact, list is a two-dimensional integer array declared in lines 9 and 10 inside the main() function body. The other two arguments, max1 and max2, are two dimension sizes of the list array.

As you can tell from the definition of DataAdd1() in lines 22–31, each element of the list array, expressed as list[i][j], is added and assigned to a local variable called sum that is returned at the end of the DataAdd1() function in line 30. Here i goes from 0 to max1 - 1, and j is within the range of 0 to max2 - 1.

The DataAdd1() function is called in line 14, with the name of the list array and the two dimension sizes, 2 and 5. The result returned by DataAdd1() is printed out by the statement in lines 13 and 14. So you see, passing a multidimensional array to a function is quite similar to passing a one-dimensional array to a function. The function, in this case, needs both dimension sizes to determine the total number of elements in the array.

Another way to do the job is to pass a pointer that contains the start address of a multidimensional array to a function. In this example, the DataAdd2() function is declared in line 5 with a pointer expression, int *list, as the function's first argument. The definition of DataAdd2() is given in lines 33–42.

Note that in line 40, each element in the list array is fetched by moving the pointer to point to the memory location of the element. That is, the dereferenced pointer *(list + i*max2 + j) evaluates to the value of an element that is located at row i and column j, if you imagine that the two-dimensional array is a matrix with both horizontal and vertical dimensions. Therefore, adding i*max2 to list calculates the address of row i (that is, skipping rows 0 through i-1), and then adding j calculates the address of element j (that is, column j) within the current row (i). In this example, the range of the row is from 0 to 1 (that is, a total of 2 rows); the range of the column is from 0 to 4 (that is, a total of 5 columns). See Figure 16.1.

The result returned by the DataAdd2() function is displayed on the screen by the printf() statement in lines 16 and 17.

FIGURE 16.1

The two-dimensional coordinate shows the locations of the elements in the list array.

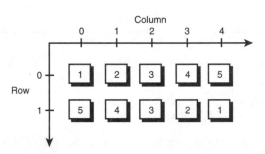

Arrays of Pointers

In many cases, it's useful to declare an array of pointers and access the contents pointed by the array by dereferencing each pointer. For instance, the following declaration declares an array of int pointers:

```
int *ptr_int[3];
```

In other words, the variable ptr_int is a three-element array of pointers to integers. In addition, you can initialize the array of pointers. For example:

```
int x1 = 10;
int x2 = 100;
int x3 = 1000;
ptr_int[0] = &x1;
ptr_int[1] = &x2;
ptr_int[2] = &x3;
```

Listing 16.7 shows another example. Here an array of pointers is used to access an array of strings.

TYPE **LISTING 16.7** Using an Array of Pointers to Character Strings

```
1:  /* 16L07.c: Using an array of pointers */
2:  #include <stdio.h>
3:  /* function declarations */
4:  void StrPrint1(char **str1, int size);
5:  void StrPrint2(char *str2);
```

```
6:  /* main() function */
7:  main()
8:  {
9:     char *str[4] = {"There's music in the sighing of a reed;",
10:                    "There's music in the gushing of a rill;",
11:                    "There's music in all things if men had ears;",
12:                    "There earth is but an echo of the spheres.\n"
13:                    };
14:     int i, size = 4;
15:
16:     StrPrint1(str, size);
17:     for (i=0; i<size; i++)
18:        StrPrint2(str[i]);
19:
20:     return 0;
21: }
22: /* function definition */
23: void StrPrint1(char **str1, int size)
24: {
25:    int i;
26:    /* Print all strings in an array of pointers to strings */
27:    for (i=0; i<size; i++)
28:       printf("%s\n", str1[i]);
29: }
30: /* function definition */
31: void StrPrint2(char *str2)
32: {
33:     /* Prints one string at a time */
34:    printf("%s\n", str2);
35: }
```

A piece of a poem written by Lord Byron is printed out after the executable (16L07.exe) of the program in Listing 16.7 is created and executed:

OUTPUT
```
There's music in the sighing of a reed;
There's music in the gushing of a rill;
There's music in all things if men had ears;
There earth is but an echo of the spheres.
There's music in the sighing of a reed;
There's music in the gushing of a rill;
There's music in all things if men had ears;
There earth is but an echo of the spheres.
```

ANALYSIS Let's first have a look at the array of pointers, str, which is declared and initialized in lines 9–13 inside the main() function body of the program in Listing 16.7. As you can see, str is a four-element array of pointers to a set of character strings. I have adopted four sentences of a poem written by Lord Byron and used them as four character strings in the program.

You can access a character string by using a corresponding pointer in the array. In fact, there are two functions, StrPrint1() and StrPrint2(), in Listing 16.7. Both of them can be called to access the character strings. From the function declaration in line 4, you can see that the StrPrint1() function takes a pointer of pointers—that is, **str1, which is dereferenced inside the StrPrint1() function to represent the four pointers that point to the four character strings. The definition of StrPrint1() is in lines 23–29.

The StrPrint2() function, on the other hand, only takes a pointer variable as its argument, and prints out a character string referenced by the pointer. Lines 31–35 give the definition of the StrPrint2() function.

Now let's move back to the main() function. The StrPrint1() function is called in line 16 with the name of the array of pointers, str, as the argument. StrPrint1() then displays the four sentences of Byron's poem on the screen. The for loop in lines 17 and 18 does the same thing by calling the StrPrint2() function four times. Each time, the start address of a sentence is passed to StrPrint2(). Therefore, you see all the sentences of the poem printed on the screen twice..

Pointing to Functions

Before you finish the course for this hour, there is one more interesting thing you need to learn about: pointers to functions.

As with pointers to arrays, you can declare a pointer that is initialized with the left value of a function. (The left value is the memory address at which the function is located.) Then you can call the function via the pointer.

The program in Listing 16.8 is an example that declares a pointer to a function.

TYPE   **LISTING 16.8**   Pointing to a Function

```
1:   /* 16L08.c: Pointing to a function */
2:   #include <stdio.h>
3:   /* function declaration */
4:   int StrPrint(char *str);
5:   /* main() function */
6:   main()
7:   {
8:      char str[24] = "Pointing to a function.";
9:      int (*ptr)(char *str);
10:
11:     ptr = StrPrint;
12:     if (!(*ptr)(str))
```

```
13:        printf("Done!\n");
14:
15:    return 0;
16: }
17: /* function definition */
18: int StrPrint(char *str)
19: {
20:    printf("%s\n", str);
21:    return 0;
22: }
```

16

OUTPUT After the executable 16L08.exe of the program in Listing 16.8 is created and executed on my computer, the following output is shown on the screen:

ANALYSIS
```
Pointing to a function.
Done!
```

As usual, a function declaration comes first in Listing 16.8. The StrPrint() function is declared with the int data type specifier and an argument of a char pointer in line 4.

The statement in line 9 gives the declaration of a pointer (ptr) to the StrPrint() function: that is, int (*ptr)(char *str);.

Note that the pointer, ptr, is specified with the int data type and passed with a char pointer. In other words, the format of the pointer declaration in line 9 is quite similar to the declaration of StrPrint() in line 4. Please remember that you have to put the *ptr expression between a pair of parentheses ((and)) so that the compiler won't confuse it with a function name.

In line 11, the left value (that is, the address) of the StrPrint() function is assigned to the ptr pointer. Then, the (*ptr)(str) expression in line 12 calls the StrPrint() function via the dereferenced pointer ptr, and passes the address of the string declared in line 8 to the function.

From the definition of the StrPrint() function in lines 18–22, you can tell that the function prints out the content of a string whose address is passed to the function as the argument. Then, 0 is returned at the end of the function.

In fact, the if statement in lines 12 and 13 checks the value returned by the StrPrint() function. When the value is 0, the printf() call in line 13 displays the string Done! on the screen.

The output of the program in Listing 16.8 shows that the StrPrint() function has been invoked successfully by using a pointer that holds the address of the function.

Summary

In this lesson you've learned the following very important concepts and applications of pointers and arrays in C:

- You should always make sure that a pointer is pointing to a legal and valid memory location before you use it.
- The position of a pointer can be moved by adding or subtracting an integer.
- The scalar size of a pointer is determined by the size of its data type, which is specified in the pointer declaration.
- For two pointers of the same type, you can subtract one pointer value from the other to obtain the offset between them.
- The elements in an array can be accessed via a pointer that holds the start address of the array.
- You can pass an unsized array as a single argument to a function.
- Also, you can pass an array to a function through a pointer. The pointer should hold the start address of the array.
- You can either pass the unsized format of a multidimensional array, or a pointer that contains the start address of the multidimensional array, to a function.
- A function that takes an array as an argument does not know how many elements are in the array. You should also pass the number of elements as another argument to the function.
- Arrays of pointers are useful in dealing with character strings.
- You can assign a pointer to the address of a function, and then call the function using that pointer.

In the next lesson you'll learn how to allocate memory in C.

Q&A

Q Why do you need pointer arithmetic?

A The beauty of using pointers is that you can move pointers around to get access to valid data that are saved in those memory locations referenced by the pointers. To do so, you can perform pointer arithmetic to add (or subtract) an integer to (or from) a pointer. For example, if a character pointer, ptr_str, holds the start address of a character string, the ptr_str+1 expression moves to the next memory location, which contains the second character in the string.

Q How does the compiler determine the scalar size of a pointer?

A The compiler determines the scalar size of a pointer by its data type, which is specified in the declaration. When an integer is added to or subtracted from a pointer, the actual value the compiler uses is the multiplication of the integer and the size of the pointer type. For instance, given an int pointer ptr_int, the expression ptr_int + 1 is interpreted by the compiler as ptr_int + 1 * sizeof(int). If the size of the int type is 2 bytes, the ptr_int + 1 expression really means to move 2 bytes higher from the memory location referenced by the ptr_int pointer.

16

Q How do you get access to an element in an array by using a pointer?

A For a one-dimensional array, you can assign the start address of an array to a pointer of the same type, and then move the pointer to the memory location that contains the value of an element in which you're interested. Then you dereference the pointer to obtain the value of the element. For multidimensional arrays, the method is similar, but you have to think about the other dimensions at the same time (See the example shown in Listing 16.6.)

Q Why do you need to use arrays of pointers?

A In many cases, it's helpful to use arrays of pointers. For instance, it's convenient to use an array of pointers to point to a set of character strings so that you can access any one of the strings referenced by a corresponding pointer in the array.

Workshop

To help solidify your understanding of this hour's lesson, you are encouraged to answer the quiz questions and finish the exercises provided in the workshop before you move to the next lesson. The answers and hints to the questions and exercises are given in Appendix B, "Answers to Quiz Questions and Exercises."

Quiz

1. Given a char pointer, ptr_ch, an int pointer, ptr_int, and a float pointer, ptr_flt, how many bytes will be added, respectively, in the following expressions on your machine?

   - ptr_ch + 4
   - ptr_int + 2
   - ptr_flt + 1
   - ptr_ch + 12
   - ptr_int + 6
   - ptr_flt + 3

2. If the address held by an `int` pointer, `ptr1`, is `0x100A`, and the address held by another `int` pointer, `ptr2`, is `0x1006`, what will you get from the subtraction of `ptr1–ptr2`?

3. Given that the size of the `double` data type is `8` bytes long, and the current address held by a `double` pointer variable, `ptr_db`, is `0x0238`, what are the addresses held, respectively, by `ptr_db–1` and `ptr_db+5`?

4. Given the following declarations and assignments:
```
char ch[] = {'a', 'b', 'c', 'd', 'A', 'B', 'C', 'D'};
char *ptr;
ptr = &ch[1];
```

what do each of these expressions do?

- `*(ptr + 3)`
- `ptr - ch`
- `*(ptr - 1)`
- `*ptr = 'F'`

Exercises

1. Given a character string, `I like C!`, write a program to pass the string to a function that displays the string on the screen.

2. Rewrite the program in exercise 1. This time, change the string of `I like C!` to `I love C!` by moving a pointer that is initialized with the start address of the string and updating the string with new characters. Then, pass the updated string to the function to display the content of the string on the screen.

3. Given a two-dimensional character array, `str`, that is initialized as
```
char str[2][15] = { "You know what,", "C is powerful." };
```
write a program to pass the start address of `str` to a function that prints out the content of the character array.

4. Rewrite the program in Listing 16.7. This time, the array of pointers is initialized with the following strings:

`"Sunday"`, `"Monday"`, `"Tuesday"`, `"Wednesday"`, `"Thursday"`, `"Friday"`, and `"Saturday"`.

Hour 17

Allocating Memory

It's just as unpleasant to get more than you bargain for as to get less.

—G. B. Shaw

So far you've learned how to declare and reserve a piece of memory space before it is used in your program. For instance, you have to specify the size of an array in your program (or the compiler has to figure out the size if you declare an unsized array) before you assign any data to it at runtime. In this lesson you'll learn to allocate memory space dynamically when your program is running. The four dynamic memory allocation functions covered in this lesson are

- The malloc() function
- The calloc() function
- The realloc() function
- The free() function

Allocating Memory at Runtime

There are many cases when you do not know the exact sizes of arrays used in your programs, until much later when your programs are actually being executed. You can specify the sizes of arrays in advance, but the arrays can be too small or too big if the numbers of data items you want to put into the arrays change dramatically at runtime.

Fortunately, C provides you with four dynamic memory allocation functions that you can employ to allocate or reallocate certain memory spaces while your program is running. Also, you can release allocated memory storage as soon as you don't need it. These four C functions, `malloc()`, `calloc()`, `realloc()`, and `free()`, are introduced in the following sections

The `malloc()` Function

You can use the `malloc()` function to allocate a specified size of memory space.

SYNTAX

The syntax for the `malloc()` function is

```
#include <stdlib.h>
void *malloc(size_t size);
```

Here `size` indicates the number of bytes of storage to allocate. The `malloc()` function returns a `void` pointer.

Note that the header file, `stdlib.h`, has to be included before the `malloc()` function can be called. Because the `malloc()` function itself returns a `void` pointer, its type is then automatically converted to the type of the pointer on the left side of an assignment operator, according to the ANSI C standard.

There are some C compilers in the market, usually old versions, which are not 100% ANSI C compliant. If you use one of those C compilers, you may get warning or error messages complaining about your declarations of `malloc()`, `calloc()`, or `realloc()`. For example, if you write something like this:

```
int *ptr;
ptr = malloc ( 10 * sizeof(int) );
```

you may get an error message about the return type from the `malloc()` function when you try to compile the code. This is because that the C compiler that you're using may not be 100% ANSI C compliant, and it does not know how to covert the return type of `malloc()`. If it is the case, what you can do is to use the casting operator `(int *)` shown here:

```
int *ptr;
ptr = (int *) malloc ( 10 * sizeof(int) );
```

This indicates to the compiler the type of the pointer returned by malloc(), and shuts off the complaint from the C compiler. Here, you have to make sure the type of the allocated memory, the type of the pointer, and the type of the casting operator, are all the same. Similarly, you can add a casting operator in front of the calloc() or realloc() functions when you use a non–ANSI C compiler.

Because this book focuses on the ANSI C, which is the industry standard, I don't use casting operators in the example programs using malloc(), calloc(), or realloc(), in the book.

If the malloc() function fails to allocate a piece of memory space, it returns a null pointer. Normally, this happens when there is not enough memory. Therefore, you should always check the returned pointer from malloc() before you use it.

Listing 17.1 demonstrates the use of the malloc() function.

TYPE **LISTING 17.1** Using the malloc() Function

```
1:  /* 17L01.c: Using the malloc function */
2:  #include <stdio.h>
3:  #include <stdlib.h>
4:  #include <string.h>
5:  /* function declaration */
6:  void StrCopy(char *str1, char *str2);
7:  /* main() function */
8:  main()
9:  {
10:    char str[] = "Use malloc() to allocate memory.";
11:    char *ptr_str;
12:    int result;
13:    /* call malloc() */
14:    ptr_str = malloc( strlen(str) + 1);
15:    if (ptr_str != NULL){
16:      StrCopy(str, ptr_str);
17:      printf("The string pointed to by ptr_str is:\n%s\n",
18:             ptr_str);
19:      result = 0;
20:    }
21:    else{
22:      printf("malloc() function failed.\n");
23:      result = 1;
24:    }
25:    return result;
```

continues

17

LISTING 17.1 continued

```
26: }
27: /* function definition */
28: void StrCopy(char *str1, char *str2)
29: {
30:    int i;
31:
32:    for (i=0; str1[i]; i++)
33:        str2[i] = str1[i];
34:    str2[i] = '\0';
35: }
```

The following output is shown on the screen after the executable program, 17L01.exe, in Listing 17.1 is created and executed.

OUTPUT
```
The string pointed to by ptr_str is:
Use malloc() to allocate memory.
```

ANALYSIS The purpose of the program in Listing 17.1 is to use the malloc() function to allocate a piece of memory space that has the same size as a character string. Then, the content of the string is copied to the allocated memory referenced by the pointer returned from the malloc() function. The content of the memory is displayed on the screen to prove that the memory space does contain the content of the string after the allocation and duplication.

Note that two more header files, stdlib.h and string.h, are included in lines 3 and 4, respectively, for the functions malloc() and strlen(), which are called in line 14.

Line 10 declares a char array, str, that is initialized with a character string of "Use malloc() to allocate memory.". A char pointer variable, ptr_str, is declared in line 11.

The statement in line 14 allocates a memory space of strlen(str)+1 bytes by calling the malloc() function. Because the strlen() function does not count the null character at the end of a string, adding 1 to the value returned by strlen(str) gives the total number of bytes that need to be allocated. The value of the returned pointer is assigned to the char pointer variable ptr_str after the malloc() function is called in line 14.

The if-else statement in lines 15–24 checks the returned pointer from the malloc() function. If it's a null pointer, an error message is printed out, and the return value of the main() function is set to 1 in lines 22 and 23. (Remember that a nonzero value returned by the return statement indicates an abnormal termination.)

But if the returned pointer is not a null pointer, the start address of the str array and the pointer ptr_str are passed to a function called StrCopy() in line 16. The StrCopy() function, whose definition is given in lines 28–35, copies the content of the str array to the allocated memory pointed to by ptr_str. Then, the printf() call in lines 17 and 18 prints out the copied content in the allocated memory. Line 19 sets the return value to 0 after the success of the memory allocation and string duplication.

The output on my screen shows that a piece of memory has been allocated and that the string has been copied to the memory.

There is a potential problem if you keep allocating memory, because there is always a limit. You can easily run out of memory when you just allocate memory without ever releasing it. In the next section, you'll learn how to use the free() function to free up memory spaces allocated for you when you don't need them anymore.

Releasing Allocated Memory with free()

Because memory is a limited resource, you should allocate an exactly sized piece of memory right before you need it, and release it as soon as you are through using it.

The program in Listing 17.2 demonstrates how to release allocated memory by calling the free() function.

TYPE   **LISTING 17.2**   Using the free() and malloc() Functions Together

```
1:  /* 17L02.c: Using the free() function */
2:  #include <stdio.h>
3:  #include <stdlib.h>
4:  /* function declarations */
5:  void DataMultiply(int max, int *ptr);
6:  void TablePrint(int max, int *ptr);
7:  /* main() function */
8:  main()
9:  {
10:     int *ptr_int, max;
11:     int termination;
12:     char key = 'c';
13:
14:     max = 0;
15:     termination = 0;
16:     while (key != 'x'){
17:         printf("Enter a single digit number:\n");
```

continues

LISTING 17.2 continued

```
18:        scanf("%d", &max);
19:
20:        ptr_int = malloc(max * max * sizeof(int));   /* call malloc() */
21:        if (ptr_int != NULL){
22:           DataMultiply(max, ptr_int);
23:           TablePrint(max, ptr_int);
24:           free(ptr_int);
25:        }
26:        else{
27:           printf("malloc() function failed.\n");
28:           termination = 1;
29:           key = 'x';  /* stop while loop */
30:        }
31:        printf("\n\nPress x key to quit; other key to continue.\n");
32:        scanf("%s", &key);
33:     }
34:     printf("\nBye!\n");
35:     return termination;
36: }
37: /* function definition */
38: void DataMultiply(int max, int *ptr)
39: {
40:     int i, j;
41:
42:     for (i=0; i<max; i++)
43:        for (j=0; j<max; j++)
44:           *(ptr + i * max + j) = (i+1) * (j+1);
45: }
46: /* function definition */
47: void TablePrint(int max, int *ptr)
48: {
49:     int i, j;
50:
51:     printf("The multiplication table of %d is:\n",
52:             max);
53:     printf("  ");
54:     for (i=0; i<max; i++)
55:        printf("%4d", i+1);
56:     printf("\n ");
57:     for (i=0; i<max; i++)
58:        printf("----", i+1);
59:     for (i=0; i<max; i++){
60:        printf("\n%d¦", i+1);
61:        for (j=0; j<max; j++)
62:           printf("%3d ", *(ptr + i * max + j));
63:     }
64: }
```

Whilethe executable 17L02.exe is being run, I enter two integers, 4 and 2 (highlighted in the following output), to obtain a multiplication table for each; then I quit running the program by pressing the x key:

OUTPUT

```
Enter a single digit number:
4
The multiplication table of 4 is:
    1   2   3   4
   ---------------
1¦ 1   2   3   4
2¦ 2   4   6   8
3¦ 3   6   9  12
4¦ 4   8  12  16
Press x key to quit; other key to continue.
c
Enter a single digit number:
2
The multiplication table of 2 is:
    1   2
   -------
1¦ 1   2
2¦ 2   4
Press x key to quit; other key to continue.
x
Bye!
```

ANALYSIS The purpose of the program in Listing 17.2 is to build a multiplication table based on the integer given by the user. The program can continue building multiplication tables until the user presses the x key to quit. The program also stops execution if the malloc() function fails.

To show you how to use the free() function, the program allocates temporary memory storage to hold the items of a multiplication table. As soon as the content of a multiplication table is printed out, the allocated memory is released by calling the free() function.

Lines 5 and 6 declare two functions, DataMultiply() and TablePrint(), respectively. The former is for performing multiplication and building a table, whereas the latter prints out the table on the screen. The definitions of the two functions are given in lines 38–45 and lines 47–64, respectively.

Inside the main() function, there is a while loop in lines 16–33 that keeps asking the user to enter an integer number (see lines 17 and 18) and then builds a multiplication table based on the integer.

To hold the result of the multiplication, the statement in line 20 allocates a memory storage that has the size of max*max*sizeof(int), where the int variable max contains the integer value entered by the user. Note that the sizeof(int) expression gives the byte size of the int data type for the computer on which the program is being run.

If the malloc() function returns a null pointer, the return value of the main() function is set to 1 to indicate an abnormal termination (see line 28), and the while loop is stopped by assigning the key variable with 'x' in line 29.

Otherwise, if the malloc() function allocates memory storage successfully, the DataMultiply() function is called in line 22 to calculate each multiplication. The results are saved into the memory storage pointed to by the ptr_int pointer. Then the multiplication table is printed out by calling the TablePrint() function in line 23.

As soon as I no longer need to keep the multiplication table, I call the free() function in line 24 to release the allocated memory storage pointed by the ptr_int pointer.

If I did not release the memory, the program would take more and more memory as the user keeps entering integer numbers to build more multiplication tables. Eventually, the program would either crash the operating system or be forced to quit. By using the free() and malloc() functions, I am able to keep running the program by taking the exact amount of memory storage I need, no more and no less.

The calloc() Function

Besides the malloc() function, you can also use the calloc() function to allocate memory storage dynamically. The differences between the two functions are that the latter takes two arguments and that the memory space allocated by calloc() is always initialized to 0. There is no such guarantee that the memory space allocated by malloc() is initialized to 0.

The syntax for the calloc() function is

```
#include <stdlib.h>
void *calloc(size_t nitem, size_t size);
```

Here nitem is the number of items you want to save in the allocated memory space. size gives the number of bytes that each item takes. The calloc() function returns a void pointer too.

If the calloc() function fails to allocate a piece of memory space, it returns a null pointer.

Listing 17.3 contains an example of using the calloc() function. The initial value of the memory space allocated by calloc() is printed out.

▼ SYNTAX

▲

TYPE   **LISTING 17.3**   Using the calloc() Function

```
 1:  /* 17L03.c: Using the calloc() function */
 2:  #include <stdio.h>
 3:  #include <stdlib.h>
 4:  /* main() function */
 5:  main()
 6:  {
 7:     float *ptr1, *ptr2;
 8:     int i, n;
 9:     int termination = 1;
10:
11:     n = 5;
12:     ptr1 = calloc(n, sizeof(float));
13:     ptr2 = malloc(n * sizeof(float));
14:     if (ptr1 == NULL)
15:        printf("malloc() failed.\n");
16:     else if (ptr2 == NULL)
17:        printf("calloc() failed.\n");
18:     else {
19:        for (i=0; i<n; i++)
20:           printf("ptr1[%d]=%5.2f,  ptr2[%d]=%5.2f\n",
21:              i, *(ptr1 + i), i, *(ptr2 + i));
22:        free(ptr1);
23:        free(ptr2);
24:        termination = 0;
25:     }
26:     return termination;
27: }
```

17

The following output appears on the screen after running the executable program
17L03.exe.

OUTPUT
```
ptr1[0] = 0.00,  ptr2[0] = 7042.23
ptr1[1] = 0.00,  ptr2[1] = 1427.00
ptr1[2] = 0.00,  ptr2[2] = 2787.14
ptr1[3] = 0.00,  ptr2[3] =    0.00
ptr1[4] = 0.00,  ptr2[4] = 5834.73
```

ANALYSIS   The purpose of the program in Listing 17.3 is to use the calloc() function to
allocate a piece of memory space. To prove that the calloc() function initializes
the allocated memory space to 0, the initial values of the memory are printed out. Also,
another piece of memory space is allocated by using the malloc() function, and the initial values of the second memory space are printed out too.

As you see in line 12, the calloc() function is called with two arguments passed to it:
the int variable n and the sizeof(float) expression. The float pointer variable ptr1 is
assigned the value returned by the calloc() function.

Likewise, the malloc() function is called in line 13. This function only takes one argument that specifies the total number of bytes that the allocated memory should have. The value returned by the malloc() function is then assigned to another float pointer variable, ptr2.

From lines 12 and 13, you can tell that the calloc() and malloc() functions actually plan to allocate two pieces of memory space with the same size.

The if-else-if-else statement in lines 14–25 checks the two values returned from the calloc() and malloc() functions and then prints out the initial values from the two allocated memory spaces if the two return values are not null.

I ran the executable program of Listing 17.3 several times. Each time, the initial value from the memory space allocated by the calloc() function was always 0. But there is no such guarantee for the memory space allocated by the malloc() function. The output shown here is one of the results from running the executable program on my machine. You can see that there is some "garbage" in the memory space allocated by the malloc() function. That is, the initial value in the memory is unpredictable. (Sometimes, the initial value in a memory block allocated by the malloc() function happens to be 0. But it is not guaranteed that the initial value is always zero each time the malloc() function is called.)

The realloc() Function

The realloc() function gives you a means to change the size of a piece memory space allocated by the malloc() function, the calloc() function, or even realloc() itself.

The syntax for the realloc() function is

```
#include <stdlib.h>
void *realloc(void *block, size_t size);
```

Here block is the pointer to the start of a piece of memory space previously allocated. size specifies the total byte number you want to change to. The realloc() function returns a void pointer.

The realloc() function returns a null pointer if it fails to reallocate a piece of memory space.

The realloc() function is equivalent to the malloc() function if the first argument passed to realloc() is NULL. In other words, the following two statements are equivalent:

```
ptr_flt = realloc(NULL, 10 * sizeof(float));
ptr_flt = malloc(10 * sizeof(float));
```

Also, you can use the `realloc()` function in place of the `free()` function. You do this by passing 0 to `realloc()` as its second argument. For instance, to release a block of memory pointed to by a pointer `ptr`, you can either call the `free()` function like this:

```
free(ptr);
```

or use the `realloc()` function in the following way:

```
realloc(ptr, 0);
```

The program in Listing 17.4 demonstrates the use of the `realloc()` function in memory reallocation.

TYPE   **LISTING 17.4**   Using the `realloc()` Function

17

```
1:  /* 17L04.c: Using the realloc() function */
2:  #include <stdio.h>
3:  #include <stdlib.h>
4:  #include <string.h>
5:  /* function declaration */
6:  void StrCopy(char *str1, char *str2);
7:  /* main() function */
8:  main()
9:  {
10:    char *str[4] = {"There's music in the sighing of a reed;",
11:                    "There's music in the gushing of a rill;",
12:                    "There's music in all things if men had ears;",
13:                    "There earth is but an echo of the spheres.\n"
14:                   };
15:    char *ptr;
16:    int i;
17:
18:    int termination = 0;
19:
20:    ptr = malloc((strlen(str[0]) + 1) * sizeof(char));
21:    if (ptr == NULL){
22:      printf("malloc() failed.\n");
23:      termination = 1;
24:    }
25:    else{
26:      StrCopy(str[0], ptr);
27:      printf("%s\n", ptr);
28:      for (i=1; i<4; i++){
29:        ptr = realloc(ptr, (strlen(str[i]) + 1) * sizeof(char));
30:        if (ptr == NULL){
31:          printf("realloc() failed.\n");
32:          termination = 1;
```

continues

LISTING 17.4   continued

```
33:            i = 4;    /* break the fro loop */
34:          }
35:          else{
36:            StrCopy(str[i], ptr);
37:            printf("%s\n", ptr);
38:          }
39:        }
40:      }
41:    free(ptr);
42:    return termination;
43: }
44: /* funciton definition */
45: void StrCopy(char *str1, char *str2)
46: {
47:    int i;
48:
49:    for (i=0; str1[i]; i++)
50:        str2[i] = str1[i];
51:    str2[i] = '\0';
52: }
```

The following output is obtained by running the executable program 17L04.exe.

```
There's music in the sighing of a reed;
There's music in the gushing of a rill;
There's music in all things if men had ears;
There earth is but an echo of the spheres.
```

ANALYSIS The purpose of the program in Listing 17.4 is to allocate a block of memory space to hold a character string. There are four strings in this example, and the length of each string may vary. I use the realloc() function to adjust the size of the previously allocated memory so it can hold a new string.

As you can see in lines 10–13, there are four character strings containing a lovely poem written by Lord Byron. (You can tell that I love Byron's poems.) Here I use an array of pointers, str, to refer to the strings.

A piece of memory space is first allocated by calling the malloc() function in line 20. The size of the memory space is determined by the (strlen(str[0])+1)*sizeof(char) expression. As mentioned earlier, because the C function strlen() does not count the null character at the end of a string, you have to remember to allocate space for one more character to hold the full size of a string. The sizeof(char) expression is used here for portability, although the char data type is 1 byte.

Exercise 4 at the end of this lesson asks you to rewrite the program in Listing 17.4 and replace the `malloc()` and `free()` functions with their equivalent formats of the `realloc()` function.

If the `malloc()` function doesn't fail, the content of the first string pointed to by the `str[0]` pointer is copied to the block of memory allocated by `malloc()`. To do this, a function called `StrCopy()` is called in line 26. Lines 45–52 give the definition of `StrCopy()`.

The `for` loop, in lines 28–39, copies the remaining three strings, one at a time, to the block of memory pointed to by `ptr`. Each time, the `realloc()` function is called in line 29 to reallocate and adjust the previously allocated memory space based on the length of the next string whose content is about to be copied to the memory block.

After the content of a string is copied to the memory block, the content is also printed out (see lines 27 and 37).

In this example, a block of memory space is allocated and adjusted based on the length of each of the four strings. The `realloc()` function, as well as the `malloc()` function, does the memory allocation and adjustment dynamically.

Summary

In this lesson you've learned the following very important functions and concepts for memory management in C:

- In C, there are four functions that can be used to allocate, reallocate, or release a block of memory space dynamically at runtime.
- The `malloc()` function allocates a block of memory whose size is specified by the argument passed to the function.
- The `free()` function is used to free up a block of memory space previously allocated by the `malloc()`, `calloc()`, or `realloc()` function.
- The `calloc()` function can do the same job as the `malloc()` function. In addition, the `calloc()` function can initialize the allocated memory space to 0.
- The `realloc()` function is used to reallocate a block of memory that has been allocated by the `malloc()` or `calloc()` function.
- If a null pointer is passed to the `realloc()` function as its first argument, the function acts like the `malloc()` function.
- If the second argument of the `realloc()` function is set to 0, the `realloc()` function is equivalent to the `free()` function that releases a block of allocated memory.

- You have to first include the header file stdlib.h before you can call the malloc(), calloc(), realloc(), or free() function.
- You should always check the values returned from the malloc(), calloc(), or realloc() function, before you use the memory allocated by these functions.

In the next lesson you'll learn more about data types in C.

Q&A

Q Why do you need to allocate memory at runtime?

A Very often, you don't know exact sizes of arrays until your program is being run. You might be able to estimate the sizes for those arrays, but if you make those arrays too big, you waste the memory. On the other hand, if you make those arrays too small, you're going to lose data. The best way is to allocate blocks of memory dynamically and precisely for those arrays when their sizes are determined at runtime. There are four C library functions, malloc(), calloc(), realloc(), and free(), which you can use for memory allocation at runtime.

Q What does it mean if the malloc() function returns a null pointer?

A If the malloc() function returns a null pointer, it means the function failed to allocate a block of memory whose size is specified by the argument passed to the function. Normally, the failure of the malloc() function is caused by the fact that there is not enough memory left to allocate. You should always check the value returned by the malloc() function to make sure that the function has succeeded before you attempt to use the block of memory allocated by the function.

Q What are the differences between the calloc() and malloc() functions?

A Basically, there are two differences between the calloc() and malloc() functions, although both functions can do the same job. The first difference is that the calloc() function takes two arguments, while the malloc() function takes only one. The second difference is that the calloc() function initializes the allocated memory space to 0, whereas there is no such guarantee made by the malloc() function.

Q Is the free() function necessary?

A Yes. The free() function is very necessary, and you should use it to free up allocated memory blocks as soon as you don't need them. As you know, memory is a limited resource in a computer. Your program shouldn't take too much memory space when it allocates blocks of memory. One way to reduce the size of memory taken by your program is to use the free() function to release the unused allocated memory in time.

Workshop

To help solidify your understanding of this hour's lesson, you are encouraged to answer the quiz questions and finish the exercises provided in the workshop before you move to the next lesson. The answers and hints to the questions and exercises are given in Appendix B, "Answers to Quiz Questions and Exercises."

Quiz

1. Provided that the `char` data type is 1 byte, the `int` data type is 2 bytes, and the `float` data type is 4 bytes, how many bytes of memory do the following functions try to allocate?

   - `malloc(100 * sizeof(int))`
   - `calloc(200, sizeof(char))`
   - `realloc(NULL, 50 * sizeof(float))`
   - `realloc(ptr, 0)`

2. Given an `int` pointer, `ptr`, that is pointing to a block of memory that can hold 100 integers, if you want to reallocate the memory block to hold up to 150 integers, which of the two following statements do you use?

   - `ptr = realloc(ptr, 50 * sizeof(int));`
   - `ptr = realloc(ptr, 150 * sizeof(int));`

3. After the following statements are executed successfully, what is the final size of the allocated memory block pointed to by the `ptr` pointer?

   ```
   . . .
   ptr = malloc(300 * sizeof(int));
   . . .
   ptr = realloc(ptr, 500 * sizeof(int));
   . . .
   ptr = realloc(ptr, 60 * sizeof(int));
   ```

4. What is the final size of the allocated memory block pointed to by the `ptr` pointer, if the following statements are executed successfully?

   ```
   . . .
   ptr = calloc(100 * sizeof(char));
   . . .
   free(ptr);
   ptr = realloc(NULL, 200 * sizeof(char));
   . . .
   ptr = realloc(ptr, 0);
   ```

17

Exercises

1. Write a program to ask the user to enter the total number of bytes he or she wants to allocate. Then, initialize the allocated memory with consecutive integers, starting from 1. Add all the integers contained by the memory block and print out the final result on the screen.

2. Write a program that allocates a block of memory space to hold 100 items of the float data type by calling the calloc() function. Then, reallocate the block of memory in order to hold 50 more items of the float data type.

3. Write a program to ask the user to enter the total number of float data. Then use the calloc() and malloc() functions to allocate two memory blocks with the same size specified by the number, and print out the initial values of the two memory blocks.

4. Rewrite the program in Listing 17.4. This time, use the two special cases of the realloc() function to replace the malloc() and free() functions.

HOUR 18

Using Special Data Types and Functions

That's all there is, there isn't any more.

—E. Barrymore

In Hour 4, "Understanding Data Types and Keywords," you learned about most of the data types, such as char, int, float, and double. In Hour 15, "Working with Functions," you learned the basics of using functions in C. In this hour, you'll learn more about data types and functions from the following topics:

- The enum data type
- The typedef statement
- Function recursion
- Command-line arguments

The enum Data Type

The C language provides you with an additional data type—the enum data type. enum is short for *enumerated*. The enumerated data type can be used to declare named integer constants. The enum data type makes the C program more readable and easier to maintain. (Another way to declare a named constant is to use the #define directive, which is introduced later in this book.)

Declaring the enum Data Type

▼ SYNTAX
▲

The general form of the enum data type declaration is

```
enum tag_name {enumeration_list} variable_list;
```

Here *tag_name* is the name of the enumeration. *variable_list* gives a list of variable names that are of the enum data type. *enumeration_list* contains defined enumerated names that are used to represent integer constants. (Both *tag_name* and *variable_list* are optional.)

For instance, the following declares an enum data type with the tag name of automobile:

```
enum automobile {sedan, pick_up, sport_utility};
```

Given this, you can define enum variables like this:

```
enum automobile  domestic, foreign;
```

Here the two enum variables, domestic and foreign, are defined.

Of course, you can always declare and define a list of enum variables in a single statement, as shown in the general form of the enum declaration. Therefore, you can rewrite the enum declaration of domestic and foreign like this:

```
enum automobile {sedan, pick_up, sport_utility} domestic, foreign;
```

Assigning Values to enum Names

By default, the integer value associated with the leftmost name in the enumeration list field, surrounded by the braces ({ and }), starts with 0, and the value of each name in the rest of the list increases by one from left to right. Therefore, in the previous example, sedan, pick_up, and sport_utility have the values of 0, 1, and 2, respectively.

In fact, you can assign integer values to enum names. Considering the previous example, you can initialize the enumerated names like this:

```
enum automobile {sedan = 60, pick_up = 30, sport_utility = 10};
```

Now, sedan represents the value of 60, pick_up has the value of 30, and sport_utility assumes the value of 10.

The program shown in Listing 18.1 prints out the values of enum names.

TYPE   **LISTING 18.1**   Defining enum Data Types

```
1:  /* 18L01.c: Defining enum data types */
2:  #include <stdio.h>
3:  /* main() function */
4:  main()
5:  {
6:     enum language {human=100,
7:                    animal=50,
8:                    computer};
9:     enum days{SUN,
10:              MON,
11:              TUE,
12:              WED,
13:              THU,
14:              FRI,
15:              SAT};
16:
17:    printf("human: %d,  animal: %d,  computer: %d\n",
18:       human, animal, computer);
19:    printf("SUN: %d\n", SUN);
20:    printf("MON: %d\n", MON);
21:    printf("TUE: %d\n", TUE);
22:    printf("WED: %d\n", WED);
23:    printf("THU: %d\n", THU);
24:    printf("FRI: %d\n", FRI);
25:    printf("SAT: %d\n", SAT);
26:
27:    return 0;
28: }
```

The following output is shown on the screen after the executable file, 18L01.exe, of the program in Listing 18.1 is created and executed on my computer:

OUTPUT
```
human: 100,  animal: 50,  computer: 51
SUN: 0
MON: 1
TUE: 2
WED: 3
THU: 4
FRI: 5
SAT: 6
```

18

ANALYSIS The purpose of the program in Listing 18.1 is to show you the default values of the enum names, as well as the values assigned to some enum names by the programmer.

As you can tell, there are two enum declarations, in lines 6–8 and lines 9–15, respectively. Note that the variable lists in the two enum declarations are omitted because there is no need for the variable lists in the program.

The first declaration has a tag name called language and three enumerated names, human, animal, and computer. In addition, human is assigned the value of 100; animal is initialized with 50. According to the enum definition, the default value of computer is the value of animal increased by 1. Therefore, in this case, the default value of computer is 51.

The output made by the statement in line 17 shows that the values of human, animal, and computer are indeed 100, 50, and 51.

The second enum declaration in the program contains seven items with their default values. Then, lines 19–25 print out these default values one at a time. It is not surprising to see that the values represented by the enumerated names, SUN, MON, TUE, WED, THU, FRI, and SAT, are 0, 1, 2, 3, 4, 5, and 6, respectively.

Now, let's look at another example, shown in Listing 18.2, which demonstrates how to use the enum data type.

TYPE   **LISTING 18.2**   Using the enum Data Type

```
1:   /* 18L02.c: Using the enum data type */
2:   #include <stdio.h>
3:   /* main() function */
4:   main()
5:   {
6:      enum units{penny = 1,
7:                 nickel = 5,
8:                 dime = 10,
9:                 quarter = 25,
10:                dollar = 100};
11:     int money_units[5] = {
12:                dollar,
13:                quarter,
14:                dime,
15:                nickel,
16:                penny};
17:     char *unit_name[5] = {
18:                "dollar(s)",
19:                "quarter(s)",
```

```
20:              "dime(s)",
21:              "nickel(s)",
22:              "penny(s)"};
23:    int cent, tmp, i;
24:
25:    printf("Enter a monetary value in cents:\n");
26:    scanf("%d", &cent);  /* get input from the user */
27:    printf("Which is equivalent to:\n");
28:    tmp = 0;
29:    for (i=0; i<5; i++){
30:       tmp = cent / money_units[i];
31:       cent -= tmp * money_units[i];
32:       if (tmp)
33:          printf("%d %s ", tmp, unit_name[i]);
34:    }
35:    printf("\n");
36:    return 0;
37: }
```

While the executable file (18L02.exe) is being executed, I enter 141 (for 141 cents) and
obtain the following output on the screen:

OUTPUT

```
Enter a monetary value in cents:
141
Which is equivalent to:
1 dollar(s) 1 quarter(s) 1 dime(s) 1 nickel(s) 1 penny(s)
```

18

ANALYSIS The purpose of the program in Listing 18.2 is to use the enum data type to represent the value of the amount of money entered by the user.

Inside the main() function, an enum declaration with a tag name of units is made in
lines 6–10. The numbers assigned to the enumerated names are based on their ratios to
the unit of cent. For instance, one dollar is equal to 100 cents. Therefore, the enum name
dollar is assigned the value of 100.

After the enum declaration, an int array, called money_units, is declared, and is initialized with the enumerated names from the enum declaration. According to the definition
of the enum data type, the declaration of the money_units array in the program is actually
equivalent to the following one:

```
int money_units[5] = {
            100,
            25,
            10,
            5,
            1};
```

So now you see that you can use enumerated names, instead of integer numbers, to make
up other expressions or declarations in your program.

In lines 17–22, an array of pointers, unit_name, is declared and initialized. (The usage of arrays of pointers was introduced in Hour 16, "Applying Pointers.")

Then, the statement in line 15 asks the user to enter an integer number in the unit of cent. The scanf() call in line 26 stores the number entered by the user to an int variable called cent.

The for loop in lines 29–34 divides the entered number and represents it in a dollar-quarter-dime-nickel-penny format.

Note that the integer constants represented by the enumerated names are used in lines 30 and 31, through the money_units array. If the value of a unit is not 0, a corresponding string pointed to by the array of pointers, unit_name, is printed out in line 33. Therefore, when I enter 141 (in unit of cent), I see its equivalent in the output: 1 dollar(s) 1 quarter(s) 1 dime(s) 1 nickel(s) 1 penny(s).

Making typedef Definitions

You can create your own names for data types with the help of the typedef keyword in C, and make those name synonyms for the data types. Then, you can use the name synonyms, instead of the data types themselves, in your programs. Often, the name synonyms defined by typedef can make your program more readable.

For instance, you can declare TWO_BYTE as a synonym for the int data type:

```
typedef  int   TWO_BYTE;
```

Then, you can start to use TWO_BYTE to declare integer variables like this:

```
TWO_BYTE i, j;
```

which is equivalent to

```
int i, j;
```

Remember that a typedef definition must be made before the synonym created in the definition is used in any declarations in your program.

Why Use typedef?

There are several advantages to using typedef definitions. First, you can consolidate complex data types into a single word and then use the word in variable declarations in your program. In this way, you don't need to type a complex declaration over and over, which helps to avoid typing errors.

The second advantage is that you just need to update a typedef definition, which fixes every use of that typedef definition if the data type is changed in the future.

typedef is so useful, in fact, that there is a header file called stddef.h included in the ANSI-standard C that contains a dozen typedef definitions. For instance, size_t is a typedef for the value returned by the sizeof operator.

The program shown in Listing 18.3 is an example of using typedef definitions.

TYPE   **LISTING 18.3**   Using typedef Definitions

```
1:  /* 18L03.c: Using typedef definitions */
2:  #include <stdio.h>
3:  #include <stdlib.h>
4:  #include <string.h>
5:
6:  enum constants{ITEM_NUM = 3,
7:                 DELT='a'-'A'};
8:  typedef char *STRING[ITEM_NUM];
9:  typedef char *PTR_STR;
10: typedef char CHAR;
11: typedef int INTEGER;
12:
13: void Convert2Upper(PTR_STR str1, PTR_STR str2);
14:
15: main()
16: {
17:    STRING str;
18:    STRING moon = {"Whatever we wear",
19:                   "we become beautiful",
20:                   "moon viewing!"};
21:    INTEGER i;
22:    INTEGER term = 0;
23:
24:    for (i=0; i<ITEM_NUM; i++){
25:      str[i] = malloc((strlen(moon[i])+1) * sizeof(CHAR));
26:      if (str[i] == NULL){
27:        printf("malloc() failed.\n");
28:        term = 1;
29:        i = ITEM_NUM;   /* break the for loop */
30:      }
31:      Convert2Upper(moon[i], str[i]);
32:      printf("%s\n", moon[i]);
33:    }
34:    for (i=0; i<ITEM_NUM; i++){
35:      printf("\n%s", str[i]);
```

continues

18

LISTING **18.3**   continued

```
36:      free (str[i]);
37:    }
38:    printf("\n");
39:    return term;
40: }
41: /* function definition */
42: void Convert2Upper(PTR_STR str1, PTR_STR str2)
43: {
44:    INTEGER i;
45:
46:    for (i=0; str1[i]; i++){
47:      if ((str1[i] >= 'a') &&
48:          (str1[i] <= 'z'))
49:        str2[i] = str1[i] - DELT;
50:      else
51:        str2[i] = str1[i];
52:    }
53:    str2[i] = '\0';  /* add null character */
54: }
```

I have the following output displayed on the screen after running the executable file, 18L03.exe, of the program in Listing 18.3:

OUTPUT

```
Whatever we wear
we become beautiful
moon viewing!

WHATEVER WE WEAR
WE BECOME BEAUTIFUL
MOON VIEWING!
```

ANALYSIS   The purpose of the program in Listing 18.3 is to show you how to create your own names for data types such as char and int. The program in Listing 18.3 converts all characters in a Japanese haiku into their uppercase counterparts.

In lines 3 and 4, two more header files, stdlib.h and string.h, are included for the malloc(), and strlen()functions that are invoked later in the program.

An enum declaration is made in lines 6 and 7 with two enumerated name, ITEM_NUM and DELT. ITEM_NUM is assigned the value of 3 because there are three strings in the haiku. DELT contains the value of the difference between a lowercase character and its uppercase counterpart in the ASCII code. In line 7, the values of 'a' and 'A' are used to calculate the difference. In lines 8–11, I define the names STRING, PTR_STR, CHAR, and INTEGER, for a char array of pointers with three elements, a char pointer, a char, and an int data type, respectively, so that I can use these names as synonyms to these data types in the program.

For instance, the prototype of the Convert2Upper() function in line 13 contains two arguments that are all char pointers declared with PTR_STR.

In lines 17–20, two arrays of pointers, str and moon, are declared with STRING. moon is initialized to point to the strings of the Japanese haiku. In lines 21 and 22, two int variables, i and term, are declared with INTEGER.

The for loop in lines 24–33 allocates enough memory space dynamically based on the size of the haiku. The Conver2Upper() function is then called in line 31 to copy strings referenced by moon to the memory locations pointed by str and to convert all lowercase characters to their uppercase counterparts as well. Line 32 prints out the strings referenced by moon. The definition of the Conver2Upper() function is shown in lines 42–54.

In lines 34–37, another for loop prints out the content from the memory locations referenced by str. There are a total of three strings with uppercase characters in the content. After a string is displayed on the screen, the memory space allocated for the string is released by calling the free() function. Because line 35 prints out each string with a newline at its beginning instead of the end, a newline that will follow the final string is printed on line 38.

On the screen, you see two copies of the haiku—the original one and the one with all-uppercase characters.

Recursive Functions

You already know that in C a function can be called by another function. But can a function call itself? The answer is yes. A function can call itself from a statement inside the body of the function itself. Such a function is said to be *recursive*.

Listing 18.4 contains an example of calling a recursive function to add integers from 1 to 100.

TYPE   **LISTING 18.4**   Calling a Recursive Function

```
1:  /* 18L04.c: Calling a recursive function */
2:  #include <stdio.h>
3:
4:  enum con{MIN_NUM = 0,
5:           MAX_NUM = 100};
6:
7:  int fRecur(int n);
8:
9:  main()
```

continues

LISTING **18.4**   continued

```
10: {
11:     int i, sum1, sum2;
12:
13:     sum1 = sum2 = 0;
14:     for (i=1; i<=MAX_NUM; i++)
15:        sum1 += i;
16:     printf("The value of sum1 is %d.\n", sum1);
17:     sum2 = fRecur(MAX_NUM);
18:     printf("The value returned by fRecur() is %d.\n", sum2);
19:
20:     return 0;
21: }
22: /* function definition */
23: int fRecur(int n)
24: {
25:     if (n == MIN_NUM)
26:        return 0;
27:     return fRecur(n - 1) + n;
28: }
```

After the executable file 18L04.exe is created and executed, the following output is displayed on the screen of my computer:

OUTPUT
```
The value of sum1 is 5050.
The value returned by fRecur() is 5050.
```

ANALYSIS
In the program in Listing 18.4, a recursive function, fRecur(), is declared in line 7 and defined in lines 23–28.

You can see from the definition of the fRecur() function that the recursion is stopped in line 26 if the incoming int variable, n, is equal to the value contained by the enum name MIN_NUM. Otherwise, the fRecur() function is called by itself over and over in line 27. Note that each time the fRecur() function is called, the integer argument passed to the function is decreased by one.

Now, let's have a look at the main() function of the program. The for loop, shown in lines 14 and 15, adds integers from 1 to the value represented by another enum name, MAX_NUM. In lines 4 and 5, MIN_NUM and MAX_NUM are respectively assigned 0 and 100 in an enum declaration. The printf() call in line 16 then prints out the sum of the addition made by the for loop.

In line 17, the recursive function, fRecur(), is called and passed an integer argument starting at the value of MAX_NUM. The value returned by the fRecur() function is then assigned to an int variable, sum2.

When the fRecur() function returns, the value of sum2 is printed out in line 18. From the output, you can see that the execution of the recursive function fRecur() produces the same result as the for loop inside the main() function.

Recursive functions are useful in making clearer and simpler implementations of algorithms. On the other hand, however, recursive functions may run slower than their iterative equivalents due to the overhead of repeated function calls.

Function arguments and local variables of a program are usually stored temporarily by the computer, in a block of memory called the *stack*. Each call to a recursive function makes a new copy of the arguments and local variables. The new copy is then put on the stack. If you see your recursive function behaving strangely, it's probably overwriting other data stored on the stack.

Although it's possible that the recursive function is simply being executed too many times and exhausting the stack resource, this kind of problem often occurs when you have a case of "runaway recursion." In Listing 18.4, the if statement in line 25 stops the recursion when n is equal to MIN_NUM. In your own recursive functions, always remember to have such a condition in place to stop the recursion so that the function will return back to the original caller.

18

Revisiting the main() Function

As you've learned, each C program must have one and only one main() function. The execution of a program starts and ends at its main() function.

As with other functions in C, you can pass arguments to a main() function. So far, I've been using the void keyword in the definition of the main() function to indicate that there are no arguments passed to the function. Now, the question is what to do if you want to pass information to the main() function.

Command-Line Arguments

Because each C program starts at its main() function, information is usually passed to the main() function via command-line arguments.

A *command-line argument* is a parameter that follows a program's name when the program is invoked from the operating system's command line. For instance, given a C program, test.c, whose executable file is called test.exe, if you are using a PC, you might run the program from a DOS prompt like this:

```
test argument1 argument2 argument3
```

argument1, argument2, and argument3 are called command-line arguments to the main() function in the test.c program.

The next subsection teaches you how to receive command-line arguments.

Receiving Command-Line Arguments

There are two built-in arguments in the main() function that can be used to receive command-line arguments. Usually, the name of the first argument is argc, and it is used to store the number of arguments on the command line. The second argument is called argv and is a pointer to an array of char pointers. Each element in the array of pointers points to a command-line argument that is treated as a string.

In order to use argc and argv, declare your main() function in your program like this:

```
main(int argc, char *argv[])
{
    . . .
}
```

Let's continue to use the example shown in the last section. Suppose that the main() function defined in the test.c program looks like this:

```
main(int argc, char *argv[])
{
    . . .
}
```

If you run the executable file of the program from a prompt like this:

```
test argument1 argument2 argument3
```

the value received by argc is 4 because the name of the program itself is counted as the first command-line argument. Accordingly, argv[0] holds a representation of the program name, and argv[1], argv[2], and argv[3] contain the strings of argument1, argument2, and argument3, respectively.

The program in Listing 18.5 is another example of passing command-line arguments to the main() function.

TYPE **LISTING 18.5** Passing Command-Line Arguments to the main() Function

```
1:  /* 18L05.c: Command-line arguments */
2:  #include <stdio.h>
3:
4:  main (int argc, char *argv[])
5:  {
```

```
6:      int i;
7:
8:      printf("The value received by argc is %d.\n", argc);
9:      printf("There are %d command-line arguments passed to main().\n",
10:            argc);
11:     if(argc) {
12:        printf("The first command-line argument is: %s\n", argv[0]);
13:        printf("The rest of the command-line arguments are:\n");
14:        for (i=1; i<argc; i++)
15:            printf("%s\n", argv[i]);
16:     }
17:     return 0;
18: }
```

After the executable file 18L05.exe is executed with several command-line arguments, the following output is displayed on the screen of my computer (I entered "Hello, world!" in this example.):

OUTPUT

```
18L05.exe  Hello, world!
The value received by argc is 3.
There are 3 command-line arguments passed to main().
The first command-line argument is: C:\app\18L05.EXE
The rest of the command-line arguments are:
Hello,
world!
```

ANALYSIS The first line of the output shown above contains the executable file 18L05.exe, and the command-line arguments, Hello, world!, from a DOS prompt on my computer. The purpose of the program in Listing 18.5 is to show you how to check the number of command-line arguments and print out the strings that hold the arguments entered by the user.

Note that there are two arguments, argc and argv, that are declared in line 4 for the main() function. Then, the statements in lines 8 and 9 print out the value of the total number of arguments held by argc. If the program was run with no command-line arguments, argc can be 0, in which case argv is a null pointer. Line 11 makes sure that argc and argv contain data; if not, we return 0 and end the program.

Line 12 prints out the first string saved in the memory location pointed to by argv[0]. As you can see from the output, the content of the first string is the executable file name of the program in Listing 18.5, plus the path to the executable file.

The for loop in lines 14 and 15 displays the rest of the strings that contain the command-line arguments entered by the user. In this example, I enter two command-line argument strings, "Hello," and "world!", which are shown back on the screen after the execution of the for loop.

argc and argv are normally used as the two built-in arguments in the main()
function, but you can use other names to replace them in their declarations.
As long as the data types are correct, your main() function will still be able
to receive the command line arguments.

Summary

In this lesson you've learned the following important data type, keywords, and concepts
in C:

- The enum (that is, enumerated) data type can be used to declare named integer con-
  stants.
- By default, the first enum name starts with the value of 0. Each name in the rest of
  the list increases by one from the value contained by the name on its left side.
- If needed, you can assign any integer values to enumerated names.
- You can create your own names for data types with the help of the typedef key-
  word. Those names can then be used as synonyms for the data types.
- In ANSI C, there is a header file called stddef.h that contains a dozen typedef
  definitions.
- A function in C can be made to call itself. Such a function is said to be recursive.
- You can use command-line arguments to pass information to the main() function
  in your program.
- There are two built-in arguments to the main() function.
- The first built-in argument receives the number of command-line arguments
  entered by the user. The second built-in argument is a pointer to an array of pointers that refers to the strings of command-line arguments.

In the next lesson you'll learn about collecting variables of different types with structures.

Q&A

Q What can you do with the enum data type?

A The enum data type can be used to declare names that represent integer constants.
You can use the default values held by enum names, or you can assign values to
enum names and use them later in the program. The enum data type makes the C
program more readable and easier to maintain because you can use words that you
understand as the names of enum, and you will only have to go to one place to
update the values when needed.

Q Why do you need to use the `typedef` keyword?

A By using the `typedef` keyword, you can define your own names to represent the data types in C. You can represent complex data types in a single word and then use that word in subsequent variable declarations. In this way, you can avoid typing errors when writing a complex declaration over and over. Also, if a data type is changed in the future, you just need to update the `typedef` definition of the data type, which fixes every use of the `typedef` definition.

Q Does a recursive function help to improve the performance of a program?

A Not really. Normally, a recursive function only makes the implementations of some algorithms clearer and simpler. A recursive function may slow down the speed of a program because of the overhead of repeated function calls.

Workshop

To help solidify your understanding of this hour's lesson, you are encouraged to answer the quiz questions and finish the exercises provided in the workshop before you move to the next lesson. The answers and hints to the questions and exercises are given in Appendix B, "Answers to Quiz Questions and Exercises."

Quiz

1. What are the values represented by the following `enum` names?

```
enum months { Jan, Feb, Mar, Apr,
              May, Jun, Jul, Aug,
              Sep, Oct, Nov, Dec };
```

2. What are the values represented by the following `enum` names?

```
enum tag { name1,
           name2 = 10,
           name3,
           name4 };
```

3. Which of the following statements have equivalent variable declarations?

   - `typedef long int BYTE32; BYTE32 x, y, z;`
   - `typedef char *STRING[16]; STRING str1, str2, str3;`
   - `long int x, y, z;`
   - `char *str1[16], *str2[16], *str3[16];`

4. Can you pass some command-line arguments to a `main()` function that has the following definition?

```
int main(void)
{
   . . .
}
```

18

Exercises

1. Write a program to print out the values represented by the enumerated names declared in Quiz question 2 in this hour.

2. Given the following declarations:
   ```
   typedef char WORD;
   typedef int SHORT;
   typedef long LONG;
   typedef float FLOAT;
   typedef double DFLOAT;
   ```
   write a program to measure the sizes of the synonyms to the data types.

3. Rewrite the program in Listing 18.4. This time, add integers starting at the value of MIN_NUM instead of the value of MAX_NUM.

4. Write a program that accepts command-line arguments. If the number of command-line arguments, not including the name of the executable itself, is less than two, print out the usage format of the program and ask the user to reenter the command-line arguments. Otherwise, display all command-line arguments entered by the user.

PART V

Structure, Union, File I/O, and More

Hour

Hour 19

Understanding Structures

The art of programming is the art of organizing complexity.

—W. W. Dijkstra

In Hour 12, "Understanding Arrays," you learned how to store data of the same type into arrays. In this hour, you'll learn to use structures to collect data items that have different data types. The following topics are covered in this lesson:

- Declaring and defining structures
- Referencing structure members
- Structures and pointers
- Structures and functions
- Arrays of structures

What Is a Structure?

As you've learned, arrays can be used to collect groups of variables of the same type. The question now is how to aggregate pieces of data that are not identically typed.

The answer is that you can group variables of different types with a data type called a *structure*. In C, a structure collects different data items in such a way that they can be referenced as a single unit.

There are several major differences between an array and a structure. Besides the fact that data items in a structure can have different types, each data item has its own name instead of a subscript value. In fact, data items in a structure are called *members* of the structure.

The next two subsections teach you how to declare structures and define structure variables.

Declaring Structures

The general form to declare a structure is

```
struct struct_tag {
    data_type1 variable1;
    data_type2 variable2;
    data_type3 variable3;
    .
    .
    .
    };
```

Here struct is the keyword used in C to start a structure declaration. *struct_tag* is the tag name of the structure. *variable1*, *variable2*, and *variable3* are the members of the structure. Their data types are specified respectively by *data_type1*, *data_type2*, and *data_type3*. As you can see, the declarations of the members have to be enclosed within the opening and closing braces ({ and }) in the structure declaration, and a semicolon (;) has to be included at the end of the declaration.

The following is an example of a structure declaration:

```
struct automobile {
    int year;
    char model[8];
    int engine_power;
    float weight;
    };
```

Here struct is used to start a structure declaration. automobile is the tag name of the structure. In this example, there are three types of variables, char, int, and float. The variables have their own names, such as year, model, engine_power, and weight.

Note that a structure tag name, like automobile, is the name of a structure. The compiler uses the tag name to identify the structure labeled by that tag name.

Defining Structure Variables

After declaring a structure, you can define the structure variables. For instance, the following structure variables are defined with the structure data type of automobile from the previous section:

```
struct automobile sedan, pick_up, sport_utility;
```

Here three structure variables, sedan, pick_up, and sport_utility, are defined by the structure of automobile. All these three structure variables contain the four members of the structure automobile.

Also, you can combine the structure declaration and definition into one statement like this:

```
struct automobile {
    int year;
    char model[8];
    int engine_power;
    float weight;
    } sedan, pick_up, sport_utility;
```

Here three structure variables, sedan, pick_up, and sport_utility, are defined along with the structure automobile in the single statement.

Referencing Structure Members with the Dot Operator

Now, let's see how to reference a structure member. Given the structure automobile and the structure variable sedan, for instance, I can access its member, year, and assign an integer to it in the following way:

```
sedan.year = 1997;
```

Here the structure name and its member's name are separated by the dot (.) operator so that the compiler knows that the integer value of 1997 is assigned to the member called year, which is a member of the structure variable called sedan.

19

Likewise, the following statement assigns the start address of the character array of model, which is another member of the structure variable sedan, to a char pointer ptr:

ptr = sedan.model;

The program in Listing 19.1 gives another example to reference the members of a structure.

TYPE   **LISTING 19.1**   Referencing the Members of a Structure

```
1:  /* 19L01.c Access to structure members */
2:  #include <stdio.h>
3:
4:  main(void)
5:  {
6:      struct computer {
7:          float cost;
8:          int year;
9:          int cpu_speed;
10:         char cpu_type[16];
11:         } model;
12:
13:     printf("The type of the CPU inside your computer?\n");
14:         gets(model.cpu_type);
15:     printf("The speed(MHz) of the CPU?\n");
16:         scanf("%d", &model.cpu_speed);
17:     printf("The year your computer was made?\n");
18:         scanf("%d", &model.year);
19:     printf("How much you paid for the computer?\n");
20:         scanf("%f", &model.cost);
21:
22:     printf("Here are what you entered:\n");
23:     printf("Year: %d\n", model.year);
24:     printf("Cost: $%6.2f\n", model.cost);
25:     printf("CPU type: %s\n", model.cpu_type);
26:     printf("CPU speed: %d MHz\n", model.cpu_speed);
27:
28:     return 0;
29: }
```

I have the following output shown on the screen after I run the executable (19L01.exe) of the program in Listing 19.1 and enter my answers to the questions (in the output, the bold characters or numbers are the answers entered from my keyboard):

OUTPUT
```
The type of the CPU inside your computer?
Pentium
The speed(MHz) of the CPU?
100
The year your computer was made?
1996
How much you paid for the computer?
1234.56
Here are what you entered:
Year: 1996
Cost: $1234.56
CPU type: Pentium
CPU speed: 100 MHz
```

ANALYSIS The purpose of the program in Listing 19.1 is to show you how to reference members of a structure. As you can see from the program, there is a structure called model that is defined with a type of struct computer in lines 6–11. The structure has one float variable, two int variables, and one char array. The statement in line 13 asks the user to enter the type of the CPU (central processing unit) used inside his or her computer. Then, line 14 receives the string of the CPU type entered by the user and saves the string into the char array called cpu_type. Because cpu_type is a member of the model structure, the model.cpu_type expression is used in line 14 to reference the member of the structure. Note that the dot operator (.) is used to separate the two names in the expression.

Lines 15 and 16 ask for the CPU speed and store the value of an integer entered by the user to another member of the model structure—the int variable cpu_speed. Note that in line 16, the address-of operator (&) is prefixed to the model.cpu_speed expression inside the scanf() function because the argument should be an int pointer.

Likewise, lines 17 and 18 receive the value of the year in which the user's computer was made, and lines 19 and 20 get the number for the cost of the computer. After the execution, the int variable year and the float variable cost in the model structure contain the corresponding values entered by the user.

Then, lines 23–26 print out all values held by the members of the model structure. From the output, you can tell that each member of the structure has been accessed and assigned a number or string correctly.

19

Initializing Structures

A structure can be initialized by a list of data called *initializers*. Commas are used to separate data items in a list of data.

Listing 19.2 contains an example of initializing a structure before it's updated by the user.

TYPE   **LISTING 19.2**   Initializing a Structure

```
1:   /* 19L02.c Initializing a structure */
2:   #include <stdio.h>
3:
4:   main(void)
5:   {
6:       struct employee {
7:           int id;
8:           char name[32];
9:           };
10:      /* structure initialization */
11:      struct employee info = {
12:          1,
13:          "B. Smith"
14:          };
15:
16:      printf("Here is a sample:\n");
17:      printf("Employee Name: %s\n", info.name);
18:      printf("Employee ID #: %04d\n\n", info.id);
19:
20:      printf("What's your name?\n");
21:          gets(info.name);
22:      printf("What's your ID number?\n");
23:          scanf("%d", &info.id);
24:
25:      printf("\nHere are what you entered:\n");
26:      printf("Name: %s\n", info.name);
27:      printf("ID #: %04d\n", info.id);
28:
29:      return 0;
30:  }
```

When the executable 19L02.exe is being run, the initial content saved in a structure is displayed. Then, I enter my answers to the questions and get the updated information shown on the screen:

OUTPUT
```
Here is a sample:
Employee Name: B. Smith
Employee ID #: 0001

What's your name?
T. Zhang
What's your ID number?
1234
```

```
Here are what you entered:
Name: T. Zhang
ID #: 1234
```

ANALYSIS The purpose of the program in Listing 19.2 is to initialize a structure and then ask the user to update the content held by the structure.

The structure data type, labeled as employee, is declared in lines 6–9. Then, the variable, info, is defined with the structure data type and initialized with the integer 1 and the string "B. Smith" in lines 11–14.

You can also combine the declaration, definition, and initialization of a structure into a single statement. Here's an example:

```
struct employee {
    int id;
    char name[32];
    } info = {
    1,
    "B. Smith"
    };
```

The statements in lines 17 and 18 display the initial contents stored by the two members of the info structure on the screen. Then, lines 20–23 ask the user to enter his or her name and employee ID number and save them into the two structure members, name and id, respectively.

Before the end of the program, the updated contents contained by the two members are printed out by the statements in lines 26 and 27.

Again, the dot operator (.) is used in the program to reference the structure members.

Structures and Function Calls

The C language allows you to pass an entire structure to a function. In addition, a function can return a structure back to its caller.

To show you how to pass a structure to a function, I rewrote the program in Listing 19.1 and created a function called DataReceive() in the program. The upgraded program is shown in Listing 19.3.

19

TYPE   **LISTING 19.3**   Passing a Structure to a Function

```
 1:  /* 19L03.c Passing a structure to a function */
 2:  #include <stdio.h>
 3:
 4:  struct computer {
 5:     float cost;
 6:     int year;
 7:     int cpu_speed;
 8:     char cpu_type[16];
 9:  };
10:  /* create synonym */
11:  typedef struct computer SC;
12:  /* function declaration */
13:  SC DataReceive(SC s);
14:
15:  main(void)
16:  {
17:     SC model;
18:
19:     model = DataReceive(model);
20:     printf("Here are what you entered:\n");
21:     printf("Year: %d\n", model.year);
22:     printf("Cost: $%6.2f\n", model.cost);
23:     printf("CPU type: %s\n", model.cpu_type);
24:     printf("CPU speed: %d MHz\n", model.cpu_speed);
25:
26:     return 0;
27:  }
28:  /* function definition */
29:  SC DataReceive(SC s)
30:  {
31:     printf("The type of the CPU inside your computer?\n");
32:        gets(s.cpu_type);
33:     printf("The speed(MHz) of the CPU?\n");
34:        scanf("%d", &s.cpu_speed);
35:     printf("The year your computer was made?\n");
36:        scanf("%d", &s.year);
37:     printf("How much you paid for the computer?\n");
38:        scanf("%f", &s.cost);
39:     return s;
40:  }
```

After I run the executable, 19L03.exe, and enter my answers to the questions, I get the
following output, which is the same as the output from the executable program of
Listing 19.1:

OUTPUT

```
The type of the CPU inside your computer?
Pentium
The speed(MHz) of the CPU?
100
The year your computer was made?
1996
How much you paid for the computer?
1234.56
Here are what you entered:
Year: 1996
Cost: $1234.56
CPU type: Pentium
CPU speed: 100 MHz
```

ANALYSIS

The purpose of the program in Listing 19.3 is to show you how to pass a structure to a function. The structure in Listing 19.3, with the tag name of computer, is declared in lines 4–9.

Note that in line 11 the typedef keyword is used to define a synonym, SC, for struct computer. Then SC is used in the sequential declarations. Here, the structure and typedef are placed outside the main() function so that SC can be used in any function in the program.

The DataReceive() function is declared in line 13, with the structure of computer as its argument (that is, the synonym SC and the variable name s), so that a copy of the structure can be passed to the function.

In addition, the DataReceive() function returns the copy of the structure back to the caller after the content of the structure is updated. To do this, SC is prefixed to the function in line 13 to indicate the data type of the value returned by the function.

The statement in line 17 defines the structure variable model with SC. The model structure is passed to the DataReceive() function in line 19, and then the value returned by the function is assigned back to model as well. Note that if the DataReceive() function return value is not assigned to model, the changes made to s in the function will not be evident in model.

The definition of the DataReceive() function is shown in lines 29–40, from which you can see that the new data values entered by the user are saved into the corresponding members of the structure that is passed to the function. At the end of the function, the copy of the updated structure is returned in line 39.

Then, back to the main() function of the program, lines 21–24 print out the updated contents held by the members of the structure. Because the program in Listing 19.3 is basically the same as the one in Listing 19.1, I see the same output on my screen after running the executable file 19L03.exe.

19

Referencing Structures with Pointers

As you can pass a pointer that refers to an array in a function call, you can also pass a pointer that points to a structure.

However, unlike passing a structure to a function, which sends an entire copy of the structure to the function, passing a pointer to a structure sends only the address of the structure to the function. The function can then use the address to access the structure members directly, avoiding the overhead of duplicating the structure. Therefore, it's more efficient to pass a pointer to a structure, than it is to pass the structure itself to a function. Accordingly, the program in Listing 19.3 can be rewritten to pass the DataReceive() function a pointer that points to the structure. The rewritten program is shown in Listing 19.4.

TYPE | **LISTING 19.4** Passing a Function with a Pointer that Points to a Structure

```
1:  /* 19L04.c Pointing to a structure */
2:  #include <stdio.h>
3:
4:  struct computer {
5:     float cost;
6:     int year;
7:     int cpu_speed;
8:     char cpu_type[16];
9:  };
10:
11: typedef struct computer SC;
12:
13: void DataReceive(SC *ptr_s);
14:
15: main(void)
16: {
17:    SC model;
18:
19:    DataReceive(&model);
20:    printf("Here are what you entered:\n");
21:    printf("Year: %d\n", model.year);
22:    printf("Cost: $%6.2f\n", model.cost);
23:    printf("CPU type: %s\n", model.cpu_type);
24:    printf("CPU speed: %d MHz\n", model.cpu_speed);
25:
26:    return 0;
27: }
28: /* function definition */
29: void DataReceive(SC *ptr_s)
30: {
```

```
31:    printf("The type of the CPU inside your computer?\n");
32:        gets((*ptr_s).cpu_type);
33:    printf("The speed(MHz) of the CPU?\n");
34:        scanf("%d", &(*ptr_s).cpu_speed);
35:    printf("The year your computer was made?\n");
36:        scanf("%d", &(*ptr_s).year);
37:    printf("How much you paid for the computer?\n");
38:        scanf("%f", &(*ptr_s).cost);
39: }
```

Similarly, I obtain output that is the same as the one from the program in Listing 19.3 after I run the executable (19L04.exe) of the program in Listing 19.4:

OUTPUT

```
The type of the CPU inside your computer?
Pentium
The speed(MHz) of the CPU?
100
The year your computer was made?
1996
How much you paid for the computer?
1234.56
Here are what you entered:
Year: 1996
Cost: $1234.56
CPU type: Pentium
CPU speed: 100 MHz
```

ANALYSIS The program in Listing 19.4 is almost identical to the one in Listing 19.3, except that the argument passed to the DataReceive() function is a pointer defined with SC—that is, struct computer. (Refer to lines 11 and 13.) Also, the DataReceive() function does not need to return a copy of the structure because the function can directly access and modify all members of the original structure, not a copy, via the pointer passed to it. That's why the void keyword is prefixed to the function name in line 13.

The statement in line 17 defines the structure variable model. And in line 19, the address of the model structure is passed to the DataReceive() function by applying the address-of operator (&).

When you look at the definition of the DataReceive() function in lines 29–39, you see that the dereferenced pointer *ptr_s is used to reference the members of the model structure. For instance, to access the char array of cpu_type, (*ptr_s) is used in the (*ptr_s).cpu_type expression to indicate to the compiler that cpu_type is a member in the structure pointed to by the pointer ptr_s. Note that the dereferenced pointer *ptr_s has to be enclosed within the parentheses ((and)). This is because the default order of operator precedence would evaluate the . (dot) operator before the * operator, which in this case is not what we intend.

19

Another example is the expression &(*ptr_s).cpu_speed in line 34, which evaluates to the address of the cpu_speed member of the structure pointed to by the pointer ptr_s. Again, the dereferenced pointer *ptr_s is surrounded by the parentheses ((and)).

The next subsection shows you how to use the arrow operator (->) to refer to a structure member with a pointer.

Referencing a Structure Member with ->

You can use the arrow operator -> to refer to a structure member associated with a pointer that points to the structure.

For instance, you can rewrite the (*ptr_s).cpu_type expression in Listing 19.4 with this:

```
ptr_s -> cpu_type
```

or you could replace the &(*ptr_s).cpu_speed expression with this:

```
&(ptr_s->cpu_speed)
```

Since the -> operator has higher precedence than the & operator, you can leave out the parentheses in the above expression, writing it instead like this:

```
&ptr_s->cpu_speed
```

Because of its better clarity, the -> operator is more frequently used in programs that access structure members via pointers, rather than the dot operator. Exercise 3, later in this hour, gives you a chance to rewrite the entire program in Listing 19.4 using the -> operator.

Arrays of Structures

In C, you can declare an array of structures by preceding the array name with the structure name. For instance, given a structure with the tag name of x, the following statement:

```
struct x array_of_structure[8];
```

declares an array, called array_of_structure, of struct x. The array has eight elements, each element being a single instance of struct x.

The program shown in Listing 19.5 demonstrates how to use an array of structs by printing out two pieces of Japanese haiku and their authors' names.

TYPE   **LISTING 19.5**   Using Arrays of Structures

```
1:   /* 19L05.c Arrays of structures */
2:   #include <stdio.h>
3:
4:   struct haiku {
5:      int start_year;
6:      int end_year;
7:      char author[16];
8:      char str1[32];
9:      char str2[32];
10:      char str3[32];
11: };
12:
13: typedef struct haiku HK;
14:
15: void DataDisplay(HK *ptr_s);
16:
17: main(void)
18: {
19:      HK poem[2] = {
20:        { 1641,
21:          1716,
22:          "Sodo",
23:          "Leading me along",
24:          "my shadow goes back home",
25:          "from looking at the moon."
26:        },
27:        { 1729,
28:          1781,
29:          "Chora",
30:          "A storm wind blows",
31:          "out from among the grasses",
32:          "the full moon grows."
33:        }
34:      };
35:      int i;
36:
37:      for (i=0; i<2; i++)
38:         DataDisplay(&poem[i]);
39:
40:      return 0;
41: }
42: /* function definition */
43: void DataDisplay(HK *ptr_s)
44: {
45:      printf("%s\n", ptr_s->str1);
46:      printf("%s\n", ptr_s->str2);
```

continues

LISTING 19.5   continued

```
47:     printf("%s\n", ptr_s->str3);
48:     printf("--- %s\n", ptr_s->author);
49:     printf("   (%d-%d)\n\n", ptr_s->start_year, ptr_s->end_year);
50: }
```

After running the executable (19L05.exe) of the program in Listing 19.5, I see the two pieces of Japanese haiku displayed on the screen of my computer:

OUTPUT

```
Leading me along
my shadow goes back home
from looking at the moon.
--- Sodo
   (1641-1716)

A storm wind blows
out from among the grasses
the full moon grows.
--- Chora
   (1729-1781)
```

ANALYSIS   In Listing 19.5, a structure data type, with the tag name of haiku, is declared in lines 4–11. The structure data type contains two int variables and four char arrays as its members. The statement in line 13 creates a synonym, HK, for the struct haiku data type.

Then, in lines 19–34, an array of two elements, poem, is declared and initialized with two pieces of haiku written by Sodo and Chora, respectively. The following is a copy of the two pieces of haiku from poem:

```
"Leading me along",
"my shadow goes back home",
"from looking at the moon."
```

and

```
"A storm wind blows",
"out from among the grasses",
"the full moon grows."
```

The initializer also includes the author's names and the years of their birth and death (refer to lines 20–22, and lines 27–29). Note that the poem array, declared with HK, is indeed an array of the haiku structure.

The DataDisplay() function is called twice in a for loop in lines 37 and 38. Each time, the address of an element of poem is passed to the DataDisplay() function. According to the definition of the function in lines 43–50, DataDisplay() prints out three strings of a haiku, the author's name, and the period of time in which he lived.

From the output, you can see that the contents stored in the poem array of the haiku structure are displayed on the screen properly.

Nested Structures

You can declare a structure member that is itself a structure. For instance, given a structure data type of x, the following statement:

```
struct y {
   int i;
   char ch[8];
   struct x nested;
};
```

declares a nested structure with tag name of y. One of the members of the y structure is a structure with the variable name of nested that is defined by the structure data type of x.

Listing 19.6 contains an example of using a nested structure to receive and print out information about an employee.

TYPE   **LISTING 19.6**   Using Nested Structures

```
 1: /* 19L06.c Using nested structures */
 2: #include <stdio.h>
 3:
 4: struct department {
 5:    int  code;
 6:    char name[32];
 7:    char position[16];
 8: };
 9:
10: typedef struct department DPT;
11:
12: struct employee {
13:    DPT d;
14:    int id;
15:    char name[32];
16: };
17:
18: typedef struct employee EMPLY;
19:
20: void InfoDisplay(EMPLY *ptr);
21: void InfoEnter(EMPLY *ptr);
22:
23: main(void)
24: {
25:    EMPLY info = {
```

19

continues

LISTING 19.6 continued

```
26:      { 1,
27:        "Marketing",
28:        "Manager"
29:      },
30:      1,
31:      "B. Smith"
32:    };
33:
34:    printf("Here is a sample:\n");
35:    InfoDisplay(&info);
36:
37:    InfoEnter(&info);
38:
39:    printf("\nHere are what you entered:\n");
40:    InfoDisplay(&info);
41:
42:    return 0;
43: }
44: /* function definition */
45: void InfoDisplay(EMPLY *ptr)
46: {
47:    printf("Name: %s\n", ptr->name);
48:    printf("ID #: %04d\n", ptr->id);
49:    printf("Dept. name: %s\n", ptr->d.name);
50:    printf("Dept. code: %02d\n", ptr->d.code);
51:    printf("Your position: %s\n", ptr->d.position);
52: }
53: /* function definition */
54: void InfoEnter(EMPLY *ptr)
55: {
56:    printf("\nPlease enter your information:\n");
57:    printf("Your name:\n");
58:      gets(ptr->name);
59:    printf("Your position:\n");
60:      gets(ptr->d.position);
61:    printf("Dept. name:\n");
62:      gets(ptr->d.name);
63:    printf("Dept. code:\n");
64:      scanf("%d", &(ptr->d.code));
65:    printf("Your employee ID #:\n");
66:      scanf("%d", &(ptr->id));
67: }
```

When the executable file, 19L06.exe, is running, the initial content of the nested structure is printed out first. Then, I enter my employment information, which is in bold in the following output and displayed back on the screen too:

OUTPUT

```
Here is a sample:
Name: B. Smith
ID #: 0001
Dept. name: Marketing
Dept. code: 01
Your position: Manager

Please enter your information:\n");
Your name:
T. Zhang
Your position:\n");
Engineer
Dept. name:
R&D
Dept. code:
3
Your employee ID #:
1234

Here are what you entered:
Name: T. Zhang
ID #: 1234
Dept. name: R&D
Dept. code: 03
Your position: Engineer
```

ANALYSIS

There are two structure data types in Listing 19.6. The first one, called depart-ment, is declared in lines 4–8. The second one, employee, declared in lines 12–16, contains a member of the department structure data type. Therefore, the employee structure data type is a nested structure data type.

Two synonyms, DPT for the struct department data type, and EMPLY for the struct employee data type, are created in two typedef statements respectively in lines 10 and 18. In the program, there are two functions, InfoDisplay() and InfoEnter(), whose prototypes are declared with a pointer to an EMPLY as an argument (see lines 20 and 21).

The statements in 25–32 initialize a nested structure, which is called info and has a data type of EMPLY. Note that the nested braces ({ and }) in lines 26 and 29 enclose the initial-izers for the d structure of DPT that is nested inside the info structure.

Then, the statement in line 35 displays the initial contents held by the nested info struc-ture by calling the InfoDisplay() function. Line 37 calls the InfoEnter() function to ask the user to enter his or her employment information and then save it into the info structure. The InfoDisplay() function is called again in line 40 to display the informa-tion that was entered by the user and is now stored in the nested structure.

The definitions for the two functions, InfoDisplay() and InfoEnter(), are listed in lines 45–52 and lines 54–67, respectively.

19

Summary

In this lesson you learned the following very important concepts about structures in C:

- You can group variables of different types with a data type called a structure.
- The data items in a structure are called members of the structure.
- The struct keyword is used to start a structure declaration or a structure variable definition.
- The dot operator (.) is used to separate a structure name and a member name in referencing the structure member.
- The arrow operator (->) is commonly used to reference a structure member using a pointer to the structure.
- A structure can be passed to a function, and a function can return a structure back to the caller.
- Passing a pointer that points to a structure when calling a function is more efficient than passing the entire structure as an argument. Also, if a pointer is used, the function can modify the structure's contents directly.
- Arrays of structures are permitted in C.
- You can enclose a structure within another structure. This is called a nested structure.

In the next lesson you'll learn to use unions to collect dissimilar data items in C.

Q&A

Q Why do you need structures?

A You often need to collect and group data items that are relevant to each other, but of different data types. The struct data type provides a convenient way to aggregate differently typed data items.

Q How do you reference a structure member?

A You can reference a structure member by prefixing the structure member's name with the structure variable name and a dot operator (.). If you are accessing the structure via a pointer, you can use the pointer name, the arrow operator (->), and then the member name to reference the structure member.

Q Why is it more efficient to pass a pointer that refers to a structure to a function?

A When an entire structure is passed to a function, a copy of the structure is made and saved in a temporary block of storage. After the copy is modified by the function, it has to be returned and written back to the storage that holds the original content of the structure. Passing a function with a pointer that points to a structure, on the other hand, simply passes the address of the structure to the function instead of passing a copy of the entire structure. The function can then access the original memory location of the structure and modify the content held by the structure without duplicating the structure in temporary storage. Therefore, it's more efficient to pass a pointer of a structure than to pass the structure itself to a function.

Workshop

To help solidify your understanding of this hour's lesson, you are encouraged to answer the quiz questions and finish the exercises provided in the workshop before you move to the next lesson. The answers and hints to the questions and exercises are given in Appendix B, "Answers to Quiz Questions and Exercises."

Quiz

1. What's wrong with the following structure declaration?

```
struct automobile {
     int year;
     char model[8];
     int engine_power;
     float weight;
     }
```

2. How many structure variables are defined in the following statement?

```
struct x {int y; char z} u, v, w;
```

3. Given a structure declaration

```
struct automobile {
     int year;
     char model[8]};
```

and two car models, Taurus and Accord, which are made in 1997, initialize an array of two elements, car, of the automobile structures.

19

Exercises

1. Given the following declaration and definition of a structure:

```
struct automobile {
      int year;
      char model[10];
      int engine_power;
      double weight;
      } sedan = {
      1997,
      "New Model",
      200,
      2345.67};
```

   write a program to display on the screen the initial values held by the structure.

2. Rewrite the program in Listing 19.2. This time, create a function that can display the content in the employee structure. Then, make calls to the function by passing the structure to it.

3. Rewrite the program in Listing 19.4. This time, use the arrow operator (->) with the pointers to structures.

4. Rewrite the program in Listing 19.5. This time, add an array of pointers that is declared with HK. Then pass each element in the array of pointers to the DataDisplay() function.

Hour **20**

Understanding Unions

Coming together is a beginning;
keeping together is progress;
working together is success.

—T. Roosevelt

In the previous hour's lesson you learned how to store data of different types into structures. In this hour you'll learn another way to collect differently typed data items by using unions. You'll learn about the following topics in this lesson:

- How to declare and define unions
- How to initialize unions
- The differences between unions and structures
- Nested unions with structures
- Manipulating the bit field with `struct`

What Is a Union?

A *union* is a block of memory that is used to hold data items of different types. In C, a union is similar to a structure, except that the data items saved in the union are overlaid in order to share the same memory location. That is, they all share the same starting address, unlike a structure where each member gets its own area of memory. More details on the differences between unions and structures are discussed in the following sections. First, let's look at the syntax of unions.

Declaring Unions

The syntax for declaring a union is similar to the syntax for a structure. The following is an example of a union declaration:

```
union automobile {
    int year;
    char model[8];
    int engine_power;
    float weight;
};
```

Here union is the keyword that specifies the union data type. automobile is the tag name of the union. The variables year, model, engine_power, and weight, are members of the union, and are declared within the braces ({ and }). The union declaration ends with a semicolon (;).

Like a structure tag name, a union tag name is a label to a union, which is used by the compiler to identify the union.

Defining Union Variables

You can define union variables after declaring a union. For instance, the following union variables are defined with the union labeled with automobile from the previous section:

```
union automobile sedan, pickup, sport_utility;
```

Here the three variables, sedan, pickup, and sport_utility, are defined as union variables.

Of course, you can declare a union and define variables of the union in a single statement. For instance, you can rewrite the previous union declaration and definition like this:

```
union automobile {
    int year;
    char model[8];
    int engine_power;
    float weight;
} sedan, pickup, sport_utility;
```

Here three union variables, sedan, pickup, and sport_utility, are defined by the union of automobile in which there are four members of different data types. If you declare a union and define variables of the union in a single statement, and there are no further union variable definitions made with the union, you can omit the tag name of the union. For instance, the tag name automobile can be omitted in the union definition like this:

```
union {
    int year;
    char model[8];
    int engine_power;
    float weight;
} sedan, pickup, sport_utility;
```

Referencing a Union with . or ->

As well as being used to reference structure members, the dot operator (.) can be used in referencing union members. For example, the following statement assigns the value of 1997 to one of the members of the sedan union:

```
sedan.year = 1997;
```

Here the dot operator is used between the union name sedan and the member name year.

In addition, if you define a pointer ptr like this:

```
union automobile *ptr;
```

you can reference one of the union members in the following way:

```
ptr->year = 1997;
```

Here the arrow operator (->) is used to reference the union member year with the pointer ptr.

The program in Listing 20.1 gives another example of how to reference and assign values to the members of a union.

TYPE   **LISTING 20.1**   Referencing the Members of a Union

20

```
1:   /* 20L01.c Referencing a union */
2:   #include <stdio.h>
3:   #include <string.h>
4:
5:   main(void)
6:   {
7:       union menu {
8:           char name[23];
```

continues

LISTING 20.1   continued

```
 9:       double price;
10:    } dish;
11:
12:    printf("The content assigned to the union separately:\n");
13:    /* reference name */
14:    strcpy(dish.name, "Sweet and Sour Chicken");
15:    printf("Dish Name: %s\n", dish.name);
16:    /* reference price */
17:    dish.price = 9.95;
18:    printf("Dish Price: %5.2f\n", dish.price);
19:
20:    return 0;
21: }
```

After running the executable 20L01.exe of the program in Listing 20.1, I have the following output shown on the screen of my computer:

```
The content assigned to the union separately:
Dish Name: Sweet and Sour Chicken
Dish Price: 9.95
```

The purpose of the program in Listing 20.1 is to show you how to reference
union members with the dot operator.

Inside the main() function, a union, called dish, is first defined with the union data type
of menu in lines 7–10. There are two members, name and price, in the union.

Then the statement in line 14 copies the string "Sweet and Sour Chicken" into the
character array name that is one of the union members. Note that the dish.name expression is used as the first argument to the strcpy() function in line 14. When the compiler
sees the expression, it knows that you want to reference the memory location of name
that is a member of the dish union.

The strcpy() function is a C function that copies the contents of a string, pointed to by
the function's second argument, into the memory storage pointed to by the function's
first argument. I included the header file string.h in the program before calling the
strcpy() function. (See line 3.)

Line 15 prints out the contents copied to the name array by using the dish.name expression one more time.

The statement in line 17 assigns the value 9.95 to the double variable price, which is
another member for the dish union. Note that the dish.price expression is used to reference the union member. Then line 18 displays the value assigned to price by calling the
printf() function and passing the dish.price expression as an argument to the function.

According to the results shown in the output, the two members of the dish union, name and price, have been successfully referenced and assigned corresponding values.

Unions versus Structures

You might notice that in Listing 20.1, I assigned a value to one member of the dish union, and then immediately printed out the assigned value before I moved to the next union member. In other words, I didn't assign values to all the union members together before I printed out each assigned value from each member in the union.

I did this purposely because of the reason that is explained in the following section. So keep reading. (In Exercise 1 at the end of this lesson, you'll see a different output when you rewrite the program in Listing 20.1 by exchanging the order between the statements in lines 15 and 17.)

Initializing a Union

As mentioned earlier in this lesson, data items in a union are overlaid at the same memory location. In other words, the starting memory location of a union is shared by all the members of the union at different times. The size of a union is at least as large as the size of the largest data item in the list of the union members. This way, it is large enough to hold any members of the union, one at a time. Therefore, it does not make sense to initialize all members of a union together because the value of the latest initialized member overwrites the value of the preceding member. You initialize a member of a union only when you are ready to use it. The value contained by a union is always the value that was last assigned to a member of the union.

For instance, if you declare and define a union on a 16-bit machine (that is, the int data type is 2 bytes long) like this:

```
union u {
   char ch;
   int x;
} a_union;
```

then the following statement initializes the char variable ch with the character constant 'H':

```
a_union.ch = 'H';
```

and the value contained by the a_union union is the character constant 'H'. However, if the int variable x is initialized by the following statement:

```
a_union.x = 365;
```

20

then the value contained by the a_union union becomes the value of 365. Figure 20.1 demonstrates the content change of the union during the two initializations.

FIGURE **20.1**

The content of the a_union union is the same as the content assigned to one of its members.

(Assume that 0x1000 is the start address of the union.)

According to the ANSI C standard, a union can be initialized by assigning the first union member with a value. For instance, in the following statement:

```
union u {
    char ch;
    int x;
} a_union = {'H'};
```

the a_union union is said to be initialized because the character constant 'H' is assigned to the first union member, ch.

If the first member of a union is a structure, the entire structure has to be initialized with a list of values before the union is said to be initialized.

Let's see what will happen if you try to assign values to all members of a union together. Listing 20.2 gives such an example.

TYPE **LISTING 20.2** The Members of a Union Share the Same Memory Location

```
1:  /* 20L02.c:  Memory sharing in unions */
2:  #include <stdio.h>
3:
4:  main(void)
5:  {
6:      union employee {
7:          int start_year;
8:          int dpt_code;
9:          int id_number;
10:     } info;
```

```
11:
12:     /* initialize start_year */
13:     info.start_year = 1997;
14:     /* initialize dpt_code */
15:     info.dpt_code = 8;
16:     /* initialize id */
17:     info.id_number = 1234;
18:
19:     /* display content of union */
20:     printf("Start Year:  %d\n", info.start_year);
21:     printf("Dpt. Code:   %d\n", info.dpt_code);
22:     printf("ID Number:   %d\n", info.id_number);
23:
24:     return 0;
25: }
```

OUTPUT After the executable 20L02.exe is created and executed, the following output is displayed on the screen:

```
Start Year:   1234
Dpt. Code:    1234
ID Number:    1234
```

ANALYSIS As you can see in Listing 20.2, a union called info has three int variable members, start_year, dpt_code, and id_number. (See lines 6–10.) Then, these three union members are assigned with different values consecutively in lines 13, 15, and 17. And in lines 20–22, you try to print out the values assigned to the three members. However, the output shows that every member in the info union has the same value, 1234, which is the integer assigned to the third member of the union, id_number. Note that id_number is the member that is assigned with 1234 last; the info union does indeed hold the latest value assigned to its members.

The Size of a Union

You've been told that the members of a union all share the same memory location. The size of a union is at least as large as the size of the largest member in the union.

In contrast with a union, all members of a structure can be initialized together without any overwriting. This is because each member in a structure has its own memory storage. The size of a structure is at least equal to the sum of the sizes of its members, instead of the size of the largest member as is the case with a union.

Listing 20.3 contains a program that measures the size of a union as well as the size of a structure. The structure has exactly the same members as the union.

20

TYPE **LISTING 20.3** Measuring the Size of a Union

```
1:  /* 20L03.c The size of a union */
2:  #include <stdio.h>
3:  #include <string.h>
4:
5:  main(void)
6:  {
7:     union u {
8:         double x;
9:         int y;
10:    } a_union;
11:
12:    struct s {
13:        double x;
14:        int y;
15:    } a_struct;
16:
17:    printf("The size of double: %d-byte\n",
18:           sizeof(double));
19:    printf("The size of int:    %d-byte\n",
20:           sizeof(int));
21:
22:    printf("The size of a_union:  %d-byte\n",
23:           sizeof(a_union));
24:    printf("The size of a_struct: %d-byte\n",
25:           sizeof(a_struct));
26:
27:    return 0;
28: }
```

The compiler on your machine may generate several warning messages, something like "unreferenced local variables." This is because the a_union union and the a_struct structure are not initialized in the program. You can ignore the warning messages because they don't apply to what we're doing here. The following output is displayed on the screen of my computer after the executable 20L03.exe is created and executed:

OUTPUT
```
The size of double: 8-byte
The size of int:    2-byte
The size of a_union:  8-byte
The size of a_struct: 10-byte
```

ANALYSIS The purpose of the program in Listing 20.3 is to show the difference between a union memory allocation and a structure memory allocation, although both the union and the structure consist of the same members.

A union, called a_union, is defined in lines 7–10; it has two members, a double variable x and an int variable y. In addition, a structure, called a_structure and defined in lines 12–15, also consists of two members, a double variable x and an int variable y.

The statements in lines 17–20 first measure the sizes of the `double` and `int` data types on the host machine. For instance, on my machine, the size of the `double` data type is 8 bytes long and the `int` data type is 2 bytes long.

Then lines 22–25 measure the sizes of the `a_union` union and the `a_structure` structure, respectively. From the output, you see that the size of `a_union` is 8 bytes long on my machine.

The size of the structure, on the other hand, is 10 bytes on my machine, because there has to be enough memory space for both the `double` and the `int` in the structure.

Using Unions

Now let's focus on the applications of unions. Basically, there are two kinds of union applications, which are introduced in the following two sections.

Referencing the Same Memory Location Differently

The first application of unions is to reference the same memory location with different union members.

To get a better idea about referencing the same memory with different union members, let's have a look at the program in Listing 20.4, which uses the two members of a union to reference the same memory location. (You assume that the `char` data type is 1 byte long, and the `int` data type is 2 bytes long.)

TYPE   **LISTING 20.4**   Referencing the Same Memory Location with Different Union Members

```
1:  /* 20L04.c: Referencing the same memory in different ways */
2:  #include <stdio.h>
3:
4:  union u{
5:     char ch[2];
6:     int num;
7:  };
8:
9:  int UnionInitialize(union u val);
10:
11: main(void)
12: {
13:    union u val;
14:    int x;
15:
```

20

continues

LISTING 20.4   continued

```
16:     x = UnionInitialize(val);
17:
18:     printf("The two characters held by the union:\n");
19:     printf("%c\n", x & 0x00FF);
20:     printf("%c\n", x >> 8);
21:
22:     return 0;
23: }
24: /* function definition */
25: int UnionInitialize(union u val)
26: {
27:     val.ch[0] = 'H';
28:     val.ch[1] = 'i';
29:
30:     return val.num;
31: }
```

The following output is displayed on the screen of my computer after the executable
`20L04.exe` is created and executed:

```
The two characters held by the union:
H
i
```

ANALYSIS   As you see from the program in Listing 20.4, a union called `val` is defined in
line 13, which contains two members. One is a `char` array `ch` and the other is an
`int` variable `num`. If a `char` data type is 1 byte long and an `int` data type is 2 bytes long,
the `ch` array and the integer variable `num` have the same length of memory storage on
those machines.

A function named `UnionInitialize()` is called and passed the union name `val` in line
16. The definition of the `UnionInitialize()` function is shown in lines 25–31.

From the function definition, you can see that the two elements of the `char` array `ch` are
initialized with two character constants, `'H'` and `'i'` (in lines 27 and 28). Because the
`char` array `ch` and the `int` variable `num` share the same memory location, you can return
the value of `num` that contains the same content as the `ch` array. (See line 30.) Here
you've used the two members, `ch` and `num`, in the `val` union to reference the same memory location and the same contents of the union.

The value returned by the `UnionInitialize()` function is assigned to an `int` variable `x`
in line 16 inside the `main()` function. The statements in lines 19 and 20 print out the two
bytes of the `int` variable `num`. Each byte of `num` corresponds to a character that was used
to initialize the `ch` array because `num` and `ch` are both in the same union and have the
same content as the union. Line 19 displays the low byte of `num`, obtained by evaluating

the x & 0x00FF expression. In line 20, the high byte of num is obtained by shifting the x variable to the right by 8 bits, that is, by using the shift-right operator in the x >> 8 expression. (The bitwise operator (&) and the shift operator (>>) were introduced in Hour 8, "Using Conditional Operators.")

From the output, you can see that the content of the val union is shown on the screen correctly.

Figure 20.2 shows the locations of the two character constants in memory.

FIGURE 20.2

The memory locations of the two character constants.

(Assume that 0x1000 is the start address.)

There are two formats to store a multiple-byte quantity, such as the int variable num in Listing 20.4. One of the formats is called the *little-endian* format; the other is the *big-endian* format.

For the little-endian format, the high bytes of a multiple-byte quantity are stored at higher memory addresses and the low bytes are saved at lower addresses. The little-endian format is used by Intel's 80x86 microprocessors. My computer's CPU is a Pentium microprocessor, which is one of the members in the 80x86 family. Therefore, in Listing 20.4, the character constant 'H', which is a low byte, is stored at the lower address. 'i' is stored at the higher address because it's a high byte.

The big-endian format is just the opposite. That is, the high bytes are stored at lower addresses; the low bytes are stored at higher addresses. Motorola's 68000 microprocessor family uses the big-endian format.

20

Making Structures Flexible

The second application of unions is to nest a union inside a structure so that the structure can hold different types of values.

For example, suppose you want to write a program that asks the user about the name of a cable company or a satellite dish company that provides service to the user. Assume that the user either uses a cable or a satellite dish at home, but not both. Then, if you define two character arrays to store the cable company and satellite dish company names respectively, one of the arrays will be empty due to the assumption. In this case, you can declare a union with the two character arrays as its members so that the union can hold either a cable company name or a satellite dish company name, depending on the user's input. Listing 20.5 demonstrates how to write a program with such a union.

TYPE   **LISTING 20.5**   Making a Structure Flexible

```c
1:  /* 20L05.c: Using unions */
2:  #include <stdio.h>
3:  #include <string.h>
4:
5:  struct survey {
6:     char name[20];
7:     char c_d_p;
8:     int age;
9:     int hour_per_week;
10:    union {
11:       char cable_company[16];
12:       char dish_company[16];
13:    } provider;
14: };
15:
16: void DataEnter(struct survey *s);
17: void DataDisplay(struct survey *s);
18:
19: main(void)
20: {
21:    struct survey tv;
22:
23:    DataEnter(&tv);
24:    DataDisplay(&tv);
25:
26:    return 0;
27: }
28: /* function definition */
29: void DataEnter(struct survey *ptr)
30: {
31:    char is_yes[4];
32:
33:    printf("Are you using cable at home? (Yes or No)\n");
34:       gets(is_yes);
35:    if ((is_yes[0] == 'Y') ||
36:       (is_yes[0] == 'y')){
37:       printf("Enter the cable company name:\n");
38:       gets(ptr->provider.cable_company);
39:       ptr->c_d_p = 'c';
40:    } else {
41:       printf("Are you using a satellite dish? (Yes or No)\n");
```

```
42:        gets(is_yes);
43:     if ((is_yes[0] == 'Y') ||
44:         (is_yes[0] == 'y')){
45:        printf("Enter the satellite dish company name:\n");
46:        gets(ptr->provider.dish_company);
47:        ptr->c_d_p = 'd';
48:     } else {
49:        ptr->c_d_p = 'p';
50:     }
51:   }
52:   printf("Please enter your name:\n");
53:     gets(ptr->name);
54:   printf("Your age:\n");
55:     scanf("%d", &ptr->age);
56:   printf("How many hours you spend on watching TV per week:\n");
57:     scanf("%d", &ptr->hour_per_week);
58: }
59: /* function definition */
60: void DataDisplay(struct survey *ptr)
61: {
62:   printf("\nHere's what you've entered:\n");
63:   printf("Name: %s\n", ptr->name);
64:   printf("Age:  %d\n", ptr->age);
65:   printf("Hour per week: %d\n", ptr->hour_per_week);
66:   if (ptr->c_d_p == 'c')
67:      printf("Your cable company is: %s\n",
68:         ptr->provider.cable_company);
69:   else if (ptr->c_d_p == 'd')
70:      printf("Your satellite dish company is: %s\n",
71:         ptr->provider.dish_company);
72:   else
73:      printf("You don't have cable or a satellite dish.\n");
74:   printf("\nThanks and Bye!\n");
75: }
```

When the executable program 20L05.exe is being run, I enter my answers to the survey and the following output is displayed (my answers are shown in bold type in the output):

OUTPUT

```
Are you using cable at home? (Yes or No)
No
Are you using a satellite dish? (Yes or No)
Yes
Enter the satellite dish company name:
ABCD company
Please enter your name:
Tony Zhang
Your age:
30
How many hours you spend on watching TV per week:
8
```

20

```
Here's what you've entered:
Name: Tony Zhang
Age: 30
Hour per week: 8
Your satellite dish company is: ABCD company

Thanks and Bye!
```

ANALYSIS As you can see in lines 5–14, a `structure` data type with the tag name `survey` is declared, and in it a nested union called `provider` has two members, the `cable_company` array and the `dish_company` array. The two members of the union are used to hold the names of cable or satellite dish companies, depending on the user's input.

The statements in lines 16 and 17 declare two functions, `DataEnter()` and `DataDisplay()`, in which a pointer with `struct survey` is passed to each function as its argument.

A structure called `tv` is defined in line 21 inside the `main()` function. Then in lines 23 and 24, the `DataEnter()` and `DataDisplay()` functions are each called with the address of the `tv` structure as the argument.

Lines 29–58 contain the definition of the `DataEnter()` function, which asks the user to enter proper information based on the survey questions. Under the assumption you made earlier, the user can use either cable or a satellite dish, but not both. If the user does use cable, line 38 receives the cable company name entered by the user and saves it into the memory storage referenced by one of the members in the `provider` union, `cable_company`.

If the user uses a satellite dish, line 46 stores the satellite dish company name entered by the user into the same location of the `provider` union. But this time the name of another union member, `dish_company`, is used to reference the memory location. Now you see how to save the memory by putting two exclusive data items into a union.

In fact, the program supports another situation in which the user neither has cable nor a satellite dish. In this case, the `char` variable `c_d_p`, which is a member of the structure, is assigned with the character constant `'p'`.

Lines 60–75 give the definition of the `DataDisplay()` function that prints out the information entered by the user back to the screen. The output shown here is a sample I made by running the executable program of Listing 20.5 on my machine.

Defining Bit Fields with `struct`

In this section, you'll revisit our old friend the `struct` keyword to declare a very small object. Then you'll use the object with unions.

As you know, `char` is the smallest data type in C. The `char` data type is one `byte` long. However, with the help of the `struct` keyword, you can declare a smaller object—a *bit field*—which allows you to access a single bit. A bit is able to hold only one of two values, 1 or 0.

The general form to declare and define bit fields is

```
struct tag_name {
   data_type name1: length1;
   data_type name2: lenght2;
   . . .
   data_type nameN: lengthN;
} variable_list;
```

Here the `struct` keyword is used to start the declaration. `tag_name` is the tag name of the `struct` data type. `data_type`, which must be either `int`, `unsigned int`, or `signed int`, specifies the data type of the bit fields. `name1`, `name2`, and `nameN` are names of bit fields. `length1`, `length2`, and `lengthN` indicate the lengths of bit fields, specified in bits. The length of any one bit field may not exceed the length of the `int` data type. `variable_list` contains the variable names of the bit field.

For instance, the following statement defines a structure called `jumpers` with three bit field members:

```
struct bf {
   int jumper1: 1;
   int jumper2: 2;
   int jumper3: 3;
} jumpers;
```

Here `jumper1`, `jumper2`, and `jumper3` are the three bit fields with lengths of 1 bit, 2 bits, and 3 bits, respectively. Figure 20.3 demonstrates the memory allocations of the 3 bit fields.

20

FIGURE 20.3

The memory allocations of jumper1, jumper2, and jumper3 in a 16-bit `int`.

The program in Listing 20.6 is an example of using the bit fields defined with `struct`. In fact, the program in Listing 20.6 is a modified version of the program in Listing 20.5.

TYPE   **LISTING 20.6**   Applying Bit Fields

```
1:  /* 20L06.c: Applying bit fields */
2:  #include <stdio.h>
3:  #include <string.h>
4:
5:  struct bit_field {
6:      int cable: 1;
7:      int dish: 1;
8:  };
9:
10: struct survey {
11:     char name[20];
12:     struct bit_field c_d;
13:     int age;
14:     int hour_per_week;
15:     union {
16:         char cable_company[16];
17:         char dish_company[16];
18:     } provider;
19: };
20:
21: void DataEnter(struct survey *s);
22: void DataDisplay(struct survey *s);
23:
24: main(void)
25: {
26:     struct survey tv;
27:
28:     DataEnter(&tv);
29:     DataDisplay(&tv);
30:
31:     return 0;
32: }
33: /* function definition */
34: void DataEnter(struct survey *ptr)
35: {
36:     char is_yes[4];
37:
38:     printf("Are you using cable at home? (Yes or No)\n");
39:         gets(is_yes);
40:     if ((is_yes[0] == 'Y') ||
41:         (is_yes[0] == 'y')){
42:         printf("Enter the cable company name:\n");
43:         gets(ptr->provider.cable_company);
```

```
44:        ptr->c_d.cable = 1;
45:        ptr->c_d.dish = 0;
46:    } else {
47:        printf("Are you using a satellite dish? (Yes or No)\n");
48:          gets(is_yes);
49:        if ((is_yes[0] == 'Y') ¦¦
50:           (is_yes[0] == 'y')){
51:           printf("Enter the satellite dish company name:\n");
52:           gets(ptr->provider.dish_company);
53:           ptr->c_d.cable = 0;
54:           ptr->c_d.dish = 1;
55:        } else {
56:           ptr->c_d.cable = 0;
57:           ptr->c_d.dish = 0;
58:        }
59:    }
60:    printf("Please enter your name:\n");
61:       gets(ptr->name);
62:    printf("Your age:\n");
63:       scanf("%d", &ptr->age);
64:    printf("How many hours you spend on watching TV per week:\n");
65:       scanf("%d", &ptr->hour_per_week);
66: }
67: /* function definition */
68: void DataDisplay(struct survey *ptr)
69: {
70:    printf("\nHere's what you've entered:\n");
71:    printf("Name: %s\n", ptr->name);
72:    printf("Age:  %d\n", ptr->age);
73:    printf("Hour per week: %d\n", ptr->hour_per_week);
74:    if (ptr->c_d.cable && !ptr->c_d.dish)
75:       printf("Your cable company is: %s\n",
76:          ptr->provider.cable_company);
77:    else if (!ptr->c_d.cable && ptr->c_d.dish)
78:       printf("Your satellite dish company is: %s\n",
79:          ptr->provider.dish_company);
80:    else
81:       printf("You don't have cable or a satellite dish.\n");
82:    printf("\nThanks and Bye!\n");
83: }
```

20

Because the program in Listing 20.6 is basically the same as the one in Listing 20.5, I have the same output shown on the screen after I run the executable 20L06.exe and enter the same answers to the survey:

OUTPUT
```
Are you using cable at home? (Yes or No)
No
Are you using a satellite dish? (Yes or No)
```

```
Yes
Enter the satellite dish company name:
ABCD company
Please enter your name:
Tony Zhang
Your age:
30
How many hours you spend on watching TV per week:
8

Here's what you've entered:
Name: Tony Zhang
Age: 30
Hour per week: 8
Your satellite dish company is: ABCD company

Thanks and Bye!
```

[ic:analysis]The purpose of the program in Listing 20.6 is to show you how to declare bit fields and how to use them. As you can see in lines 5–8, two bit fields, cable and dish, are declared with the struct data type. Each of the bit fields is 1 bit long. Then a structure called c_d is defined with the two bit fields in line 12, which is within another structure declaration from line 10 to line 19.

The bit fields cable and dish are used as flags to indicate whether the user is using cable or a satellite dish based on the answers made by the user. If the user has cable, the cable bit field is set to 1 and the dish bit field is set to 0. (See lines 44 and 45.) On the other hand, if the user has a satellite dish, dish is set to 1 and cable is set to 0, as shown in lines 53 and 54. If, however, the user has neither cable nor a satellite dish, both cable and dish are set to 0 in lines 56 and 57.

So you see, you've used the combinations of the two bit fields, cable and dish, to represent the three situations: having cable, having a satellite dish, or having neither cable nor a satellite dish.

Because the program in Listing 20.6 is basically the same as the one in Listing 20.5, I get the same output after I run the executable program of Listing 20.6 and enter the same information as I did to the executable 20L05.exe.

Summary

In this hour you've learned the following very important concepts about unions in C:

- A union is a block of memory that is used to hold data items of different types.

- A union is similar to a structure, except that data items saved in the union are overlaid in order to share the same starting memory location.

- The size of a union is at least the size of the size of the largest member in the union.

- The union keyword is used to specify the union data type in a union declaration or a union variable definition.

- To reference a union member, you can use either a dot operator (.) to separate the union name and the union member name or an arrow operator (->) to separate the name of a pointer that points to the union and the union member name.

- The ANSI C standard allows you to initialize a union by assigning the first union member a value.

- You can access the same memory location with different union members.

- To make a structure flexible, you can nest a union inside a structure so that the structure can hold different types of values.

- You can define bit fields, which can be a single bit or any number of bits up to the number of bits in an integer, by using the struct data type.

In the next hour you'll learn how to read from and write to disk files.

Q&A

Q What are the differences between a union and a structure?

A Basically, the difference between a union and a structure is that the members in a union are overlaid and they share the same starting memory location, whereas the members in a structure have their own memory locations. Like a structure, you reference a union's members by using one of its member names.

Q What will happen if you initialize all members of a union together?

A The value that is assigned to a union member last will be the value that stays in the memory storage of the union until the next assignment to the union. In ANSI C, you can initialize a union by initializing its first member.

Q How do you reference a union member?

A If the name of a union is used to reference the union members, the dot operator (.) can be used in between the union name and the name of a union member. If it is a pointer which points to a union, the arrow operator (->) can be used between the pointer name and the name of a union member.

20

Q Can you access the same memory location with different union members?

A Yes. Because all union members in a union share the same memory location, you can access the memory location with different union members. For example, in the program in Listing 20.4, two character constants are assigned to a union memory storage through one of the union members, and then the two characters saved at the memory location of the union are printed out with the help of another union member.

Workshop

To help solidify your understanding of this hour's lesson, you are encouraged to answer the quiz questions and finish the exercises provided in the workshop before you move to the next lesson. The answers and hints to the questions and exercises are given in Appendix B, "Answers to Quiz Questions and Exercises."

Quiz

1. Of the following two statements, which one is the declaration of a union and which one is the definition of union variables?

```
union a_union {
    int x;
    char y;
    };

union a_union x, y;
```

2. What's wrong with the following union declaration?

```
union automobile {
    int year;
    char model[8]
    float weight;
    }
```

3. In the following statement, what are the values contained by the two union members?

```
union u {
    int date;
    char year;
} a_union = {1997};
```

Exercises

1. Rewrite the program in Listing 20.1 by switching the order between the statement in line 15 and the statement in line 17. What do you get after running the rewritten program? Why?

2. Rewrite the program in Listing 20.2. This time, print out values held by all the members in the `info` union each time one of the members is assigned a value.

3. Write a program to ask the user to enter his or her name. Then ask the user whether he or she is a U.S. citizen. If the answer is `Yes`, ask the user to enter the name of the state where he or she comes from. Otherwise, ask the user to enter the name of the country he or she comes from. (You're required to use a union in your program.)

4. Modify the program you wrote in Exercise 3. Add a bit field and use it as a flag. If the user is a U.S. citizen, set the bit field to `1`. Otherwise, set the bit field to `0`. Print out the user's name and the name of country or state by checking the value of the bit field.

20

Hour 21

Reading and Writing with Files

I can only assume that a "Do Not File" document is filed in a "Do Not File" file.

—F. Church

In Hour 5, "Handling Standard Input and Output," you learned how to read and write characters through standard input or output. In this lesson you'll learn to read data from and write data to disk files. The following topics are discussed in this lesson:

- Files and streams
- Opening a file with `fopen()`
- Closing a file with `fclose()`
- The `fgetc()` and `fputc()` functions
- The `fgets()` and `fputs()` functions
- The `fread()` and `fwrite()` functions
- The `feof()` function

Files Versus Streams

The C language provides a rich set of library functions to perform input and output (I/O) operations. Those functions can read or write any type of data to files. Before we go any further in discussing the C I/O functions, let's first understand the definitions of files and streams in C.

What Is a File?

In C, a *file* can refer to a disk file, a terminal, a printer, or a tape drive. In other words, a file represents a concrete device with which you want to exchange information. Before you perform any communication to a file, you have to open the file. Then you need to close the opened file after you finish exchanging information with it.

What Is a Stream?

The data flow you transfer from your program to a file, or vice versa, is called a *stream*, which is a series of bytes. Unlike a file, which targets a specific I/O device, a stream is device independent. All streams have the same behavior regardless of whatever device they are associated with. To perform I/O operations, you can read from or write to any type of file by simply associating a stream to the file.

There are two formats of streams. The first one is called the *text stream*, which consists of a sequence of characters (that is, text data). Depending on the system, each line of characters in a text stream may be terminated by a newline character ('\n'). Text streams are used for textual data, which has a consistent appearance from one environment to another, or from one machine to another.

The second format of streams is called the *binary stream*, which is a series of bytes, for example, the content of an `executable program` file. Binary streams are primarily used for nontextual data, where the exact contents of the data are maintained without regard to appearance.

Buffered I/O

In C, a memory area that is temporarily used to store data before it is sent to its destination is called a *buffer*. With the help of buffers, the operating system can improve efficiency by reducing the number of accesses to I/O devices (that is, files).

Access to a disk or other I/O device is generally much slower than direct access to memory. Several I/O operations can be performed on a buffer that represents the I/O file, instead of the file itself. For example, if several write operations are sent to a buffer, they are kept in memory until it is time to save, or commit, the new data to the actual device.

(This process is known as *flushing* the buffer.) So instead of several write operations in a row, each going to the slow disk device, they all take place in the memory buffer and the disk device will only be accessed once—when the buffer is flushed.

By default, all I/O streams are buffered. Buffered I/O is also called high-level I/O, whereas unbuffered I/O (directly to the device) is called low-level I/O.

The Basics of Disk File I/O

Now let's focus on how to open and close a disk data file and how to interpret error messages returned by I/O functions.

Pointers of FILE

The FILE structure is the file control structure defined in the header file stdio.h. A pointer of type FILE is called a file pointer, which references a disk file. A file pointer is used by a stream to conduct the operation of the I/O functions. For instance, the following defines a file pointer called fptr:

```
FILE *fptr;
```

In the FILE structure there is a member, called the *file position indicator*, which points to the position in a file where data will next be read from or written to. You'll learn how to move the file position indicator in the next lesson.

Opening a File

The C I/O function fopen() opens a file and associates a stream with the opened file. You need to specify the method of opening the file and the filename as arguments to the fopen() function.

The syntax for the fopen() function is

```
#include <stdio.h>
FILE *fopen(const char *filename, const char *mode);
```

Here *filename* is a char pointer that references a string containing a filename. The filename is given to the file that is about to be opened by the fopen() function. *mode* points to another string that specifies the way to open the file. The fopen() function returns a pointer of type *FILE*. If an error occurs during the procedure to open a file, the fopen() function returns a null pointer.

The *mode* parameter is made by a combination of the characters r (read), w (write), b (binary), a (append), and + (update). When you use append mode, and the file already exists, the contents of the file will be preserved and new data that you write will be added to the end. If the file does not already exist, it will be created. This is in contrast to w, which always attempts to create a new file, and will discard whatever data may already be in the file. Using the + character sets the mode to both reading and writing. When you use r, the file must already exist; if it does not, the call will fail.

The following list shows the possible ways to open a file by various strings of modes:

- "r" opens an existing text file for reading.
- "w" creates a text file for writing.
- "a" opens an existing text file for appending.
- "r+" opens an existing text file for reading or writing.
- "w+" creates a text file for reading or writing.
- "a+" opens or create a text file for appending.
- "rb" opens an existing binary file for reading.
- "wb" creates a binary file for writing.
- "ab" opens an existing binary file for appending.
- "r+b" opens an existing binary file for reading or writing.
- "w+b" creates a binary file for reading or writing.
- "a+b" opens or creates a binary file for appending.

Note that you might see code where the mode is given as "rb+" instead of "r+b". These two strings are equivalent. Similarly, "wb+" is the same as "w+b"; "ab+" is equivalent to "a+b".

The following statements try to open a file called test.txt:

```
FILE *fptr;
if ((fptr = fopen("test.txt", "r")) == NULL){
   printf("Cannot open test.txt file.\n");
   exit(1);
}
```

Here "r" is used to indicate that a text file is about to be opened for reading only. If an error occurs when the fopen() function tries to open the file, the function returns a null pointer. (This will happen if test.txt does not already exist.) Then an error message is printed out by the printf() function and the program is aborted by calling the exit() function with a nonzero value.

Closing a File

After a disk file is read, written, or appended with some new data, you have to disassociate the file from a specified stream by calling the fclose() function.

▼ SYNTAX

The syntax for the `fclose()` function is

```
#include <stdio.h>
int fclose(FILE *stream);
```

Here *stream* is a file pointer that is associated with a stream to the opened file. If `fclose()` closes a file successfully, it returns 0. Otherwise, the function returns EOF. Normally, the `fclose()` function fails only when the disk is removed before the function

▲ is called or there is no more space left on the disk.

Because all high-level I/O operations are buffered, the `fclose()` function flushes data left in the buffer to ensure that no data will be lost before it disassociates a specified stream with the opened file.

Note that a file that is opened and associated with a stream has to be closed after the I/O operation. Otherwise, the data saved in the file may be lost; some unpredictable errors might occur during the execution of your program. In addition, failing to close a file when you are done with it may prevent other programs (or users of your program) from accessing the file later.

The program in Listing 21.1 shows you how to open and close a text file and how to check the value of the file pointer returned from `fopen()` as well.

TYPE   **LISTING 21.1**   Opening and Closing a Text File

```
1:  /* 21L01.c: Opening and closing a file */
2:  #include <stdio.h>
3:
4:  enum {SUCCESS, FAIL};
5:
6:  main(void)
7:  {
8:     FILE *fptr;
9:     char filename[]= "haiku.txt";
10:    int reval = SUCCESS;
11:
12:    if ((fptr = fopen(filename, "r")) == NULL){
13:       printf("Cannot open %s.\n", filename);
14:       reval = FAIL;
15:    } else {
16:       printf("The value of fptr: 0x%p\n", fptr);
17:       printf("Ready to close the file.");
18:       fclose(fptr);
19:    }
20:
21:    return reval;
22: }
```

21

The following output displays onscreen after running the executable `21L01.exe` of the program in Listing 21.1 on my computer. (Note that the value of the `fptr` is likely to be different on your machine. That's okay.)

OUTPUT
```
The value of fptr: 0x013E
Ready to close the file.
```

ANALYSIS The purpose of the program in Listing 21.1 is to show you how to open a text file. From the expression in line 12, you can see that the `fopen()` function tries to open a text file with the name contained by the character array `filename` for reading. The `filename` array is defined and initialized with the name `haiku.txt` in line 9.

If an error occurs when you try to open the text file, the `fopen()` function returns a null pointer. Line 13 then prints a warning message, and line 14 assigns the value represented by the enum name `FAIL` to the `int` variable `reval`. From the declaration of the enum data type in line 4, you know that the value of `FAIL` is `1`.

If, however, the `fopen()` function opens the text file successfully, the statement in line 16 prints the value contained by the file pointer `fptr`. Line 17 tells the user that the program is about to close the file, and line 18 then closes the file by calling the `fclose()` function.

In line 21, the `return` statement returns the value of `reval` that contains `0` if the text file has been opened successfully, or `1` otherwise.

From the output shown on my screen, I see that the value held by the file pointer `fptr` is `0x013E` after the text file is opened.

Reading and Writing Disk Files

The program in Listing 21.1 does not do anything with the text file, `haiku.txt`, except open and close it. In fact, there are two pieces of Japanese haiku, written by Sodo and Chora, saved in the `haiku.txt` file. So how can you read them from the file?

In C, you can perform I/O operations in the following ways:

- Read or write one character at a time.
- Read or write one line of text (that is, one character line) at a time.
- Read or write one block of characters at a time.

The following three sections explain the three ways to read from, and write to, disk files.

One Character at a Time

Among the C I/O functions, there is a pair of functions, `fgetc()` and `fputc()`, that can be used to read from or write to a disk file one character at a time.

SYNTAX

The syntax for the fgetc() function is

```
#include <stdio.h>
int fgetc(FILE *stream);
```

Here *stream* is the file pointer that is associated with a stream. The fgetc() function fetches the next character from the stream specified by *stream*. The function then returns the value of an int that is converted from the character. EOF is returned if fgetc() encounters the end of the file, or if there is an error.

▲

SYNTAX

The syntax for the fputc() function is

```
#include <stdio.h>
int fputc(int c , FILE *stream);
```

Here *c* is an int value that represents a character. In fact, the int value is converted to an unsigned char before being outputted. *stream* is the file pointer that is associated with a stream. The fputc() function returns the character written if the function is successful; otherwise, it returns EOF. After a character is written, the fputc() function advances the associated file pointer.

▲

To learn how to use the fgetc() and fputc() functions, let's have a look at Listing 21.2, which contains a program that opens a text file, and then reads and writes one character at a time.

TYPE　**LISTING 21.2**　Reading and Writing One Character at a Time

```
1:  /* 21L02.c: Reading and writing one character at a time */
2:  #include <stdio.h>
3:
4:  enum {SUCCESS, FAIL};
5:
6:  void CharReadWrite(FILE *fin, FILE *fout);
7:
8:  main(void)
9:  {
10:    FILE *fptr1, *fptr2;
11:    char filename1[]= "outhaiku.txt";
12:    char filename2[]= "haiku.txt";
13:    int reval = SUCCESS;
14:
15:    if ((fptr1 = fopen(filename1, "w")) == NULL){
16:       printf("Cannot open %s.\n", filename1);
17:       reval = FAIL;
18:    } else if ((fptr2 = fopen(filename2, "r")) == NULL){
19:       printf("Cannot open %s.\n", filename2);
```

continues

21

LISTING 21.2   continued

```
20:         reval = FAIL;
21:      } else {
22:         CharReadWrite(fptr2, fptr1);
23:         fclose(fptr1);
24:         fclose(fptr2);
25:      }
26:
27:      return reval;
28: }
29: /* function definition */
30: void CharReadWrite(FILE *fin, FILE *fout)
31: {
32:      int c;
33:
34:      while ((c=fgetc(fin)) != EOF){
35:         fputc(c, fout);   /* write to a file */
36:         putchar(c);       /* put the character to the screen */
37:      }
38: }
```

After running the executable, `21L02.exe`, on my machine, I get the following output:

 OUTPUT

```
Leading me along
my shadow goes back home
from looking at the moon.
--- Sodo
   (1641-1716)

A storm wind blows
out from among the grasses
the full moon grows.
--- Chora
   (1729-1781)
```

ANALYSIS   The purpose of the program in Listing 21.2 is to read one character from a file, write the character to another file, and then display the character on the screen. Before running the program, you need to create a text file called `haiku.txt` with the contents shown above, and save it in the same directory as the executable program.

In Listing 21.2 there is a function called `CharReadWrite()`, which has two file pointers as its arguments. (See the declaration of the `CharReadWrite()` function in line 6.)

The statement in line 10 defines two file pointers, `fptr1` and `fptr2`, which are used later in the program. Lines 11 and 12 define two character arrays, `filename1` and `filename2`, and initialize the two arrays with two strings containing filenames, `outhaiku.txt` and `haiku.txt`.

In line 15, a text file with the name `outhaiku.txt` is opened for writing. `outhaiku.txt` is contained by the `filename1` array. The file pointer `fptr1` is associated with the file. If the `fopen()` function returns `NULL`, which means an error has occurred, a warning message is printed out in line 16. Also, in line 17, the `reval` variable is assigned 1 and is represented by the `enum` name `FAIL`.

If the file `outhaiku.txt` is opened successfully, another text file, called `haiku.txt`, is opened for reading in line 18. The file pointer `fptr2` is associated with the opened text file.

If no error occurs, the `CharReadWrite()` function is called in line 22 with two file pointers, `fptr1` and `fptr2`, passed to the function as arguments. From the definition of the `CharReadWrite()` function in lines 30 and 38, you see that there is a `while` loop that keeps calling the `fgetc()` function to read the next character from the `haiku.txt` text file until the function reaches the end of the file (see line 34).

Within the `while` loop, the `fputc()` function in line 35 writes each character read from the `haiku.txt` file to another text file, `outhaiku.txt`, which is pointed to by `fout`. In addition, `putchar()` is called in line 36 in order to put the character returned by the `fgetc()` function on the screen.

After the `CharReadWrite()` function finishes its job, the two opened files, which are associated with `fptr1` and `fptr2`, are each closed with a call to the `fclose()` function respectively in lines 23 and 24.

As mentioned earlier, the `haiku.txt` file contains two pieces of Japanese haiku written by Sodo and Chora. If the program in Listing 21.2 is run successfully, you will see the two pieces of haiku shown on the screen, and they are written into the `outhaiku.txt` file as well. You can view `outhaiku.txt` in a text editor to confirm that the content of `haiku.txt` has been correctly copied to `outhaiku.txt`.

One Line at a Time

Besides reading or writing one character at a time, you can also read or write one character line at time. There is a pair of C I/O functions, `fgets()` and `fputs()`, that allows you to do so.

The syntax for the `fgets()` function is

```
#include <stdio.h>
char *fgets(char *s, int n, FILE *stream);
```

Here *s* references a character array that is used to store characters read from the opened file pointed to by the file pointer *stream*. *n* specifies the maximum number of array elements. If it is successful, the `fgets()` function returns the `char` pointer *s*. If `EOF` is

21

▼ encountered, the fgets() function returns a null pointer and leaves the array untouched. If an error occurs, the function returns a null pointer, and the contents of the array are ▲ unknown.

The fgets() function can read up to n-1 characters, and can append a null character after the last character fetched, until a newline or an EOF is encountered. Note that if a newline is encountered during the read operation, the fgets() function includes the newline in the array. This is different from what the gets() function does. The gets() function just replaces the newline character with a null character. (The gets() function was introduced in Hour 13, "Manipulating Strings.")

SYNTAX

The syntax for the fputs() function is

```
#include <stdio.h>
int fputs(const char *s, FILE *stream);
```

Here s points to the array that contains the characters to be written to a file associated with the file pointer stream. The const modifier indicates that the content of the array pointed to by s cannot be changed by the fputs() function. (You learned about the const modifier in Hour 14, " Understanding Scope and Storage Classes.") If it fails, the ▲ fputs() function returns a nonzero value; otherwise, it returns zero.

Note that the character array must include a null character at the end of the string as the terminator to the fputs() function. Also, unlike the puts() function, the fputs() function does not insert a newline character to the string written to the file. (The puts() function was introduced in Hour 13, "Manipulating Strings.")

You can modify the program in Listing 21.2 to read or write one character line at a time by calling the fgets() and fputs() functions. The modified version is shown in Listing 21.3.

TYPE   **LISTING 21.3**   Reading and Writing One Character Line at a Time

```
1:  /* 21L03.c: Reading and writing one line at a time */
2:  #include <stdio.h>
3:
4:  enum {SUCCESS, FAIL, MAX_LEN = 81};
5:
6:  void LineReadWrite(FILE *fin, FILE *fout);
7:
8:  main(void)
9:  {
10:    FILE *fptr1, *fptr2;
11:    char filename1[]= "outhaiku.txt";
12:    char filename2[]= "haiku.txt";
13:    int reval = SUCCESS;
14:
```

```
15:    if ((fptr1 = fopen(filename1, "w")) == NULL){
16:       printf("Cannot open %s for writing.\n", filename1);
17:       reval = FAIL;
18:    } else if ((fptr2 = fopen(filename2, "r")) == NULL){
19:       printf("Cannot open %s for reading.\n", filename2);
20:       reval = FAIL;
21:    } else {
22:       LineReadWrite(fptr2, fptr1);
23:       fclose(fptr1);
24:       fclose(fptr2);
25:    }
26:
27:    return reval;
28: }
29: /* function definition */
30: void LineReadWrite(FILE *fin, FILE *fout)
31: {
32:    char buff[MAX_LEN];
33:
34:    while (fgets(buff, MAX_LEN, fin) != NULL){
35:       fputs(buff, fout);
36:       printf("%s", buff);
37:    }
38: }
```

Because the program in Listing 21.3 reads the same text file, haiku.txt, as the program in Listing 21.2 did, I get the same output on the screen:

OUTPUT

```
Leading me along
my shadow goes back home
from looking at the moon.
--- Sodo
   (1641-1716)

A storm wind blows
out from among the grasses
the full moon grows.
--- Chora
   (1729-1781)
```

ANALYSIS From the program in Listing 21.3, you can see that a function called LineReadWrite() has replaced the CharReadWrite() function.

The definition of the LineReadWrite() function is shown in lines 30–38. The fgets() function is called repeatedly in a while loop to read one character line at a time from the haiku.txt text file, until it reaches the end of the text file. In line 34, the array name buff and the maximum number of the array elements MAX_LEN are passed to the fgets() function, along with the file pointer fin that is associated with the opened haiku.txt file.

21

Meanwhile, each line read by the `fgets()` function is written to another opened text file called `outhaiku.txt` that is associated with the file pointer `fout`. This is done by calling the `fputs()` function in line 35.

The statement in line 36 prints the contents of each string on the screen so that you see the two pieces of Japanese verses after running the program in Listing 21.3. Also, you can view the `outhaiku.txt` file in a text editor to make sure that the content of the `haiku.txt` file has been copied to the `outhaiku.txt` file.

> In the previous hour, we used the `gets()` function to read data input from the keyboard. Since `gets()` does not know the size of the character array you pass to it, it simply reads data until a newline is encountered. This is actually quite dangerous, since the user could very easily type more characters than your array will hold. As a result, your other variables would get overwritten and your program will crash or, at best, behave unpredictably.
>
> Fortunately, `fgets()` provides a much safer way of reading input from the keyboard, if you pass `stdin` as the stream from which to read.
>
> The following code uses `fgets()` to read input from `stdin` into a string str.
>
> ```
> int length = 80;
> char str[80];
> fgets(str, length, stdin);
> if (str[(length = strlen(str) - 1)] == '\n')
>   str[length] = '\0';  /* replace the '\n' */
> else
>   while (getchar() != '\n')
>     ;  /* discard input until the newline */
> ```
>
> As you can see, this method involves a little more work than `gets()` because we have to get rid of the newline character which `fgets()` stores in our array. However, it is well worth it because this is a much safer, cleaner way of dealing with user input than using `gets()`.

One Block at a Time

If you like, you can also read or write a block of data at a time. In C, there are two I/O functions, `fread()` and `fwrite()`, that can be used to perform block I/O operations. The `fread()` and `fwrite()` functions are mirror images of each other.

SYNTAX

The syntax for the `fread()` function is

```
#include <stdio.h>
size_t fread(void *ptr, size_t size, size_t n, FILE *stream);
```

Here `ptr` is a pointer to an array in which the data is stored. `size` indicates the size of each array element. `n` specifies the number of elements to read. `stream` is a file pointer

▼ that is associated with the opened file for reading. *size_t* is an integral type defined in the header file stdio.h. The fread() function returns the number of elements actually read.

▲ The number of elements read by the fread() function should be equal to the value specified by the third argument to the function, unless an error occurs or an EOF (end-of-file) is encountered. The fread() function returns the number of elements that are actually read during the attempt, if an error occurs or an EOF is encountered.

SYNTAX ▼

The syntax for the fwrite() function is

```
#include <stdio.h>
size_t fwrite(const void *ptr, size_t size, size_t n, FILE *stream);
```

Here *ptr* references the array that contains the data to be written to an opened file pointed to by the file pointer *stream*. *size* indicates the size of each element in the array. *n* specifies the number of elements to be written. The fwrite() function returns the

▲ number of elements actually written.

If no error has occurred, the value returned by fwrite() should equal the third argument in the function. The return value may be less than the specified value if an error occurs.

Note that it's the programmer's responsibility to ensure that the array is large enough to hold data for either the fread() function or the fwrite() function.

In C, a function called feof() can be used to determine when the end of a file is encountered. This function is more useful when you're reading a binary file because the values of some bytes may be equal to the value of EOF. That is to say, the character which is used as an end-of-file marker in a text file can easily occur in a binary file, but in that case it is not intended to mark end of the file. If you try to determine the end of a binary file by checking the value returned by fread(), you may end up at a wrong position. Using the feof() function helps you to avoid mistakes in determining the end of a file, because it checks whether the file position indicator has actually reached the end of the file, regardless of any EOF character present.

SYNTAX ▼

The syntax for the feof() function is

```
#include <stdio.h>
int feof(FILE *stream);
```

Here *stream* is the file pointer that is associated with an opened file. The feof() function returns 0 if the end of the file has not been reached; otherwise, it returns a nonzero

▲ integer.

21

The program in Listing 21.4 demonstrates how to read and write one block of characters at a time by calling the `fread()` and `fwrite()` functions. In fact, the program in Listing 21.4 is another modified version of the program from Listing 21.2.

TYPE   **LISTING 21.4**   Reading and Writing One Block of Characters at a Time

```
1:  /* 21L04.c: Reading and writing one block at a time */
2:  #include <stdio.h>
3:
4:  enum {SUCCESS, FAIL, MAX_LEN = 80};
5:
6:  void BlockReadWrite(FILE *fin, FILE *fout);
7:  int ErrorMsg(char *str);
8:
9:  main(void)
10: {
11:    FILE *fptr1, *fptr2;
12:    char filename1[]= "outhaiku.txt";
13:    char filename2[]= "haiku.txt";
14:    int reval = SUCCESS;
15:
16:    if ((fptr1 = fopen(filename1, "w")) == NULL){
17:       reval = ErrorMsg(filename1);
18:    } else if ((fptr2 = fopen(filename2, "r")) == NULL){
19:       reval = ErrorMsg(filename2);
20:    } else {
21:       BlockReadWrite(fptr2, fptr1);
22:       fclose(fptr1);
23:       fclose(fptr2);
24:    }
25:
26:    return reval;
27: }
28: /* function definition */
29: void BlockReadWrite(FILE *fin, FILE *fout)
30: {
31:    int num;
32:    char buff[MAX_LEN + 1];
33:
34:    while (!feof(fin)){
35:       num = fread(buff, sizeof(char), MAX_LEN, fin);
36:       buff[num * sizeof(char)] = '\0';  /* append a null character */
37:       printf("%s", buff);
38:       fwrite(buff, sizeof(char), num, fout);
39:    }
40: }
41: /* function definition */
42: int ErrorMsg(char *str)
43: {
```

```
44:     printf("Cannot open %s.\n", str);
45:     return FAIL;
46: }
```

Again, I get the same output on the screen because the program in Listing 21.4 also reads the same text file, haiku.txt:

OUTPUT
```
Leading me along
my shadow goes back home
from looking at the moon.
--- Sodo
    (1641-1716)

A storm wind blows
out from among the grasses
the full moon grows.
--- Chora
    (1729-1781)
```

ANALYSIS The purpose of the program in Listing 21.4 is to show you how to invoke the fread() and fwrite() functions in your program to perform block I/O operations. In Listing 21.4, the haiku.txt file is read by the fread() function, and then the fwrite() function is used to write the contents read from haiku.txt to another file called outhaiku.txt. You call the two C I/O functions from your own function, BlockReadWrite().

From the definition of the BlockReadWrite() function in lines 29–40, you can see that a character array called buff is defined with the number of elements of MAX_LEN + 1 in line 32, although you only read MAX_LEN number of characters by calling the fread() function in line 35. The reason is that you append a null character in line 36 after the last character read so that you ensure the block of characters saved in buff is treated as a string and can be printed out on the screen properly by the printf() function which is called in line 37.

The while loop, shown in lines 34–39, keeps calling the fread() function to read a character block with MAX_LEN elements, until the feof() function in line 34 returns 0, which means that the end of the text file has been reached. As shown in lines 35 and 38, you use the sizof operator to measure the size of the char data type because the elements in the buff array are all characters.

If everything goes smoothly, you should see the Japanese verses again on the screen or in the outhaiku.txt file after running the program in Listing 21.4.

21

Summary

In this lesson you learned the following important concepts and functions regarding disk file input and output in C:

- In C, a file can refer to a disk file, a terminal, a printer, or a tape drive.
- The data flow you transfer from your program to a file, or vice versa, is called a stream.
- A stream is a series of ordered bytes.
- Unlike a file, a stream is device independent.
- There are two stream formats: text stream and binary stream.
- The file position indicator in the FILE structure points to the position in a file where data will next be read from or written to.
- The fopen() function is used to open a file and associate a stream to the opened file.
- You can specify different modes for opening a file.
- The fclose() function is responsible for closing an opened file and disassociating a stream with the file.
- The fgetc() and fputc() functions read or write one character at a time.
- The fgets() and fputs() functions read or write one line at a time.
- The fread() and fwrite() functions read or write one block of data at a time.
- The feof() function can determine when the end of a file has been reached.
- In a binary file, the feof() function should be used to detect EOF.

In the next lesson you'll learn more about disk file I/O in C.

Q&A

Q What are the differences between a text stream and a binary stream?

A A text stream is a sequence of characters that may not have a one-to-one relationship with the data on the device. Text streams are normally used for textual data, which have a consistent appearance from one environment to another, or from one machine to another. For this reason, the data in a text file may be interpreted so that it appears correctly on the screen. A binary stream, on the other hand, is a sequence of bytes that has a one-to-one correspondence to those on the device. Binary streams are primarily used for nontextual data that is needed to keep the exact contents on the device.

Q Why do you need a file pointer?

A A file pointer is used to associate a stream with an opened file for reading or writing purpose. A pointer of the type FILE is called a file pointer. FILE is a typedef for a structure that contains overhead information about a disk file. A file pointer plays an important role in the communication between programs and disk files.

Q What does the fclose() function do before it closes an opened file?

A As you know, all high-level I/O operations are buffered. One of the jobs of the fclose() function is to flush data left in the buffer to commit the I/O operations and ensure that no data is lost. For instance, when you finish writing several blocks of characters to an opened text file, you call the fclose() function to disassociate a specified stream and close the text file. The fclose() function will first flush all characters left in the buffer and write them into the text file before it closes the file. In this way, all characters you write to the file will be saved properly.

Q What is the difference between fgets() and gets()?

A The major difference between the fgets() and gets() functions is that the fgets() function includes a newline character in the array if the newline is encountered during the read operation, whereas the gets() function just replaces the newline character with a null character. Additionally, fgets() is much safer than gets() because it lets you specify the size of the array where the string is stored.

Workshop

To help solidify your understanding of this lesson, you are encouraged to answer the quiz questions and finish the exercises provided in the workshop before you move to the next lesson. The answers and hints to the questions and exercises are given in Appendix B, "Answers to Quiz Questions and Exercises."

Quiz

1. What do the following expressions do?
   ```
   fopen("test.bin", "r+b")
   fopen("test.txt" "a")
   fopen("test.ini", "w+")
   ```

2. What's wrong with the following code segment?
   ```
   FILE *fptr;
   int c;
   if ((fptr = fopen("test1.txt", "r")) == NULL){
      while ((c=fgetc(fptr)) != EOF){
         putchar(c);
      }
   }
   fclose(fptr);
   ```

21

3. What's wrong with the following code segment?

```
FILE *fptr;
int c;
if ((fptr = fopen("test2.txt", "r")) != NULL){
   while ((c=fgetc(fptr)) != EOF){
      fputc(c, fptr);
   }
   fclose(fptr);
}
```

4. What's wrong with the following code segment?

```
FILE *fptr1, *fptr2;
int c;
if ((fptr1 = fopen("test1.txt", "r")) != NULL){
   while ((c=fgetc(fptr1)) != EOF){
      putchar(c);
   }
}
fclose(fptr1);
if ((fptr2 = fopen("test2.txt", "w")) != NULL){
   while ((c=fgetc(fptr1)) != EOF){
      fputc(c, fptr2);
   }
}
fclose(fptr2);
```

Exercises

1. Write a program to read the text file haiku.txt and count the number of characters in the file. Also, print out the content of the file and the total character number on the screen.

2. Write a program to receive a string entered by the user, and then save the string into a file with the name also given by the user.

3. Given the string "Disk file I/O is fun." write a program to write the string into a file called test_21.txt by writing one character at a time. Meanwhile, print out the string on the screen.

4. Rewrite exercise 3. This time, try to write one block of characters (that is, one string) at a time.

HOUR 22

Using Special File Functions

Disk space: the final frontier.

—Captain Kirk's younger brother

In last hour's lesson you learned the basics of reading and writing disk data files. In this lesson you'll learn more about communication with disk data files. The main topics discussed in this hour are

- Random access to files
- Reading or writing binary data
- Redirecting the standard streams

In addition, the following C I/O functions are introduced in this lesson:

- The fseek(), ftell(), and rewind() functions
- The fscanf() and fprintf() functions
- The freopen() function

Random Access to Disk Files

So far you've learned how to read or write data sequentially to an opened disk file, known as *sequential access*. In other words, you start with the first byte and keep reading or writing each successive byte in order. In many cases, however, you need to access particular data somewhere in the middle of a disk file. One way to do it is to keep reading data from the file until the particular data is fetched. Obviously, this is not an efficient way, especially when the file contains many data items.

Random access is another way to read or write data to disk files. In random access, specific file elements can be accessed in random order (that is, without reading through all the preceding data).

In C there are two I/O functions, fseek() and ftell(), that are designed to deal with random access.

The `fseek()` and `ftell()` Functions

As just mentioned, you need functions that enable you to access files randomly. The fseek() and ftell() functions provide you with such a capability.

In the previous lesson you learned that one of the members in the FILE structure is called the *file position indicator*. The file position indicator has to point to the desired position in a file before data can be read from or written to there. You can use the fseek() function to move the file position indicator to the spot you want to access in a file.

The syntax for the fseek() function is

```
#include <stdio.h>
int fseek(FILE *stream, long offset, int whence);
```

Here *stream* is the file pointer associated with an opened file. *offset* indicates the number of bytes from a fixed position specified by *whence* that can have one of the following integral values represented by SEEK_SET, SEEK_CUR, and SEEK_END. If it is successful, the fseek() function returns 0; otherwise, the function returns a nonzero value.

You can find the values represented by SEEK_SET, SEEK_CUR, and SEEK_END in the header file stdio.h.

If SEEK_SET is chosen as the third argument to the fseek() function, the offset is counted from the beginning of the file and the value of the offset should be greater than or equal to zero. If, however, SEEK_END is used, the offset starts from the end of the file, and the value of the offset should be negative. When SEEK_CUR is passed to the fseek() function, the offset is calculated from the current value of the file position indicator.

▼ SYNTAX

▲

22

You can obtain the current value of the file position indicator by calling the `ftell()` function.

SYNTAX

The syntax for the `ftell()` function is

```
#include <stdio.h>
long ftell(FILE *stream);
```

▲ Here *stream* is the file pointer associated with an opened file. The `ftell()` function returns the current value of the file position indicator.

The value returned by the `ftell()` function represents the number of bytes from the beginning of the file to the current position pointed to by the file position indicator.

If the `ftell()` function fails, it returns -1L (that is, a `long` value of minus 1). One thing that can cause the failure of the `ftell()` function is that the file is a terminal or some other type for which the file position indicator becomes meaningless.

The program in Listing 22.1 shows how to randomly access a disk file by using the `fseek()` and `ftell()` functions.

TYPE   **LISTING 22.1**   Random Access to a File

```
1:  /* 22L01.c: Random access to a file */
2:  #include <stdio.h>
3:
4:  enum {SUCCESS, FAIL, MAX_LEN = 80};
5:
6:  void PtrSeek(FILE *fptr);
7:  long PtrTell(FILE *fptr);
8:  void DataRead(FILE *fptr);
9:  int ErrorMsg(char *str);
10:
11: main(void)
12: {
13:    FILE *fptr;
14:    char filename[]= "haiku.txt";
15:    int reval = SUCCESS;
16:
17:    if ((fptr = fopen(filename, "r")) == NULL){
18:        reval = ErrorMsg(filename);
19:    } else {
20:        PtrSeek(fptr);
21:        fclose(fptr);
22:    }
23:
```

continues

LISTING **22.1**   continued

```
24:     return reval;
25: }
26: /* function definition */
27: void PtrSeek(FILE *fptr)
28: {
29:     long offset1, offset2, offset3;
30:
31:     offset1 = PtrTell(fptr);
32:     DataRead(fptr);
33:     offset2 = PtrTell(fptr);
34:     DataRead(fptr);
35:     offset3 = PtrTell(fptr);
36:     DataRead(fptr);
37:
38:     printf("\nRe-read the haiku:\n");
39:     /* re-read the third verse of the haiku */
40:     fseek(fptr, offset3, SEEK_SET);
41:     DataRead(fptr);
42:     /* re-read the second verse of the haiku */
43:     fseek(fptr, offset2, SEEK_SET);
44:     DataRead(fptr);
45:     /* re-read the first verse of the haiku */
46:     fseek(fptr, offset1, SEEK_SET);
47:     DataRead(fptr);
48: }
49: /* function definition */
50: long PtrTell(FILE *fptr)
51: {
52:     long reval;
53:
54:     reval = ftell(fptr);
55:     printf("The fptr is at %ld\n", reval);
56:
57:     return reval;
58: }
59: /* function definition */
60: void DataRead(FILE *fptr)
61: {
62:     char buff[MAX_LEN];
63:
64:     fgets(buff, MAX_LEN, fptr);
65:     printf("---%s", buff);
66: }
67: /* function definition */
68: int ErrorMsg(char *str)
69: {
70:     printf("Cannot open %s.\n", str);
71:     return FAIL;
72: }
```

I have the following output shown on the screen of my computer after running the executable `22L01.exe` of the program in Listing 22.1:

OUTPUT

```
The fptr is at 0
---Leading me along
The fptr is at 18
---my shadow goes back home
The fptr is at 44
---from looking at the moon.

Re-read the haiku:
---from looking at the moon.
---my shadow goes back home
---Leading me along
```

ANALYSIS The purpose of the program in Listing 22.1 is to move the file position indicator around in order to read different verses from the `haiku.txt` file.

Inside the `main()` function, a file pointer `fptr` is defined in line 13, and the name of the `haiku.txt` file is assigned to the array called `filename` in line 14. Then, in line 17, you try to open the `haiku.txt` file for reading by calling the `fopen()` function. If successful, you invoke the `PtrSeek()` function with the `fptr` file pointer as the argument in line 20.

The definition of your first function, `PtrSeek()`, is shown in lines 27–48. The statement in line 31 obtains the original value of the `fptr` file pointer by calling your other function, `PtrTell()`, which is defined in lines 50–58. The `PtrTell()` function finds and prints out the value of the file position indicator with the help of the `ftell()` function. The original value of the file position indicator contained by `fptr` is assigned to the `long` variable `offset1` in line 31.

In line 32, the third function, `DataRead()`, is called to read one line of characters from the opened file and print out the line of characters on the screen. Line 33 gets the value of the `fptr` file position indicator right after the read operation and assigns the value to another `long` variable `offset2`.

Then the `DataRead()` function in line 34 reads the second line of characters from the opened file. Line 35 obtains the value of the file position indicator that points to the first byte of the third verse and assigns the value to the third `long` variable, `offset3`. Line 36 calls the `DataRead()` function to read the third verse and print it out on the screen.

Therefore, from the first portion of the output, you can see the three different values of the file position indicator at three different positions, and the three verses of the haiku written by Sodo. The three values of the file position indicator are saved respectively by `offset1`, `offset2`, and `offset3`.

Now, starting from line 40 to line 47, you read Sodo's haiku backward, one verse at a time. That is, you read the third verse first, and then the second verse, and finally the first verse. To do so, you first call the `fseek()` function to move the file position indicator to the beginning of the third verse by passing the value contained by `offset3` to the function. Then you call `fseek()` again and pass the value of `offset2` to the function so that the file position indicator is set to point to the first byte of the second verse. Finally, you move the file position indicator to the beginning of the first verse by passing the value of `offset1` to the `fseek()` function. Therefore, in the second portion of the output, you see the three verses of the haiku in reverse order.

The `rewind()` Function

Sometimes you might want to reset the file position indicator and put it at the beginning of a file. There is a handy C function, called `rewind()`, which can be used to rewind the file position indicator.

SYNTAX

The syntax for the `rewind()` function is

```
#include <stdio.h>
void rewind(FILE *stream);
```

Here `stream` is the file pointer associated with an opened file. No value is returned by the `rewind()` function.

▲

In fact, the following statement of the `rewind()` function:

```
rewind(fptr);
```

is equivalent to this:

```
fseek(fptr, 0L, SEEK_SET);
```

Listing 22.2 contains an example that calls the `rewind()` function to move the file position indicator to the beginning of an opened file.

More Examples of Disk File I/O

The following sections show several more examples of disk file I/O, such as reading and writing binary data and redirecting the standard streams. Three more I/O functions, `fscanf()`, `fprintf()`, and `freopen()`, are introduced too.

Reading and Writing Binary Data

As you learned in Hour 21, "Reading and Writing with Files," you can indicate to the compiler that you're going to open a binary file by setting a proper mode when calling

the fopen() function. For instance, the following statement tries to open an existing
binary file for reading:

```
fptr = fopen("test.bin", "rb");
```

Note that the "rb" mode is used to indicate that the file you're going to open for reading
is a binary file.

Listing 22.2 contains an example of reading and writing binary data.

TYPE   LISTING 22.2   Reading and Writing Binary Data

```
1:  /* 22L02.c: Reading and writing binary data */
2:  #include <stdio.h>
3:
4:  enum {SUCCESS, FAIL, MAX_NUM = 3};
5:
6:  void DataWrite(FILE *fout);
7:  void DataRead(FILE *fin);
8:  int ErrorMsg(char *str);
9:
10: main(void)
11: {
12:    FILE *fptr;
13:    char filename[]= "double.bin";
14:    int reval = SUCCESS;
15:
16:    if ((fptr = fopen(filename, "wb+")) == NULL){
17:       reval = ErrorMsg(filename);
18:    } else {
19:       DataWrite(fptr);
20:       rewind(fptr);  /* reset fptr */
21:       DataRead(fptr);
22:       fclose(fptr);
23:    }
24:
25:    return reval;
26: }
27: /* function definition */
28: void DataWrite(FILE *fout)
29: {
30:    int i;
31:    double buff[MAX_NUM] = {
32:                123.45,
33:                567.89,
34:                100.11};
35:
```

continues

LISTING 22.2 continued

```
36:     printf("The size of buff: %d-byte\n", sizeof(buff));
37:     for (i=0; i<MAX_NUM; i++){
38:         printf("%5.2f\n", buff[i]);
39:         fwrite(&buff[i], sizeof(double), 1, fout);
40:     }
41: }
42: /* function definition */
43: void DataRead(FILE *fin)
44: {
45:     int i;
46:     double x;
47:
48:     printf("\nRead back from the binary file:\n");
49:     for (i=0; i<MAX_NUM; i++){
50:         fread(&x, sizeof(double), (size_t)1, fin);
51:         printf("%5.2f\n", x);
52:     }
53: }
54: /* function definition */
55: int ErrorMsg(char *str)
56: {
57:     printf("Cannot open %s.\n", str);
58:     return FAIL;
59: }
```

After running the executable 22L02.exe, I have the following output on the screen of my computer:

OUTPUT
```
The size of buff: 24-byte
123.45
567.89
100.11

Read back from the binary file:
123.45
567.89
100.11
```

ANALYSIS The purpose of the program in Listing 22.2 is to write three values of the double data type into a binary file and then rewind the file position indicator and read back the three double values from the binary file. The two functions, DataWrite() and DataRead(), that perform the writing and reading, are declared in lines 6 and 7.

The enum names, SUCCESS, FAIL, and MAX_NUM, are defined in line 4 with values of 0, 1, and 3, respectively.

Inside the main() function, the statement in line 16 tries to create and open a binary file called double.bin for both reading and writing. Note that the "wb+" mode is used in the fopen() function in line 16.

If the fopen() function is successful, the DataWrite() function is called in line 19 to write three double data items, 123.45, 567.89, and 100.11, into the opened binary file, according to the definition of the DataWrite() function in lines 28–41. The fwrite() function in line 39 does the writing. Because the three double data items are saved in an array named buff, you also measure and print out the size of the buff array in line 36. On my machine, the size of the buff array is 24 bytes because each double data item is 8 bytes.

Right after the execution of the DataWrite() function, the file position indicator is reset to the beginning of the binary file by calling the rewind() function in line 20 because you want to read back all the three double data items written to the file.

Then in line 21, the DataRead() function reads the three double data items from the opened binary file double.bin. From the definition of the DataRead() function in lines 43–53, you can see that the fread() function is used to perform the reading operation (see line 50).

The output from running the program in Listing 22.2 shows the three double data items before the writing and after the reading as well.

The fscanf() and fprintf() Functions

As you have learned, the two C library functions scanf() and printf() can be used to read or write formatted data through the standard I/O (that is, stdin and stdout). Among the C disk file I/O functions, there are two equivalent functions, fscanf() and fprintf(), that can do the same jobs as the scanf() and printf() functions. In addition, the fscanf() and fprintf() functions allow the programmer to specify I/O streams other than stdin and stdout.

The syntax for the fscanf() function is

```
#include <stdio.h>
int fscanf(FILE *stream, const char *format, …);
```

Here *stream* is the file pointer associated with an opened file. *format*, whose usage is the same as in the scanf() function, is a char pointer pointing to a string that contains the format specifiers. If successful, the fscanf() function returns the number of data items read. Otherwise, the function returns EOF.

SYNTAX

The syntax for the `fprintf()` function is

```
#include <stdio.h>
int fprintf(FILE *stream, const char *format, ...);
```

Here *stream* is the file pointer associated with an opened file. *format*, whose usage is the same as in the `printf()` function, is a char pointer pointing to a string that contains the format specifiers. If successful, the `fprintf()` function returns the number of formatted expressions. Otherwise, the function returns a negative value.

To know more about the `fprintf()` and `fscanf()` functions, you can review the explanations on the `printf()` and `scanf()` functions in Hour 5, "Handling Standard Input and Output," and Hour 13, "Manipulating Strings."

The program in Listing 22.3 demonstrates how to use the `fscanf()` and `fprintf()` functions to read and write differently typed data items.

TYPE **LISTING 22.3** Using the `fscanf()` and `fprintf()` Functions

```
1:  /* 22L03.c: Using the fscanf() and fprintf() functions */
2:  #include <stdio.h>
3:
4:  enum {SUCCESS, FAIL,
5:        MAX_NUM = 3,
6:        STR_LEN = 23};
7:
8:  void DataWrite(FILE *fout);
9:  void DataRead(FILE *fin);
10: int ErrorMsg(char *str);
11:
12: main(void)
13: {
14:    FILE *fptr;
15:    char filename[]= "strnum.mix";
16:    int reval = SUCCESS;
17:
18:    if ((fptr = fopen(filename, "w+")) == NULL){
19:       reval = ErrorMsg(filename);
20:    } else {
21:       DataWrite(fptr);
22:       rewind(fptr);
23:       DataRead(fptr);
24:       fclose(fptr);
25:    }
26:
27:    return reval;
28: }
29: /* function definition */
30: void DataWrite(FILE *fout)
```

```
31: {
32:    int i;
33:    char cities[MAX_NUM][STR_LEN] = {
34:              "St.Louis->Houston:",
35:              "Houston->Dallas:",
36:              "Dallas->Philadelphia:"};
37:    int miles[MAX_NUM] = {
38:              845,
39:              243,
40:              1459};
41:
42:    printf("The data written:\n");
43:    for (i=0; i<MAX_NUM; i++){
44:       printf("%-23s  %d miles\n", cities[i], miles[i]);
45:       fprintf(fout, "%s  %d", cities[i], miles[i]);
46:    }
47: }
48: /* function definition */
49: void DataRead(FILE *fin)
50: {
51:    int i;
52:    int miles;
53:    char cities[STR_LEN];
54:
55:    printf("\nThe data read:\n");
56:    for (i=0; i<MAX_NUM; i++){
57:       fscanf(fin, "%s%d", cities, &miles);
58:       printf("%-23s  %d miles\n", cities, miles);
59:    }
60: }
61: /* function definition */
62: int ErrorMsg(char *str)
63: {
64:    printf("Cannot open %s.\n", str);
65:    return FAIL;
66: }
```

The following output is shown on the screen after the executable 22L03.exe is created and run on my computer:

OUTPUT
```
The data written:
St.Louis->Houston:      845 miles
Houston->Dallas:        243 miles
Dallas->Philadelphia:   1459 miles

The data read:
St.Louis->Houston:      845 miles
Houston->Dallas:        243 miles
Dallas->Philadelphia:   1459 miles
```

ANALYSIS The purpose of the program in Listing 22.3 is to write data items of different types into a file with the help of the `fprintf()` function and read back the data items in the same format by calling the `fscanf()` function. The two functions declared in lines 8 and 9, `DataWrite()` and `DataRead()`, actually perform the writing and reading.

The statement of the `main()` function in line 18 tries to create and open a text file called `strnum.mix` for both reading and writing by specifying the second argument to the `fopen()` function as `"w+"`. If `fopen()` does not return a null pointer, the `DataWrite()` function is called in line 21 to write strings and `int` data items into the `strnum.mix` file. Note that the `fprintf()` function is invoked inside the `DataWrite()` function in line 45 to write the formatted data into the text file.

From the definition of the `DataWrite()` function in lines 30–47, you can see that there are two arrays, `cities` and `miles`. The `cities` array contains three strings that indicate three pairs of cities, and the `miles` array has three `int` values representing the corresponding distances between the cities shown in the `cities` array. For instance, `845` in the `miles` array is the distance (in miles) between the two cities expressed by the string `St.Louis->Houston:` in the `cities` array.

In line 22, the `rewind()` function is called to rewind the file position indicator and reset it to the beginning of the `strnum.mix` file. Then the `DataRead()` function in line 23 reads back what has been saved in `strnum.mix` with the help of the `fscanf()` function. The definition of the `DataRead()` function is shown in lines 49–60.

From this example, you see that it is convenient to use the `fprintf()` and `fscanf()` functions together to perform formatted disk file I/O operations.

Redirecting the Standard Streams with `freopen()`

In Hour 5 you learned how to read from or write to standard I/O. Also, you were told that the C functions, such as `getc()`, `gets()`, `putc`, and `printf()`, direct their I/O operations automatically to either `stdin` or `stdout`.

In this section you're going to learn how to redirect the standard streams, such as `stdin` and `stdout`, to disk files. A new C function you're going to use is called `freopen()`, which can associate a standard stream with a disk file.

▼ SYNTAX

The syntax for the `freopen()` function is

```
#include <stdio.h>
FILE *freopen(const char *filename, const char *mode, FILE *stream);
```

Here *filename* is a `char` pointer referencing the name of a file that you want to associate with the standard stream represented by *stream*. *mode* is another `char` pointer pointing to a string that defines the way to open a file. The values that *mode* can have in freopen() are the same as the mode values in the fopen() function. (The definitions of all mode values are given in Hour 21.)

The freopen() function returns a null pointer if an error occurs. Otherwise, the function returns the standard stream that has been associated with a disk file identified by *filename*.

Listing 22.4 demonstrates an example of redirecting the standard output, stdout, with the help of the freopen() function.

TYPE **LISTING 22.4** Redirecting the Standard Stream stdout

```
1:  /* 22L04.c: Redirecting a standard stream */
2:  #include <stdio.h>
3:
4:  enum {SUCCESS, FAIL,
5:       STR_NUM = 4};
6:
7:  void StrPrint(char **str);
8:  int ErrorMsg(char *str);
9:
10: main(void)
11: {
12:    char *str[STR_NUM] = {
13:          "Be bent, and you will remain straight.",
14:          "Be vacant, and you will remain full.",
15:          "Be worn, and you will remain new.",
16:          "--- by Lao Tzu"};
17:    char filename[]= "LaoTzu.txt";
18:    int reval = SUCCESS;
19:
20:    StrPrint(str);
21:    if (freopen(filename, "w", stdout) == NULL){
22:       reval = ErrorMsg(filename);
23:    } else {
24:       StrPrint(str);
25:       fclose(stdout);
26:    }
27:    return reval;
28: }
29: /* function definition */
30: void StrPrint(char **str)
31: {
32:    int i;
33:
```

continues

LISTING 22.4   continued

```
34:    for (i=0; i<STR_NUM; i++)
35:        printf("%s\n", str[i]);
36: }
37: /* function definition */
38: int ErrorMsg(char *str)
39: {
40:    printf("Cannot open %s.\n", str);
41:    return FAIL;
42: }
```

After the executable 22L04.exe is created and run, the following output is printed out on the screen of my computer:

```
Be bent, and you will remain straight.
Be vacant, and you will remain full.
Be worn, and you will remain new.
--- by Lao Tzu
```

ANALYSIS   The purpose of the program in Listing 22.4 is to save a paragraph of *Tao Te Ching* written by a Chinese philosopher, Lao Tzu, into a text file, LaoTzu.txt. To do so, you call the printf() function instead of the fprintf() function or other disk I/O functions after you redirect the default stream, stdout, of the printf() function to point to the text file.

The function that actually does the writing is called StrPrint(), which calls the C function printf() to send out formatted character strings to the output stream. (See the definition of the StrPrint() function in lines 30–36.)

Inside the main() function, you call the StrPrint() function in line 20 before you redirect stdout to the LaoTzu.txt file. It's not surprising to see that the paragraph adopted from *Tao Te Ching* is printed on the screen because the printf() function automatically sends out the paragraph to stdout, which directs to the screen by default.

Then, in line 21, you redirect stdout to the LaoTzu.txt text file by calling the freopen() function. There the "w" is used as the mode that indicates to open the text file for writing. If freopen() is successful, you then call the StrPrint() function in line 24. However, this time, the StrPrint() function writes the paragraph into the opened text file, LaoTzu.txt. The reason is that stdout is now associated with the text file, not the screen, so that strings sent out by the printf() call inside StrPrint() are directed to the text file.

After the execution of the program in Listing 22.4, you can open the LaoTzu.txt file in a text editor and see that the paragraph of *Tao Te Ching* has been saved in the file.

As mentioned previously, the I/O streams are buffered by default. Occasionally, you may want to turn off the buffering so that you can process the input immediately. In C there are two functions, setbuf() and setvbuf(), that can be used to turn off the buffering, although unbuffered I/O is beyond the scope of this book.

Also, there is a set of low-level I/O functions, such as open(), create(), close(), read(), write(), lseek(), and tell(), which are not supported by the ANSI C standard. You may still see them in some platform-dependent C programs. To use them, you need to read your C compiler's reference manual to make sure they're available.

Summary

In this lesson you learned the following important concepts and functions regarding disk file input and output in C:

- The file position indicator can be reset by the fseek() function.
- The ftell() function can tell you the value of the current file position indicator.
- The rewind() function can set the file position indicator to the beginning of a file.
- After you specify the mode of the fopen() function for a binary file, you can use the fread() or fwrite() functions to perform I/O operations on binary data.
- Besides the fact that the fscanf() and fprintf() functions can do the same jobs as the scanf() and printf() functions, the fscanf() and fprintf() functions also allow the programmer to specify I/O streams.
- You can redirect the standard streams, such as stdin and stdout, to a disk file with the help of the freopen() function.

In the next lesson you'll learn about the C preprocessor.

Q&A

Q Why is random access to a disk file necessary?

A When you want to fetch a piece of information from a large file that contains a huge amount of data, random access to the file is a more efficient way than sequential access to the file. The functions that perform random access can put the file position indicator directly to the right place in the file, and then you can simply start to fetch the required information from there. In C, the fseek() and ftell() functions are two handy functions that help you to carry out the random access operation.

Q How do you specify the format of a new disk file you're going to create by calling `fopen()`?

A You have to add b into the mode argument to the `fopen()` function to specify that the file you're going to create is a binary file. You can use `"wb"` to create a new file for writing and `"wb+"` to create a new file for writing and reading. If, however, the file to be created is a text file, no b is needed in the mode argument.

Q What is the difference between the `printf()` and `fprintf()` functions?

A Basically, the `printf()` and `fprintf()` functions can do a similar job: send the formatted data items to the output streams. However, the `printf()` function automatically sends formatted data to `stdout`, whereas the `fprintf()` function can be assigned a file pointer that is associated with a specified output stream.

Q Can you redirect a standard stream to a disk file?

A Yes. With the help of the `freopen()` function, you can redirect a standard stream and associate the stream with a disk file.

Workshop

To help solidify your understanding of this hour's lesson, you are encouraged to answer the quiz questions and finish the exercises provided in the workshop before you move to the next lesson. The answers and hints to the questions and exercises are given in Appendix B, "Answers to Quiz Questions and Exercises."

Quiz

1. Are the following two statements equivalent?
   ```
   rewind(fptr);
   fseek(fptr, 0L, SEEK_SET);
   ```

2. Are the following two statements equivalent?
   ```
   rewind(fptr);
   fseek(fptr, 0L, SEEK_CUR);
   ```

3. After the statement
   ```
   freopen("test.txt", "r", stdin);
   ```
   is executed successfully, where does the `scanf()` function in the following statement read from?
   ```
   scanf("%s%d", str, &num);
   ```

4. Given that the size of the `double` data type is 8 bytes long, and you have four `double` data items, if you write the four `double` data items into a binary file, how many bytes do the four data items take in the file?

Exercises

1. Assume that the following paragraph of *Tao Te Ching* is saved in a text file called LaoTzu.txt:

   ```
   Be bent, and you will remain straight.
   Be vacant, and you will remain full.
   Be worn, and you will remain new.
   ```

   Write a program to use `ftell()` to find the positions of the three strings in the file, and then call `fseek()` to set the file position indicator in such a way that the three strings are printed out in reverse order.

2. Rewrite the program you made in exercise 1 by calling the `rewind()` function to reset the file position indicator at the beginning of the LaoTzu.txt file.

3. Given a `double` value of `123.45`, and an `int` value of `10000`, write a program to save them into a binary file, called data.bin, and then read them back from the binary file. Also, print out what you're writing or reading. What do you think the size of the binary file will be?

4. Read the text file strnum.mix, which is created by the program in Listing 22.3. Redirect the input stream so that you can use the `scanf()` function to perform the reading operation.

22

HOUR **23**

Compiling Programs: The C Preprocessor

Intelligence is the faculty of making artificial objects, especially tools to make tools.

—H. Bergson

In Hour 2, "Your First C Program," you learned how to use the `#include` preprocessor directive to include C header files. Since then, the `#include` directive has been used in every program in this book. In this lesson you'll learn more about the C preprocessor and making macro definitions with the preprocessor directives. The following topics are discussed in this hour:

- What the C preprocessor can do
- Macro definitions and macro substitutions
- The `#define` and `#undef` directives
- How to define function-like macros with `#define`
- The `#ifdef`, `#ifndef`, and `#endif` directives
- The `#if`, `#elif`, and `#else` directives
- How to nest `#if` and `#elif` directives

What Is the C Preprocessor?

If there is a constant appearing in several places in your program, it's a good idea to associate a symbolic name to the constant, and then use the symbolic name to replace the constant throughout the program. There are two advantages to doing so. First, your program will be more readable. Second, it's easier to maintain your program. For instance, if the value of the constant needs to be changed, you just find the statement that associates the constant with the symbolic name and replace the constant with the new one. Without using the symbolic name, you have to look everywhere in your program to replace the constant. Sounds great, but can you do this in C?

Well, C has a special program called the C preprocessor that allows you to define and associate symbolic names with constants. In fact, the C preprocessor uses the terminology *macro names* and *macro body* to refer to the symbolic names and the constants. The C preprocessor runs before the compiler. During the preprocessing, the operation to replace a macro name with its associated macro body is called *macro substitution* or *macro expansion*.

You can put a macro definition anywhere in your program. However, a macro name has to be defined before it can be used in your program.

In addition, the C preprocessor gives you the ability to include other source files. For instance, you've been using the preprocessor directive `#include` to include C header files, such as `stdio.h`, `stdlib.h`, and `string.h`, in the programs throughout this book. Also, the C preprocessor enables you to compile different sections of your program under specified conditions.

The C Preprocessor versus the Compiler

One important thing you need to remember is that the C preprocessor is not part of the C compiler.

The C preprocessor uses a different syntax. All directives in the C preprocessor begin with a pound sign (#). In other words, the pound sign denotes the beginning of a preprocessor directive, and it must be the first nonspace character on the line.

The C preprocessor is line-oriented. Each macro statement ends with a newline character, not a semicolon. (Only C statements end with semicolons.) One of the most common mistakes made by the programmer is to place a semicolon at the end of a macro statement. Fortunately, many C compilers can catch such errors.

The following sections describe some of the most frequently used directives, such as `#define`, `#undef`, `#if`, `#elif`, `#else`, `#ifdef`, `#ifndef`, and `#endif`.

Macro names, especially those that will be substituted by constants, are normally represented with uppercase letters so that they can be distinguished from other variable names in the program.

The #define and #undef Directives

23

The #define directive is the most common preprocessor directive, which tells the preprocessor to replace every occurrence of a particular character string (that is, macro name) with a specified value (that is, macro body).

SYNTAX

The syntax for the #define directive is

```
#define macro_name  macro_body
```

Here *macro_name* is an identifier that can contain letters, numerals, or underscores. *macro_body* may be a string or a data item, which is used to substitute each *macro_name* found in the program.

As mentioned earlier, the operation to replace occurrences of *macro_name* with the value specified by *macro_body* is known as *macro substitution* or *macro expansion*.

The value of the macro body specified by a #define directive can be any character string or number. For example, the following definition associates STATE_NAME with the string "Texas" (including the quotation marks):

```
#define STATE_NAME    "Texas"
```

Then, during the preprocessing, all occurrences of STATE_NAME will be replaced by "Texas".

Likewise, the following statement tells the C preprocessor to replace SUM with the string (12 + 8):

```
#define SUM  (12 + 8)
```

On the other hand, you can use the #undef directive to remove the definition of a macro name that has been previously defined.

SYNTAX

The syntax for the #undef directive is

```
#undef macro_name
```

Here *macro_name* is an identifier that has been previously defined by a #define directive.

You can think of the #undef directive as "undefining" a macro name. For instance, the following segment of code:

```
#define STATE_NAME "Texas"
   printf("I am moving out of %s.\n", STATE_NAME);
#undef STATE_NAME
```

defines the macro name STATE_NAME first, and uses the macro name in the printf() function; then it removes the macro name. From that point in the program, STATE_NAME cannot be used again (unless, of course, it is redefined first).

Defining Function-Like Macros with #define

You can specify one or more arguments to a macro name defined by the #define directive, so that the macro name can be treated like a simple function that accepts arguments.

For instance, the following macro name, MULTIPLY, takes two arguments:

```
#define MULTIPLY(val1, val2)  ((val1) * (val2))
```

When the following statement:

```
result = MULTIPLY(2, 3) + 10;
```

is preprocessed, the preprocessor substitutes the expression 2 for val1 and 3 for val2, and then produces the following equivalent:

```
result = ((2) * (3)) + 10;
```

The program in Listing 23.1 is an example of using the #define directive to perform macro substitution.

TYPE   **LISTING 23.1**   Using the #define Directive

```
 1:  /* 23L01.c:  Using #define */
 2:  #include <stdio.h>
 3:
 4:  #define METHOD        "ABS"
 5:  #define ABS(val)      ((val) < 0 ? -(val) : (val))
 6:  #define MAX_LEN       8
 7:  #define NEGATIVE_NUM -10
 8:
 9:  main(void)
10:  {
11:     char *str = METHOD;
12:     int array[MAX_LEN];
13:     int i;
14:
15:     printf("The orignal values in array:\n");
16:     for (i=0; i<MAX_LEN; i++){
```

```
17:        array[i] = (i + 1) * NEGATIVE_NUM;
18:        printf("array[%d]: %d\n", i, array[i]);
19:     }
20:
21:     printf("\nApplying the %s macro:\n", str);
22:     for (i=0; i<MAX_LEN; i++){
23:        printf("ABS(%d): %3d\n", array[i], ABS(array[i]));
24:     }
25:
26:     return 0;
27: }
```

The following output appears on the screen of my computer after I run the executable
23L01.exe of the program in Listing 23.1:

OUTPUT
```
The orignal values in array:
array[0]: -10
array[1]: -20
array[2]: -30
array[3]: -40
array[4]: -50
array[5]: -60
array[6]: -70
array[7]: -80

Applying the ABS macro:
ABS(-10):  10
ABS(-20):  20
ABS(-30):  30
ABS(-40):  40
ABS(-50):  50
ABS(-60):  60
ABS(-70):  70
ABS(-80):  80
```

ANALYSIS The purpose of the program in Listing 23.1 is to define different macro names,
including a function-like macro, and use them in the program.

In lines 4–7, four macro names, METHOD, ABS, MAX_LEN, and NEGATIVE_NUM are defined
with the #define directive. Among them, ABS can accept one argument. The definition of
ABS in line 5 checks the value of the argument and returns the absolute value of the argument. Note that the conditional operator ?: is used to find the absolute value for the
incoming argument. (The ?: operator was introduced in Hour 8, "Using Conditional
Operators.")

Then, inside the main() function, the char pointer str is defined and assigned with
METHOD in line 11. As you can see, METHOD is associated with the string "ABS". In line 12,
an int array called array is defined with the element number specified by MAX_LEN.

In lines 16–19, each element of array is initialized with the value represented by the (i + 1) * NEGATIVE_NUM expression that produces a series of negative integer numbers.

The for loop in lines 22–24 applies the function-like macro ABS to each element of array and obtains the absolute value for each element. Then, all of the absolute values are displayed on the screen. The output from the program in Listing 23.1 proves that each macro defined in the program works very well.

Nested Macro Definitions

A previously defined macro can be used as the value in another #define statement. The following is an example:

```
#define ONE      1
#define TWO      (ONE + ONE)
#define THREE    (ONE + TWO)
result = TWO * THREE;
```

Here the macro ONE is defined to be equivalent to the value 1, and TWO is defined to be equivalent to (ONE + ONE), where ONE has been defined in the previous macro definition. Likewise, THREE is defined to be equivalent to (ONE + TWO), where both ONE and TWO are previously defined.

Therefore, the assignment statement following the macro definitions is expanded to the following statement:

```
result = (1 + 1) * (1 + (1 + 1));
```

When you are using the #define directive with a macro body that is an expression, you need to enclose the macro body in parentheses. For example, if the macro definition is

```
#define SUM   12 + 8
```

then the following statement:

```
result = SUM * 10;
```

becomes this:

```
result = 12 + 8 * 10;
```

which assigns 92 to result.

However, if you enclose the macro body in parentheses like this:

```
#define SUM   (12 + 8)
```

then the assignment statement becomes this:

```
result = (12 + 8) * 10;
```

and produces the result 200, which is likely what you want.

Compiling Your Code Under Conditions

You can select portions of your C program that you want to compile by using a set of preprocessor directives. This technique is called *conditional compilation*. This is useful, especially when you're testing a piece of new code or debugging a portion of code.

The #ifdef and #endif Directives

The #ifdef and #endif directives control whether a given group of statements is to be included as part of your program.

The general form to use the #ifdef and #endif directives is

```
#ifdef macro_name
   statement1
   statement2
   . . .
   statementN
#endif
```

Here *macro_name* is any character string that can be defined by a #define directive. *statement1*, *statement2*, and *statementN* are statements that are included in the program only if *macro_name* has already been defined. If *maccro_name* has not been defined, *statement1*, *statement2*, and everything up to *statementN* skipped.

Unlike an if statement in C, the statements under the control of the #ifdef directive are not enclosed in braces; instead, the #endif directive must be used to mark the end of the #ifdef block.

For instance, the #ifdef directive in the following code segment:

```
. . .
#ifdef DEBUG
   printf("The contents of the string pointed to by str: %s\n", str);
#endif
. . .
```

indicates that if the macro name DEBUG is defined, the printf() function in the statement following the #ifdef directive is included in the program. The compiler will compile the statement so that the contents of a string pointed to by str will be printed by the statement. However if DEBUG has not been defined, the printf() call will be entirely left out of your compiled program.

The #ifndef Directive

The #ifndef directive enables you to define code that is to be executed when a particular macro name is not defined.

23

The general format to use #ifndef is the same as for #ifdef:

```
#ifndef macro_name
   statement1
   statement2
   . . .
   statementN
#endif
```

Here *macro_name*, *statement1*, *statement2*, and *statementN* have the same meanings as those in the form of #ifdef introduced in the previous section. Again, the #endif directive is needed to mark the end of the #ifndef block.

Listing 23.2 contains a program that demonstrates how to use the #ifdef, #ifndef, and #endif directives together.

TYPE   **LISTING 23.2**   Using the #ifdef, #ifndef, and #endif Directives

```
1:  /* 23L02.c:  Using #ifdef, #ifndef, and #endif */
2:  #include <stdio.h>
3:
4:  #define UPPER_CASE   0
5:  #define NO_ERROR     0
6:
7:  main(void)
8:  {
9:     #ifdef UPPER_CASE
10:      printf("THIS LINE IS PRINTED OUT,\n");
11:      printf("BECAUSE UPPER_CASE IS DEFINED.\n");
12:     #endif
13:     #ifndef LOWER_CASE
14:      printf("\nThis line is printed out,\n");
15:      printf("because LOWER_CASE is not defined.\n");
16:     #endif
17:
18:     return NO_ERROR;
19: }
```

The following output is shown on the screen after the executable 23L02.exe is created and run on my computer:

OUTPUT
```
THIS LINE IS PRINTED OUT,
BECAUSE UPPER_CASE IS DEFINED.

This line is printed out,
because LOWER_CASE is not defined.
```

ANALYSIS   The purpose of the program in Listing 23.2 is to use #ifdef and #ifndef directives to control whether a message will be displayed.

Two macro names, UPPER_CASE and NO_ERROR, are defined in lines 4 and 5.

The #ifdef directive in line 9 checks whether the UPPER_CASE macro name has been defined. Because the macro name has been defined in line 4, the two statements in lines 10 and 11 (until the #endif directive in line 12 marks the end of the #ifdef block) are included in the compiled program.

In line 13, the #ifndef directive tells the preprocessor to include the two statements in lines 14 and 15 in the program if the LOWER_CASE macro name has not been defined. As you can see, LOWER_CASE is not defined in the program at all. Therefore, the two statements in lines 14 and 15 are compiled as part of the program.

The output from running the program in Listing 23.2 shows that the printf() functions in lines 10, 11, 14, and 15 are compiled and executed accordingly, under the control of the #ifdef and #ifndef directives. You can try modifying the program by changing line 4 so that it defines LOWER_CASE rather than UPPER_CASE. The #ifdef and #ifndef directives will then remove all four printf() calls from the program.

The #if, #elif, and #else Directives

The #if directive specifies that certain statements are to be included only if the value represented by the conditional expression is nonzero. The conditional expression can be an arithmetic expression.

The general form to use the #if directive is

```
#if expression
   statement1
   statement2
   . . .
   statementN
#endif
```

Here *expression* is the conditional expression to be evaluated. *statement1*, *statement2*, and *statementN* represent the code to be included if *expression* is nonzero.

Note that the #endif directive is included at the end of the definition to mark the end of the #if block, as it does for an #ifdef or #ifndef block.

In addition, the #else directive provides an alternative to choose. The following general form uses the #else directive to put *statement_1*, *statement_2*, and *statement_N* into the program if *expression* is zero:

```
#if expression
   statement1
   statement2
   . . .
```

```
   statementN
#else
   statement_1
   statement_2
   . . .
   statement_N
#endif
```

Again, the #endif directive is used to mark the end of the #if block.

Also, a macro definition can be used as part of the conditional expression evaluated by the #if directive. If the macro is defined, it has a nonzero value in the expression; otherwise, it has the value 0.

For example, look at the following portion of code:

```
#ifdef DEBUG
   printf("The value of the debug version: %d\n", debug);
#else
   printf("The value of the release version: %d\n", release);
#endif
```

If DEBUG has been defined by a #define directive, the value of the debug version is printed out by the printf() function in the following statement:

```
printf("The value of the debug version: %d\n", debug);
```

Otherwise, if DEBUG has not been defined, the following statement is executed:

```
printf("The value of the release version: %d\n", release);
```

Now consider another example:

```
#if 1
 printf("The line is always printed out.\n");
#endif
```

The printf() function is always executed because the expression 1 evaluated by the #if directive never returns 0.

In the following example:

```
#if MACRO_NAME1 || MACRO_NAME2
   printf("MACRO_NAME1 or MACRO_NAME2 is defined.\n");
#else
   printf("MACRO_NAME1 and MACRO_NAME2 are not defined.\n");
#endif
```

the logical operator || is used, along with MACRO_NAME1 and MACRO_NAME2 in the expression evaluated by the #if directive. If one of the macro names, MACRO_NAME1 or MACRO_NAME2, has been defined, the expression evaluates to a nonzero value; otherwise, 0 is produced.

The C preprocessor has another directive, #elif, which stands for "else if." You can use #if and #elif together to build an if-else-if chain for multiple conditional compilation.

The program shown in Listing 23.3 is an example of using the #if, #elif, and #else directives.

TYPE **LISTING 23.3** Using the #if, #elif, and #else Directives

23

```
 1:  /* 23L03.c:  Using #if, #elif, and #else */
 2:  #include <stdio.h>
 3:
 4:  #define C_LANG     'C'
 5:  #define B_LANG     'B'
 6:  #define NO_ERROR   0
 7:
 8:  main(void)
 9:  {
10:     #if C_LANG == 'C' && B_LANG == 'B'
11:        #undef C_LANG
12:        #define C_LANG "I know the C language.\n"
13:        #undef B_LANG
14:        #define B_LANG "I know BASIC.\n"
15:        printf("%s%s", C_LANG, B_LANG);
16:     #elif C_LANG == 'C'
17:        #undef C_LANG
18:        #define C_LANG "I only know C language.\n"
19:        printf("%s", C_LANG);
20:     #elif B_LANG == 'B'
21:        #undef B_LANG
22:        #define B_LANG "I only know BASIC.\n"
23:        printf("%s", B_LANG);
24:     #else
25:        printf("I don't know C or BASIC.\n");
26:     #endif
27:
28:     return NO_ERROR;
29:  }
```

After the executable 23L03.exe is created and run, the following output is displayed on the screen of my computer:

OUTPUT
```
I know C language.
I know BASIC.
```

ANALYSIS The purpose of the program in Listing 23.3 is to use the #if, #elif, and #else directives to select portions of code that are going to be compiled.

Inside the main() function, the #if directive in line 10 evaluates the conditional expression C_LANG == 'C' && B_LANG == 'B'. If the expression evaluates to nonzero, statements in lines 11–15 are selected to be compiled.

In line 11 the #undef directive is used to remove the C_LANG macro name. Line 12 then redefines C_LANG with the string "I know the C language.\n". Likewise, line 13 removes the B_LANG macro name and line 14 redefines B_LANG with another character string. The printf() call in line 15 prints the two newly assigned strings associated with C_LANG and B_LANG.

The #elif directive in line 16 starts to evaluate the expression C_LANG == 'C' if the expression in line 10 has evaluated to 0. If the C_LANG == 'C' expression evaluates to nonzero, the statements in lines 17–19 are compiled.

If, however, the expression in line 16 also fails to evaluate to a nonzero value, the B_LANG == 'B' expression is evaluated by another #elif directive in line 20. The statements in lines 21–23 are skipped, and the statement in line 25 is compiled finally if the B_LANG == 'B' expression evaluates to 0.

In line 26 the #endif directive marks the end of the #if block that started on line 10.

From the program in Listing 23.3 you can tell that C_LANG and B_LANG have been properly defined in lines 4 and 5. Therefore, the statements in lines 11–15 are selected as part of the program and compiled by the C compiler. The two character strings assigned to C_LANG and B_LANG during the redefinition are displayed after the program in Listing 23.3 is executed.

You can change the value of the macros C_LANG and B_LANG to experiment with other executions of the program.

Nested Conditional Compilation

According to the ANSI C standard, the #if and #elif directives can be nested at least eight levels.

For example, the #if directive is nested in the following code segment:

```
#if MACRO_NAME1
   #if MACRO_NAME2
     #if MACRO_NAME3
         printf("MACRO_NAME1, MACRO_NAME2, and MACRO_NAME3\n");
     #else
         printf("MACRO_NAME1 and MACRO_NAME2\n");
     #endif
   #else
     printf("MACRO_NAME1\n");
```

```
   #endif
#else
   printf("No macro name defined.\n");
#endif
```

Here the #if directive is nested to three levels. Note that each #else or #endif is associated with the nearest #if.

Now let's have a look at another example in Listing 23.4, in which the #if directives are nested.

23

TYPE   **LISTING 23.4**   Nesting the #if Directive

```
1:  /* 23L04.c: Nesting #if    */
2:  #include <stdio.h>
3:
4:  /* macro definitions */
5:  #define ZERO      0
6:  #define ONE       1
7:  #define TWO       (ONE + ONE)
8:  #define THREE     (ONE + TWO)
9:  #define TEST_1    ONE
10: #define TEST_2    TWO
11: #define TEST_3    THREE
12: #define MAX_NUM   THREE
13: #define NO_ERROR  ZERO
14: /* function declaration */
15: void StrPrint(char **ptr_s, int max);
16: /* the main() function */
17: main(void)
18: {
19:    char *str[MAX_NUM] = {"The choice of a point of view",
20:                          "is the initial act of culture.",
21:                          "--- by O. Gasset"};
22:
23:    #if TEST_1 == 1
24:       #if TEST_2 == 2
25:          #if TEST_3 == 3
26:             StrPrint(str, MAX_NUM);
27:          #else
28:             StrPrint(str, MAX_NUM - ONE);
29:          #endif
30:       #else
31:          StrPrint(str, MAX_NUM - TWO);
32:       #endif
33:    #else
34:       printf("No TEST macro has been set.\n");
35:    #endif
```

continues

LISTING 23.4   continued

```
36:
37:    return NO_ERROR;
38: }
39: /* function definition */
40: void StrPrint(char **ptr_s, int max)
41: {
42:    int i;
43:
44:    for (i=0; i<max; i++)
45:        printf("Content: %s\n",
46:                ptr_s[i]);
47: }
```

The following output is shown on the screen after the executable 23L04.exe is created
and run on my machine:

```
Content: The choice of a point of view
Content: is the initial act of culture.
Content: --- by O. Gasset
```

The purpose of the program in Listing 23.4 is to print the content of character
strings controlled by the nested #if directives.

At the beginning of the program, nine macro names are defined in lines 5–13. The prototype of a function, StrPrint(), is given in line 15. Lines 19–21 define and initialize an
array of char pointers called str.

The #if directives in lines 23–25 evaluate macro names, TEST_1, TEST_2, and TEST_3,
respectively. If the three macro names all evaluate to nonzero values, thenStrPrint() is
called in line 26 to print the content of all character strings pointed to by the pointers in
the str array.

If, however, only TEST_1 and TEST_2 are nonzero, the statement in line 28 prints out the
content of the MAX_NUM-ONE strings. Likewise, if only TEST_1 evaluates to a nonzero
value, the StrPrint() function is called in line 31 to print out the content of the
MAX_NUM-TWO strings.

The last case is that TEST_1, TEST_2, and TEST_3 all return zero. Then the printf() call
in line 34 is executed to display onscreen the message No TEST macro has been set.

As you can tell from the program in Listing 23.4, TEST_1, TEST_2, and TEST_3 are all
defined with nonzero constants; the content of all character strings referenced by the
pointers of the str array are printed out as the output from the program.

You can experiment with the effects of these nested directives by changing the values of
the macros TEST_1, TEST_2, and TEST_3.

Summary

In this lesson you learned the following important concepts and directives regarding the preprocessor in C:

- The C preprocessor runs before the compiler. During the preprocessing stage, all occurrences of a macro name are replaced by the macro body that is associated with the macro name.

- The C preprocessor also enables you to include additional source files in the program or compile sections of C code conditionally.

- The C preprocessor is not part of the C compiler.

- A macro statement ends with a newline character, not a semicolon.

- The #define directive tells the preprocessor to replace every occurrence of a macro name defined by the directive with a macro body that is associated with the macro name.

- The #undef directive is used to remove the definition of a macro name that has been previously defined.

- You can specify one or more arguments to a macro name defined by the #define directive.

- The #ifdef directive enables you to specify code that is to be included only when a particular macro name is defined.

- The #ifndef directive is a mirror directive to the #ifdef directive. With #ifndef, you specify code that is to be included when a particular macro name is not defined.

- The #endif directive is used to mark the end of an #ifdef, an #ifndef, or an #if block.

- The #if, #elif, and #else directives enable you to select alternate portions of code to compile.

In the next lesson you'll see a summary of what you've learned and what you can do after studying this book.

Q&A

Q Is the C preprocessor part of the C compiler?

A No. The C preprocessor is not part of the C compiler. With its own line-oriented grammar and syntax, the C preprocessor runs before the compiler in order to handle named constants, macros, and inclusion of files.

Q How do you remove a macro name?

A By using the `#undef` directive with a macro name, that macro name can be removed, or "undefined." According to the ANSI C standard, a macro name has to be removed before it can be redefined.

Q Why do you need the `#endif` directive?

A The `#endif` directive is used with an `#if`, `#ifdef`, or `#ifndef` directives because statements under the control of a conditional preprocessor directive are not enclosed in braces (`{` and `}`). Therefore, `#endif` must be used to mark the end of the block of statements.

Q Can the conditional expression following the `#if` directive be an arithmetic expression?

A Yes. The conditional expression evaluated by the `#if` directive can be an arithmetic expression. If the expression evaluates to a nonzero value, the code between the `#if` directive and the next nearest conditional directive are included for compilation. Otherwise, the code is skipped entirely and will not be part of the compiled program.

Workshop

To help solidify your understanding of this hour's lesson, you are encouraged to answer the quiz questions and finish the exercises provided in the workshop before you move to the next lesson. The answers and hints to the questions and exercises are given in Appendix B, "Answers to Quiz Questions and Exercises."

Quiz

1. What's wrong with the following macro definition?

   ```
   #define  ONE   1;
   ```

2. What is the final value assigned to `result` after the assignment statement is executed?

   ```
   #define ONE       1
   #define NINE      9
   #define EXPRESS   ONE + NINE
   result = EXPRESS * NINE;
   ```

3. What message will be displayed by the following code segment?

   ```
   #define MACRO_NAME  0
   #if MACRO_NAME
      printf("Under #if.\n");
   #else
      printf("Under #else.\n");
   #endif
   ```

4. What message will be displayed by the following code segment?

```
#define MACRO_NAME  0
#ifdef MACRO_NAME
   printf("Under #ifdef.\n");
#endif
#ifndef MACRO_NAME
   printf("Under #ifndef.\n");
#endif
```

Exercises

1. In Hour 18, "Using Special Data Types and Functions," you learned how to define enum data. Rewrite the program in Listing 18.1 with the #define directive.

2. Define a macro name that can multiply two arguments. Write a program to calculate the multiplication of 2 and 3 with the help of the macro. Print out the result of the multiplication.

3. Rewrite the program in Listing 23.2 with the #if, #elif, and #else directives.

4. Rewrite the program in Listing 23.3 with nested #if directives.

23

HOUR 24

Where Do You Go from Here?

It's not what you know, but what you can.

—A. Alekhine

Congratulations! You're now in the last chapter of this book. You just need to spend one more hour to complete your 24-hour journey. In this lesson you'll learn more about the C language from the following topics:

- Programming style
- Modular programming
- Debugging

Also, a brief review on what you've learned from this book is included in this lesson. Before you start to cover these topics, let's have a look at the last example in this book.

Creating a Linked List

In this section, I'm going to build functions that can create a linked list, and add items to or delete items from the created linked list. I save those functions into a source file (that is, a *module*; refer to the section "Modular Programming" in this lesson). In addition, I will set up an interface between the module file and the user. In other words, the user can call one of the functions saved in the module via the interface. The interface is invoked in the main() function that is saved in another source file. I will put data declarations and function prototypes in a separate header file.

A *linked list* is a chain of nodes (or elements). Each node consists of data items and a pointer that points to the next node in the list. The last item has a null pointer to signify the end of the list.

A linked list is a very powerful, and very versatile, data structure. No matter what programming project you eventually undertake, it's likely that you'll want to use a linked list at some point. Why are linked lists so popular? For starters, they are relatively easy to implement, unlike some other data structures that may be more powerful but get complicated quickly. Secondly, it is easy to "walk" a linked list by simply following the pointers along. It's almost as easy as using an array, but with a linked list you have the flexibility of dynamic memory allocation.

A linked list with N nodes is shown in Figure 24.1.

FIGURE 24.1

A linked list with N nodes.

As you can see from Figure 24.1, a start pointer points to the first node in the list. The pointer in the last (*N*th) node is a null pointer.

The linked list I'm going to build is a very simple one, in which each element only contains two items: a student name and an ID number. Listing 24.1 contains the module program, which is saved in the source file named 24L01.c.

TYPE   **LISTING 24.1**   Putting Cohesive Functions in the Module Program

```
1:   /* 24L01.c: A module file */
2:   #include "24L02.h"
3:
4:   static NODE *head_ptr = NULL;
5:
```

```
6:   /**
7:    ** main_interface()
8:    **/
9:   void main_interface(int ch)
10:  {
11:     switch (ch){
12:       case 'a':
13:          list_node_add();
14:          break;
15:       case 'd':
16:          if (!list_node_delete())
17:             list_node_print();
18:          break;
19:       case 'p':
20:          list_node_print();
21:          break;
22:       default:
23:          break;
24:     }
25:  }
26:  /**
27:   ** list_node_create()
28:   **/
29:  NODE *list_node_create(void)
30:  {
31:     NODE *ptr;
32:
33:     if ((ptr=(NODE *)malloc(sizeof(NODE))) == NULL)
34:        ErrorExit("malloc() failed.\n");
35:
36:     ptr->next_ptr = NULL;  /* set the next pointer to NULL */
37:     ptr->id = 0; /* initialization */
38:     return ptr;
39:  }
40:
41:  /**
42:   ** list_node_add()
43:   **/
44:  void list_node_add(void)
45:  {
46:     NODE *new_ptr, *ptr;
47:
48:     new_ptr = list_node_create();
49:     printf("Enter the student name and ID: ");
50:     scanf("%s%ld", new_ptr->name, &new_ptr->id);
51:
52:     if (head_ptr == NULL){
53:        head_ptr = new_ptr;
54:     } else {
```

continues

LISTING 24.1   continued

```
55:        /* find the last node in the list */
56:        for (ptr=head_ptr;
57:              ptr->next_ptr != NULL;
58:              ptr=ptr->next_ptr)
59:           ; /* doing nothing here */
60:        /* link to the last node */
61:        ptr->next_ptr = new_ptr;
62:     }
63: }
64: /**
65:  ** list_node_delete()
66:  **/
67: int list_node_delete(void)
68: {
69:    NODE *ptr, *ptr_saved;
70:    unsigned long id;
71:    int deleted = 0;
72:    int reval = 0;
73:
74:    if (head_ptr == NULL){
75:       printf("Sorry, nothing to delete.\n");
76:       reval = 1;
77:    } else {
78:       printf("Enter the student ID: ");
79:       scanf("%ld", &id);
80:
81:       if (head_ptr->id == id){
82:          ptr_saved = head_ptr->next_ptr;
83:          free(head_ptr);
84:          head_ptr = ptr_saved;
85:          if (head_ptr == NULL){
86:             printf("All nodes have been deleted.\n");
87:             reval = 1;
88:          }
89:       } else {
90:          for (ptr=head_ptr;
91:                ptr->next_ptr != NULL;
92:                ptr=ptr->next_ptr){
93:             if (ptr->next_ptr->id == id){
94:                ptr_saved = ptr->next_ptr->next_ptr;
95:                free(ptr->next_ptr);
96:                ptr->next_ptr = ptr_saved;
97:                deleted = 1;
98:                break;
99:             }
100:         }
101:         if (!deleted){
102:            printf("Can not find the student ID.\n");
103:         }
```

```
104:       }
105:    }
106:    return reval;
107: }
108: /**
109:  ** list_node_print()
110:  **/
111: void list_node_print(void)
112: {
113:    NODE *ptr;
114:
115:    if (head_ptr == NULL){
116:       printf("Nothing to display.\n");
117:    } else {
118:       printf("The content of the linked list:\n");
119:       for (ptr = head_ptr;
120:             ptr->next_ptr != NULL;
121:             ptr = ptr->next_ptr){
122:          printf("%s:%d -> ",
123:                ptr->name,
124:                ptr->id);
125:       }
126:       printf("%s:%d ->|",
127:             ptr->name,
128:             ptr->id);
129:       printf("\n");
130:    }
131: }
132: /**
133:  ** list_node_free()
134:  **/
135: void list_node_free()
136: {
137:    NODE *ptr, *ptr_saved;
138:
139:    for (ptr=head_ptr; ptr != NULL; ){
140:       ptr_saved = ptr->next_ptr;
141:       free(ptr);
142:       ptr = ptr_saved;
143:    }
144:    free(ptr);
145: }
146: /**
147:  ** ErrorExit()
148:  **/
149: void ErrorExit(char *str)
150: {
151:    printf("%s\n", str);
152:    exit(ERR_FLAG);
153: }
```

There is no direct output from the module program in Listing 24.1.

ANALYSIS The purpose of the program in Listing 24.1 is to provide a module program that contains all cohesive functions for linked list creation, node addition, and node reduction. Figure 24.2 demonstrates the tasks performed by functions, such as `list_node_create()`, `list_node_add()`, and `list_node_delete()`, from the program.

FIGURE 24.2

Use functions defined in 24L01.c (refer to the following paragraphs for explanation).

As you can see in Figure 24.2 (a), the first linked list node is created by calling the `list_node_create()` function, and the data items are added with the help of the `list_node_add()` function. Also, the `head_ptr` pointer points to the node. Here `Peter` is the student name; `1234` is his ID number. Because there are no more nodes linked, the `next_ptr` pointer of the first node is set to be null.

In Figure 24.2 (b), another node is added to the linked list, with `Paul` as the student name and `5678` as the ID number. Note that the `next_ptr` pointer of the first node is reset to point to the second node, while the `next_ptr` pointer of the second node is set to be null.

Likewise, in Figure 24.2 (c), the third node is added to the linked list. The next_ptr pointer of the third node is a null pointer. The pointer in the second node is reset to point to the third node.

If you want to delete one of the nodes, you can call the list_node_delete() function. As shown in Figure 24.2 (d), the second node is deleted, so the pointer of the first node has to be reset to point to the former third node that contains the student name Mary and her ID number, 7777.

In Figure 24.2 (e), the first node is deleted by applying the list_node_delete() function again. There is only one node left in the linked list. The head_ptr pointer has to be reset to point to the last node.

The header file, 24L02.h, included in the module program 24L01.c, is shown in Listing 24.2. (The header file is also included by the driver program in Listing 24.3.)

24

LISTING 24.2   Putting Data Declarations and Function Prototypes into
TYPE   the Header File

```
 1: /* 24L02.h: the header file */
 2: #include <stdio.h>
 3: #include <stdlib.h>
 4:
 5: #ifndef LNK_LIST_H
 6: #define LNK_LIST_H
 7: #define ERR_FLAG   1
 8: #define MAX_LEN    16
 9:
10: struct lnk_list_struct
11: {
12:    char name[MAX_LEN];
13:    unsigned long id;
14:    struct lnk_list_struct *next_ptr;
15: };
16:
17: typedef struct lnk_list_struct NODE;
18:
19: NODE *list_node_create(void);
20: void list_node_add(void);
21: int list_node_delete(void);
22: void list_node_print(void);
23: void list_node_free(void);
24: void ErrorExit(char *);
25: void main_interface(int);
26:
27: #endif /* for LNK_LIST_H */
```

There is no direct output from the program in Listing 24.2.

ANALYSIS The purpose of the program in Listing 24.2 is to declare a structure with the tag name of `lnk_list_struct` in lines 10–15, and define a new variable name, of the structure `NODE`, in line 17.

The prototypes of the functions defined in the module program in Listing 24.1, such as `list_node_create()`, `list_node_add()`, and `list_node_delete()`, are listed in lines 19–25.

Note that the `#ifndef` and `#endif` preprocessor directives are used in lines 5 and 27. The declarations and definitions located between the two directives are compiled only if the macro name `LNK_LIST_H` has not been defined. Also, line 6 defines the macro name if it has not been defined. It's a good idea to put the `#ifndef` and `#endif` directives in a header file so as to avoid cross inclusions when the header file is included by more than one source file. In this case, the declarations and definitions in the `24L02.h` header file will not be included more than one time.

The module program in Listing 24.3 provides an interface that the user can use to call the functions saved in the source file (`24L01.c`).

TYPE **LISTING 24.3** Calling Functions Saved in the Module File

```
1:  /* 24L03.c:  The driver file */
2:  #include "24L02.h"    /* include header file */
3:
4:  main(void)
5:  {
6:    int ch;
7:
8:    printf("Enter a for adding, d for deleting,\n");
9:    printf("p for displaying, and q for exit:\n");
10:   while ((ch=getchar()) != 'q'){
11:     main_interface(ch);   /* process input from the user */
12:   }
13:
14:   list_node_free();
15:   printf("\nBye!\n");
16:
17:   return 0;
18: }
```

I compile the source files, `24L01.c` and `24L03.c`, separately with Microsoft Visual C++, and then link their object files and C library functions together to produce a single executable program called `24L03.exe`. I have the following output displayed after I run the executable 24L03.exe and enter or delete several student names and their ID numbers (the bold characters or numbers in the output section are what I entered from the keyboard):

OUTPUT

```
Enter a for adding, d for deleting,
p for displaying, and q for exit:
a
Enter the student name and ID: Peter 1234
a
Enter the student name and ID: Paul 5678
a
Enter the student name and ID: Mary 7777
p
The content of the linked list:
Peter:1234 -> Paul:5678 -> Mary:7777 ->¦
d
Enter the student ID: 1234
The content of the linked list:
Paul:5678 -> Mary:7777 ->¦
d
Enter the student ID: 5678
The content of the linked list:
Mary:7777 ->¦
d
Enter the student ID: 7777
All nodes have been deleted.
q

Bye!
```

ANALYSIS The purpose of the program in Listing 24.3 is to provide the user with an interface to call other functions. The functions, such as list_node_create(), list_node_add(), and list_node_delete(), can be invoked through the interface. Also, the main() function is located inside the program of Listing 24.3.

The content of a linked list node can be printed out in the format of

name:id ->

The following is an example:

Peter:1234 -> Paul:5678 -> Mary:7777 ->¦

Here the sign ¦ is used to indicate the pointer of the last node is a null pointer.

Figure 24.3 shows the relationship among the 24L01.c, 24L02.h, and 24L03.c files.

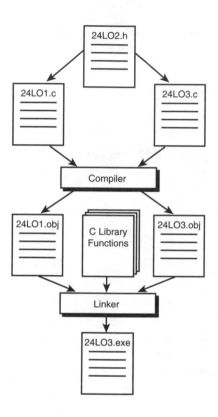

FIGURE 24.3
The relationship among the 24L01.c, 24L02.h, and 24L03.c files.

To learn to compile separate source files and link their object files together to make a single executable program, you need to check the technical reference from your C compiler vendor.

Programming Style

In this section, I'd like to briefly highlight some points that can help you write clean programs that can easily be read, understood, and maintained.

First, make sure the variable or function names in your program describe the meanings of the variables or tasks of the functions precisely and concisely.

Put comments into your code so that you or the other readers can have clues about what your code is doing, or at least what the code intends to do but might do incorrectly.

Whenever possible, keep using local variables, not global variables. Try to avoid sharing global data among functions; instead, pass the shared data as arguments to functions.

You should be careful in the use of C operators which use the same symbols, especially the assignment operator (=) and the conditional operator (==), because any misuse of these two operators can lead to an unexpected result and make debugging very difficult.

Avoid using the goto statement; instead, use other control flow statements whenever needed.

Use named constants in your program, instead of numeric constants, because named constants can make your program more readable, and you will only have to go to one place to update the values of constants.

You should put parentheses around each constant expression or argument defined by a preprocessor directive to avoid side effects.

Also, you should set up a reasonable rule for spacing and indentation so that you can follow the rule consistently in all the programs you write. The rule should help make your programs easy to read.

Modular Programming

It's not a good programming practice to try to solve a complex problem with a single function. The proper way to approach it is to break the problem into several smaller and simpler problems that can be understood in more detail, and then start to define and build functions to solve those smaller and simpler problems. Keep in mind that each of your functions should do only one task, but do it well.

When your program becomes larger and larger, you should consider breaking it into several source files, with each source file containing a small group of cohesive functions. Such source files are also called *modules*. Put data declarations and function prototypes into header files so that any changes to the declarations or prototypes can be automatically signified to all source files that include the header file.

For instance, in the section "Creating a Linked List," all functions that can be used to create a linked list and add or delete a node are put into the same module (24L01.c). Data structure and variable declarations and function prototypes are saved into a header file (24L02.h). The main() function and the interface are saved into another module (24L03.c).

You can use a software engineering technique known as *information hiding* to reduce the complexity of programming. Simply speaking, information hiding requires a module to not provide information to other modules unless it's very necessary.

The C compiler enables you to compile and debug different source files separately. In this way, you can focus on one source file at a time, and complete the compiling before you move to the next one. With the separate compilation, you can compile only those source files that have been changed and leave the source files that have already been compiled and debugged unattached.

If you're interested in knowing more details about software engineering, you should study Ian Sommerville's classic book, *Software Engineering*, which I've put into the list of recommended books at the end of this lesson.

Debugging

I've mentioned debugging several times in this lesson. What is a bug, anyway?

A *bug* in this context refers to any erroneous behavior of a computer system or a software program. *Debugging* means to find bugs and fix them. Please be aware that no computer system or software program is immune from bugs. Programmers, like you and me, make bugs because we're human beings.

When you're debugging your program, you should learn to isolate the erroneous behavior performed by your program. Many C compilers provide built-in debuggers that you can use to debug your program. Also, there are quite a few debugging tools made by third-party software vendors.

As it's said, debugging requires patience, ingenuity, and experience. I recommend that you read a good book that will teach you all the techniques on debugging; in fact, I recommend one in the list of the books in the next section.

What You Have Learned

The following subsections provide you with a brief review on the basics of the C language. The review is a summary that you will find useful to brush up what you've learned in the previous hours.

C Keywords

In C, certain words have been reserved. These reserved words, called C *keywords*, have special meanings to the C language. The following are the C keywords:

```
auto                          int

break                         long

case                          register
```

char	return
const	short
continue	signed
default	sizeof
do	static
double	struct
else	switch
enum	typedef
extern	union
float	unsigned
for	void
goto	volatile
if	while

24

Operators

Operators can help you to manipulate data. C provides you with a rich set of operators. Table 24.1 contains a list of the operators used in C.

TABLE 24.1   The Operators in C

Operator	Description
=	Assignment operator
+=	Addition assignment operator
-=	Subtraction assignment operator
*=	Multiplication assignment operator
/=	Division assignment operator
%=	Remainder assignment operator
-	Unary minus operator
++	Increment operator
--	Decrement operator
==	Equal to
!=	Not equal to
>	Greater than

continues

TABLE 24.1 continued

Operator	Description
<	Less than
>=	Greater than or equal to
<=	Less than or equal to
sizeof	Size-of operator
&&	Logical AND operator
¦¦	Logical OR operator
!	Logical NEGATION operator
&	Bitwise AND operator
¦	Bitwise OR operator
^	Bitwise eXclusive OR (XOR) operator
~	Bitwise complement operator
>>	Right shift operator
<<	Left shift operator
?:	Conditional operator

Constants

Constants are elements whose values do not change in the program. In C, there are several different types of constants.

Integer Constants

Integer constants are decimal numbers. You can suffix an integer constant with u or U to specify that the constant is of the unsigned data type. An integer constant suffixed with l or L is a long int constant.

An integer constant is prefixed with a 0 (zero) to indicate that the constant is in the octal format. If an integer constant is prefixed with 0X or 0x, the constant is a hexadecimal number.

Character Constants

A character constant is a character enclosed by single quotes. For instance, 'C' is a character constant.

In C, there are several character constants that represent certain special characters (see Table 24.2).

TABLE 24.2   Special Characters in C

Character	Meaning
\a	Audible alert
\b	Backspace
\f	Form feed
\n	New line
\r	Carriage return
\t	Horizontal tab
\v	Vertical tab
\"	Double quote
\'	Single quote
\0	Null
\\	Backslash
\N	Octal constant (here N is an octal constant)
\xN	Hexadecimal constant (here N is a hexadecimal constant)

Floating-Point Constants

Floating-point constants are decimal numbers that can be suffixed with f, F, l, or L to specify float or long double. A floating-point constant without a suffix is of the double data type by default. For instance, the following statements declare and initialize a float variable (flt_num) and a double variable (db_num):

```
float   flt_num = 1234.56f;
double  db_num = 1234.56;
```

A floating-point can also be represented in scientific notation.

String Constants

A *string constant* is a sequence of characters enclosed by double quotes. For instance, "This is a string constant." is a string constant. Note that the double quotes are not part of the content of the string. Also, the C compiler automatically adds a null character (\0) at the end of a string constant to indicate the end of the string.

Data Types

The basic *data types* provided by the C language are char, int, float, and double. In addition, there are array, enum, struct, and union data types that you can declare and use in your C programs.

The general form to define a list of variables with a specified data type is

```
data_type    variable_name_list;
```

Here `data_type` can be one of the keywords of the data types. `variable_name_list` represents a list of variable names separated by commas.

The Array Data Type

An *array* is a collection of variables that are of the same data type. The following is the general form to declare an array:

```
data-type   array-name[array-size];
```

Here `data-type` is the type specifier that indicates the data type of the array elements. `array-name` is the name of the declared array. `array-size` defines how many elements the array can contain. Note that the brackets (`[` and `]`) are required in declaring an array. The pair of `[` and `]` is also called the *array subscript operator*.

In addition, C supports multidimensional arrays.

The enum Data Type

enum is a short name for *enumerated*. The enumerated data type is used to declare named integer constants. The general form of the `enum` data type declaration is

```
enum tag_name {enumeration_list} variable_list;
```

Here `tag_name` is the name of the enumeration. `variable_list` gives a list of variable names that are of the enum data type. Both `tag_name` and `variable_list` are optional. `enumeration_list` contains defined enumerated names that are used to represent integer constants. Names represented by `variable_list` or `enumeration_list` are separated by commas.

The struct Data Type

In C, a structure collects different data items in such a way that they can be referenced as a single unit. The general form to declare a structure is

```
struct struct_tag {
    data_type1 variable1;
    data_type2 variable2;
    data_type3 variable3;
    .
    .
    .
    };
```

Here `struct` is the keyword used in C to start a structure declaration. *struct_tag* is the tag name of the structure. *variable1*, *variable2*, and *variable3* are the members of the structure. Their data types are specified respectively by *data_type1*, *data_type2*, and *data_type3*. The declarations of the members have to be enclosed within the opening and closing braces (`{` and `}`) in the structure declaration, and a semicolon (`;`) has to be included at the end of the declaration.

The following is an example of a structure declaration:

```
struct automobile {
    int year;
    char model[8];
    int engine_power;
    float weight;
    };
```

Here `struct` is used to start a structure declaration. `automobile` is the tag name of the structure. In the example here, there are three types of variables, `char`, `int`, and `float`. The variables have their own names, such as `year`, `model`, `engine_power`, and `weight`. They are all the members of the structure, and are declared with the braces (`{` and `}`).

The union Data Type

A *union* is a block of memory that is used to hold data items of different types. In C, a union is similar to a structure, except that data items saved in the union are overlaid in order to share the same memory location. The syntax for declaring a union is similar to the syntax for a structure. The general form to declare a union is

```
union union_tag {
    data_type1 variable1;
    data_type2 variable2;
    data_type3 variable3;
    .
    .
    .
    };
```

Here `union` is the keyword used in C to start a union declaration. *union_tag* is the tag name of the union. *variable1*, *variable2*, and *variable3* are the members of the union. Their data types are specified respectively by *data_type1*, *data_type2*, and *data_type3*. The union declaration is ended with a semicolon (`;`).

The following is an example of a union declaration:

```
union automobile {
    int year;
    char model[8];
    int engine_power;
    float weight;
};
```

Here union specifies the union data type. automobile is the tag name of the union. The variables, such as year, model, engine_power, and weight, are the members of the union and are declared within the braces ({ and }).

Defining New Type Names with typedef

You can create your own names for data types with the help of the typedef keyword, and use those names as synonyms for the data types. For instance, you can declare NUMBER as a synonym for the int data type:

```
typedef  int  NUMBER;
```

Then, you can start to use NUMBER to declare integer variables like this,

```
NUMBER i, j;
```

which is equivalent to

```
int i, j;
```

Remember that a typedef definition must be made before the synonym made in the definition is used in any declarations in your program.

Expressions and Statements

An *expression* is a combination of constants or variables that is used to denote computations.

For instance,

```
(2 + 3) * 10
```

is an expression that adds 2 and 3 first, and then multiplies the result of the addition by 10.

In the C language, a *statement* is a complete instruction, ended with a semicolon. In many cases, you can turn an expression into a statement by simply adding a semicolon at the end of the expression.

A *null statement* is represented by an isolated semicolon.

A group of statements can form a *statement block* that starts with an opening brace ({) and ends with a closing brace (}). A statement block is treated as a single statement by the C compiler.

Control Flow Statements

In C, there is a set of control flow statements that can be divided into two categories: looping and conditional branching.

The `for`, `while`, and `do-while` Loops

The general form of the `for` statement is

```
for (expression1; expression2; expression3) {
   statement1;
   statement2;
   .
   .
   .
}
```

The `for` statement first evaluates *expression1*, which is usually an expression that initializes one or more variables. The second expression, *expression2*, is the conditional part that is evaluated and tested by the `for` statement for each iteration. If *expression2* evaluates to a nonzero value, the statements within the braces, such as *statement1* and *statement2*, are executed. If *expression2* evaluates to 0 (zero), the looping is stopped and the execution of the `for` statement is finished. The third expression in the `for` statement, *expression3*, is evaluated after each looping before the statement goes back to test *expression2* again. This third expression is often used to increment an index variable.

The following `for` statement makes an infinite loop because all three expressions are empty:

```
for ( ; ; ){
  /* statement block */
}
```

The general form of the `while` statement is

```
while (expression) {
   statement1;
   statement2;
   .
   .
   .
}
```

Here *expression* is the conditional expression in the `while` statement. The expression is evaluated first. If it evaluates to a nonzero value, the looping continues; that is, the statements inside the statement block, such as *statement1* and *statement2*, are executed. After the execution, the expression is evaluated again. Then the statements are executed one more time if the expression still evaluates to a nonzero value. The process is repeated over and over until the expression evaluates to zero.

24

You can also make a `while` loop infinite by putting 1 (one) in the expression field like this:

```
while (1) {
    /* statement block */
}
```

The general form for the `do-while` statement is

```
do {
    statement1;
    statement2;
        .
        .
        .
} while (expression);
```

Here `expression` is the conditional expression that is evaluated in order to determine whether the statements inside the statement block are executed one more time. If the expression evaluates to a nonzero value, the do-while loop continues; otherwise, the looping stops. Note that the `do-while` statement ends with a semicolon, which is an important distinction. The statements controlled by the do-while statement are guaranteed to execute at least once before the conditional expression is evaluated.

Conditional Branching

The `if`, `if-else`, `switch`, `break`, `continue`, and `goto` statements fall into the conditional branching category.

The general form of the `if` statement is

```
if (expression) {
    statement1;
    statement2;
        .
        .
        .
}
```

Here `expression` is the conditional expression. If `expression` evaluates to nonzero, the statements inside the braces ({ and }), such as `statement1` and `statement2`, are executed. If `expression` evaluates to 0, the statements are skipped.

As an expansion of the `if` statement, the `if-else` statement has the following form:

```
if (expression) {
    statement1;
    statement2;
        .
        .
        .
```

```
}
else {
   statement_A;
   statement_B;
   .
   .
   .
}
```

Here if *expression* evaluates to nonzero, the statements controlled by if, including *statement1* and *statement2*, are executed. Otherwise, the statements, such as *statement_A* and *statement_B*, inside the statement block following the else keyword are executed.

The general form of the switch statement is

```
switch (expression) {
   case expression1:
        statement1;
   case expression2:
        statement2;
   .
   .
   .
   default:
        statement-default;
}
```

Here the conditional expression, *expression*, is evaluated first. If the value produced by *expression* is equal to the constant expression *expression1*, execution begins at the statement *statement1*. If the value of *expression* is the same as the value of *expression2*, execution then begins at *statement2*. If, however, the value of *expression* is not equal to any values of the constant expressions labeled by the case keyword, the statement *statement-default*, following the default keyword, is executed.

You can add a break statement at the end of the statement list following each case label if you want to exit the switch construct after the statements within a selected case have been executed.

The break statement can also be used to break out of an infinite loop.

There are times when you want to stay in a loop but skip over some of the statements within the loop. To do this, you can use the continue statement.

The following gives the general form of the goto statement:

```
label-name:
   statement1;
   statement2;
```

24

```
        .
        .
        .
    goto   label-name;
```

Here *label-name* is a label name that tells the goto statement where to jump. You have to place *label-name* in two places: at the place where the goto statement is going to jump and at the place following the goto keyword. Also, the place for the goto statement to jump to can appear either before or after the statement. Note that a colon (:) must follow the label name at the place where the goto statement will jump to. The use of goto is not recommended, however, because it makes your program hard to debug.

Pointers

A *pointer* is a variable whose value is used to point to another variable. The general form of a pointer declaration is

```
data-type  *pointer-name;
```

Here *data-type* specifies the type of data to which the pointer points. *pointer-name* is the name of the pointer variable, which can be any valid variable name in C. When the compiler sees the asterisk (*) prefixed to the variable name in the declaration, it makes a note that the variable can be used as a pointer.

Usually, the address associated with a variable name is called the *left value* of the variable. When a variable is assigned with a value, the value is stored into the reserved memory location of the variable as the content. The content is also called the *right value* of the variable.

A pointer is said to be a *null pointer* when it has been assigned the right value of 0. Remember that a null pointer can never point to valid data, so you can use it to test for the validity of a pointer.

The dereference operator (*) is a unary operator that requires only one operand. For instance, the *ptr_name expression produces the value pointed to by the pointer variable ptr_name, where ptr_name can be any valid variable name in C.

The & operator is called the *address-of operator* because it can return the address (that is, left value) of a variable.

Several pointers can point to the same location of a variable in memory. In C, you can move the position of a pointer by adding or subtracting integers to or from the pointer.

Note that for pointers of different data types, the integers added to or subtracted from the pointers have different scalar sizes.

Pointing to Objects

You can access an element in an array by using a pointer. For instance, given an array, an_array, and a pointer, ptr_array, if an_array and ptr_array are of the same data type, and ptr_array is assigned with the start address of the array like this:

```
ptr_array = an_array;
```

the expression

```
an_array[n]
```

is equivalent to the expression

```
*(ptr_array + n)
```

Here n is a subscript number in the array.

In many cases, it's useful to declare an array of pointers and access the contents pointed to by the array through dereferencing each pointer. For instance, the following declaration declares an int array of pointers:

```
int *ptr_int[3];
```

In other words, the variable ptr_int is a three-element array of pointers with the int type.

Also, you can define a pointer of struct and refer to an item in the structure via the pointer. For example, given the following structure declaration:

```
struct computer {
   float cost;
   int year;
   int cpu_speed;
   char cpu_type[16];
};
```

a pointer can be defined like this:

```
struct computer *ptr_s;
```

Then, the items in the structure can be accessed by dereferencing the pointer. For instance, to assign the value of 1997 to the int variable year in the computer structure, you can use the following assignment statement:

```
(*ptr_s).year = 1997;
```

Or, you can use the arrow operator (->) for the assignment, like this:

```
ptr_s->year = 1997;
```

24

Note that the arrow operator (->) is commonly used to reference a structure member with a pointer.

Functions

Functions are the building blocks of C programs. Besides the standard C library functions, you can also use other functions made by you or by another programmer in your C program. The opening brace ({) signifies the start of a function body, while the closing brace (}) marks the end of the function body.

According to the ANSI standard, the *declaration* of a variable or function specifies the interpretation and attributes of a set of identifiers. The *definition*, on the other hand, requires the C compiler to reserve storage for a variable or function named by an identifier.

In fact, a variable declaration is a definition. But the same is not true for functions. A *function declaration* alludes to a function that is defined elsewhere, and specifies what kind of value is returned by the function. A *function definition* defines what the function does, as well as the number and type of arguments passed to the function.

The ANSI standard allows the number and types of arguments passed to a function to be added into the function declaration. The number and types of arguments are called the *function prototype*.

The general form of a function declaration, including its prototype, is as follows:

```
data_type_specifier  function_name(
     data_type_specifier argument_name1,
     data_type_specifier argument_name2,
     data_type_specifier argument_name3,
     .
     .
     .
     data_type_specifier argument_nameN,
);
```

Here `data_type_specifier` determines the type of the value returned by the function or specifies the data types of arguments, such as `argument_name1`, `argument_name2`, `argument_name3`, and `argument_nameN`, passed to the function named `function_name`.

The purpose of using a function prototype is to help the compiler to check whether the data types of arguments passed to a function match what the function expects. The compiler issues an error message if the data types do not match. The `void` data type is needed in the declaration of a function that takes no argument.

To declare a function that takes a variable number of arguments, you have to specify at least the first argument and use the ellipsis (...) to represent the rest of the arguments passed to the function.

A function call is an expression that can be used as a single statement or within other expressions or statements.

It's often more efficient to pass the address of an argument, instead of its copy, to a function so that the function can access and manipulate the original value of the argument. Therefore, it's a good idea to pass the name of a pointer, which points to an array, as an argument to a function, instead of the array elements themselves.

You can also call a function via a pointer that holds the address of the function.

Input and Output (I/O)

24

In C, a *file* refers to a disk file, a terminal, a printer, or a tape drive. In other words, a file represents a concrete device with which you want to exchange information. A *stream*, on the other hand, is a series of bytes through which you read or write data to a file. Unlike a file, a stream is device independent. All streams have the same behavior.

In addition, there are three file streams that are pre-opened for you:

- stdin—The standard input for reading.
- stdout—The standard output for writing.
- stderr—The standard error for writing error messages.

Usually, the standard input stdin links to the keyboard, while the standard output stdout and the standard error stderr point to the screen. Also, many operating systems allow you to redirect these file streams.

By default, all I/O streams are buffered. Buffered I/O is also called *high-level I/O*.

The FILE structure is the file control structure defined in the header file stdio.h. A pointer of type FILE is called a *file pointer* and references a disk file. A file pointer is used by a stream to conduct the operation of the I/O functions. For instance, the following defines a file pointer called fptr:

```
FILE *fptr;
```

In the FILE structure, there is a member, called the *file position indicator*, which points to the position in a file where data will be read from or written to.

The C language provides a rich set of library functions to perform I/O operations. Those functions can read or write any types of data to files. Among them, fopen(), fclose(), fgetc(), fputc(), fgets(), fputs(), fread(), fwrite(), feof(), fscanf(), `fprintf()`, `fseek()`, `ftell()`, `rewind()`, and `freopen()` have been introduced in this book.

The C Preprocessor

The *C preprocessor* is not part of the C compiler. The C preprocessor runs before the compiler. During the preprocessing stage, all occurrences of a macro name are replaced by the macro body that is associated with the macro name. Note that a macro statement ends with a newline character, not a semicolon.

The C preprocessor also enables you to include additional source files to the program or compile sections of C code conditionally.

The `#define` directive tells the preprocessor to replace every occurrence of a macro name defined by the directive with a macro body that is associated with the macro name. You can specify one or more arguments to a macro name defined by the `#define` directive.

The `#undef` directive is used to remove the definition of a macro name that has been previously defined.

The `#ifdef` directive controls whether a given group of statements is to be included as part of the program. The `#ifndef` directive is a mirror directive to the `#ifdef` directive; it enables you to define code that is to be included when a particular macro name is not defined.

The `#if`, `#elif`, and `#else` directives enable you to filter out portions of code to compile. `#endif` is used to mark the end of an `#ifdef`, `#ifndef`, or `#if` block because the statements under the control of these preprocessor directives are not enclosed in braces.

The Road Ahead...

I believe that you can start to run now after you have learned to walk in the world of C language programming through this book. Although you're on your own, you're not alone. You can revisit this book whenever you feel you need to. The following books, which I recommend to you, can also guide you in your continuous journey in the C world:

The C Programming Language
by Brian Kernighan and Dennis Ritchie, published by Prentice Hall

C Interfaces and Implementations
by David Hanson, published by Addison-Wesley

Practical C Programming

by Steve Oualline, published by O'Reilly & Associates, Inc.

No Bugs!—Delivering Error-Free Code in C and C++

by David Thielen, published by Addison-Wesley

Software Engineering

by Ian Sommerville, published by Addison-Wesley

The Mythical Man-Month: Essays on Software Engineering

by F. P. Brooks, Jr., published by Addison-Wesley

Dynamics of Software Development: "Don't Flip the Bozo Bit" and 53 More Rules for Delivering Great Software on Time
by Jim McCarthy, published by Microsoft Press
ISBN: 1-55615-823-8

Code Complete: A Practical Handbook of Software Construction
by Steve McConnell, published by Microsoft Press
ISBN: 1-55615-484-4

24

Summary

Before you close this book, I'd like to thank you for your patience and the effort you have put into learning the basics of the C language in the past 24 hours. (I think most of you may have spent more than 24 hours. It is quite normal. There are still a lot more things about C programming that you will learn as you go. But if you have already mastered the basic concepts, operators, and functions taught in this book, you can learn the new things quickly.) Now, it's your turn to apply what you've learned from this book to solving the problems in the real world. Good luck!

PART VI
Appendixes

Hour

APPENDIX **A**

ANSI Standard Header Files

As you have learned in the past 24 hours, the C standard library comes with a set of include files called *header files*. These header files contain the declarations for the C library functions and macros, as well as relevant data types. Whenever a C function is invoked, the header file(s) with which the C function is associated has to be included in your programs.

The following are the ANSI standard header files:

File	Description
assert.h	Contains diagnostic functions.
ctype.h	Contains character testing and mapping functions.
errno.h	Contains constants for error processing.
float.h	Contains constants for floating-point values.
limits.h	Contains implementation-dependent values.

continues

File	Description
locale.h	Contains the setlocale() function, and is used to set locale parameters.
math.h	Contains mathematics functions.
setjmp.h	Contains the setjmp() and longjmp() functions, and is used to bypass the normal function call and return discipline.
signal.h	Contains signal-handling functions.
stdarg.h	Contains functions and macros for implementing functions that accept a variable number of arguments.
stddef.h	Contains definitions for the ptrdiff_t, size_t, NULL, and errno macros.
stdio.h	Contains input and output functions.
stdlib.h	Contains general utility functions.
string.h	Contains functions that are used to manipulate strings.
time.h	Contains functions for manipulating time.

If the C compiler on your machine is not 100 percent ANSI-conformable, some of the ANSI header files might not be available with the compiler.

APPENDIX B

Answers to Quiz Questions and Exercises

Hour 1, "Taking the First Step"

Quiz

1. The lowest language mentioned in this hour that a computer can understand directly is the machine language—that is, the binary code. On the other hand, the highest language is the human language, such as Chinese, English, French, and so on. Most high-level programming languages, such as C, Java, and Perl, are close to the human language.

2. A computer cannot directly understand a program written in C. You have to compile the program and translate it into binary code so that the computer can read it.

3. Yes. That's the beauty of the C language; you can write a program in C and save it into a library file. Later, you can invoke the program in another C program by including the library file.

4. We need the ANSI standard for C to guarantee the portability of the programs written in C. Most C compiler vendors support the ANSI standard. If you write your program by following the rules set up by the ANSI standard, you can port your program to any machine by simply recompiling your program with a compiler that supports those machines.

Hour 2, "Writing Your First C Program"

Quiz

1. No. Actually, the C preprocessor will filter out all comments you put into your program before the compiler can see them. Comments are written for you or other programmers who look at your program.

2. An .obj file is created after a program is compiled by the C compiler. You still need a linker to link all .obj files and other library files together to make the final executable file.

3. No, the exit() function doesn't return any values. However, the return statement does. In the main() function, if the return statement returns a value of 0, it indicates to the operating system that the program has terminated normally; otherwise, an error occurs.

4. A file that is required by the #include directive and ends with the extension .h is called a *header file* in C. Later in this book, you'll learn that a header file contains the data or function declarations.

Exercises

1. No. The angle brackets (< and >) in the #include <stdio.h> expression ask the C preprocessor to look for a header file in a directory other than the current one. On the other hand, the #include "stdio.h" expression tells the C preprocessor to check the current directory first for the header file stdio.h, and then look for the header file in another directory.

2. The following is one possible solution:

```
/* 02A02.c */
#include <stdio.h>

main()
{
   printf ("It's fun to write my own program in C.\n");
   return 0;
}
```

OUTPUT The output of the program is:

```
It's fun to write my own program in C.
```

3. The following is one possible solution:

```
/* 02A03.c */
#include <stdio.h>

main()
{
   printf ("Howdy, neighbor!\nThis is my first C program.\n");
   return 0;
}
```

OUTPUT The output of the program is:

```
Howdy, neighbor!
This is my first C program.
```

4. The warning message I get when I try to compile the program is that the `main()` function should return a value of integer because, by default, the `main()` function returns an integer. Because the `exit()` function doesn't return any values, you can replace `exit()` with the `return` statement.

5. I got two error (warning) messages on my machine. The first one is `'printf'` `undefined`; the second one is `'main'` : `'void' function returning a value`. To fix the first error, the header file, `stdio.h`, has to be included first before the `printf()` function can be called from the `main()` function; otherwise, you'll get an error message during the linking stage. To fix the second error, you can remove the `void` keyword from the code.

B

Hour 3, "Learning the Structure of a C Program"

Quiz

1. Yes. Both `74` and `571` are constants in C.

2. Yes. Both `x = 571 + 1` and `x = 12 + y` are expressions.

3. `2methods`, `*start_function`, and `.End_Exe` are not valid function names.

4. No. `2 + 5 * 2` is equivalent to `2 + 10`, which gives `12`; `(2 + 5) * 2` is equivalent to `7 * 2`, which produces `14`.

5. Yes. Both `7 % 2` and `4 % 3` produce `1`.

Exercises

1. The following is one possible solution:

   ```
   {
     x = 3;
     y = 5 + x;
   }
   ```

2. The function name, `3integer_add`, is illegal in C.

3. The second statement inside the function needs a semicolon at the end of the statement.

4. The following are two possible solutions:

   ```
   /* Method 1: a C function */
   int MyFunction( int x, int y)
   {
      int result;
      result = x * y;
      return result;
   }
   ```

   or

   ```
   /* Method 2: a C function */
   int MyFunction( int x, int y)
   {
      return (x * y);
   }
   ```

5. The following is one possible solution:

   ```
   /* 03A05.c */
   #include <stdio.h>

   int integer_multiply( int x, int y )
   {
      int result;
      result = x * y;
      return result;
   }

   int main()
   {
      int sum;

      sum = integer_multiply(3, 5);
      printf("The multiplication of 3 and 5 is %d\n", sum);
      return 0;
   }
   ```

Hour 4, "Understanding Data Types and Keywords"

Quiz

1. Yes. Both 134/100 and 17/10 give the same result of 1.

2. Yes. The results of both 3000 + 1.0 and 3000/1.0 are floating-point values.

3. In scientific notation, we have the following expressions:

   - 3.5e3
   - 3.5e-3
   - -3.5e-3

4. Among the four names, 7th_calculation and Tom's_method are not valid names in C.

Exercises

1. The following is one possible solution:

```
/* 04A01.c */
#include <stdio.h>

main()
{
   char c1;
   char c2;

   c1 = 'Z';
   c2 = 'z';
   printf("The numeric value of Z: %d.\n", c1);
   printf("The numeric value of z: %d.\n", c2);
   return 0;
}
```

   OUTPUT The output of the program is:

```
The numeric value of Z: 90.
The numeric value of z: 122.
```

2. The following is one possible solution:

```
/* 04A02.c */
#include <stdio.h>

main()
{
   char c1;
```

```
        char c2;

        c1 = 72;
        c2 = 104;
        printf("The character of 72 is: %c\n", c1);
        printf("The character of 104 is: %c\n", c2);
        return 0;
    }
```

OUTPUT

The output of the program is:

```
The character of 72 is: H
The character of 104 is: h
```

3. No. 72368 is beyond the range of the int data type of 16 bits. If you assign a value that is too large for the data type, the resulting value will wrap around and the result will be incorrect.

4. The following is one possible solution:

```
/* 04A04.c */
#include <stdio.h>

main()
{
    double dbl_num;;

    dbl_num = 123.456;
    printf("The floating-point format of 123.456 is: %f\n",
            dbl_num);
    printf("The scientific notation format of 123.456 is: %e\n",
            dbl_num);

    return 0;
}
```

OUTPUT

The output of the program from my machine is:

```
The floating-point format of 123.456 is: 123.456000
The scientific notation format of 123.456 is: 1.234560e+002
```

5. The following is one possible solution:

```
/* 04A05.c */
#include <stdio.h>

main()
{
    char ch;

    ch = '\n';
    printf("The numeric value of newline is: %d\n", ch);

    return 0;
}
```

OUTPUT The output of the program is:

```
The numeric value of newline is: 10
```

Hour 5, "Handling Standard Input and Output"

Quiz

1. Yes. By prefixing the minimum field specifier with the minus sign -.

2. The main difference between putc() and putchar() is that putc() requires the user to specify the file stream. For putchar(), the user doesn't need to do so because the standard output (stdout) is used as the file stream.

3. The getchar() function returns a value of the int data type.

4. Within the %10.3f expression, 10 is the value of the minimum field width specifier; .3 is called the precision specifier.

Exercises

1. The following is one possible solution:

```
/* 05A01.c */
#include <stdio.h>

main()
{
    char c1, c2, c3;

    c1 = 'B';
    c2 = 'y';
    c3 = 'e';

    /* Method I */
    printf("%c%c%c\n", c1, c2, c3);

    /* Method II */
    putchar(c1);
    putchar(c2);
    putchar(c3);

    return 0;
}
```

2. The following is one possible solution:

```
/* 05A02.c */
#include <stdio.h>
```

B

```
main()
{
    int x;
    double y;

    x = 123;
    y = 123.456;
    printf("x: %-3d\n", x);
    printf("y: %-6.3f\n", y);

    return 0;
}
```

OUTPUT   The output of the program is:
```
x: 123
y: 123.456
```

3. The following is one possible solution:

```
/* 05A03.c */
#include <stdio.h>

main()
{
    int num1, num2, num3;

    num1 = 15;
    num2 = 150;
    num3 = 1500;
    printf("The hex format of 15 is: 0x%04X\n", num1);
    printf("The hex format of 150 is: 0x%04X\n", num2);
    printf("The hex format of 1500 is: 0x%04X\n", num3);

    return 0;
}
```

OUTPUT   The output of the program is:
```
The hex format of 15 is: 0x000F
The hex format of 150 is: 0x0096
The hex format of 1500 is: 0x05DC
```

4. The following is one possible solution:

```
/* 05A04.c */
#include <stdio.h>

main()
{
    int ch;

    printf("Enter a character:\n");
    ch = getchar();
```

```
        putchar(ch);

        return 0;
}
```

5. You will probably get two error (warning) messages; one stating that `getchar()` is undefined and another saying that `putchar()` is undefined. The reason is that the header file, `stdio.h`, is missing in the code.

Hour 6, "Manipulating Data"

Quiz

1. The = operator is an assignment operator that assigns the value of the operand on the right side of the operator to the one on the left side. On the other hand, == is one of the relational operators; it just tests the values of two operands on both sides and finds out whether they are equal to each other.

2. In the x + - y - - z expression, the first and third minus signs are unary minus operators; the second minus sign is a subtraction operator.

3. `15/4` evaluates to 3. `(float)15/4` evaluates to `3.750000`.

4. No. The y `*=` x + 5 expression is actually equal to the y = y `*` (x + 5) expression.

Exercises

1. The following is one possible solution:
```
/* 06A01.c */
#include <stdio.h>

main()
{
    int x, y;

    x = 1;
    y = 3;
    x += y;
    printf("The result of x += y is: %d\n", x);

    x = 1;
    y = 3;
    x += -y;
    printf("The result of x += -y is: %d\n", x);

    x = 1;
    y = 3;
```

B

```
    x -= y;
    printf("The result of x -= y is: %d\n", x);

    x = 1;
    y = 3;
    x -= -y;
    printf("The result of x -= -y is: %d\n", x);

    x = 1;
    y = 3;
    x *= y;
    printf("The result of x *= y is: %d\n", x);

    x = 1;
    y = 3;
    x *= -y;
    printf("The result of x *= -y is: %d\n", x);

    return 0;
}
```

OUTPUT   The output of the program is:

```
The result of x += y is: 4
The result of x += -y is: -2
The result of x -= y is: -2
The result of x -= -y is: 4
The result of x *= y is: 3
The result of x *= -y is: -3
```

2. The value of z is 1 (one), after the expression z=x*y==18 expression is evaluated.

3. The following is one possible solution:

```
/* 06A03.c */
#include <stdio.h>

main()
{
    int x;

    x = 1;
    printf("x++ produces:   %d\n", x++);
    printf("Now x contains: %d\n", x);

    return 0;
}
```

OUTPUT   The output of the program is:

```
x++ produces:   1
Now x contains: 2
```

4. The following is one possible solution:

```c
/* 06A04.c */
#include <stdio.h>

main()
{
    int x;

    x = 1;
    printf("x = x++ produces: %d\n", x = x++);
    printf("Now x contains:   %d\n", x);

    return 0;
}
```

I get 1 and 1 from the two `printf()` calls in this program. The reason is that, in the `x = x++` expression, the original value of x is copied into a temporary location first, and then x is incremented by 1. Last, the value saved in the temporary location is assigned back to x. That's why the final value saved in x is still 1.

5. The program incorrectly uses an assignment operator =, instead of an "equal to" relational operator (==).

Hour 7, "Working with Loops"

Quiz

1. No.

2. Yes. The `do-while` loop prints out the character d, whose numeric value is `100`.

3. Yes. Both `for` loops iterate `8` times.

4. Yes.

Exercises

1. The first `for` loop contains a statement:

```c
printf("%d + %d = %d\n", i, j, i+j);
```

But the second `for` loop has a semicolon right after the for statement. This is a null statement—a semicolon by itself, which is a statement that does nothing.

2. The following is one possible solution:

```c
/* 07A02.c */
#include <stdio.h>

main()
{
```

```
   int i, j;

   for (i=0, j=1; i<8; i++, j++)
      printf("%d + %d = %d\n", i, j, i+j);

   printf("\n");
   for (i=0, j=1; i<8; i++, j++);
      printf("%d + %d = %d\n", i, j, i+j);

   return 0;
}
```

3. The following is one possible solution:

```
/* 07A03.c */
#include <stdio.h>

main()
{
   int c;

   printf("Enter a character:\n(enter K to exit)\n");
   c = ' ';

   while( c != 'K' ) {
      c = getc(stdin);
      putchar(c);
   }
   printf("\nOut of the for loop. Bye!\n");

   return 0;
}
```

4. The following is one possible solution:

```
/* 07A04.c: Use a for loop */
#include <stdio.h>

main()
{
   int i;

   i = 65;
   for (i=65; i<72; i++){
      printf("The numeric value of %c is %d.\n", i, i);
   }

   return 0;
}
```

5. The following is one possible solution:

```c
/* 07A05.c */
#include <stdio.h>

main()
{
   int i, j;

   i = 1;
   while (i<=3) {   /* outer loop */
      printf("The start of iteration %d of the outer loop.\n", i);
      j = 1;
      do{   /* inner loop */
         printf("   Iteration %d of the inner loop.\n", j);
         j++;
      } while (j<=4);
      i++;
      printf("The end of iteration %d of the outer loop.\n", i);
   }

   return 0;
}
```

Hour 8, "Using Conditional Operators"

Quiz

1. The `(x=1)&&(y=10)` expression returns 1; `(x=1)&(y=10)` returns 0.

2. In the `!y ? x == z : y` expression, `!y` produces 0, thus the value of the third operand y is taken as the value of the expression. That is, the expression evaluates to 1.

3. `1100111111000110` and `0011000000111001`.

4. The `(x%2==0)||(x%3==0)` expression yields 1, and the `(x%2==0)&&(x%3==0)` expression evaluates to 0.

5. Yes. `8 >> 3` is equivalent to $8/2^3$. `1 << 3` is equivalent to 2^3.

Exercises

1. `~x` yields `0x1000` because `~0xEFFF` is equivalent to `~0111111111111111` (in binary), which produces `1000000000000000` (in binary), (that is, `0x1000` in hex format). Likewise, `~y` evaluates to `0xEFFF` because `~0x1000` is equivalent to `~1000000000000000` (in binary), which yields `0111111111111111` (in binary) (that is, `0xEFFF` in hex format).

2. The following is one possible solution:

```
/* 08A02.c */
#include <stdio.h>

int main()
{
    int x, y;

    x = 0xEFFF;
    y = 0x1000;

    printf("!x yields: %d (i.e., %u)\n", !x, !x);
    printf("!y yields: %d (i.e., %u)\n", !y, !y);

    return 0;
}
```

The output of the program is:

```
!x yields: 0 (i.e., 0)
!y yields: 0 (i.e., 0)
```

3. The following is one possible solution:

```
/* 08A03.c */
#include <stdio.h>

int main()
{
    int x, y;

    x = 123;
    y = 4;
    printf("x << y yields: %d\n", x << y);
    printf("x >> y yields: %d\n", x >> y);

    return 0;
}
```

[ic:output]The output of the program is:

```
x << y yields: 1968
x >> y yields: 7
```

4. The following is one possible solution:

```
/* 08A04.c */
#include <stdio.h>

int main()
{
    printf("0xFFFF ^ 0x8888 yields: 0x%X\n",
```

```
            0xFFFF ^ 0x8888);
    printf("0xABCD & 0x4567 yields: 0x%X\n",
            0xABCD & 0x4567);
    printf("0xDCBA ¦ 0x1234 yields: 0x%X\n",
            0xDCBA ¦ 0x1234);

    return 0;
}
```

OUTPUT The output of the program is:

```
0xFFFF ^ 0x8888 yields: 0x7777
0xABCD & 0x4567 yields: 0x145
0xDCBA ¦ 0x1234 yields: 0xDEBE
```

5. The following is one possible solution:

```
/* 08A05.c */
#include <stdio.h>

main()
{
    int x;

    printf("Enter a character:\n(enter q to exit)\n");
    for ( x=' '; x != 'q' ? 1 : 0; ) {
        x = getc(stdin);
        putchar(x);
    }
    printf("\nOut of the for loop. Bye!\n");

    return 0;
}
```

Hour 9, "Working with Data Modifiers and Math Functions"

Quiz

1. No. x contains a negative number that is not the same as the number contained by the unsigned int variable y.

2. You can use the long modifier, which increases the range of values that the int can hold. Or, if you are storing a positive number, you can also use the unsigned modifier to store a larger value.

3. %lu.

4. The header file is math.h.

Exercises

1. The following is one possible solution:

```
/* 09A01 */
#include <stdio.h>

main()
{
    int x;
    unsigned int y;

    x = 0xAB78;
    y = 0xAB78;

    printf("The decimal value of x is %d.\n", x);
    printf("The decimal value of y is %u.\n", y);

    return 0;
}
```

> **OUTPUT** The output of the program from my machine is:
> ```
> The decimal value of x is -21640.
> The decimal value of y is 43896.
> ```

2. The following is one possible solution:

```
/* 09A02 */
#include <stdio.h>

main()
{
    printf("The size of short int is %d.\n",
            sizeof(short int));
    printf("The size of long int is %d.\n",
            sizeof(long int));
    printf("The size of long double is %d.\n",
            sizeof(long double));

    return 0;
}
```

3. The following is one possible solution:

```
/* 09A03 */
#include <stdio.h>

main()
{
    int x, y;
    long int result;

    x = 7000;
```

```
   y = 12000;
   result = x * y;
   printf("x * y == %lu.\n", result);

   return 0;
}
```

OUTPUT The output of the program from my machine is:

```
x * y == 84000000.
```

4. The following is one possible solution:

```
/* 09A04 */
#include <stdio.h>

main()
{
   int x;

   x = -23456;
   printf("The hex value of x is  0x%X.\n", x);

   return 0;
}
```

OUTPUT The output of the program from my machine is:

```
The hex value of x is  0xA460.
```

5. The following is one possible solution:

```
/* 09A05.c */
#include <stdio.h>
#include <math.h>

main()
{
   double x;

   x = 30.0;                 /* 45 degrees */
   x *= 3.141593 / 180.0;    /* convert to radians */
   printf("The sine of 30 is:    %f.\n", sin(x));
   printf("The tangent of 30 is: %f.\n", tan(x));

   return 0;
}
```

6. The following is one possible solution (note that I've used the type casting (double) in the assignment statement x=(double)0x19A1;):

```
/* 09A06.c */
#include <stdio.h>
#include <math.h>
```

B

```
main()
{
   double x;

   x = (double)0x19A1;
   printf("The square root of x is: %2.0f\n", sqrt(x));

   return 0;
}
```

Hour 10, "Controlling Program Flow"

Quiz

1. No.

2. The final result saved in x is 2, after the execution of three cases, '-', '*', and '/'.

3. The final result saved in x is 2. This time, only the case of operator = '-' is executed due to the break statement.

4. The result saved by x is 27.

Exercises

1. The following is one possible solution:

```
/* 10A01.c  Use the if statement */
#include <stdio.h>

main()
{
   int i;

   printf("Integers that can be divided by both 2 and 3\n");
   printf("(within the range of 0 to 100):\n");
   for (i=0; i<=100; i++)
      if (i%6 == 0)
         printf("   %d\n", i);

   return 0;
}
```

2. The following is one possible solution:

```
/* 10A02.c  Use the if statement */
#include <stdio.h>
```

```
main()
{
   int i;

   printf("Integers that can be divided by both 2 and 3\n");
   printf("(within the range of 0 to 100):\n");
   for (i=0; i<=100; i++)
      if (i%2 == 0)
        if (i%3 == 0)
          printf("   %d\n", i);

   return 0;
}
```

3. The following is one possible solution:

```
/* 10A03.c */
#include <stdio.h>

main()
{
   int letter;

   printf("Please enter a letter:\n");
   letter = getchar();
   switch (letter){
      case 'A':
         printf("The numeric value of A is: %d\n", 'A');
         break;
      case 'B':
         printf("The numeric value of B is: %d\n", 'B');
         break;
      case 'C':
         printf("The numeric value of C is: %d\n", 'C');
         break;
      default:
         break;
   }

   return 0;
}
```

4. The following is one possible solution:

```
/* 10A04.c */
#include <stdio.h>

main()
{
   int c;
```

```
        printf("Enter a character:\n(enter q to exit)\n");
        while ((c = getc(stdin)) != 'q') {

           /* no statements inside the while loop */
        }
        printf("\nBye!\n");

        return 0;
    }
```

5. The following is one possible solution:

```
/* 10A05.c */
#include <stdio.h>

main()
{
    int i, sum;

    sum = 0;
    for (i=1; i<8; i++){
        if ((i%2 == 0) && (i%3 == 0))
            continue;
        sum += i;
    }
    printf("The sum is: %d\n", sum);
    return 0;
}
```

Hour 11, "Understanding Pointers"

Quiz

1. By using the address-of operator, &. That is, the &ch expression gives the left value (the address) of the character variable ch.

2. The answers are as follows:

   • Dereference operator

   • Multiplication operator

   • Multiplication operator

   • The first and third asterisks are dereference operators; the second asterisk is a multiplication operator.

3. ptr_int yields the value of the address 0x1A38; *ptr_int yields the value of 10.

4. x now contains the value of 456.

Exercises

1. The following is one possible solution:

```c
/* 11A01.c */
#include <stdio.h>

main()
{
   int x, y, z;

   x = 512;
   y = 1024;
   z = 2048;

   printf("The left values of x, y, and z are:\n");
   printf("0x%p,  0x%p,  0x%p\n", &x, &y, &z);
   printf("The right values of x, y, and z are:\n");
   printf("%d,  %d,  %d\n", x, y, z);

   return 0;
}
```

2. The following is one possible solution:

```c
/* 11A02.c */
#include <stdio.h>

main()
{
   int *ptr_int;
   char *ptr_ch;

   ptr_int = 0; /* null pointer */
   ptr_ch = 0;  /* null pointer */

   printf("The left value of ptr_int is: 0x%p\n",
          ptr_int);
   printf("The right value of ptr_int is: %d\n",
          *ptr_int);
   printf("The left value of ptr_ch is: 0x%p\n",
          ptr_ch);
   printf("The right value of ptr_ch is: %d\n",
          *ptr_ch);

   return 0;
}
```

3. The following is one possible solution:

```c
/* 11A03.c */
#include <stdio.h>
```

```
main()
{
   char ch;
   char *ptr_ch;

   ch = 'A';
   printf("The right value of ch is: %c\n",
          ch);
   ptr_ch = &ch;
   *ptr_ch = 'B';   /* decimal 66 */
   /* prove ch has been updated */
   printf("The left value of ch is: 0x%p\n",
          &ch);
   printf("The right value of ptr_ch is: 0x%p\n",
          ptr_ch);
   printf("The right value of ch is: %c\n",
          ch);

   return 0;
}
```

4. The following is one possible solution:

```
/* 11A04.c */
#include <stdio.h>

main()
{
   int x, y;
   int *ptr_x, *ptr_y;

   x = 5;
   y = 6;
   ptr_x = &x;
   ptr_y = &y;

   *ptr_x *= *ptr_y;

   printf("The result is: %d\n",
          *ptr_x);

   return 0;
}
```

Hour 12, "Understanding Arrays"

Quiz

1. It declares an int array called array_int with four elements. The statement also initializes the array with four integers, 12, 23, 9, and 56.

2. Because there are only three elements in the int array data, and the last element is data[2], the third statement is illegal. It may overwrite some valid data in the memory location of data[3].

3. The first array, array1, is a two-dimensional array, the second one, array2, is one-dimensional, the third one, array3, is three-dimensional, and the last one, array4, is a two-dimensional array.

4. In a multidimensional array declaration, only the size of the leftmost dimension can be omitted. Therefore, this declaration is wrong. The correct declaration looks like this:

```
char list_ch[][2] = {
        'A', 'a',
        'B', 'b',
        'C', 'c',
        'D', 'd',
        'E', 'e'};
```

Exercises

1. The following is one possible solution:

```
/* 12A01.c */
#include <stdio.h>

main()
{
   int i;
   char array_ch[5] = {'A', 'B', 'C', 'D', 'E'};

   for (i=0; i<5; i++)
     printf("%c ", array_ch[i]);

   return 0;
}
```

2. The following is one possible solution:

```
/* 12A02.c */
#include <stdio.h>

main()
{
   int i;
   char array_ch[5];

   for (i=0; i<5; i++)
      array_ch[i] = 'a' + i;
   for (i=0; i<5; i++)
     printf("%c ", array_ch[i]);

   return 0;
}
```

B

3. The following is one possible solution:

```c
/* 12A03.c */
#include <stdio.h>

main()
{
   int i, size;
   char list_ch[][2] = {
       '1', 'a',
       '2', 'b',
       '3', 'c',
       '4', 'd',
       '5', 'e',
       '6', 'f'};

   /* method I */
   size = &list_ch[5][1] - &list_ch[0][0] + 1;
   size *= sizeof(char);
   printf("Method I: The total bytes are %d.\n", size);

   /* method II */
   size = sizeof(list_ch);
   printf("Method II: The total bytes are %d.\n", size);

   for (i=0; i<6; i++)
     printf("%c  %c\n",
         list_ch[i][0], list_ch[i][1]);

   return 0;
}
```

4. The following is one possible solution:

```c
/* 12A04.c */
#include <stdio.h>

main()
{
    char array_ch[11] = {'I', ' ',
                         'l', 'i', 'k', 'e', ' ',
                         'C', '!', '\0'};
    int i;
    /*  array_ch[i] in logical test */
    for (i=0; array_ch[i]; i++)
      printf("%c", array_ch[i]);

    return 0;
}
```

5. The following is one possible solution:

```
/* 12A05.c */
#include <stdio.h>

main()
{
   double list_data[6] = {
          1.12345,
          2.12345,
          3.12345,
          4.12345,
          5.12345};
   int size;

   /* Method I */
   size = sizeof(double) * 6;
   printf("Method I:  The size is %d.\n", size);

   /* Method II */
   size = sizeof(list_data);
   printf("Method II: The size is %d.\n", size);

   return 0;
}
```

Hour 13, "Manipulating Strings"

Quiz

1. The following two statements are legal:
   - `char str2[] = "A character string";`
   - `char str3 = "A";`

2. The following two statements are illegal:
   - `ptr_ch = 'x';`
   - `*ptr_ch = "This is Quiz 2.";`

3. No. The puts() function appends a newline character to replace the null character at the end of a character array.

4. The %s format specifier is used for reading in a string; the %f is for a float number.

B

Exercises

1. The following is one possible solution:

```c
/* 13A01.c: Copy a string to another */
#include <stdio.h>
#include <string.h>

main()
{
   int i;
   char str1[] = "This is Exercise 1.";
   char str2[20];

   /* Method I */
   strcpy(str2, str1);

   /* confirm the copying */
   printf("from Method I: %s\n", str2);

   /* Method II */
   for (i=0; str1[i]; i++)
      str2[i] = str1[i];
   str2[i] = '\0';
   /* confirm the copying */
   printf("from Method II: %s\n", str2);

   return 0;
}
```

2. The following is one possible solution:

```c
/* 13A02.c: Measure a string */
#include <stdio.h>
#include <string.h>

main()
{
   int i, str_length;
   char str[] = "This is Exercise 2.";

   /* Method I */
   str_length = 0;
   for (i=0; str[i]; i++)
      str_length++;
   printf("The string length is %d.\n", str_length);

   /* Method II */
   printf("The string length is %d.\n",
        strlen(str));

   return 0;
}
```

3. The following is one possible solution:

```
/* 13A03.c: Use gets() and puts() */
#include <stdio.h>

main()
{
   char str[80];
   int i, delt;

   printf("Enter a string less than 80 characters:\n");
   gets( str );
   delt = 'a' - 'A';
   i = 0;
   while (str[i]){
     if ((str[i] >= 'A') && (str[i] <= 'Z'))
       str[i] += delt;  /* convert to lowercase */
     ++i;
   }
   printf("The entered string is (in lowercase):\n");
   puts( str );

   return 0;
}
```

4. The following is one possible solution:

```
/* 13A04.c: Use scanf() */
#include <stdio.h>

main()
{
   int x, y, sum;

   printf("Enter two integers:\n");
   scanf("%d%d", &x, &y);
   sum = x + y;
   printf("The sum is %d\n", sum);

   return 0;
}
```

Hour 14, "Understanding Scope and Storage Classes"

Quiz

1. The int variable x and float variable y, declared outside the myFunction() function, are global variables. The int variables, i and j, and the float variable y,

declared inside the function, are local variables. Also, the two int variables, x and y, declared within a block inside myFunction(), are local variables with scope limited to the block.

2. For two variables sharing the same name, the compiler can figure out which one to use by checking their scopes. The latest declared variable becomes visible by replacing the variable that has the same name but is declared in the outer block. If, however, two variables sharing the same name are declared in the same block, the compiler will issue an error message.

3. The int variable i declared outside the myFunction() function has the same static storage class as the int variable x. The float variable y has an extern storage class.

   Inside the myFunction() function, the two integer variables, i and j, have the auto storage class. The float variable z has an extern storage class, and the long variable s has a register storage class. index is an integer variable with a static storage class. The content of the character array str cannot be changed due to the const specifier.

4. No, it's not legal. You cannot change the content of an array specified by the const specifier.

Exercises

1. The answers are as follows:
   - `{ int x; }`
   - `{ const char ch; }`
   - `{ static float y; }`
   - `register int z;`
   - `char *ptr_str = 0;`

2. The following is one possible solution:
```
/* 14A02.c */
#include <stdio.h>

int x = 1234;            /* program scope */
float y = 1.234567f;  /* program scope */

void function_1(int x, double y)
{
    printf("From function_1:\n  x=%d, y=%f\n", x, y);
}

main()
```

```
{
    int x = 4321;   /* block scope 1*/

    function_1(x, y);
    printf("Within the main block:\n  x=%d, y=%f\n", x, y);
    /* a nested block */
    {
        float y = 7.654321f;  /* block scope 2 */
        function_1(x, y);
        printf("Within the nested block:\n  x=%d, y=%f\n", x, y);
    }
    return 0;
}
```

3. The following is what I obtained from running the C program given in this exercise:

```
x=0, y=0
x=0, y=1
x=0, y=2
x=0, y=3
x=0, y=4
```

Because x has a temporary storage with the block scope, and y has a permanent storage, x is set to 0 every time the program execution enters the for loop, but the value saved in y is kept.

4. The following is one possible solution:

```
/* 14A04.c: Use the static specifier */
#include <stdio.h>
/* the add_two function */
int add_two(int x, int y)
{
    static int counter = 1;
    static int sum = 0;

    printf("This is the function call of %d,\n", counter++);
    printf("the previous value of sum is %d,\n", sum);
    sum = x + y;
    return sum;
}
/* the main function */
main()
{
    int i, j;

    for (i=0, j=5; i<5; i++, j--)
      printf("the addition of %d and %d is %d.\n\n",
             i, j, add_two(i, j));
    return 0;
}
```

B

Hour 15, "Working with Functions"

Quiz

1. The answers are as follows:

   - `int function_1(int x, int y);` is a function declaration with a fixed number of arguments.

   - `void function_2(char *str);` is a function declaration with a fixed number of arguments.

   - `char *asctime(const struct tm *timeptr);` is a function declaration with a fixed number of arguments.

   - `int function_3(void);` is a function declaration with no arguments.

   - `void function_5(void);` is a function declaration with no arguments.

   - `char function_4(char c, ...);` is a function declaration with a variable number of arguments.

2. The second expression is a function definition; that is,

   `int function_2(int x, int y) {return x+y;}`

3. The `int` data type is the default data type returned by a function if a type specifier is omitted.

4. The third one, `char function_3(...);`, is illegal.

Exercises

1. The following is one possible solution:

```c
/* 15A01.c: */
#include <stdio.h>
#include <time.h>

void GetDateTime(void);

main()
{
   printf("Before the GetDateTime() function is called.\n");
   GetDateTime();
   printf("After the GetDateTime() function is called.\n");
   return 0;
}
/* GetDateTime() definition */
void GetDateTime(void)
{
   time_t now;
   int i;
```

```c
    char *str;

    printf("Within GetDateTime().\n");
    time(&now);
    str = asctime(localtime(&now));
    printf("Current date and time is: ");
    for (i=0; str[i]; i++)
        printf("%c", str[i]);
}
```

2. The following is one possible solution:

```c
/* 15A02.c */
#include <stdio.h>

int MultiTwo(int x, int y);

main ()
{
    printf("The result returned by MultiTwo() is: %d\n",
        MultiTwo(32, 10));
    return 0;
}

/* function definition */
int MultiTwo(int x, int y)
{
    return x * y;
}
```

3. The following is one possible solution:

```c
/* 15A03.c */
#include <stdio.h>
#include <stdarg.h>

int MultiInt(int x, ...);

main ()
{
    int d1 = 1;
    int d2 = 2;
    int d3 = 3;
    int d4 = 4;

    printf("Given an argument: %d\n", d1);
    printf("The result returned by MultiInt() is: %d\n\n",
        MultiInt(1, d1));
    printf("Given an argument: %d, %d, %d, and %d\n", d1, d2, d3, d4);
    printf("The result returned by MultiInt() is: %d\n\n",
        MultiInt(4, d1, d2, d3, d4));

    return 0;
```

B

```
    }

    /* definition of MultiInt() */
    int MultiInt(int x, ...)
    {
        va_list    arglist;
        int i;
        int result = 1;

        printf("The number of arguments is: %d\n", x);
        va_start (arglist, x);
        for (i=0; i<x; i++)
            result *= va_arg(arglist, int);
        va_end (arglist);
        return result;
    }
```

4. The va_arg() fetches arguments from left to right on my machine. The following
   is one possible solution:

```
/* 15A04.c */
#include <stdio.h>
#include <stdarg.h>

double AddDouble(int x, ...);

main ()
{
    double d1 = 1.5;
    double d2 = 2.5;
    double d3 = 3.5;
    double d4 = 4.5;

    printf("Given an argument: %2.1f\n", d1);
    printf("The result returned by AddDouble() is: %2.1f\n\n",
        AddDouble(1, d1));
    printf("Given arguments: %2.1f and %2.1f\n", d1, d2);
    printf("The result returned by AddDouble() is: %2.1f\n\n",
        AddDouble(2, d1, d2));
    printf("Given arguments: %2.1f, %2.1f and %2.1f\n", d1, d2, d3);
    printf("The result returned by AddDouble() is: %2.1f\n\n",
        AddDouble(3, d1, d2, d3));
    printf("Given arguments: %2.1f, %2.1f, %2.1f, and %2.1f\n", d1, d2, d3,
d4);
    printf("The result returned by AddDouble() is: %2.1f\n",
        AddDouble(4, d1, d2, d3, d4));
    return 0;
}

/* definition of AddDouble() */
```

```
double AddDouble(int x, ...)
{
    va_list    arglist;
    int i;
    double argument, result = 0.0;

    printf("The number of arguments is: %d\n", x);
    va_start (arglist, x);
    for (i=0; i<x; i++){
        argument = va_arg(arglist, double);
        printf("Argument passed to this function: %f\n", argument);
        result += argument;
    }

    va_end (arglist);

    return result;
}
```

Hour 16, "Applying Pointers"

Quiz

1. I obtain the following answers from my machine:

   - 4 bytes
   - 4 bytes
   - 4 bytes
   - 12 bytes
   - 12 bytes
   - 12 bytes

2. Because 0x100A - 0x1006 gives 4, and one int takes 2 bytes, ptr1 and ptr2 are two integers apart. Therefore, the answer is 2.

3. 0x0230 and 0x0260.

4. The answers are as follows:

   - *(ptr + 3) fetches 'A'.
   - ptr - ch gives 1.
   - *(ptr - 1) fetches 'a'.
   - *ptr = 'F' replaces 'b' with 'F'.

Exercises

1. The following is one possible solution:

```c
/* 16A01.c */
#include <stdio.h>

void StrPrint(char *str);
main()
{
    char string[] = "I like C!";

    StrPrint(string);

    return 0;
}
void StrPrint(char *str)
{
    printf("%s\n", str);
}
```

2. The following is one possible solution:

```c
/* 16A02.c */
#include <stdio.h>

void StrPrint(char *str);
main()
{
    char string[] = "I like C!";
    char *ptr;
    int i;

    ptr = string;
    for (i=0; ptr[i]; i++){
      if (ptr[i] == 'i')
        ptr[i] = 'o';
      if (ptr[i] == 'k')
        ptr[i] = 'v';
    }
    StrPrint(ptr);

    return 0;
}

void StrPrint(char *str)
{
    printf("%s\n", str);
}
```

3. The following is one possible solution:

```c
/* 16A03.c */
#include <stdio.h>

void StrPrint(char str[][15], int max);
main()
{
   char str[2][15] = {
        "You know what,",
        "C is powerful." };

   StrPrint(str, 2);

   return 0;
}
void StrPrint(char str[][15], int max)
{
   int i;

   for (i=0; i<max; i++)
     printf("%s\n", str[i]);
}
```

4. The following is one possible solution:

```c
* 16A04.c */
#include <stdio.h>

/* function declarations */
void StrPrint1(char **str1, int size);
void StrPrint2(char *str2);

/* main() function */
main()
{
   char *str[7] = {
        "Sunday",
        "Monday",
        "Tuesday",
        "Wednesday",
        "Thursday",
        "Friday",
        "Saturday"};
   int i, size;

   size = 7;
   StrPrint1(str, size);
   for (i=0; i<size; i++)
     StrPrint2(str[i]);
```

B

```
      return 0;
   }

   /* function definition */
   void StrPrint1(char **str1, int size)
   {
      int i;

      for (i=0; i<size; i++)
         printf("%s\n", str1[i]);
   }

   /* function definition */
   void StrPrint2(char *str2)
   {
      printf("%s\n", str2);
   }
```

Hour 17, "Allocating Memory"

Quiz

1. The answers are as follows:

   - 200 bytes

   - 200 bytes

   - 200 bytes

   - 0 bytes

2. The statement is

   ```
   ptr = realloc(ptr, 150 * sizeof(int));
   ```

3. The final size is 120 bytes, provided the `int` data type is one byte long.

4. The final size is 0. In other words, all allocated memory blocks have been released by the last statement.

Exercises

1. The following is one possible solution:

   ```
   /* 17A01.c */
   #include <stdio.h>
   #include <stdlib.h>

   /* main() function */
   main()
   {
   ```

```c
    int *ptr_int;
    int i, sum;
    int max = 0;
    int termination = 0;

    printf("Enter the total number of integers:\n");
       scanf("%d", &max);
    /* call malloc() */
    ptr_int = malloc(max * sizeof(int));
    if (ptr_int == NULL){
      printf("malloc() function failed.\n");
      termination = 1;
    }
    else{
       for (i=0; i<max; i++)
          ptr_int[i] = i + 1;
    }
    sum = 0;
    for (i=0; i<max; i++)
      sum += ptr_int[i];
    printf("The sum is %d.\n", sum);
    free(ptr_int);

    return termination;
}
```

2. The following is one possible solution:

```c
/* 17A02.c */
#include <stdio.h>
#include <stdlib.h>

/* main() function */
main()
{
   float *ptr_flt;
   int termination = 0;

   /* call calloc() */
   ptr_flt = calloc(100, sizeof(float));
   if (ptr_flt == NULL){
     printf("calloc() function failed.\n");
     termination = 1;
   }
   else{
     ptr_flt = realloc(ptr_flt, 150 * sizeof(float));
     if (ptr_flt == NULL){
       printf("realloc() function failed.\n");
       termination = 1;
     }
```

B

```
      else
         free(ptr_flt);
   }
   printf("Done!\n");

   return termination;
}
```

3. The following is one possible solution:

```
/* 17A03.c */
#include <stdio.h>
#include <stdlib.h>

/* main() function */
main()
{
   float *ptr1, *ptr2;
   int i;
   int termination = 1;
   int max = 0;

   printf("Enter the total number:\n");
      scanf("%d", &max);

   ptr1 = malloc(max * sizeof(float));
   ptr2 = calloc(max, sizeof(float));

   if (ptr1 == NULL)
      printf("malloc() failed.\n");
   else if (ptr2 == NULL)
      printf("calloc() failed.\n");
   else{
      for (i=0; i<max; i++)
         printf("ptr1[%d]=%5.2f,  ptr2[%d]=%5.2f\n",
            i, *(ptr1 + i), i, *(ptr2 + i));
      free(ptr1);
      free(ptr2);
      termination = 0;
   }
   printf ("\nBye!\n");

   return termination;
}
```

4. The following is one possible solution:

```
/* 17A04.c: Use the realloc() function */
#include <stdio.h>
#include <stdlib.h>
```

```c
#include <string.h>
/* function declaration */
void StrCopy(char *str1, char *str2);
/* main() function */
main()
{
   char *str[4] = {"There's music in the sighing of a reed;",
                   "There's music in the gushing of a rill;",
                   "There's music in all things if men had ears;",
                   "There earth is but an echo of the spheres.\n"
                  };
   char *ptr;
   int i;

   int termination = 0;

   ptr = realloc(NULL, strlen((str[0]) + 1) * sizeof(char));
   if (ptr == NULL){
     printf("realloc() failed.\n");
     termination = 1;
   }
   else{
     StrCopy(str[0], ptr);
     printf("%s\n", ptr);
     for (i=1; i<4; i++){
       ptr = realloc(ptr, (strlen(str[i]) + 1) * sizeof(char));
       if (ptr == NULL){
         printf("realloc() failed.\n");
         termination = 1;
         i = 4;   /* break the for loop */
       }
       else{
         StrCopy(str[i], ptr);
         printf("%s\n", ptr);
       }
     }
   }
   realloc(ptr, 0);
   return termination;
}
/* funciton definition */
void StrCopy(char *str1, char *str2)
{
   int i;

   for (i=0; str1[i]; i++)
      str2[i] = str1[i];
   str2[i] = '\0';
}
```

Hour 18, "Using Special Data Types and Functions"

Quiz

1. The enumerated names Jan, Feb, Mar, Apr, May, Jun, Jul, Aug, Sep, Oct, Nov, and Dec represent the values of 0 to 11, respectively.

2. The values of 0, 10, 11, and 12 are represented by the enumerated names name1, name2, name3, and name4, respectively.

3. The typedef long int BYTE32; and BYTE32 x, y, z; statements are equivalent to long int x, y, z;.

   typedef char *STRING[16]; and STRING str1, str2, str3; are equivalent to char *str1[16], *str2[16], *str3[16];

4. No. The void keyword in the main() function indicates that there is no argument passed to the function.

Exercises

1. The following is one possible solution:

```
/* 18A01.c */
#include <stdio.h>

main(void)
{
   enum tag {name1,
             name2 = 10,
             name3,
             name4 };

   printf("The value represented by name1 is: %d\n",
           name1);
   printf("The value represented by name2 is: %d\n",
           name2);
   printf("The value represented by name3 is: %d\n",
           name3);
   printf("The value represented by name4 is: %d\n",
           name4);

   return 0;
}
```

2. The following is one possible solution:

```
/* 18A02.c */
#include <stdio.h>
```

```
main(void)
{
   typedef char WORD;
   typedef int SHORT;
   typedef long LONG;
   typedef float FLOAT;
   typedef double DFLOAT;

   printf("The size of WORD is: %d-byte\n", sizeof(WORD));
   printf("The size of SHORT is: %d-byte\n", sizeof(SHORT));
   printf("The size of LONG is: %d-byte\n", sizeof(LONG));
   printf("The size of FLOAT is: %d-byte\n", sizeof(FLOAT));
   printf("The size of DFLOAT is: %d-byte\n", sizeof(DFLOAT));

   return 0;
}
```

3. The following is one possible solution:

```
/* 18A03.c */
#include <stdio.h>

enum con{MIN_NUM = 0,
         MAX_NUM = 100};

int fRecur(int n);

main()
{
   int i, sum1, sum2;

   sum1 = sum2 = 0;
   for (i=1; i<=MAX_NUM; i++)
     sum1 += i;
   printf("The value of sum1 is %d.\n", sum1);
   sum2 = fRecur(MIN_NUM);
   printf("The value returned by fRecur() is %d.\n", sum2);

   return 0;
}
int fRecur(int n)
{
   if (n > MAX_NUM)
     return 0;
   return  fRecur(n + 1) + n;
}
```

4. The following is one possible solution:

```
/* 18A04.c: Command-line arguments */
#include <stdio.h>

main (int argc, char *argv[])
```

B

```
{
   int i;

   if (argc < 2){
     printf("The usage of this program is:\n");
     printf("18A04.EXE argument1 argument2 [...argumentN]\n");
   }
   else {
     printf("The command-line arguments are:\n");
     for (i=1; i<argc; i++)
       printf("%s ", argv[i]);
     printf("\n");
   }

   return 0;
}
```

Hour 19, "Understanding Structures"

Quiz

1. The semicolon (;) should be included at the end of the structure declaration.

2. u, v, and w are three structure variables.

3. You can initialize the array of the automobile structure like this:

```
struct automobile {
   int year;
   char model[8]} car[2] = {
       {1997, "Taurus"},
       {1997, "Accord"}};
```

Exercises

1. The following is one possible solution:

```
/* 19A01.c */
#include <stdio.h>

main(void)
{
   struct automobile {
     int year;
     char model[10];
     int engine_power;
     double weight;
     } sedan = {
         1997,
         "New Model",
```

```
        200,
        2345.67};

    printf("year: %d\n", sedan.year);
    printf("model: %s\n", sedan.model);
    printf("engine_power: %d\n", sedan.engine_power);
    printf("weight: %6.2f\n", sedan.weight);

    return 0;
}
```

2. The following is one possible solution:

```
/* 19A02.c */
#include <stdio.h>

struct employee {
   int id;
   char name[32];
};

void Display(struct employee s);

main(void)
{
    /* structure initialization */
    struct employee info = {
       0001,
       "B. Smith"
       };

    printf("Here is a sample:\n");
    Display(info);

    printf("What's your name?\n");
       gets(info.name);
    printf("What's your ID number?\n");
       scanf("%d", &info.id);

    printf("\nHere are what you entered:\n");
    Display(info);

    return 0;
}

/* function definition */
void Display(struct employee s)
{
    printf("Employee Name: %s\n", s.name);
    printf("Employee ID #: %04d\n\n", s.id);
}
```

3. The following is one possible solution:

```c
/* 19A03.c Use the -> operator */
#include <stdio.h>

struct computer {
   float cost;
   int year;
   int cpu_speed;
   char cpu_type[16];
};

typedef struct computer SC;

void DataReceive(SC *ptr_s);

main(void)
{
   SC model;

   DataReceive(&model);
   printf("Here are what you entered:\n");
   printf("Year: %d\n", model.year);
   printf("Cost: %6.2f\n", model.cost);
   printf("CPU type: %s\n", model.cpu_type);
   printf("CPU speed: %d MHz\n", model.cpu_speed);

   return 0;
}

void DataReceive(SC *ptr_s)
{
   printf("The type of the CPU inside your computer?\n");
      gets(ptr_s->cpu_type);
   printf("The speed(MHz) of the CPU?\n");
      scanf("%d", &(ptr_s->cpu_speed));
   printf("The year your computer was made?\n");
      scanf("%d", &(ptr_s->year));
   printf("How much you paid for the computer?\n");
      scanf("%f", &(ptr_s->cost));
}
```

4. The following is one possible solution:

```c
/* 19L04.c Arrays of structures */
#include <stdio.h>

struct haiku {
   int start_year;
   int end_year;
```

```
      char author[16];
      char str1[32];
      char str2[32];
      char str3[32];
   };

   typedef struct haiku HK;

   void DataDisplay(HK *ptr_s);

   main(void)
   {
      HK poem[2] = {
         { 1641,
           1716,
           "Sodo",
           "Leading me along",
           "my shadow goes back home",
           "from looking at the moon."
         },
         { 1729,
           1781,
           "Chora",
           "A storm wind blows",
           "out from among the grasses",
           "the full moon grows."
         }
      };

      /* define an array of pointers with HK */
      HK *ptr_poem[2] = {&poem[0], &poem[1]};
      int i;

      for (i=0; i<2; i++)
         DataDisplay(ptr_poem[i]);

      return 0;
   }

   void DataDisplay(HK *ptr_s)
   {
      printf("%s\n", ptr_s->str1);
      printf("%s\n", ptr_s->str2);
      printf("%s\n", ptr_s->str3);
      printf("--- %s\n", ptr_s->author);
      printf("   (%d-%d)\n\n", ptr_s->start_year, ptr_s->end_year);
   }
```

B

Hour 20, "Understanding Unions"

Quiz

1. The first statement is the declaration of a union with the tag name of _union. The second statement defines two union variables, x and y, with the a_union data type.

2. The semicolon (;) is missed in two places: at the end of the declaration of char model[8] and at the end of the declaration of the union.

3. The two union members have the same value, 1997.

Exercises

1. The following is the modified version. The content of the name array is partially overwritten by the value assigned to the double variable price.

```
/* 20A01.c */
#include <stdio.h>
#include <string.h>

main(void)
{
   union menu {
      char name[23];
      double price;
   } dish;

   printf("The content assigned to the union separately:\n");
   /* access to name */
   strcpy(dish.name, "Sweet and Sour Chicken");
   /* access to price */
   dish.price = 9.95;
   printf("Dish Name: %s\n", dish.name);
   printf("Dish Price: %5.2f\n", dish.price);

   return 0;
}
```

2. The following is one possible solution:

```
/* 20A02.c */
#include <stdio.h>

union employee {
   int start_year;
   int dpt_code;
   int id_number;
};

void DataDisplay(union employee u);
```

```
main(void)
{
    union employee info;

    /* initialize start_year */
    info.start_year = 1997;
    DataDisplay(info);

    /* initialize dpt_code */
    info.dpt_code = 8;
    DataDisplay(info);

    /* initialize id */
    info.id_number = 1234;
    DataDisplay(info);

    return 0;
}

/* function definition */
void DataDisplay(union employee u)
{
    printf("Start Year:  %d\n", u.start_year);
    printf("Dpt. Code:   %d\n", u.dpt_code);
    printf("ID Number:   %d\n", u.id_number);
}
```

OUTPUT The output of the program is

```
Start Year:    1997
Dpt. Code:     1997
ID Number:     1997
Start Year:    8
Dpt. Code:     8
ID Number:     8
Start Year:    1234
Dpt. Code:     1234
ID Number:     1234
```

3. The following is one possible solution:

```
/* 20A03.c */
#include <stdio.h>
#include <string.h>

struct survey {
    char name[20];
    union {
        char state[32];
        char country[32];
    } place;
};
```

```
void DataEnter(struct survey *s);
void DataDisplay(struct survey *s);

main(void)
{
   struct survey citizen;

   DataEnter(&citizen);
   DataDisplay(&citizen);

   return 0;
}

/* definition of DataDisplay() */
void DataDisplay(struct survey *ptr)
{
   printf("\nHere is what you entered: \n");
   printf("Your name is %s.\n", ptr->name);
   printf("You are from %s.\n", ptr->place.state);
   printf("\nThank you!\n");
}

/* definition of DataEnter() */
void DataEnter(struct survey *ptr)
{
   char is_yes[4];

   printf("Please enter your name:\n");
      gets(ptr->name);

   printf("Are you a U. S. citizen? (Yes or No)\n");
      gets(is_yes);
   if ((is_yes[0] == 'Y') ||
       (is_yes[0] == 'y')){
      printf("Enter the name of the state:\n");
      gets(ptr->place.state);
   } else {
      printf("Enter the name of your country:\n");
      gets(ptr->place.country);
   }
}
```

OUTPUT   The following is the output of the program on my machine:

```
Please enter your name:
Tony
Are you a U. S. citizen? (Yes or No)
Yes
Enter the name of the state:
Texas
```

```
                    Here is what you entered:
                    Your name is Tony.
                    You are from Texas.

                    Thank you!
```

4. The following is one possible solution:

```c
/* 20A04.c */
#include <stdio.h>
#include <string.h>

struct bit_field {
   int yes: 1;
};

struct survey {
   struct bit_field flag;
   char name[20];
   union {
       char state[32];
       char country[32];
   } place;
};

void DataEnter(struct survey *s);
void DataDisplay(struct survey *s);

main(void)
{
   struct survey citizen;

   DataEnter(&citizen);
   DataDisplay(&citizen);

   return 0;
}

/* function definition */
void DataEnter(struct survey *ptr)
{
   char is_yes[4];

   printf("Please enter your name:\n");
      gets(ptr->name);

   printf("Are you a U.S. citizen? (Yes or No)\n");
      gets(is_yes);
   if ((is_yes[0] == 'Y') ||
      (is_yes[0] == 'y')){
      printf("Enter the name of the state:\n");
      gets(ptr->place.state);
```

B

```
        ptr->flag.yes = 1;
    } else {
        printf("Enter the name of your country:\n");
        gets(ptr->place.country);
        ptr->flag.yes = 0;
    }
}
/* function definition */
void DataDisplay(struct survey *ptr)
{
    printf("\nHere is what you've entered:\n");
    printf("Name: %s\n", ptr->name);
    if (ptr->flag.yes)
        printf("The state is: %s\n",
            ptr->place.state);
    else
        printf("Your country is: %s\n",
            ptr->place.country);
    printf("\nThanks and Bye!\n");
}
```

Hour 21, "Reading and Writing with Files"

Quiz

1. The first expression tries to open an existing binary file called `test.bin` for reading and writing. The second expression tries to open an existing text file called `test.txt` for appending. The last expression tries to create a text file, called `test.ini`, for reading and writing.

2. The `fopen()` function returns a null pointer when an error occurs during the procedure of opening a file. It's not legal to do any reading or writing with a null file pointer. Therefore, the code is wrong because it calls `fgetc()` when `fopen()` returns a null pointer.

3. The mode is set to read only, but the code tries to write a character to the opened file by calling the `fputc()` function.

4. The code still reads a text file by using the file pointer `fptr1`, even though the file pointer `fptr1` has been closed.

Exercises

1. The following is one possible solution:
```
/* 21A01.c */
#include <stdio.h>
```

```
enum {SUCCESS, FAIL};

int CharRead(FILE *fin);

main(void)
{
   FILE *fptr;
   char filename[]= "haiku.txt";
   int reval = SUCCESS;

   if ((fptr = fopen(filename, "r")) == NULL){
      printf("Cannot open %s.\n", filename);
      reval = FAIL;
   } else {
      printf("\nThe total character number is %d.\n",
         CharRead(fptr));
      fclose(fptr);
   }

   return reval;
}

/* definition of CharRead() */
int CharRead(FILE *fin)
{
   int c, num;

   num = 0;
   while ((c=fgetc(fin)) != EOF){
      putchar(c);
      ++num;
   }

   return num;
}
```

2. The following is one possible solution:

```
/* 21A02.c */
#include <stdio.h>
#include <string.h>

enum {SUCCESS, FAIL, MAX_LEN = 80};

void LineWrite(FILE *fout, char *str);

main(void)
{
   FILE *fptr;
   char str[MAX_LEN+1];
   char filename[32];
   int reval = SUCCESS;
```

```c
      printf("Please enter the file name:\n");
      gets(filename);

      printf("Enter a string:\n");
      gets(str);

      if ((fptr = fopen(filename, "w")) == NULL){
         printf("Cannot open %s for writing.\n", filename);
         reval = FAIL;
      } else {
         LineWrite(fptr, str);
         fclose(fptr);
      }

      return reval;
   }

   /* definition of LineWrite() */
   void LineWrite(FILE *fout, char *str)
   {
      fputs(str, fout);
      printf("Done!\n");
   }
```

3. The following is one possible solution:

```c
   /* 21A03.c */
   #include <stdio.h>

   enum {SUCCESS, FAIL};

   void CharWrite(FILE *fout, char *str);

   main(void)
   {
      FILE *fptr;
      char filename[]= "test_21.txt";
      char str[]= "Disk file I/O is fun.";
      int reval = SUCCESS;

      if ((fptr = fopen(filename, "w")) == NULL){
         printf("Cannot open %s.\n", filename);
         reval = FAIL;
      } else {
         CharWrite(fptr, str);
         fclose(fptr);
      }

      return reval;
   }
```

```
/* function definition */
void CharWrite(FILE *fout, char *str)
{
   int i, c;

   i = 0;
   while ((c=str[i]) != '\0'){
      putchar(c);
      fputc(c, fout);
      i++;
   }
}
```

4. The following is one possible solution:

```
/* 21A04.c */
#include <stdio.h>
#include <string.h>

enum {SUCCESS, FAIL};

void BlkWrite(FILE *fout, char *str);

main(void)
{
   FILE *fptr;
   char filename[]= "test_21.txt";
   char str[]= "Disk file I/O is tricky.";
   int reval = SUCCESS;

   if ((fptr = fopen(filename, "w")) == NULL){
      printf("Cannot open %s.\n", filename);
      reval = FAIL;
   } else {
      BlkWrite(fptr, str);
      fclose(fptr);
   }

   return reval;
}

/* function definition */
void BlkWrite(FILE *fout, char *str)
{
   int num;

   num = strlen(str);
   fwrite(str, sizeof(char), num, fout);
   printf("%s\n", str);
}
```

B

Hour 22, "Using Special File Functions"

Quiz

1. Yes. The two statements are equivalent.

2. No. The two statements are not equivalent, unless the current file position indicator is indeed at the beginning of the file.

3. The scanf() function reads from the test.txt file, instead of the default input stream, because the freopen() function has redirected the input stream and associated it with the test.txt file.

4. The four double data items together are going to take 32 bytes in the binary file, if the size of the double data type is eight bytes long.

Exercises

1. The following is one possible solution:

```c
/* 22A01.c */
#include <stdio.h>

enum {SUCCESS, FAIL, MAX_LEN = 80};

void PtrSeek(FILE *fptr);
long PtrTell(FILE *fptr);
void DataRead(FILE *fptr);
int ErrorMsg(char *str);

main(void)
{
    FILE *fptr;
    char filename[]= "LaoTzu.txt";
    int reval = SUCCESS;

    if ((fptr = fopen(filename, "r")) == NULL){
        reval = ErrorMsg(filename);
    } else {
        PtrSeek(fptr);
        fclose(fptr);
    }

    return reval;
}

/* function definition */
void PtrSeek(FILE *fptr)
{
    long offset1, offset2, offset3;
```

```
        offset1 = PtrTell(fptr);
        DataRead(fptr);
        offset2 = PtrTell(fptr);
        DataRead(fptr);
        offset3 = PtrTell(fptr);
        DataRead(fptr);
        printf("\nRe-read the paragraph:\n");

        /* re-read the third sentence */
        fseek(fptr, offset3, SEEK_SET);
        DataRead(fptr);

        /* re-read the second sentence */
        fseek(fptr, offset2, SEEK_SET);
        DataRead(fptr);

        /* re-read the first sentence */
        fseek(fptr, offset1, SEEK_SET);
        DataRead(fptr);
}

/* function definition */
long PtrTell(FILE *fptr)
{
        long reval;

        reval = ftell(fptr);
        printf("The fptr is at %ld\n", reval);

        return reval;
}

/* function definition */
void DataRead(FILE *fptr)
{
        char buff[MAX_LEN];

        fgets(buff, MAX_LEN, fptr);
        printf("%s", buff);
}

/* function definition */
int ErrorMsg(char *str)
{
        printf("Cannot open %s.\n", str);

        return FAIL;
}
```

B

2. The following is one possible solution:

```
/* 22A02.c */
#include <stdio.h>

enum {SUCCESS, FAIL, MAX_LEN = 80};

void PtrSeek(FILE *fptr);
long PtrTell(FILE *fptr);
void DataRead(FILE *fptr);
int ErrorMsg(char *str);

main(void)
{
    FILE *fptr;
    char filename[]= "LaoTzu.txt";
    int reval = SUCCESS;

    if ((fptr = fopen(filename, "r")) == NULL){
       reval = ErrorMsg(filename);
    } else {
       PtrSeek(fptr);
       fclose(fptr);
    }

    return reval;
}

/* function definition */
void PtrSeek(FILE *fptr)
{
    long offset1, offset2, offset3;

    offset1 = PtrTell(fptr);
    DataRead(fptr);
    offset2 = PtrTell(fptr);
    DataRead(fptr);
    offset3 = PtrTell(fptr);
    DataRead(fptr);
    printf("\nRe-read the paragraph:\n");
    /* re-read the third sentence */
    fseek(fptr, offset3, SEEK_SET);
    DataRead(fptr);
    /* re-read the second sentence */
    fseek(fptr, offset2, SEEK_SET);
    DataRead(fptr);
    /* re-read the first sentence */
    rewind(fptr);  /* rewind the file position indicator */
    DataRead(fptr);
}
```

```
/* function definition */
long PtrTell(FILE *fptr)
{
    long reval;

    reval = ftell(fptr);
    printf("The fptr is at %ld\n", reval);

    return reval;
}

/* function definition */
void DataRead(FILE *fptr)
{
    char buff[MAX_LEN];

    fgets(buff, MAX_LEN, fptr);
    printf("%s", buff);
}

/* function definition */
int ErrorMsg(char *str)
{
    printf("Cannot open %s.\n", str);
    return FAIL;
}
```

3. On my machine, the data.bin binary file is 10 bytes. The following is one possible solution:

```
/* 22A03.c */
#include <stdio.h>

enum {SUCCESS, FAIL};

void DataWrite(FILE *fout);
void DataRead(FILE *fin);
int ErrorMsg(char *str);

main(void)
{
    FILE *fptr;
    char filename[]= "data.bin";
    int reval = SUCCESS;

    if ((fptr = fopen(filename, "wb+")) == NULL){
        reval = ErrorMsg(filename);
    } else {
        DataWrite(fptr);
        rewind(fptr);
        DataRead(fptr);
```

B

```
      fclose(fptr);
   }

   return reval;
}

/* function definition */
void DataWrite(FILE *fout)
{
   double dnum;
   int inum;

   dnum = 123.45;
   inum = 10000;

   printf("%5.2f\n", dnum);
   fwrite(&dnum, sizeof(double), 1, fout);
   printf("%d\n", inum);
   fwrite(&inum, sizeof(int), 1, fout);
}

/* function definition */
void DataRead(FILE *fin)
{
   double x;
   int y;

   printf("\nRead back from the binary file:\n");
   fread(&x, sizeof(double), (size_t)1, fin);
   printf("%5.2f\n", x);
   fread(&y, sizeof(int), (size_t)1, fin);
   printf("%d\n", y);
}

/* function definition */
int ErrorMsg(char *str)
{
   printf("Cannot open %s.\n", str);
   return FAIL;
}
```

4. The following is one possible solution:

```
/* 22A04.c */
#include <stdio.h>

enum {SUCCESS, FAIL,
      MAX_NUM = 3,
      STR_LEN = 23};

void DataRead(FILE *fin);
int ErrorMsg(char *str);
```

```
main(void)
{
   FILE *fptr;
   char filename[]= "strnum.mix";
   int reval = SUCCESS;

   if ((fptr = freopen(filename, "r", stdin)) == NULL){
      reval = ErrorMsg(filename);
   } else {
      DataRead(fptr);
      fclose(fptr);
   }

   return reval;
}

/* function definition */
void DataRead(FILE *fin)
{
   int i;
   int miles;
   char cities[STR_LEN];

   printf("The data read:\n");
   for (i=0; i<MAX_NUM; i++){
      scanf("%s%d", cities, &miles);
      printf("%-23s  %d\n", cities, miles);
   }
}

/* function definition */
int ErrorMsg(char *str)
{
   printf("Cannot open %s.\n", str);
   return FAIL;
}
```

B

Hour 23, "Compiling Programs: The C Preprocessor"

Quiz

1. The semicolon (;) should not be included at the end of the macro definition because a macro definition ends with a newline, not a semicolon.

2. The value of 82 is assigned to result due to the assignment expression result = 1 + 9 * 9.

3. The message of Under #else. is printed out.

4. The message of Under #ifdef. is printed out.

Exercises

1. The following is one possible solution:

```c
/* 23A01.c */
#include <stdio.h>
/* main() function */
main()
{
   #define human     100
   #define animal    50
   #define computer  51
   #define SUN       0
   #define MON       1
   #define TUE       2
   #define WED       3
   #define THU       4
   #define FRI       5
   #define SAT       6


   printf("human: %d,  animal: %d,  computer: %d\n",
      human, animal, computer);
   printf("SUN: %d\n", SUN);
   printf("MON: %d\n", MON);
   printf("TUE: %d\n", TUE);
   printf("WED: %d\n", WED);
   printf("THU: %d\n", THU);
   printf("FRI: %d\n", FRI);
   printf("SAT: %d\n", SAT);

   return 0;
}
```

2. The following is one possible solution:

```c
/* 23A02.c */
#include <stdio.h>

#define MULTIPLY(val1, val2)  ((val1) * (val2))
#define NO_ERROR  0

main(void)
{
   int result;

   result = MULTIPLY(2, 3);
```

```
      printf("MULTIPLY(2, 3) produces value of %d.\n", result);

      return NO_ERROR;
   }
```

3. The following is one possible solution:

```
/* 23A03.c */
#include <stdio.h>

#define UPPER_CASE  0
#define NO_ERROR    0

main(void)
{
   #if UPPER_CASE
     printf("THIS LINE IS PRINTED OUT,\n");
     printf("BECAUSE UPPER_CASE IS DEFINED.\n");
   #elif LOWER_CASE
     printf("This line is printed out,\n");
     printf("because LOWER_CASE is defined.\n");
   #else
     printf("This line is printed out,\n");
     printf("because neither UPPER_CASE nor LOWER_CASE is defined.\n");
   #endif

   return NO_ERROR;
}
```

4. The following is one possible solution:

```
/* 23A04.c:   */
#include <stdio.h>

#define C_LANG   'C'
#define B_LANG   'B'
#define NO_ERROR  0

main(void)
{
   #if C_LANG == 'C'
     #if B_LANG == 'B'
       #undef C_LANG
       #define C_LANG "I know C language.\n"
       #undef B_LANG
       #define B_LANG "Also, I know BASIC.\n"
       printf("%s%s", C_LANG, B_LANG);

     #else
       #undef C_LANG
       #define C_LANG "I only know C language.\n"
       printf("%s", C_LANG);
```

B

```
      #endif
#elif B_LANG == 'B'
  #undef B_LANG
  #define B_LANG "I only know BASIC.\n"
  printf("%s", B_LANG);
#else
  printf("I don't know C or BASIC.\n");
#endif

  return NO_ERROR;
}
```

INDEX

Other Related Titles

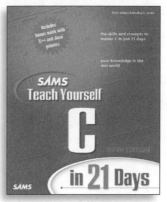

Sams Teach Yourself C in 21 Days, Fifth Edition
Peter Aitken
ISBN: 0-672-31766-4
$29.99 US

Visual C++ Unleashed
*Mickey Milliams,
Viktor Toth*
ISBN: 0-672-31241-7
$49.99 USA/$74.95 CAN

**Visual Basic 6
Unleashed: Professional
Reference**
Rob Thayer
ISBN: 0-672-31508-4
$49.99 USA/$74.95 CAN

SAMS

www.samspublishing.com

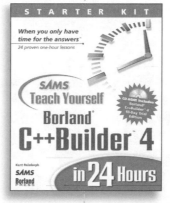

**Sams Teach Yourself
Borland C++ Builder 4 in
24 Hours**
Kent Reisdorph
ISBN: 0-672-31626-9
$24.99 US/$37.95 CAN

**Borland C++ Builder 4
Unleashed**
Kent Reisdorph
ISBN: 0-672-31510-6
$59.99 US/$89.95 CAN

All prices are subject to change.